# *Arthurian Romances*

by

## Chrétien de Troyes

Fl. th Century A.D.

Originally written in Old French, sometime in the second half of the th Century A.D., by the court poet Chretien DeTroyes.

# Table of Contents

Introduction . . . . . . . . . . . . . . . . . . . . . . . . . . . . . . . . . . . . . . . . . . . . . . . . . . . . 4

1. Erec Et Enide . . . . . . . . . . . . . . . . . . . . . . . . . . . . . . . . . . . . . . . . . . . . . . . . 11

2. Cliges . . . . . . . . . . . . . . . . . . . . . . . . . . . . . . . . . . . . . . . . . . . . . . . . . . . . . . 61

3. Yvain: The Knight with the Lion . . . . . . . . . . . . . . . . . . . . . . . . . . . . . 111

4. Lancelot: The Knight of the Cart . . . . . . . . . . . . . . . . . . . . . . . . . . . . 161

# Introduction

Chretien De Troyes has had the peculiar fortune of becoming the best known of the old French poets to students of mediaeval literature, and of remaining practically unknown to any one else. The acquaintance of students with the work of Chretien has been made possible in academic circles by the admirable critical editions of his romances undertaken and carried to completion during the past thirty years by Professor Wendelin Foerster of Bonn. At the same time the want of public familiarity with Chretien's work is due to the almost complete lack of translations of his romances into the modern tongues. The man who, so far as we know, first recounted the romantic adventures of Arthur's knights, Gawain. Yvain, Erec, Lancelot, and Perceval, has been forgotten; whereas posterity has been kinder to his debtors, Wolfram yon Eschenbach, Malory, Lord Tennyson, and Richard Wagner. The present volume has grown out of the desire to place these romances of adventure before the reader of English in a prose version based directly upon the oldest form in which they exist.

Such extravagant claims for Chretien's art have been made in some quarters that one feels disinclined to give them even an echo here. The modem reader may form his own estimate of the poet's art, and that estimate will probably not be high. Monotony, lack of proportion, vain repetitions, insufficient motivation, wearisome subtleties, and threatened, if not actual, indelicacy are among the most salient defects which will arrest, and mayhap confound, the reader unfamiliar with mediaeval literary craft. No greater service can be performed by an editor in such a case than to prepare the reader to overlook these common faults, and to set before him the literary significance of this twelfth-century poet.

Chretien de Troyes wrote in Champagne during the third quarter of the twelfth century. Of his life we know neither the beginning nor the end, but we know that between  and  he lived, perhaps as herald-at-arms (according to Gaston Paris, based on "Lancelot" -) at Troyes, where was the court of his patroness, the Countess Marie de Champagne. She was the daughter of Louis VII, and of that famous Eleanor of Aquitaine, as she is called in English histories, who, coming from the South of France in , first to Paris and later to England, may have had some share in the introduction of those ideals of courtesy and woman service which were soon to become the cult of European society. The Countess Marie, possessing her royal mother's tastes and gifts, made of her court a social experiment station, where these Provencal ideals of a perfect society were planted afresh in congenial soil. It appears from contemporary testimony that the authority of this celebrated feudal dame was weighty, and widely felt. The old city of Troyes, where she held her court, must be set down large in any map of literary history. For it was there that Chretien was led to write four romances which together form the most complete expression we possess from a single author of the ideals of French chivalry. These romances, written in eight-syllable rhyming couplets, treat respectively of Erec and Enide, Cliges, Yvain, and Lancelot. Another poem, "Perceval le Gallois", was composed about  for Philip, Count of Flanders, to whom Chretien was attached during his last years. This last poem is not included in the present translation because of its extraordinary length of , verses, because Chretien wrote only the first  verses, and because Miss Jessie L. Weston has given us an English version of Wolfram's well-known "Parzival", which tells substantially the same story, though in a different spirit. To have included this poem, of which he wrote less than one-third, in the works of Chretien would have been unjust to him. It is true the romance of "Lancelot" was not completed by Chretien, we are told, but the poem is his in such large part that one would be over-scrupulous not to call it his. The other three poems mentioned are his entire. In addition, there are quite generally assigned to the poet two insignificant lyrics, the pious romance of "Guillaume d'Angleterre", and the elaboration of an episode from Ovid's "Metamorphoses" (vi., -) called "Philomena" by its recent editor (C. de Boer, Paris, ). All these are extant and accessible. But since "Guillaume d'Angleterre" and "Philomena" are not universally attributed to Chretien, and since they have nothing to do with the Arthurian material, it seems reasonable to limit the present enterprise to "Erec and Enide", "Cliges", "Yvain", and "Lancelot".

Professor Foerster, basing his remark upon the best knowledge we possess of an obscure matter, has called "Erec and Enide" the oldest Arthurian romance extant. It is not possible to dispute this significant claim, but let us make it a little more intelligible. Scholarship has shown that from the early Middle Ages popular tradition was rife in Britain and Brittany. The existence of these traditions common to the Brythonic peoples was called to the attention of the literary world by William of Malmesbury ("Gesta regum Anglorum") and Geoffrey of Monmouth ("Historia regum Britanniae") in their Latin histories about  and  respectively, and by the Anglo-Norman poet Wace immediately afterward. Scholars have waged war over the theories of transmission of the so-called Arthurian material during the centuries which elapsed between the time of the fabled chieftain's activity in  A.D. and his appearance as a great literary personage in the twelfth century. Documents are lacking for the dark ages of popular tradition before the Norman Conquest, and the theorists may work their will. But Arthur and his knights, as we see them in the earliest French romances, have little in common with their Celtic prototypes, as we dimly catch sight of them in Irish, Welsh, and Breton legend. Chretien belonged to a generation of French poets who rook over a great mass of Celtic folk-lore they imperfectly understood, and made of what, of course, it had never been before: the vehicle to carry a rich freight of chivalric customs and ideals. As an ideal of social conduct, the code of chivalry never touched the middle and lower classes, but it was the religion of the aristocracy and of the twelfth-century "honnete homme". Never was literature in any age closer to the ideals of a social class. So true is this that it is difficult to determine whether social practices called forth the literature, or whether, as in the case of the seventeenth-century pastoral romance in France, it is truer to say that literature suggested to society its ideals. Be that as it may, it is proper to observe that the French romances of adventure portray late mediaeval aristocracy as it fain would be. For the glaring inconsistencies between the reality and the ideal, one may turn to the chronicles of the period. Yet, even history tells of many an ugly sin rebuked and of many a gallant deed performed because of the courteous ideals of chivalry. The debt of our own social code to this literature of courtesy and frequent self-sacrifice is perfectly manifest.

What Chretien's immediate and specific source was for his romances is of deep interest to the student. Unfortunately, he has left us in doubt. He speaks in the vaguest way of the materials he used. There is no evidence that he had any Celtic written source. We are thus thrown back upon Latin or French literary originals which are lost, or upon current continental lore going back to a Celtic source. This very difficult problem is as yet unsolved in the case of Chretien, as it is in the case of the Anglo-Norman Beroul, who wrote of Tristan about . The material evidently was at hand and Chretien appropriated it, without much understanding of its primitive spirit, but appreciating it as a setting for the ideal society dreamed of but not realised in his own day. Add to this literary perspicacity, a good foundation in classic fable, a modicum of ecclesiastical doctrine, a remarkable facility in phrase, figure, and rhyme and we have the foundations for Chretien's art as we shall find it upon closer examination.

A French narrative poet of the twelfth century had three categories of subject-matter from which to choose: legends connected with the history of France ("matiere de France"), legends connected with Arthur and other Celtic heroes ("matiere de Bretagne"), and stories culled from the history or mythology of Greece and Rome, current in Latin and French translations ("matiere de Rome la grant"). Chretien tells us in "Cliges" that his first essays as a poet were the translations into French of certain parts of Ovid's most popular works: the "Metamorphoses", the "Ars Amatoria", and perhaps the "Remedia Amoris". But he appears early to have chosen as his special field the stories of Celtic origin dealing with Arthur, the Round Table, and other features of Celtic folk-lore. Not only was he alive to the literary interest of this material when rationalised to suit the taste of French readers; his is further the credit of having given to somewhat crude folk-lore that polish and elegance which is peculiarly French, and which is inseparably associated with the Arthurian legends in all modern literature. Though Beroul, and perhaps other poets, had previously based romantic poems upon individual Celtic heroes like Tristan, nevertheless to Chretien, so far as we can see, is due the considerable honour of having constituted Arthur's court as a literary centre and rallying-point for an innumerable company of knights and ladies engaged in a never-ending series of amorous adventures and dangerous quests. Rather than unqualifiedly attribute to Chretien this important literary convention, one should bear in mind that all his poems imply familiarity on the part of his readers with the heroes of the court of which he speaks. One would suppose that other stories, told before his versions, were current. Some critics would go so far as to maintain that Chretien came toward the close, rather than at the beginning, of a school of French writers of Arthurian romances. But, if so, we do not possess these earlier versions, and for lack of rivals Chretien may be hailed as an innovator in the current schools of poetry.

And now let us consider the faults which a modern reader will not be slow to detect in Chretien's style. Most of his salient faults are common to all mediaeval narrative literature. They may be ascribed to the extraordinary leisure of the class for whom it was composed- -a class which was always ready to read an old story told again, and which would tolerate any description, however detailed. The pastimes of this class of readers were jousting, hunting, and making love. Hence the preponderance of these matters in the literature of its leisure hours. No detail of the joust or hunt was unfamiliar or unwelcome to these readers; no subtle arguments concerning the art of love were too abstruse to delight a generation steeped in amorous casuistry and allegories. And if some scenes seem to us indelicate, yet after comparison with other authors of his times, Chretien must be let off with a light sentence. It is certain he intended to avoid what was indecent, as did the writers of narrative poetry in general. To appreciate fully the chaste treatment of Chretien one must know some other forms of mediaeval literature, such as the fabliaux, farces, and morality plays, in which courtesy imposed no restraint. For our poet's lack of sense of proportion, and for his carelessness in the proper motivation of many episodes, no apology can be made. He is not always guilty; some episodes betoken poetic mastery. But a poet acquainted, as he was, with some first-class Latin poetry, and who had made a business of his art, ought to have handled his material more intelligently, even in the twelfth century. The emphasis is not always laid with discrimination, nor is his yarn always kept free of tangles in the spinning.

Reference has been made to Chretien's use of his sources. The tendency of some critics has been to minimise the French poet's originality by pointing out striking analogies in classic and Celtic fable. Attention has been especially directed to the defence of the fountain and the service of a fairy mistress in "Yvain", to the captivity of Arthur's subjects in the kingdom of Gorre, as narrated in "Lancelot", reminding one so insistently of the treatment of the kingdom of Death from which some god or hero finally delivers those in durance, and to the reigned death of Fenice in "Cliges", with its many variants. These episodes are but examples of parallels which will occur to the observant reader. The difficult point to determine, in speaking of conceptions so widespread in classic and mediaeval literature, is the immediate source whence these conceptions reached Chretien. The list of works of reference appended to this volume will enable the student to go deeper into this much debated question, and will permit us to dispense with an examination of the arguments in this place. However, such convincing parallels for many of Chretien's fairy and romantic episodes have been adduced by students of Irish and Welsh legend that one cannot fail to be impressed by the fact that Chretien was in touch, either by oral or literary tradition, with the populations of Britain and of Brittany, and that we have here his most immediate inspiration. Professor Foerster, stoutly opposing the so-called Anglo-Norman theory which supposes the existence of lost Anglo-Norman romances in French as the sources of Chretien de Troyes, is, nevertheless, well within the truth when he insists upon what is, so far as we are concerned, the essential originality of the French poet. The general reader will to-day care as little as did the reader of the twelfth century how the poet came upon the motives and episodes of his stories, whether he borrowed them or invented them himself. Any poet should be judged not as a "finder" but as a "user" of the common stock of ideas. The study of sources of mediaeval poetry, which is being so doggedly carried on by scholars, may well throw light upon the main currents of literary tradition, but it casts no reflection, favourable or otherwise, upon the personal art of the poet in handling his stuff. On that count he may plead his own cause before the jury.

Chretien's originality, then, consists in his portrayal of the social ideal of the French aristocracy in the twelfth century. So far as we know he was the first to create in the vulgar tongues a vast court, where men and women lived in conformity with the rules of courtesy, where the truth was told, where generosity was open-handed, where the weak and the innocent were protected by men who dedicated themselves to the cult of honour and to the quest of a spotless reputation. Honour and love combined to engage the attention of this society; these were its religion in a far more real sense than was that of the Church. Perfection was attainable under this code of ethics: Gawain, for example, was a perfect knight. Though the ideals of this court and those of Christianity are in accord at many points, yet courtly love and Christian morality are irreconcilable. This Arthurian material, as used by Chretien, is fundamentally immoral as judged by Christian standards. Beyond question, the poets and the public alike knew this to be the case, and therein lay its charm for a society in which the actual relations or the sexes were rigidly prescribed by the Church and by feudal practice, rather than by the sentiments of the individuals concerned. The passionate love of Tristan for Iseut, of Lancelot for Guinevere, of Cliges for Fenice, fascinate the conventional Christian society of the twelfth century and of the twentieth century alike, but there-is only one name among men for such relations as theirs, and neither righteousness nor reason lie that way. Even Tennyson, in spite of all he has done to spiritualise this material, was compelled to portray the inevitable dissolution and ruin of Arthur's court. Chretien well knew the difference between right and wrong, between reason and passion, as the reader of "Cliges" may learn for himself. Fenice was not Iseut, and she would not have her Cliges to be a Tristan. Infidelity, if you will, but not "menage a trois". Both "Erec" and "Yvain" present a conventional morality. But "Lancelot" is flagrantly immoral, and the poet is careful to state that for this particular romance he is indebted to his patroness Marie de Champagne. He says it was she who furnished him with both the "matiere" and the "san", the material of the story and its method of treatment.

Scholars have sought to fix the chronology of the poet's works, and have been tempted to speculate upon the evolution of his literary and moral ideas. Professor Foerster's chronology is generally accepted, and there is little likelihood of his being in error when he supposes Chretien's work to have been done as follows: the lost "Tristan" (the existence of which is denied by Gaston Paris in "Journal des Savants", , pp. f.), "Erec and Enide", "Cliges", "Lancelot", "Yvain", "Perceval". The arguments for this chronology, based upon external as well as internal criticism, may be found in the Introductions to Professor Foerster's recent editions. When we speculate upon the development of Chretien's moral ideas we are not on such sure ground. As we have seen, his standards vary widely in the different romances. How much of this variation is due to chance circumstance imposed by the nature of his subject or by the taste of his public, and how much to changing conviction it is easy to see, when we consider some contemporary novelist, how dangerous it is to judge of moral convictions as reflected in literary work. "Lancelot" must be the keystone of any theory constructed concerning the moral evolution of Chretien. The following supposition is tenable, if the chronology of Foerster is correct. After the works of his youth, consisting of lyric poems and translations embodying the ideals of Ovid and of the school of contemporary trouba-dour poets, Chretien took up the Arthurinn material and started upon a new course. "Erec" is the oldest Arthurinn romance to have survived in any language, but it is almost certainly not the first to have been written. It is a perfectly clean story: of love, estrangement, and reconciliation in the persons of Erec and his charming sweetheart Enide. The psychological analysis of Erec's motives in the rude testing of Enide is worthy of attention, and is more subtle than anything previous in French literature with which we are acquainted. The poem is an episodical romance in the biography of an Arthurinn hero, with the usual amount of space given to his adventures. "Cliges" apparently connects a Byzantine tale of doubtful origin in an arbitrary fashion with the court of Arthur. It is thought that the story embodies the same motive as the widespread tale of the deception practised upon Solomon by his wife, and that Chretien's source, as he himself claims, was literary (cf. Gaston Paris in "Journal des Savants", , pp. -). The scene where Fenice feigns death in order to rejoin her lover is a parallel of many others in literary history, and will, of course, suggest the situation in Romeo and Juliet. This romance well illustrates the drawing power of Arthur's court as a literary centre, and its use as a rallying-point for courteous knights of whatever extraction. The poem has been termed an "Anti-Tristan", because of its disparaging reference to the love of Tristan and Iseut, which, it is generally supposed, had been narrated by Chretien in his earlier years. Next may come "Lancelot", with its significant dedication to the Countess of Champagne. Of all the poet's work, this tale of the rescue of Guinevere by her lover seems to express most closely the ideals of Marie's court ideals in which devotion and courtesy but thinly disguise free love. "Yvain" is a return to the poet's natural bent, in an episodical romance, while "Perceval" crowns his production with its pure and exalted note, though without a touch of that religious mysticism which later marked Wolfram von Eschenbach's "Parzival". "Guillaime d'Angleterre" is a pseudo-historical romance of adventure in which the worldly distresses and the final reward of piety are conventionally exposed. It is unin-spired, its place is difficult to determine, and its authorship is questioned by some. It is aside from the Arthurian material, and there is no clue to its place in the evolution of Chretien's art, if indeed it be his work.

A few words must be devoted to Chretien's place in the history of mediaeval narrative poetry. The heroic epic songs of France, devoted either to the conflict of Christendom un-der the leadership of France against the Saracens, or else to the strife and rivalry of French vassals among themselves, had been current for perhaps a century before our poet began to write. These epic poems, of which some three score have survived, portray a warlike, virile, unsentimental feudal society, whose chief occupation was fighting, and whose dominant ideals were faith in God, loyalty to feudal family ties, and bravery in battle. Woman's place is comparatively obscure, and of love-making there is little said. It is a poetry of vigorous manhood, of uncompromising morality, and of hard knocks given and taken for God, for Christendom, and the King of France. This poetry is written in ten- or twelve- syllable verses grouped, at first in assonanced, later in rhymed, "tirades" of unequal length. It was intended for a society which was still homogeneous, and to it at the outset doubtless all classes of the population listened with equal interest. As poetry it is monotonous, without sense of propor-tion, padded to facilitate memorisation by professional reciters, and unadorned by figure, fancy, or imagination. Its pretention to historic accuracy begot prosaicness in its approach to the style of the chronicles. But its inspiration was noble, its conception of human duties was lofty. It gives a realistic portrayal of the age which produced it, the age of the first crusades, and to this day we would choose as our models of citizenship Roland and Oliver rather than Tristan and Lancelot. The epic poems, dealing with the pseudo-historical characters who had fought in civil and foreign wars under Charlemagne, remained the favourite literary pabulum of the middle classes until the close of the thirteenth century. Professor Bedier is at present engaged in explaining the extraordinary hold which these poems had upon the public, and in proving that they exercised a distinct function when exploited by the Church throughout the period of the crusades to celebrate local shrines and to promote muscular Christianity. But the refinement which began to penetrate the ideals of the French aristocracy about the middle of the twelfth century craved a different expression in narrative literature. Greek and Roman mythology and history were seized upon with some effect to satisfy the new demand. The "Roman de Thebes", the "Roman d'Alexandre", the "Roman de Troie", and its logical continuation, the "Roman d'Eneas", are all twelfth-century attempts to clothe classic legend in the dress of mediaeval chivalry. But better fitted to satisfy the new demand was the discovery by the alert Anglo-Normans perhaps in Brittany, perhaps in the South of England, of a vast body of legendary material which, so far as we know, had never before this century received any elaborate literary treatment. The existence of the literary demand and this discovery of the material for its prompt satisfaction is one of the most remarkable coincidences in literary history. It would seem that the pride of the Celtic populations in a Celtic hero, aided and abetted by Geoffrey of Monmouth, who first showed the romantic possibilities of the material, made of the obscure British chieftain Arthur a world conqueror. Arthur thus became already in Geoffrey's "Historia regum Britaniae" a conscious protagonist of Charlemagne and his rival in popularity. This grandiose conception of Arthur persisted in England, but this conception of the British chieftain did not interest the French. For Chretien Arthur had no political significance. He is simply the arbiter of his court in all affairs of justice and courtesy. Charlemagne's very realistic entourage of virile and busy barons is replaced by a court of elegant chevaliers and unemployed ladies. Charlemagne's setting is historical and geographical; Arthur's setting is ideal and in the air. In the oldest epic poems we find only God-fearing men and a few self-effacing women; in the Arthurian romances we meet gentlemen and ladies, more elegant and seductive than any one in the epic poems, but less fortified by faith and sense of duty against vice because breathing an enervating atmosphere of leisure and decadent morally. Though the Church made the attempt in "Parzival", it could never lay its hands so effectively upon this Celtic material, because it contained too many elements which were root and branch inconsistent with the essential teachings of Christianity. A fleeting comparison of the noble end of Charlemagne's Peers fighting for their God and their King at Ronceval with the futile and dilettante careers of Arthur's knights in joust and hunt, will show better than mere words where the difference lies.

The student of the history of social and moral ideals will find much to interest him in Chretien's romances. Mediaeval references show that he was held by his immediate successors, as he is held to-day when fairly viewed, to have been a master of the art of story-telling. More than any other single narrative poet, he was taken as a model both in France and abroad. Professor F. M. Warren has set forth in detail the finer points in the art of poetry as practised by Chretien and his contemporary craftsmen (see "Some Features of Style in Early French Narrative Poetry, - in "Modern Philology", iii., -; iii., -; iv., -). Poets in his own land refer to him with reverence, and foreign poets complimented him to a high degree by direct translation and by embroidering upon the themes which he had made popular. The knights made famous by Chretien soon crossed the frontiers and obtained rights of citizenship in counties so diverse as Germany, England, Scandinavia, Holland, Italy, and to a lesser extent in Spain and Portugal. The inevitable tendency of the fourteenth and fifteenth centuries to reduce poetry to prose affected the Arthurian material; vast prose compilations finally embodied in print the matter formerly expressed in verse, and it was in this form that the stories were known to later generations until revived interest in the Middle Ages brought to light the manuscripts in verse.

Aside from certain episodes of Chretien's romances, the student will be most interested in the treatment of love as therein portrayed. On this topic we may hear speaking the man of his time. "Cliges" contains the body of Chretien's doctrine of love, while Lancelot is his most perfect lover. His debt to Ovid has not yet been indicated with sufficient preciseness. An elaborate code to govern sentiment and its expression was independently developed by the troubadours of Provence in the early twelfth century. These Provencal ideals of the courtly life were carried into Northern France partly as the result of a royal marriage in and of the crusade of , and there by such poets as Chretien they were gathered up and fused with the Ovidian doctrine into a highly complicated but perfectly definite statement of the ideal relations of the sexes. Nowhere in the vulgar tongues can a better statement of these relations be found than in "Cliges."

So we leave Chretien to speak across the ages for himself and his generation. He is to be read as a story-teller rather than as a poet, as a casuist rather than as a philosopher. But when all deductions are made, his significance as a literary artist and as the founder of a precious literary tradition distinguishes him from all other poets of the Latin races between the close of the Empire and the arrival of Dante.

W. W. COMFORT.

# Erec Et Enide

The rustic's proverb says that many a thing is despised that is worth much more than is supposed. Therefore he does well who makes the most of whatever intelligence he may possess. For he who neglects this concern may likely omit to say something which would subsequently give great pleasure. So Chretien de Troyes maintains that one ought always to study and strive to speak well and teach the right; and he derives from a story of adventure a pleasing argument whereby it may be proved and known that he is not wise who does not make liberal use of his knowledge so long as God may give him grace. The story is about Erec the son of Lac--a story which those who earn a living by telling stories are accustomed to mutilate and spoil in the presence of kings and counts. And now I shall begin the tale which will be remembered so long as Christendom endures. This is Chretien's boast.

One Easter Day in the Springtime, King Arthur held court in his town of Cardigan. Never was there seen so rich a court; for many a good knight was there, hardy, bold, and brave, and rich ladies and damsels, gentle and fair daughters of kings. But before the court was disbanded, the King told his knights that he wished to hunt the White Stag, in order to observe worthily the ancient custom. When my lord Gawain heard this, he was sore displeased, and said: "Sire, you will derive neither thanks nor goodwill from this hunt. We all know long since what this custom of the White Stag is: whoever can kill the White Stag must forsooth kiss the fairest maiden of your court, come what may. But of this there might come great ill, for there are here five hundred damsels of high birth, gentle and prudent daughters of kings, and there is none of them but has a bold and valiant knight for her lover who would be ready to contend, whether fight or wrong, that she who is his lady is the fairest and gentlest of them all." The King replies: "That I know well; yet will I not desist on that account; for a king's word ought never to be gainsaid. To-morrow morning we shall all gaily go to hunt the White Stag in the forest of adventure. And very delightful this hunt will be."

And so the affair is arranged for the next morning at daybreak. The morrow, as soon as it is day, the King gets up and dresses, and dons a short jacket for his forest ride. He commands the knights to be aroused and the horses to be made ready. Already they are ahorse, and off they go, with bows and arrows. After them the Queen mounts her horse, taking a damsel with her. A maid she was, the daughter of a king, and she rode a white palfrey. After them there swiftly followed a knight, named Erec, who belonged to the Round Table, and had great fame at the court. Of all the knights that ever were there, never one received such praise; and he was so fair that nowhere in the world need one seek a fairer knight than he. He was very fair, brave, and courteous, though not yet twenty-five years old. Never was there a man of his age of greater knighthood. And what shall I say of his virtues? Mounted on his horse, and clad in an ermine mantle, he came galloping down the road, wearing a coat of splendid flowered silk which was made at Constantinople. He had put on hose of brocade, well made and cut, and when his golden spurs were well attached, he sat securely in his stirrups. He carried no arm with him but his sword. As he galloped along, at the corner of a street he came up with the Queen, and said: "My lady, if it please you, I should gladly accompany you along this road, having come for no other purpose than to bear you

11

company." And the Queen thanks him: "Fair friend, I like your company well, in truth; for better I could not have."

Then they ride along at full speed until they come into the forest, where the party who had gone before them had already started the stag. Some wind the horns and others shout; the hounds plunge ahead after the stag, running, attacking, and baying; the bowmen shoot amain. And before them all rode the King on a Spanish hunter.

Queen Guinevere was in the wood listening for the dogs; beside her were Erec and the damsel, who was very courteous and fair. But those who had pursued the stag were so far from them that, however intently they might listen to catch the sound of horn or baying of hound, they no longer could hear either horse, huntsman, or hound. So all three of them drew rein in a clearing beside the road. They had been there but a short time when they saw an armed knight along on his steed, with shield slung about his neck, and his lance in hand. The Queen espied him from a distance By his right side rode a damsel of noble bearing, and before them, on a hack, came a dwarf carrying in his hand a knotted scourge. When Queen Guinevere saw the comely and graceful knight, she desired to know who he and his damsel were. So she bid her damsel go quickly and speak to him.

"Damsel," says the Queen, "go and bid yonder knight come to me and bring his damsel with him." The maiden goes on amble straight toward the knight. But the spiteful dwarf sallies forth to meet her with his scourge in hand, crying: "Halt, maiden, what do you want here? You shall advance no farther." "Dwarf," says she, "let me pass. I wish to speak with yonder knight; for the Queen sends me hither." The dwarf, who was rude and mean, took his stand in the middle of the road, and said: "You have no business here. Go back. It is not meet that you should speak to so excellent a knight." The damsel advanced and tried to pass him by force, holding the dwarf in slight esteem when she saw that he was so small. Then the dwarf raised his whip, when he saw her coming toward him and tried to strike her in the face. She raised her arm to protect herself, but he lifted his hand again and struck her all unprotected on her bare hand: and so hard did he strike her on the back of her hand that it turned all black and blue. When the maiden could do nothing else, in spite of herself she must needs return. So weeping she turned back. The tears came to her eyes and ran down her cheeks. When the Queen sees her damsel wounded, she is sorely grieved and angered and knows not what to do. "Ah, Erec, fair friend," she says, "I am in great sorrow for my damsel whom that dwarf has wounded. The knight must be discourteous indeed, to allow such a monster to strike so beautiful a creature. Erec, fair friend, do you go to the knight and bid him come to me without delay. I wish to know him and his lady." Erec starts off thither, giving spurs to his steed, and rides straight toward the knight. The ignoble dwarf sees him coming and goes to meet him. "Vassal," says he, "stand back! For I know not what business you have here. I advise you to withdraw." "Avaunt," says Erec, "provoking dwarf! Thou art vile and troublesome. Let me pass." "You shall not." "That will I." "You shall not." Erec thrusts the dwarf aside. The dwarf had no equal for villainy: he gave him a great blow with his lash right on the neck, so that Erec's neck and face are scarred with the blow of the scourge; from top to bottom appear the lines which the thongs have raised on him. He knew well that he could not have the satisfaction of striking the dwarf; for he saw that the knight was armed, arrogant, and of evil intent, and he was afraid that he would soon kill him, should he strike the dwarf in his presence. Rashness is not bravery. So Erec acted wisely in retreating without more ado. "My lady," he says, "now matters stand worse; for the rascally dwarf has so wounded me that he has badly cut my face. I did not dare to strike or touch him; but none ought to reproach me, for I was completely unarmed. I mistrusted the armed knight, who, being an ugly fellow and violent, would take it as no jest, and would soon kill me in his pride. But this much I will promise you; that if I can, I shall yet avenge my disgrace, or increase it. But my arms are too far away to avail me in this time of need; for at Cardigan did I leave them this morning when I came away. And if I should go to fetch them there, peradventure I should never again find the knight who is riding off apace. So I must follow him at once, far or near, until I find some arms to hire or borrow. If I find some one who will lend me arms, the knight will quickly find me ready for battle. And you may be sure without fail that we two shall fight until he defeat me, or I him. And if possible, I shall be back by the third day, when you will see me home again either joyous or sad, I know not which. Lady, I cannot delay longer, for I must follow after the knight. I go. To God I commend you." And the Queen in like manner more than five hundred rimes commends him to God, that he may defend him from harm.

Erec leaves the Queen and ceases not to pursue the knight. The Queen remains in the wood, where now the King had come up with the Stag. The King himself outstripped the others at the death. Thus they killed and took the White Stag, and all returned, carrying the Stag, till they came again to Cardigan. After supper, when the knights were all in high spirits throughout the hall, the King, as the custom was, because he had taken the Stag, said that he would bestow the kiss and thus observe the custom of the Stag. Throughout the court a great murmur is heard: each one vows and swears to his neighbour that it shall not be done without the protest of sword or ashen lance. Each one gallantly desires to contend that his lady is the fairest in the hall. Their conversation bodes no good, and when my lord Gawain heard it, you must know that it was not to his liking. Thus he addressed the King: "Sire," he says, "your knights here are greatly aroused, and all their talk is of this kiss. They say that it shall never be bestowed without disturbance and a fight." And the King wisely replied to him: "Fair nephew Gawain, give me counsel now, sparing my honour and my dignity, for I have no mind for any disturbance."

To the council came a great part of the best knights of the court. King Yder arrived, who was the first to be summoned, and after him King Cadoalant, who was very wise and bold. Kay and Girflet came too, and King Amauguin was there, and a great number of other knights were there with them. The discussion was in process when the Queen arrived and told them of the adventure which she had met in the forest, of the armed knight whom she saw, and of the malicious little dwarf who had struck her damsel on the bare hand with his whip, and who struck Erec, too, in the same way an ugly blow on the face; but that Erec followed the knight to obtain vengeance, or increase his shame, and how he said that if possible he would be back by the third day. "Sire," says the Queen to the King, "listen to me a moment. If these knights approve what I say, postpone this kiss until the third day, when Erec will be back." There is none who does not agree with her, and the King himself approves her words.

Erec steadily follows the knight who was armed and the dwarf who had struck him until they come to a well placed town, strong and fine . They enter straight through the gate. Within the town there was great joy of knights and ladies, of whom there were many and fair. Some were feeding in the streets their sparrow-hawks and moulting falcons; others were giving an airing to their tercels, their mewed birds, and young yellow hawks; others play at dice or other game of chance, some at chess, and some at backgammon. The grooms in front of the stables are rubbing down and currying the horses. The ladies are bedecking themselves in their boudoirs. As soon as they see the knight coming, whom they recognised with his dwarf and damsel, they go out three by three to meet him. The knight they all greet and salute, but they give no heed to Erec, for they did not know him. Erec follows close upon the knight through the town, until he saw him lodged. Then, very joyful, he passed on a little farther until he saw reclining upon some steps a vavasor well on in years. He was a comely man, with white locks, debonair, pleasing, and frank. There he was seated all alone, seeming to be engaged in thought. Erec took him for an honest man who would at once give him lodging. When he turned through the gate into the yard, the vavasor ran to meet him, and saluted him before Erec had said a word. "Fair sir," says he, "be welcome. If you will deign to lodge with me, here is my house all ready for you." Erec replies: "Thank you! For no other purpose have I come; I need a lodging place this night."

Erec dismounts from his horse, which the host himself leads away by the bridle, and does great honour to his guest. The vavasor summons his wife and his beautiful daughter, who were busy in a work-room--doing I know not what. The lady came out with her daughter, who was dressed in a soft white under-robe with wide skirts hanging loose in folds. Over it she wore a white linen garment, which completed her attire. And this garment was so old that it was full of holes down the sides. Poor, indeed, was her garb without, but within her body was fair.

The maid was charming, in sooth, for Nature had used all her skill in forming her. Nature herself had marvelled more than five hundred times how upon this one occasion she had succeeded in creating such a perfect thing. Never again could she so strive successfully to reproduce her pattern. Nature bears witness concerning her that never was so fair a creature seen in all the world. In truth I say that never did Iseut the Fair have such radiant golden tresses that she could be compared with this maiden. The complexion of her forehead and face was clearer and more delicate than the lily. But with wondrous art her face with all its delicate pallor was suffused with a fresh crimson which Nature had bestowed upon her. Her eyes were so bright that they seemed like two stars. God never formed better nose, mouth, and eyes. What shall I say of her beauty? In sooth, she was made to be looked at; for in her one could have seen himself as in a mirror. So she came forth from the work-room: and when she saw the knight whom she had never seen before, she drew back a little, because she did not know him, and in her modesty she blushed. Erec, for his part, was amazed when he beheld such beauty in her, and the vavasor said to her: "Fair daughter dear, take this horse and lead him to the stable along with my own horses. See that he lack for nothing: take off his saddle and bridle, give him oats and hay, look after him and curry him, that he may be in good condition."

The maiden takes the horse, unlaces his breast-strap, and takes off his bridle and saddle. Now the horse is in good hands, for she takes excellent care of him. She throws a halter over his head, rubs him down, curries him, and makes him comfortable. Then she ties him to the manger and puts plenty of fresh sweet hay and oats before him. Then she went back to her father, who said to her: "Fair daughter dear, take now this gentleman by the hand and show him all honour. Take him by the hand upstairs." The maiden did not delay (for in her there was no lack of courtesy) and led him by the hand upstairs. The lady had gone before and prepared the house. She had laid embroidered cushions and spreads upon the couches, where they all three sat down Erec with his host beside him, and the maiden opposite. Before them, the fire burns brightly. The vavasor had only one man-servant, and no maid for chamber or kitchen work. This one man was busy in the kitchen preparing meat and birds for supper. A skilful cook was he, who knew how to prepare meal in boiling water and birds on the spit. When he had the meal prepared in accordance with the orders which had been given him, he brought them water for washing in two basins. The table was soon set, cloths, bread, and wine set out, and they sat down to supper. They had their fill of all they needed. When they had finished and when the table was cleared, Erec thus addressed his host, the master of the house: "Tell me, fair host." he asked, "why your daughter, who is so passing fair and clever, is so poorly and unsuitably attired." "Fair friend," the vavasor replies, "many a man is harmed by poverty, and even so am I. I grieve to see her so poorly clad, and yet I cannot help it, for I have been so long involved in war that I have lost or mortgaged or sold all my land. And yet she would be well enough dressed if I allowed her to accept everything that people wish to give her. The lord of this castle himself would have dressed her in becoming fashion and would have done her every manner of favour, for she is his niece and he is a count. And there is no nobleman in this region, however rich and powerful, who would not willingly have taken her to wife had I given my consent. But I am waiting yet for some better occasion, when God shall bestow still greater honour upon her, when fortune shall bring hither some king or count who shall lead her away, for there is under Heaven no king or count who would be ashamed of my daughter, who is so wondrous fair that her match cannot be found. Fair, indeed, she is; but yet greater far than her beauty, is her intelligence. God never created any one so discreet and of such open heart. When I have my daughter beside me, I don't care a marble about all the rest of the world. She is my delight and my pastime, she is my joy and comfort, my wealth and my treasure, and I love nothing so much as her own precious self."

When Erec had listened to all that his host told him, he asked him to inform him whence came all the chivalry that was quartered in the town. For there was no street or house so poor and small but it was full of knights and ladies and squires. And the vavasor said to him: "Fair friend, these are the nobles of the country round; all, both young and old, have come to a fete which is to be held in this town tomorrow; therefore the houses are so full. When they shall all have gathered, there will be a great stir to-morrow; for in the presence of all the people there will be set upon a silver perch a sparrow-hawk of five or six moultings--the best you can imagine. Whoever wishes to gain the hawk must have a mistress who is fair, prudent, and courteous. And if there be a knight so bold as to wish to defend the worth and the name of the fairest in his eyes, he will cause his mistress to step forward and lift the hawk from the perch, if no one dares to interpose. This is the custom they are observing, and for this each year they gather here." Thereupon Erec speaks and asks him: "Fair host, may it not displease you, but tell me, if you know, who is a certain knight bearing arms of azure and gold, who passed by here not long ago, having close beside him a courtly damsel, preceded by a hump-backed dwarf." To him the host then made reply: "That is he who will win the hawk without any opposition from the other knights. I don't believe that any one will offer opposition; this time there will be no blows or wounds. For two years already he has won it without being challenged; and if he wins it again this year, he will have gained permanent possession of it. Every succeeding year he may keep it without contest or challenge." Quickly Erec makes reply: "I do not like that knight. Upon my word, had I some arms I should challenge him for the hawk. Fair host, I beg you as a boon to advise me how I may be equipped with arms whether old or new, poor or rich, it matters not." And he replies to him generously: "It were a pity for you to feel concern on that score! I have good fine arms which I shall be glad to lend you. In the house I have a triple-woven hauberk, which was selected from among five hundred. And I have some fine valuable greaves, polished, handsome, and light in weight. The helmet is bright and handsome, and the shield fresh and new. Horse, sword, and lance all I will lend you, of course; so let no more be said." "Thank you kindly, fair gentle host! But I wish for no better sword that this one which I have brought with me, nor for any other horse than my own, for I can get along well enough with him. If you will lend me the rest, I shall esteem it a great favour. But there is one more boon I wish to ask of you, for which I shall make just return if God grant that I come off from the battle with honour." And frankly he replies to him: "Ask confidently for what you want, whatever it be, for nothing of mine shall lack you." Then Erec said that he wished to defend the hawk on behalf of his daughter; for surely there will be no damsel who is one hundredth part as beautiful as she. And if he takes her with him, he will have good and just reason to maintain and to prove that she is entitled to carry away the hawk. Then he added: "Sire, you know not what guest you have sheltered here, nor do you know my estate and kin. I am the son of a rich and puissant king: my father's name is King Lac, and the Bretons call me Erec. I belong to King Arthur's court, and have been with him now three years. I know not if any report of my father or of me has ever reached this land. But I promise you and vow that if you will fit me out with arms, and will give me your daughter to-morrow when I strive for the hawk, I will take her to my country, if God grant me the victory, and I will give her a crown to wear, and she shall be queen of three cities." "Ah, fair sir! Is it true that you are Erec, the son of Lac?" "That is who I am, indeed" quoth he. Then the host was greatly delighted and said: "We have indeed heard of you in this country. Now I think all the more of you, for you are very valiant and brave. Nothing now shall you be refused by me. At your request I give you my fair daughter." Then taking her by the hand, he says: "Here, I give her to you." Erec received her joyfully, and now has all he desired. Now they are all happy there: the father is greatly delighted, and the mother weeps for joy. The maiden sat quiet;

but she was very happy and glad that she was betrothed to him, because he was valiant and courteous: and she knew that he would some day be king, and she should receive honour and be crowned rich queen.

They had sat up very late that night. But now the beds were prepared with white sheets and soft pillows, and when the conversation flagged they all went to bed in happy frame. Erec slept little that night, and the next morn, at crack of dawn, he and his host rose early. They both go to pray at church, and hear a hermit chant the Mass of the Holy Spirit, not forgetting to make an offering. When they had heard Mass both kneel before the altar and then return to the house. Erec was eager for the battle; so he asks for arms, and they are given to him. The maiden herself puts on his arms (though she casts no spell or charm), laces on his iron greaves, and makes them fast with thong of deer-hide. She puts on his hauberk with its strong meshes, and laces on his ventail. The gleaming helmet she sets upon his head, and thus arms him well from tip to toe. At his side she fastens his sword, and then orders his horse to be brought, which is done. Up he jumped clear of the ground. The damsel then brings the shield and the strong lance: she hands him the shield, and he takes it and hangs it about his neck by the strap. She places the lance in his hand, and when he had grasped it by the butt-end, he thus addressed the gentle vavasor: "Fair sire," quoth he, "if you please, make your daughter ready now; for I wish to escort her to the sparrow-hawk in accordance with our agreement." The vavasor then without delay had saddled a bay palfrey. There can nothing be said of the harness because of the dire poverty with which the vavasor was afflicted. Saddle and bridle were put on, and up the maiden mounted all free and in light attire, without waiting to be urged. Erec wished to delay no longer; so off he starts with the host's daughter by his side, followed by the gentleman and his lady.

Erec rides with lance erect and with the comely damsel by his side. All the people, great and small, gaze at them with wondering eyes as they pass through the streets. And thus they question each other: "Who is yonder knight? He must be doughty and brave, indeed, to act as escort for this fair maid. His efforts will be well employed in proving that this damsel is the fairest of them all." One man to another says: "In very truth, she ought to have the sparrow-hawk." Some praised the maid, while many said: "God! who can this knight be, with the fair damsel by his side?" "I know not." "Nor I." Thus spake each one. "But his gleaming helmet becomes him well, and the hauberk, and shield, and his sharp steel sword. He sits well upon his steed and has the bearing of a valiant vassal, well-shapen in arm, in limb and foot." While all thus stand and gaze at them, they for their part made no delay to take their stand by the sparrow-hawk, where to one side they awaited the knight. And now behold! they see him come, attended by his dwarf and his damsel. He had heard the report, that a knight had come who wished to obtain the sparrow-hawk, but he did not believe there could be in the world a knight so bold as to dare to fight with him. He would quickly defeat him and lay him low. All the people knew him well, and all welcome him and escort him in a noisy crowd: knights, squires, ladies, and damsels make haste to run after him. Leading them all the knight rides proudly on, with his damsel and his dwarf at his side, and he makes his way quickly to the sparrow-hawk. But all about there was such a press of the rough and vulgar crowd that it was impossible to touch the hawk or to come near where it was. Then the Count arrived on the scene, and threatened the populace with a switch which he held in his hand. The crowd drew back, and the knight advanced and said quietly to his lady: "My lady, this bird, which is so perfectly moulted and so fair, should be yours as your just portion; for you are wondrous fair and full of charm. Yours it shall surely be so long as I live. Step forward, my dear, and lift the hawk from the perch." The damsel was on the point of stretching forth her hand when Erec hastened to challenge her, little heeding the other's arrogance. "Damsel," he cries, "stand back! Go dally with some other bird, for to this one you have no right. In spite of all, I say this hawk shall never be yours. For a better one than you claims it--aye, much more fair and more courteous." The other knight is very wroth; but Erec does not mind him, and bids his own maiden step forward.

16

"Fair one." he cries, "come forth. Lift the bird from the perch, for it is right that you should have it. Damsel, come forth! For I will make boast to defend it if any one is so bold as to intervene. For no woman excels you in beauty or worth, in grace or honour any more than the moon outshines the sun." The other could suffer it no longer, when he hears him so manfully offer himself to do battle. "Vassal," he cries, "who art thou who dost thus dispute with me the hawk?" Erec boldly answers him: "A knight I am from another land. This hawk I have come to obtain; for it is right, I say it in spite of all, that this damsel of mine should have it." "Away!" cries the other, "it shall never be. Madness has brought thee here. If thou dost wish to have the hawk, thou shalt pay fight dearly for it." "Pay, vassal; and how?" "Thou must fight with me, if thou dost not resign it to me." "You talk madness," cries Erec; "for me these are idle threats; for little enough do I fear you." "Then I defy thee here and now. The battle is inevitable." Erec replies: "God help me now; for never did I wish for aught so much." Now soon you will hear the noise of battle.

The large place was cleared, with the people gathered all around. They draw off from each other the space of an acre, then drive their horses together; they reach for each other with the tips of their lances, and strike each other so hard that the shields are pierced and broken; the lances split and crack; the saddle-bows are knocked to bits behind. They must needs lose their stirrups, so that they both fall to the ground, and the horses run off across the field. Though smitten with the lances, they are quickly on their feet again, and draw their swords from the scabbards. With great fierceness they attack each other, and exchange great sword blows, so that the helmets are crushed and made to ring. Fierce is the clash of the swords, as they rain great blows upon neck and shoulders. For this is no mere sport: they break whatever they touch, cutting the shields and shattering the hauberks. The swords are red with crimson blood. Long the battle lasts; but they fight so lustily that they become weary and listless. Both the damsels are in tears, and each knight sees his lady weep and raise her hands to God and pray that He may give the honours of the battle to the one who strives for her. "Ha! vassal," quoth the knight to Erec, "let us withdraw and rest a little; for too weak are these blows we deal. We must deal better blows than these; for now it draws near evening. It is shameful and highly discreditable that this battle should last so long. See yonder that gentle maid who weeps for thee and calls on God. Full sweetly she prays for thee, as does also mine for me. Surely we should do our best with our blades of steel for the sake of our lady-loves." Erec replies: "You have spoken well." Then they take a little rest, Erec looking toward his lady as she softly prays for him. While he sat and looked on her, great strength was recruited within him. Her love and beauty inspired him with great boldness. He remembered the Queen, to whom he pledged his word that he would avenge the insult done him, or would make it greater yet. "Ah! wretch," says he, "why do I wait? I have not yet taken vengeance for the injury which this vassal permitted when his dwarf struck me in the wood." His anger is revived within him as he summons the knight: "Vassal," quoth he, "I call you to battle anew. Too long we have rested; let us now renew our strife." And he replies: "That is no hardship to me." Whereupon, they again fall upon each other. They were both expert fencers. At his first lunge the knight would have wounded Erec had he not skilfully parried. Even so, he smote him so hard over the shield beside his temple that he struck a piece from his helmet. Closely shaving his white coif, the sword descends, cleaving the shield through to the buckle, and cutting more than a span from the side of his hauberk. Then he must have been well stunned, as the cold steel penetrated to the flesh on his thigh. May God protect him now! If the blow had not glanced off, it would have cut right through his body. But Erec is in no wise dismayed: he pays him back what is owing him, and. attacking him boldly, smites him upon the shoulder so violently a blow that the shield cannot withstand it, nor is the hauberk of any use to prevent the sword from penetrating to the bone. He made the crimson blood flow down to his waist-band. Both of the vassals are hard fighters: they fight with honours even, for one cannot gain from the other a single foot of ground. Their hauberks are so torn and their shields so hacked, that there is actually not enough of them left to serve as a protection. So they fight all exposed. Each one loses a deal of blood, and both grow weak. He strikes Erec and Erec strikes him. Erec deals him such a tremendous blow upon the helmet that he quite stuns him. Then he lets him have it again and again, giving him three blows in quick succession, which entirely split the helmet and cut the coif beneath it. The sword even reaches the skull and cuts a bone of his head, but without penetrating the brain. He stumbles and totters, and while he staggers, Erec pushes him over, so that he falls upon his right side. Erec grabs him by the helmet and forcibly drags it from his head, and unlaces the ventail, so that his head and face are completely exposed. When Erec thinks of the insult done him by the dwarf in the wood, he would have cut off his head, had he not cried for mercy. "Ah! vassal," says he, "thou hast defeated me. Mercy now, and do not kill me, after having overcome me and taken me prisoner: that would never bring thee praise or glory. If thou shouldst touch me more, thou wouldst do great villainy. Take here my sword; I yield it thee." Erec, however, does not take it, but says in reply: "I am within an ace of killing thee." "Ah! gentle knight, mercy! For what crime, indeed, or for what wrong shouldst thou hate me with mortal hatred? I never saw thee before that I am aware, and never have I been engaged in doing thee any shame or wrong." Erec replies: "Indeed you have." "Ah, sire, tell me when! For I never saw you, that I can remember, and if I have done you any wrong, I place myself at your mercy." Then Erec said: "Vassal, I am he who was in the forest yesterday with Queen Guinevere, when thou didst allow thy ill-bred dwarf to strike my lady's damsel. It is disgraceful to strike a woman. And afterwards he struck me, taking me for some common fellow. Thou wast guilty of too great insolence when thou sawest such an outrage and didst complacently permit such a monster of a lout to strike the damsel and myself. For such a crime I may well hate thee; for thou hast committed a grave offence. Thou shalt now constitute thyself my prisoner, and without delay go straight to my lady whom thou wilt surely find at Cardigan, if thither thou takest thy way. Thou wilt reach there this very night, for it is not seven leagues from here, I think. Thou shalt hand over to her thyself, thy damsel, and thy dwarf, to do as she may dictate; and tell her that I send her word that to-morrow I shall come contented, bringing with me a damsel so fair and wise and fine that in all the world she has not her match. So much thou mayst tell her truthfully. And now I wish to know thy name." Then he must needs say in spite of himself: "Sire, my name is Yder, son of Nut. This morning I had not thought that any single man by force of arms could conquer me. Now I have found by experience a man who is better than I. You are a very valiant knight, and I pledge you my faith here and now that I will go without delay and put myself in the Queen's hands. But tell me without reserve what your name may be. Who shall I say it is that sends me? For I am ready to start." And he replies: "My name I will tell thee without disguise: it is Erec. Go, and tell her that it is I who have sent thee to her." "Now I'll go, and I promise you that I will put my dwarf, my damsel, and myself altogether at her disposal (you need have no fear), and I will give her news of you and of your damsel." Then Erec received his plighted word, and the Count and all the people round about the ladies and the gentlemen were present at the agreement. Some were joyous, and some downcast; some were sorry, and others glad. The most rejoiced for the sake of the damsel with the white raiment, the daughter of the poor vavasor she of the gentle and open heart; but his damsel and those who were devoted to him were sorry for Yder.

Yder, compelled to execute his promise, did not wish to tarry longer, but mounted his steed at once. But why should I make a long story? Taking his dwarf and his damsel, they traversed the woods and the plain, going on straight until they came to Cardigan. In the bower outside the great hall, Gawain and Kay the seneschal and a great number of other lords were gathered. The seneschal was the first to espy those approaching, and said to my lord Gawain: "Sire, my heart divines that the vassal who yonder comes is he of whom the Queen spoke as having yesterday done her such an insult. If I am not mistaken, there are three in the party, for I see the dwarf and the damsel." "That is so," says my lord Gawain; "it is surely a damsel and a dwarf who are coming straight toward us with the knight. The knight himself is fully armed, but his shield is not whole. If the Queen should see him, she would know him. Hello, seneschal, go call her now!" So he went straightway and found her in one of the apartments. "My lady," says he, "do you remember the dwarf who yesterday angered you by wounding your damsel?" "Yes, I remember him right well. Seneschal, have you any news of him? Why have you mentioned him?" "Lady, because I have seen a knight-errant armed coming upon a grey horse, and if my eyes have not deceived me, I saw a damsel with him; and it seems to me that with him comes the dwarf, who still holds the scourge from which Erec received his lashing." Then the Queen rose quickly and said: "Let us go quickly, seneschal, to see if it is the vassal. If it is he, you may be sure that I shall tell you so, as soon as I see him." And Kay said: "I will show him to you. Come up into the bower where your knights are assembled. It was from there we saw him coming, and my lord Gawain himself awaits you there. My lady, let us hasten thither, for here we have too long delayed." Then the Queen bestirred herself, and coming to the windows she took her stand by my lord Gawain, and straightway recognised the knight. "Ha! my lords," she cries, "it is he. He has been through great danger. He has been in a battle. I do not know whether Erec has avenged his grief, or whether this knight has defeated Erec. But there is many a dent upon his shield, and his hauberk is covered with blood, so that it is rather red than white." "In sooth, my lady," quoth my lord Gawain, "I am very sure that you are quite right. His hauberk is covered with blood, and pounded and beaten, showing plainly that he has been in a fight. We can easily see that the battle has been hot. Now we shall soon hear from him news that will give us joy or gloom: whether Erec sends him to you here as a prisoner at your discretion, or whether he comes in pride of heart to boast before us arrogantly that he has defeated or killed Erec. No other news can he bring, I think." The Queen says: "I am of the same opinion." And all the others say: "It may well be so."

Meanwhile Yder enters the castle gate, bringing them news. They all came down from the bower, and went to meet him. Yder came up to the royal terrace and there dismounted from his horse. And Gawain took the damsel and helped her down from her palfrey; the dwarf, for his part, dismounted too. There were more than one hundred knights standing there, and when the three newcomers had all dismounted they were led into the King's presence. As soon as Yder saw the Queen, he bowed low and first saluted her, then the King and his knights, and said: "Lady, I am sent here as your prisoner by a gentleman, a valiant and noble knight, whose face yesterday my dwarf made smart with his knotted scourge. He has overcome me at arms and defeated me. Lady, the dwarf I bring you here: he has come to surrender to you at discretion. I bring you myself, my damsel, and my dwarf to do with us as you please." The Queen keeps her peace no longer, but asks him for news of Erec: "Tell me," she says, "if you please, do you know when Erec will arrive?" "To-morrow, lady, and with him a damsel he will bring, the fairest of all I ever knew." When he had delivered his message, the Queen, who was kind and sensible, said to him courteously: "Friend, since thou hast thrown thyself upon my mercy, thy confinement shall be less harsh; for I have no desire to seek thy harm. But tell me now, so help thee God, what is thy name?" And he replies: "Lady, my name is Yder, son of Nut." And they knew that he told the truth. Then the Queen arose, and going before the King, said: "Sire, did you hear? You have done well to wait for Erec, the valiant knight. I gave you good advice yesterday, when I counselled you to await his return. This proves that it is wise to take advice." The King replies: "That is no lie; rather is it perfectly true that he who takes advice is no fool. Happily we followed your advice yesterday. But if you care anything for me, release this knight from his durance, provided he consent to join henceforth my household and court; and if he does not consent, let him suffer the consequence." When the King had thus spoken, the Queen straightway released the knight; but it was on this condition, that he should remain in the future at the court. He did not have to be urged before he gave his consent to stay. Now he was of the court and household to which he had not before belonged. Then valets were at hand to run and relieve him of his arms.

Now we must revert to Erec, whom we left in the field where the battle had taken place. Even Tristan, when he slew fierce Morhot on Saint Samson's isle , awakened no such jubilee as they celebrated here over Erec. Great and small, thin and stout--all make much of him and praise his knighthood. There is not a knight but cries: "Lord what a vassal! Under Heaven there is not his like!" They follow him to his lodgings, praising him and talking much. Even the Count himself embraces him, who above the rest was glad, and said: "Sire, if you please, you ought by right to lodge in my house, since you are the son of King Lac. If you would accept of my hospitality you would do me a great honour, for I regard you as my liege. Fair sire, may it please you, I beg you to lodge with me." Erec answers: "May it not displease you, but I shall not desert my host to-night, who has done me much honour in giving me his daughter. What say you, sir? Is it not a fair and precious gift?" "Yes, sire," the Count replies; "the gift, in truth, is fine and good. The maid herself is fair and clever, and besides is of very noble birth. You must know that her mother is my sister. Surely, I am glad at heart that you should deign to take my niece. Once more I beg you to lodge with me this night." Erec replies: "Ask me no more. I will not do it." Then the Count saw that further insistence was useless, and said: "Sire, as it please you! We may as well say no more about it; but I and my knights will all be with you to-night to cheer you and bear you company." When Erec heard that, he thanked him, and returned to his host's dwelling, with the Count attending him. Ladies and knights were gathered there, and the vavasor was glad at heart. As soon as Erec arrived, more than a score of squires ran quickly to remove his arms. Any one who was present in that house could have witnessed a happy scene. Erec went first and took his seat; then all the others in order sit down upon the couches, the cushions, and benches. At Erec's side the Count sat down, and the damsel with her radiant face, who was feeding the much disputed hawk upon her wrist with a plover's wing. Great honour and joy and prestige had she gained that day, and she was very glad at heart both for the bird and for her lord. She could not have been happier, and showed it plainly, making no secret of her joy. All could see how gay she was, and throughout the house there was great rejoicing for the happiness of the maid they loved.

Erec thus addressed the vavasor: "Fair host, fair friend, fair sire! You have done me great honour, and richly shall it be repaid you. To-morrow I shall take away your daughter with me to the King's court, where I wish to take her as my wife; and if you will tarry here a little, I shall send betimes to fetch you. I shall have you escorted into the country which is my father's now, but which later will be mine. It is far from here--by no means near. There I shall give you two towns, very splendid, rich, and fine. You shall be lord of Roadan, which was built in the time of Adam, and of another town close by, which is no less valuable. The people call it Montrevel, and my father owns no better town. And before the third day has passed, I shall send you plenty of gold and silver, of dappled and grey furs, and precious silken stuffs wherewith to adorn yourself and your wife my dear lady. To-morrow at dawn I wish to take your daughter to court, dressed and arrayed as she is at present. I wish my lady, the Queen, to dress her in her best dress of satin and scarlet cloth."

There was a maiden near at hand, very honourable, prudent, and virtuous. She was seated on a bench beside the maid with the white shift, and was her own cousin the niece of my lord the Count. When she heard how Erec intended to take her cousin in such very poor array to the Queen's court, she spoke about it to the Count. "Sire," she says, "it would be a shame to you more than to any one else if this knight should take your niece away with him in such sad array." And the Count made answer: "Gentle niece, do you give her the best of your dresses." But Erec heard the conversation, and said: "By no means, my lord. For be assured that nothing in the world would tempt me to let her have another robe until the Queen shall herself bestow it upon her." When the damsel heard this, she replied: "Alas! fair sire, since you insist upon leading off my cousin thus dressed in a white shift and chemise, and since you are determined that she shall have none of my dresses, a different gift I wish to make her. I have three good palfreys, as good as any of king or count, one sorrel, one dappled, and the other black with white forefeet. Upon my word, if you had a hundred to pick from, you would not find a better one than the dappled mount. The birds in the air do not fly more swiftly than the palfrey; and he is not too lively, but just suits a lady. A child can ride him, for he is neither skittish nor balky, nor does he bite nor kick nor become unmanageable. Any one who is looking for something better does not know what he wants. And his pace is so easy and gentle that a body is more comfortable and easy on his back than in a boat." Then said Erec: "My dear, I have no objection to her accepting this gift; indeed, I am pleased with the offer, and do not wish her to refuse it." Then the damsel calls one of her trusty servants, and says to him: "Go, friend, saddle my dappled palfrey, and lead him here at once." And he carries out her command: he puts on saddle and bridle and strives to make him appear well. Then he jumps on the maned palfrey, which is now ready for inspection. When Erec saw the animal, he did not spare his praise, for he could see that he was very fine and gentle. So he bade a servant lead him back and hitch him in the stable beside his own horse. Then they all separated, after an evening agreeably spent. The Count goes off to his own dwelling, and leaves Erec with the vavasor, saying that he will bear him company in the morning when he leaves. All that night they slept well. In the morning, when the dawn was bright, Erec prepares to start, commanding his horses to be saddled. His fair sweetheart, too, awakes, dresses, and makes ready. The vavasor and his wife rise too, and every knight and lady there prepares to escort the damsel and the knight. Now they are all on horseback, and the Count as well. Erec rides beside the Count, having beside him his sweetheart ever mindful of her hawk. Having no other riches, she plays with her hawk. Very merry were they as they rode along; but when the time came to part, the Count wished to send along with Erec a party of his knights to do him honour by escorting him. But he announced that none should bide with him, and that he wanted no company but that of the damsel. Then, when they had accompanied them some distance, he said: "In God's name, farewell!" Then the Count kisses Erec and his niece, and commends them both to merciful God. Her father and mother, too, kiss them again and again, and could not keep back their tears: at parting, the mother weeps, the father and the daughter too. For such is love and human nature, and such is affection between parents and children. They wept from sorrow, tenderness, and love which they had for their child; yet they knew full well that their daughter was to fill a place from which great honour would accrue to them. They shed tears of love and pity when they separated from their daughter, but they had no other cause to weep. They knew well enough that eventually they would receive great honour from her marriage. So at parting many a tear was shed, as weeping they commend one another to God, and thus separate without more delay.

Erec quit his host; for he was very anxious to reach the royal court. In his adventure he took great satisfaction; for now he had a lady passing fair, discreet, courteous, and debonair. He could not look at her enough: for the more he looks at her, the more she pleases him. He cannot help giving her a kiss. He is happy to ride by her side, and it does him good to look at her. Long he gazes at her fair hair, her laughing eyes, and her radiant forehead, her nose, her face, and mouth, for all of which gladness fills his heart. He gazes upon her down to the waist, at her chin and her snowy neck, her bosom and sides, her arms and hands. But no less the damsel looks at the vassal with a clear eye and loyal heart, as if they were in competition. They would not have ceased to survey each other even for promise of a reward! A perfect match they were in courtesy, beauty, and gentleness. And they were so alike in quality, manner, and customs, that no one wishing to tell the truth could choose the better of them, nor the fairer, nor the more discreet. Their sentiments, too, were much alike; so that they were well suited to each other. Thus each steals the other's heart away. Law or marriage never brought together two such sweet creatures. And so they rode along until just on the stroke of noon they approached the castle of Cardigan, where they were both expected. Some of the first nobles of the court had gone up to look from the upper windows and see if they could see them. Queen Guinevere ran up, and even the King came with Kay and Perceval of

Wales, and with them my lord Gawain and Tor, the son of King Ares; Lucan the cupbearer was there, too, and many another doughty knight. Finally, they espied Erec coming along in company with his lady. They all knew him well enough from as far as they could see him. The Queen is greatly pleased, and indeed the whole court is glad of his coming, because they all love him so. As soon as he was come before the entrance hall, the King and Queen go down to meet him, all greeting him in God's name. They welcome Erec and his maiden, commending and praising her great beauty. And the King himself caught her and lifted her down from her palfrey. The King was decked in fine array and was then in cheery mood. He did signal honour to the damsel by taking her hand and leading her up into the great stone hall. After them Erec and the Queen also went up hand in hand, and he said to her: "I bring you, lady, my damsel and my sweetheart dressed in poor garb. As she was given to me, so have I brought her to you. She is the daughter of a poor vavasor. Through poverty many an honourable man is brought low: her father, for instance, is gentle and courteous, but he has little means. And her mother is a very gentle lady, the sister of a rich Count. She has no lack of beauty or of lineage, that I should not marry her. It is poverty that has compelled her to wear this white linen garment until both sleeves are torn at the side. And yet, had it been my desire, she might have had dresses rich enough. For another damsel, a cousin of hers, wished to give her a robe of ermine and of spotted or grey silk. But I would not have her dressed in any other robe until you should have seen her. Gentle lady, consider the matter now and see what need she has of a fine becoming gown." And the Queen at once replies: "You have done quite right; it is fitting that she should have one of my gowns, and I will give her straightway a rich, fair gown, both fresh and new." The Queen then hastily took her off to her own private room, and gave orders to bring quickly the fresh tunic and the greenish-purple mantle, embroidered with little crosses, which had been made for herself. The one who went at her behest came bringing to her the mantle and the tunic, which was lined with white ermine even to the sleeves. At the wrists and on the neck-band there was in truth more than half a mark's weight of beaten gold, and everywhere set in the gold there were precious stones of divers colours, indigo and green, blue and dark brown. This tunic was very rich, but not a writ less precious, I trow, was the mantle. As yet, there were no ribbons on it; for the mantle like the tunic was brand new. The mantle was very rich and fine: laid about the neck were two sable skins, and in the tassels there was more than an ounce of gold; on one a hyacinth, and on the other a ruby flashed more bright than burning candle. The fur lining was of white ermine; never was finer seen or found. The cloth was skilfully embroidered with little crosses, all different, indigo, vermilion, dark blue, white, green, blue, and yellow. The Queen called for some ribbons four ells long, made of silken thread and gold. The ribbons are given to her, handsome and well matched. Quickly she had them fastened to the mantle by some one who knew how to do it, and who was master of the art. When the mantle needed no more touches, the gay and gentle lady clasped the maid with the white gown and said to her cheerily: "Mademoiselle, you must change this frock for this tunic which is worth more than a hundred marks of silver. So much I wish to bestow upon you. And put on this mantle, too. Another time I will give you more." Not able to refuse the gift, she takes the robe and thanks her for it. Then two maids took her aside into a room, where she took off her frock as being of no further value; but she asked and requested that it be given away (to some poor woman) for the love of God. Then she dons the tunic, and girds herself, binding on tightly a golden belt, and afterwards puts on the mantle. Now she looked by no means ill; for the dress became her so well that it made her look more beautiful than ever. The two maids wove a gold thread in amongst her golden hair: but her tresses were more radiant than the thread of gold, fine though it was. The maids, moreover, wove a fillet of flowers of many various colours and placed it upon her head. They strove as best they might to adorn her in such wise that no fault should be found with her attire. Strung upon a ribbon around her neck, a damsel hung two brooches of enamelled gold. Now she looked so charming and fair that I do not believe that you could find her equal in any land, search as you might, so skilfully had Nature wrought in her. Then she stepped out of the dressing-room into the Queen's presence. The Queen made much of her, because she liked her and was glad that she was beautiful and had such gentle manners. They took each other by the hand and passed into the King's presence. And when the King saw them, he got up to meet them. When they came into the great hall, there were so many knights there who rose before them that I cannot call by name the tenth part of them, or the thirteenth, or the fifteenth. But I can tell you the names of some of the best of the knights who belonged to the Round Table and who were the best in the world.

Before all the excellent knights, Gawain ought to be named the first, and second Erec the son of Lac, and third Lancelot of the Lake. Gornemant of Gohort was fourth, and the fifth was the Handsome Coward. The sixth was the Ugly Brave, the seventh Meliant of Liz, the eighth Mauduit the Wise, and the ninth Dodinel the Wild. Let Gandelu be named the tenth, for he was a goodly man. The others I shall mention without order, because the numbers bother me. Eslit was there with Briien, and Yvain the son of Uriien. And Yvain of Loenel was there, as well as Yvain the Adulterer. Beside Yvain of Cavaliot was Garravain of Estrangot. After the Knight with the Horn was the Youth with the Golden Ring. And Tristan who never laughed sat beside Bliobleheris, and beside Brun of Piciez was his brother Gru the Sullen. The Armourer sat next, who preferred war to peace. Next sat Karadues the Shortarmed, a knight of good cheer; and Caveron of Robendic, and the son of King Quenedic and the Youth of Quintareus and Yder of the Dolorous Mount. Gaheriet and Kay of Estraus, Amauguin and Gales the Bald, Grain, Gornevain, and Carabes, and Tor the son of King Aras, Girflet the son of Do, and Taulas, who never wearied of arms: and a young man of great merit, Loholt the son of King Arthur, and Sagremor the Impetuous, who should not be forgotten, nor Bedoiier the Master of the Horse, who was skilled at chess and trictrac, nor Bravain, nor King Lot, nor Galegantin of Wales, nor Gronosis, versed in evil, who was son of Kay the Seneschal, nor Labigodes the Courteous, nor Count Cadorcaniois, nor Letron of Prepelesant, whose manners were so excellent, nor Breon the son of Canodan, nor the Count of Honolan who had such a head of fine fair hair; he it was who received the King's horn in an evil day; he never had any care for truth.

When the stranger maiden saw all the knights arrayed looking steadfastly at her, she bowed her head in embarrassment; nor was it strange that her face blushed all crimson. But her confusion was so becoming to her that she looked all the more lovely. When the King saw that she was embarrassed, he did not wish to leave her side. Taking her gently by the hand, he made her sit down on his right hand; and on his left sat the Queen, speaking thus to the King the while. "Sire, in my opinion he who can win such a fair lady by his arms in another land ought by right to come to a royal court. It was well we waited for Erec; for now you can bestow the kiss upon the fairest of the court. I should think none would find fault with you! for none can say, unless he lie, that this maiden is not the most charming of all the damsels here, or indeed in all the world." The King makes answer: "That is no lie; and upon her, if there is no remonstrance, I shall bestow the honour of the White Stag." Then he added to the knights: "My lords, what say you? What is your opinion? In body, in face, and in whatever a maid should have, this one is the most charming and beautiful to be found, as I may say, before you come to where Heaven and earth meet. I say it is meet that she should receive the honour of the Stag. And you, my lords, what do you think about it? Can you make any objection? If any one wishes to protest, let him straightway speak his mind. I am King, and must keep my word and must not permit any baseness, falsity, or arrogance. I must maintain truth and righteousness. It is the business of a loyal king to support the law, truth, faith, and justice. I would not in any wise commit a disloyal deed or wrong to either weak or strong. It is not meet that any one should complain of me; nor do I wish the custom and the practice to lapse, which my family has been wont to foster. You, too, would doubtless regret to see me strive to introduce other customs and other laws than those my royal sire observed. Regardless of consequences, I am bound to keep and maintain the institution of my father Pendragon, who was a just king and emperor. Now tell me fully what you think! Let none be slow to speak his mind, if this damsel is not the fairest of my household and ought not by right to receive the kiss of the White Stag: I wish to know what you truly think." Then they all cry with one accord: "Sire, by the Lord and his Cross! you may well kiss her with good reason, for she is the fairest one there is. In this damsel there is more beauty than there is of radiance in the sun. You may kiss her freely, for we all agree in sanctioning it." When the King hears that this is well pleasing to them all, he will no longer delay in bestowing the kiss, but turns toward her and embraces her. The maid was sensible, and perfectly willing that the King should kiss her; she would have been discourteous, indeed, to resent it. In courteous fashion and in the presence of all his knights the King kissed her, and said: "My dear. I give you my love in all honesty. I will love you with true heart, without malice and without guile." By this adventure the King carried out the practice and the usage to which the White Stag was entitled at his court.

Here ends the first part of my story.

When the kiss of the Stag was taken according to the custom of the country, Erec, like a polite and kind man, was solicitous for his poor host. It was not his intention to fail to execute what he had promised. Hear how he kept his covenant: for he sent him now five sumpter mules, strong and sleek, loaded with dresses and clothes, buckrams and scarlets, marks of gold and silver plate, furs both vair and grey, skins of sable, purple stuffs, and silks. When the mules were loaded with all that a gentleman can need, he sent with them an escort of ten knights and sergeants chosen from his own men, and straightly charged them to salute his host and show great honour both to him and to his lady, as if it were to himself in person; and when they should have presented to them the sumpters which they brought them, the gold, the silver, and money, and all the other furnishings which were in the boxes, they should escort the lady and the vavasor with great honour into his kingdom of Farther Wales. Two towns there he had promised them, the most choice and the best situated that there were in all his land, with nothing to fear from attack. Montrevel was the name of one, and the other's name was Roadan. When they should arrive in his kingdom, they should make over to them these two towns, together with their rents and their jurisdiction, in accordance with what he had promised them. All was carried out as Erec had ordered. The messengers made no delay, and in good time they presented to his host the gold and the silver and the sumpters and the robes and the money, of which there was great plenty. They escorted them into Erec's kingdom, and strove to serve them well. They came into the country on the third day, and transferred to them the towers of the towns; for King Lac made no objection. He gave them a warm welcome and showed them honour, loving them for the sake of his son Erec. He made over to them the title to the towns, and established their suzerainty by making knights and bourgeois swear that they would reverence them as their true liege lords. When this was done and accomplished, the messengers returned to their lord Erec, who received them gladly. When he asked for news of the vavasor and his lady, of his own father and of his kingdom, the report they gave him was good and fair.

Not long after this, the time drew near when Erec was to celebrate his marriage. The delay was irksome to him, and he resolved no longer to suffer and wait. So he went and asked of the King that it might please him to allow him to be married at the court. The King vouchsafed him the boon, and sent through all his kingdom to search for the kings and counts who were his liege-men, bidding them that none be so bold as not to be present at Pentecost. None dares to hold back and not go to court at the King's summons. Now I will tell you, and listen well, who were these counts and kings. With a rich escort and one hundred extra mounts Count Brandes of Gloucester came. After him came Menagormon, who was Count of Clivelon. And he of the Haute Montagne came with a very rich following. The Count of Treverain came, too, with a hundred of his knights, and Count Godegrain with as many more. Along with those whom I have just mentioned came Maheloas, a great baron, lord of the Isle of Voirre. In this island no thunder is heard, no lightning strikes, nor tempests rage, nor do toads or serpents exist there, nor is it ever too hot or too cold. Graislemier of Fine Posterne brought twenty companions, and had with him his brother Guigomar, lord of the Isle of Avalon. Of the latter we have heard it said that he was a friend of Morgan the Fay, and such he was in very truth. Davit of Tintagel came, who never suffered woe or grief. Guergesin, the Duke of Haut Bois, came with a very rich equipment. There was no lack of counts and dukes, but of kings there were still more. Garras of Cork, a doughty king, was there with five hundred knights clad in mantles, hose, and tunics of brocade and silk. Upon a Cappadocian steed came Aguisel, the Scottish king, and brought with him his two sons, Cadret and Coi--two much respected knights. Along with those whom I have named came King Ban of Gomeret, and he had in his company only young men, beardless as yet on chin and lip. A numerous and gay band he brought two hundred of them in his suite; and there was none, whoever he be, but had a falcon or tercel, a merlin or a sparrow-hawk, or some precious pigeon-hawk, golden or mewed. Kerrin, the old King of Riel, brought no youth, but rather three hundred companions of whom the youngest was seven score years old. Because of their great age, their heads were all as white as snow, and their beards reached down to their girdles. Arthur held them in great respect. The lord of the dwarfs came next, Bilis, the king of Antipodes. This king of whom I speak was a dwarf himself and own brother of Brien. Bilis, on the one hand, was the smallest of all the dwarfs, while his brother Brien was a half-foot or full palm taller than any other knight in the kingdom. To display his wealth and power, Bilis brought with him two kings who were also dwarfs and who were vassals of his, Grigoras and Glecidalan. Every one looked at them as marvels. When they had arrived at court, they were treated with great esteem. All three were honoured and served at the court like kings, for they were very perfect gentlemen. In brief, when King Arthur saw all his lords assembled, his heart was glad. Then, to heighten the joy, he ordered a hundred squires to be bathed whom he wished to dub knights. There was none of them but had a parti-coloured robe of rich brocade of Alexandria, each one choosing such as pleased his fancy. All had arms of a uniform pattern, and horses swift and full of mettle, of which the worst was worth a hundred livres.

When Erec received his wife, he must needs call her by her right name. For a wife is not espoused unless she is called by her proper name. As yet no one knew her name, but now for the first time it was made known: Enide was her baptismal name. The Archbishop of Canterbury, who had come to the court, blessed them, as is his right. When the court was all assembled, there was not a minstrel in the countryside who possessed any pleasing accomplishment that did not come to the court. In the great hall there was much merry-making, each one contributing what he could to the entertainment: one jumps, another tumbles, another does magic; there is story-telling, singing, whistling, playing from notes; they play on the harp, the rote, the fiddle, the violin, the flute, and pipe. The maidens sing and dance, and outdo each other in the merry-making. At the wedding that day everything was done which can give joy and incline man's heart to gladness. Drums are beaten, large and small, and there is playing of pipes, fifes, horns, trumpets, and bagpipes. What more shall I say? There was not a wicket or a gate kept closed; but the exits and entrances all stood ajar, so that no one, poor or rich, was turned away. King Arthur was not miserly, but gave orders to the bakers, the cooks, and the butlers that they should serve every one generously with bread, wine, and venison. No one asked anything whatever to be passed to him without getting all he desired.

There was great merriment in the palace. But I will pass over the rest, and you shall hear of the joy and pleasure in the bridal chamber. Bishops and archbishops were there on the night when the bride and groom retired. At this their first meeting, Iseut was not filched away, nor was Brangien put in her place. The Queen herself took charge of their preparations for the night; for both of them were dear to her. The hunted stag which pants for thirst does not so long for the spring, nor does the hungry sparrow-hawk return so quickly when he is called, as did these two come to hold each other in close embrace. That night they had full compensation for their long delay. After the chamber had been cleared, they allow each sense to be gratified: the eyes, which are the entrance-way of love, and which carry messages to the heart, take satisfaction in the glance, for they rejoice in all they see; after the message of the eyes comes the far surpassing sweetness of the kisses inviting love; both of them make trial of this sweetness, and let their hearts quaff so freely that hardly can they leave off. Thus, kissing was their first sport. And the love which is between them emboldened the maid and left her quite without her fears; regardless of pain, she suffered all. Before she rose, she no longer bore the name of maid; in the morning she was a new-made dame. That day the minstrels were in happy mood, for they were all well paid. They were fully compensated for the entertainment they had given, and many a handsome gift was bestowed upon them: robes of grey squirrel skin and ermine, of rabbit skins and violet stuffs, scarlets and silken stuffs. Whether it be a horse or money, each one got what he deserved according to his skill. And thus the wedding festivities and the court lasted almost a fortnight with great joy and magnificence. For his own glory and satisfaction, as well as to honour Erec the more, King Arthur made all the knights remain a full fortnight. When the third week began, all together by common consent agreed to hold a tournament. On the one side, my lord Gawain offered himself as surety that it would take place between Evroic and Tenebroc: and Meliz and Meliadoc were guarantors on the other side. Then the court separated.

A month after Pentecost the tournament assembled, and the jousting began in the plain below Tenebroc. Many an ensign of red, blue, and white, many a veil and many a sleeve were bestowed as tokens of love. Many a lance was carried there, flying the colours argent and green, or gold and azure blue. There were many, too, with different devices, some with stripes and some with dots. That day one saw laced on many a helmet of gold or steel, some green, some yellow, and others red, all aglowing in the sun; so many scutcheons and white hauberks; so many swords girt on the left side; so many good shields, fresh and new, some resplendent in silver and green, others of azure with buckles of gold; so many good steeds marked with white, or sorrel, tawny, white, black, and bay: all gather hastily. And now the field is quite covered with arms. On either side the ranks tremble, and a roar rises from the fight. The shock of the lances is very great. Lances break and shields are riddled, the hauberks receive bumps and are torn asunder, saddles go empty and horsemen ramble, while the horses sweat and foam. Swords are quickly drawn on those who tumble noisily, and some run to receive the promise of a ransom, others to stave off this disgrace. Erec rode a white horse, and came forth alone at the head of the line to joust, if he may find an opponent. From the opposite side there rides out to meet him Orguelleus de la Lande, mounted on an Irish steed which bears him along with marvellous speed. On the shield before his breast Erec strikes him with such force that he knocks him from his horse: he leaves him prone and passes on. Then Raindurant opposed him, son of the old dame of Tergalo, covered with blue cloth of silk; he was a knight of great prowess. Against one another now they charge and deal fierce blows on the shields about their neck. Erec from lance's length lays him over on the hard ground. While riding back he met the King of the Red City, who was very valiant and bold. They grasp their reins by the knots and their shields by the inner straps. They both had fine arms, and strong swift horses, and good shields, fresh and new. With such fury they strike each other that both their lances fly in splinters. Never was there seen such a blow. They rush together with shields, arms, and horses. But neither girth nor rein nor breast-strap could prevent the king from coming to earth. So he flew from his steed, carrying with him saddle and stirrup, and even the reins of his bridle in his hand. All those who witnessed the jousting were filled with amazement, and said it cost him dear to joust with such a goodly knight. Erec did not wish to stop to capture either horse or rider, but rather to joust and distinguish himself in order that his prowess might appear. He thrills the ranks in front of him. Gawain animates those who were on his side by his prowess, and by winning horses and knights to the discomfiture of his opponents. I speak of my lord Gawain, who did right well and valiantly. In the fight he unhorsed Guincel, and took Gaudin of the Mountain; he captured knights and horses alike: my lord Gawain did well. Girtlet the son of Do, and Yvain, and Sagremor the Impetuous, so evilly entreated their adversaries that they drove them back to the gates, capturing and unhorsing many of them. In front of the gate of the town the strife began again between those within and those without. There Sagremor was thrown down, who was a very gallant knight. He was on the point of being detained and captured, when Erec spurs to rescue him, breaking his lance into splinters upon one of the opponents. So hard he strikes him on the breast that he made him quit the saddle. Then he made of his sword and advances upon them, crushing and splitting their helmets. Some flee, and others make way before him, for even the boldest fears him. Finally, he distributed so many blows and thrusts that he rescued Sagremor from them, and drove them all in confusion into the town. Meanwhile, the vesper hour drew to a close. Erec bore himself so well that day that he was the best of the combatants. But on the morrow he did much better yet: for he took so many knights and left so many saddles empty that none could believe it except those who had seen it. Every one on both sides said that with his lance and shield he had won the honours of the tournament. Now was Erec's renown so high that no one spoke save of him, nor was any one of such goodly favour. In countenance he resembled Absalom, in language he seemed a Solomon, in boldness he equalled Samson, and in generous giving and spending he was the equal of Alexander. On his return from the tourney Erec went to speak with the King. He went to ask him for leave to go and visit his own land; but first he thanked him like a frank, wise, and courteous man for the honour which he had done him; for very deep was his gratitude. Then he asked his permission to leave, for he wished to visit his own country, and he wished to take his wife with him. This request the King could not deny, and yet he would have had him stay. He gives him leave and begs him to return as soon as possible: for in the whole court there was no better or more gallant knight, save only his dear nephew Gawain; with him no one could be compared. But next after him, he prized Erec most, and held him more dear than any other knight.

Erec wished to delay no longer. As soon as he had the King's leave, he bid his wife make her preparations, and he retained as his escort sixty knights of merit with horses and with dappled and grey furs. As soon as he was ready for his journey, he tarried little further at court, but took leave of the Queen and commended the knights to God. The Queen grants him leave to depart. At the hour of prime he set out from the royal palace. In the presence of them all he mounted his steed, and his wife mounted the dappled horse which she had brought from her own country; then all his escort mounted. Counting knights and squires, there were full seven score in the train. After four long days' journey over hills and slopes, through forests, plains, and streams, they came on the fifth day to Camant, where King Lac was residing in a very charming town. No one ever saw one better situated; for the town was provided with forests and meadow-land, with vineyards and farms, with streams and orchards, with ladies and knights, and fine, lively youths, and polite, well-mannered clerks who spent their incomes freely, with fair and charming maidens, and with prosperous burghers. Before Erec reached the town, he sent two knights ahead to announce his arrival to the King. When he heard the news, the King had clerks, knights, and damsels quickly mount, and ordered the bells to be rung, and the streets to be hung with tapestries and silken stuffs, that his son might be received with joy; then he himself got on his horse. Of clerks there were present fourscore, gentle and honourable men, clad in grey cloaks bordered with sable. Of knights there were full five hundred, mounted on bay, sorrel, or white-spotted steeds. There were so many burghers and dames that no one could tell the number of them. The King and his son galloped and rode on till they saw and recognised each other. They both jump down from their horses and embrace and greet each other for a long time, without stirring from the place where they first met. Each party wished the other joy: the King makes much of Erec, but all at once breaks off to turn to Enide. On all sides he is in clover: he embraces and kisses them both, and knows not which of the two pleases him the more. As they gaily enter the castle, the bells all ring their peals to honour Erec's arrival. The streets are all strewn with reeds, mint, and iris, and are hung overhead with curtains and tapestries of fancy silk and satin stuffs. There was great rejoicing; for all the people came together to see their new lord, and no one ever saw greater happiness than was shown alike by young and old. First they came to the church, where very devoutly they were received in a procession. Erec kneeled before the altar of the Crucifix, and two knights led his wife to the image of Our Lady. When she had finished her prayer, she stepped back a little and crossed herself with her right hand, as a well-bred dame should do. Then they came out from the church and entered the royal palace, when the festivity began. That day Erec received many presents from the knights and burghers: from one a palfrey of northern stock, and from another a golden cup. One presents him with a golden pigeon-hawk, another with a setter-dog, this one a greyhound, this other a sparrowhawk, and another a swift Arab steed, this one a shield, this one an ensign, this one a sword, and this a helmet. Never was a king more gladly seen in his kingdom, nor received with greater joy, as all strove to serve him well. Yet greater joy they made of Enide than of him, for the great beauty which they saw in her, and still more for her open charm. She was seated in a chamber upon a cushion of brocade which had been brought from Thessaly. Round about her was many a fair lady; yet as the lustrous gem outshines the brown flint, and as the rose excels the poppy, so was Enide fairer than any other lady or damsel to be found in the world, wherever one might search. She was so gentle and honourable, of wise speech and affable, of pleasing character and kindly mien. No one could ever be so watchful as to detect in her any folly, or sign of evil or villainy. She had been so schooled in good manners that she had learned all virtues which any lady can possess, as well as generosity and knowledge. All loved her for her open heart, and whoever could do her any service was glad and esteemed himself the more. No one spoke any ill of her, for no one could do so. In the realm or empire there was no lady of such good manners. But Erec loved her with such a tender love that he cared no more for arms, nor did he go to tournaments, nor have any desire to joust; but he spent his time in cherishing his wife. He made of her his mistress and his sweetheart. He devoted all his heart and mind to fondling and kissing her, and sought no delight in other pastime. His friends grieved over this, and often regretted among themselves that he was so deep in love. Often it was past noon before he left her side; for there he was happy, say what they might. He rarely left her society, and yet he was as open-handed as ever to his knights with arms, dress, and money. There was not a tournament anywhere to which he did not send them well apparelled and equipped. Whatever the cost might be, he gave them fresh steeds for the tourney and joust. All the knights said it was a great pity and misfortune that such a valiant man as he was wont to be should no longer wish to bear arms. He was blamed so much on all sides by the knights and squires that murmurs reached Enide's ears how that her lord had turned craven about arms and deeds of chivalry, and that his manner of life was greatly changed. She grieved sorely over this, but she did not dare to show her grief; for her lord at once would take affront, if she should speak to him. So the matter remained a secret, until one morning they lay in bed where they had had sport together. There they lay in close embrace, like the true lovers they were. He was asleep, but she was awake, thinking of what many a man in the country was saying of her lord. And when she began to think it all over, she could not keep back the tears. Such was her grief and her chagrin that by mischance she let fall a word for which she later felt remorse, though in her heart there was no guile. She began to survey her lord from head to foot, his well-shaped body and his clear countenance, until her tears fell fast upon the bosom of her lord, and she said: "Alas, woe is me that I ever left my country! What did I come here to seek? The earth ought by right to swallow me up when the best knight, the most hardy, brave, fair, and courteous that ever was a count or king, has completely abjured all his deeds of chivalry because of me. And thus, in truth, it is I who have brought shame upon his head, though I would fain not have done so at any price." Then she said to him: "Unhappy thou!" And then kept silence and spoke no more. Erec was not sound asleep and, though dozing, heard plainly what she said. He aroused at her words, and much surprised to see her weeping, he asked her: "Tell me, my precious beauty, why do you weep thus? What has caused you woe or sorrow? Surely it is my wish to know. Tell me now, my gentle sweetheart; and raise care to keep nothing back, why you said that woe was me? For you said it of me and of no one else. I heard your words plainly enough." Then was Enide in a great plight, afraid and dismayed. "Sire," says she, "I know nothing of what you say." "Lady, why do you conceal it? Concealment is of no avail. You hare been crying; I can see that, and you do not cry for nothing. And in my sleep I heard what you said." "Ah! fair sire, you never heard it, and I dare say it was a dream." "Now you are coming to me with lies. I hear you calmly lying to me. But if you do not tell me the truth now, you will come to repent of it later." "Sire, since you torment me thus, I will tell you the whole truth, and keep nothing back. But I am afraid that you will not like it. In this land they all say--the dark, the fair, and the ruddy--that it is a great pity that you should renounce your arms; your reputation has suffered from it. Every one used to say not long ago that in all the world there was known no better or more gallant knight. Now they all go about making game of you-- old and young, little and great--calling you a recreant. Do you suppose it does not give me pain to hear you thus spoken of with scorn? It grieves me when I hear it said, and yet it grieves me more that they put the blame for it on me. Yes, I am blamed for it, I regret to say, and they all assert it is because I have so ensnared and caught you that you are losing all your merit, and do not care for aught but me. You must choose another course, so that you may silence this reproach and regain your former fame; for I have heard too much of this reproach, and yet I did not dare to disclose it to you. Many a time, when I think of it, I have to weep for very grief. Such chagrin I felt just now that I could not keep myself from saying that you were ill-starred." "Lady," said he, "you were in the right, and those who blame me do so with reason. And now at once prepare yourself to take the road. Rise up from here, and dress yourself in your richest robe, and order your saddle to be put on your best palfrey." Now Enide is in great distress: very sad and pensive, she gets up, blaming and upbraiding herself for the foolish words she spoke: she had now made her bed, and must lie in it. "Ah!" said she, "poor fool! I was too happy, for there lacked me nothing. God! why was I so for- ward as to dare to utter such folly? God! did not my lord love me to excess? In faith, alas, he was too fond of me. And now I must go away into exile. But I have yet a greater grief, that I shall no longer see my lord, who loved me with such tenderness that there was nothing he held so dear. The best man that was ever born had become so wrapped up in me that he cared for nothing else. I lacked for nothing then. I was very happy. But pride it is that stirred me up: because of my pride, I must suffer woe for telling him such insulting words, and it is right that I should suffer woe. One does not know what good fortune is until he has made trial of evil." Thus the lady bemoaned her fate, while she dressed herself fitly in her richest robe. Yet nothing gave her any pleasure, but rather cause for deep chagrin. Then she had a maid call one of her squires, and bids him saddle her precious palfrey of northern stock, than which no count or king ever had a better. As soon as she had given him the command, the fellow asked for no delay, but straightway went and saddled the dappled palfrey. And Erec summoned another squire and bade him bring his arms to arm his body withal. Then he went up into a bower, and had a Limoges rug laid out before him on the floor. Meanwhile, the squire ran to fetch the arms and came back and laid them on the rug. Erec took a seat opposite, on the figure of a leopard which was portrayed on the rug. He prepares and gets ready to put on his arms: first, he had laced on a pair of greaves of polished steel; next, he dons a hauberk, which was so fine that not a mesh could be cut away from it. This hauberk of his was rich, indeed, for neither inside nor outside of it was there enough iron to make a needle, nor could it gather any rust; for it was all made of worked silver in tiny meshes triple- wove; and it was made with such skill that I can assure you that no one who had put it on would have been more uncomfortable or sore because of it, than if he had put on a silk jacket over his undershirt. The knights and squires all began to wonder why he was being armed; but no one dared to ask him why. When they had put on his hauberk, a valet laces about his head a helmet fluted with a band of gold, shining brighter than a mirror. Then he takes the sword and girds it on, and orders them to bring him saddled his bay steed of Gascony. Then he calls a valet to him, and says: "Valet, go quickly, run to the chamber beside the tower where my wife is, and tell her that she is keeping me waiting here too long. She has spent too much time on her attire. Tell her to come and mount at once, for I am awaiting her." And the fellow goes and finds her all ready, weeping and making moan: and he straightway addressed her thus: "Lady, why do you so delay? My lord is awaiting you outside yonder, already fully armed. He would have mounted some time ago, had you been ready." Enide wondered greatly what her lord's intention was; but she very wisely showed herself with as cheerful a countenance as possible, when she appeared before him. In the middle of the courtyard she found him, and King Lac comes running out. Knights come running, too, striving with each other to reach there first. There is neither young nor old but goes to learn and ask if he will take any of them with him. So each offers and presents himself. But he states definitely and affirms that he will take no companion except his wife, asserting that he will go alone. Then the King is in great distress. "Fair son," says he, "what dost thou intend to do? Thou shouldst tell me thy business and keep nothing back. Tell me whither thou will go; for thou art unwilling on any account to be accompanied by an escort of squires or knights. If thou hast undertaken to fight some knight in single combat, yet shouldst thou not for that reason fail to take a part of thy knights with thee to betoken thy wealth and lordship. A king's son ought not to fare alone. Fair son, have thy sumpters loaded now, and take thirty or forty or more of thy knights, and see that silver and gold is taken, and whatever a gentleman needs." Finally Erec makes reply and tells him all in detail how he has planned his journey. "Sire," says he, "it must be so. I shall take no extra horse, nor have I any use for gold or silver, squire or sergeant; nor do I ask for any company save that of my wife alone. But I pray you, whatever may happen, should I die and she come back, to love her and hold her dear for love of me and for my prayer, and give her so long as she live, without contention or any strife, the half of your land to be her own." Upon hearing his son's request, the King said: "Fair son, I promise it. But I grieve much to see thee thus go off without escort, and if I had my way, thou shouldst not thus depart." "Sire, it cannot be otherwise. I go now, and to God commend you. But keep in mind my companions, and give them horses and arms and all that knight may need." The King cannot keep back the tears when he is parted from his son. The people round about weep too; the ladies and knights shed tears and make great moan for him. There is not one who does not mourn, and many a one in the courtyard swoons. Weeping, they kiss and embrace him, and are almost beside themselves with grief. I think they would not have been more sad if they had seen him dead or wounded. Then Erec said to comfort them: "My lords, why do you weep so sore? I am neither in prison nor wounded. You gain nothing by this display of grief. If I go away, I shall come again when it please God and when I can. To God I commend you one and all; so now let me go; too long you keep me here. I am sorry and grieved to see you weep." To God he commends them and they him.

So they departed, leaving sorrow behind them. Erec starts, and leads his wife he knows not whither, as chance dictates. "Ride fast," he says, "and take good care not to be so rash as to speak to me of anything you may see. Take care never to speak to me, unless I address you first. Ride on now fast and with confidence." "Sire," says she, "it shall be done." She rode ahead and held her peace. Neither one nor the other spoke a word. But Enide's heart is very sad, and within herself she thus laments, soft and low that he may not hear: "Alas," she says, "God had raised and exalted me to such great joy; but now He has suddenly cast me down. Fortune who had beckoned me has quickly now withdrawn her hand. I should not mind that so much, alas, if only I dared to address my lord. But I am mortified and distressed because my lord has turned against me, I see it clearly, since he will not speak to me. And I am not so bold as to dare to look at him." While she thus laments, a knight who lived by robbery issued forth from the woods. He had two companions with him, and all three were armed. They covet the palfrey which Enide rides. "My lords, do you know the news I bring?" says he to his two companions. "If we do not now make a haul, we are good-for-nothing cowards and are playing in bad luck. Here comes a lady wondrous fair, whether married or not I do not know, but she is very richly dressed. The palfrey and saddle, with the breast-strap and reins, are worth a thousand livres of Chartres. I will take the palfrey for mine, and the rest of the booty you may have. I don't want any more for my share. The knight shall not lead away the lady, so help me God. For I intend to give him such a thrust as he will dearly pay. I it was who saw him first, and so it is my right to go the first and offer battle." They give him leave and he rides off, crouching well beneath his shield, while the other two remain aloof. In those days it was the custom and practice that in an attack two knights should not join against one; thus if they too had assailed him, it would seem that they had acted treacherously. Enide saw the robbers, and was seized with great fear. "God," says she, "what can I say? Now my lord will be either killed or made a prisoner; for there are three of them and he is alone. The contest is not fair between one knight and three. That fellow will strike him now at a disadvantage; for my lord is off his guard. God, shall I be then such a craven as not to dare to raise my voice? Such a coward I will not be: I will not fail to speak to him." On the spot she turns about and calls to him: "Fair sire, of what are you thinking? There come riding after you three knights who press you hard. I greatly fear they will do you harm." "What?" says Erec, "what's that you say? You have surely been very bold to disdain my command and prohibition. This time you shall be pardoned; but if it should happen another time, you would not be forgiven." Then turning his shield and lance, he rushes at the knight. The latter sees him coming and challenges him. When Erec hears him, he defies him. Both give spur and clash together, holding their lances at full extent. But he missed Erec, while Erec used him hard; for he knew well the right attack. He strikes him on the shield so fiercely that he cracks it from top to bottom. Nor is his hauberk any protection: Erec pierces and crushes it in the middle of his breast, and thrusts a foot and a half of his lance into his body. When he drew back, he pulled out the shaft. And the other fell to earth. He must needs die, for the blade had drunk of his life's blood. Then one of the other two rushes forward, leaving his companion behind, and spurs toward Erec, threatening him. Erec firmly grasps his shield, and attacks him with a stout heart. The other holds his shield before his breast. Then they strike upon the emblazoned shields. The knight's lance flies into two bits, while Erec drives a quarter of lance's length through the other's breast. He will give him no more trouble. Erec unhorses him and leaves him in a faint, while he spurs at an angle toward the third robber. When the latter saw him coming on he began to make his escape. He was afraid, and did not dare to face him; so he hastened to take refuge in the woods. But his flight is of small avail, for Erec follows him close and cries aloud: "Vassal, vassal, turn about now, and prepare to defend yourself, so that I may not slay you in act of flight. It is useless to try to escape." But the fellow has no desire to turn about, and continues to flee with might and main. Following and overtaking him, Erec hits him squarely on his painted shield, and throws him over on the other side. To these three robbers he gives no further heed: one he has killed, another wounded, and of the third he got rid by throwing him to earth from his steed. He took the horses of all three and tied them together by the bridles. In colour they were not alike: the first was white as milk, the second black and not at all bad looking, while the third was dappled all over. He came back to the road where Enide was awaiting him. He bade her lead and drive the three horses in front of her, warning her harshly never again to be so bold as to speak a single word unless he give her leave. She makes answer: "I will never do so, fair sire, if it be your will." Then they ride on, and she holds her peace.

They had not yet gone a league when before them in a valley there came five other knights, with lances in rest, shields held close in to the neck, and their shining helmets laced up tight; they, too, were on plunder bent. All at once they saw the lady approach in charge of the three horses, and Erec who followed after. As soon as they saw them, they divided their equipment among themselves, just as if they had already taken possession of it. Covetousness is a bad thing. But it did not turn out as they expected; for vigorous defence was made. Much that a fool plans is not executed, and many a man misses what he thinks to obtain. So it befell them in this attack. One said that he would take the maid or lose his life in the attempt; and another said that the dappled steed shall be his, and that he will be satisfied with that. The third said that he would take the black horse. "And the white one for me," said the fourth. The fifth was not at all backward, and vowed that he would have the horse and arms of the knight himself. He wished to win them by himself, and would fain attack him first, if they would give him leave: and they willingly gave consent. Then he leaves them and rides ahead on a good and nimble steed. Erec saw him, but made pretence that he did not yet notice him. When Enide saw them, her heart jumped with fear and great dismay. "Alas!" said she, "I know not what to say or do; for my lord severely threatens me, and says that he will punish me, if I speak a word to him. But if my lord were dead now, there would be no comfort for me. I should be killed and roughly treated. God! my lord does not see them! Why, then, do I hesitate, crazed as I am? I am indeed too chary of my words, when I have not already spoken to him. I know well enough that those who are coming yonder are intent upon some wicked deed. And God! how shall I speak to him? He will kill me. Well, let him kill me! Yet I will not fail to speak to him." Then she softly calls him: "Sire!" "What?" says he, "what do you want?" "Your pardon, sire. I want to tell you that five knights have emerged from yonder thicket, of whom I am in mortal fear. Having noticed them, I am of the opinion that they intend to fight with you. Four of them have stayed behind, and the other comes toward you as fast as his steed can carry him. I am afraid every moment lest he will strike you. 'Tis true, the four have stayed behind; but still they are not far away, and will quickly aid him, if need arise." Erec replies: "You had an evil thought, when you transgressed my command--a thing which I had forbidden you. And yet I knew all the time that you did not hold me in esteem. Your service has been ill employed; for it has not awakened my gratitude, but rather kindled the more my ire. I have told you that once, and I say it again. This once again I will pardon you; but another time restrain yourself, and do not again turn around to watch me: for in doing so you would be very foolish. I do not relish your words." Then he spurs across the field toward his adversary, and they come together. Each seeks out and assails the other. Erec strikes him with such force that his shield flies from his neck, and thus he breaks his collar-bone. His stirrups break, and he falls without the strength to rise again, for he was badly bruised and wounded. One of the others then appeared, and they attack each other fiercely. Without difficulty Erec thrusts the sharp and well forged steel into his neck beneath the chin, severing thus the bones and nerves. At the back of his neck the blade protrudes, and the hot red blood flows down on both sides from the wound. He yields his spirit, and his heart is still. The third sallies forth from his hiding-place on the other side of a ford. Straight through the water, on he comes. Erec spurs forward and meets him before he came out of the water, striking him so hard that he beats down flat both rider and horse. The steed lay upon the body long enough to drown him in the stream, and then struggled until with difficulty he got upon his feet. Thus he conquered three of them, when the other two thought it wise to quit the conflict and not to strive with him. In flight they follow the stream, and Erec after them in hot pursuit, until he strikes one upon the spine so hard that he throws him forward upon the saddle-bow. He put all his strength into the blow, and breaks his lance upon his body, so that the fellow fell head foremost. Erec makes him pay dearly for the lance which he has broken on him, and drew his sword from the scabbard. The fellow unwisely straightened up; for Erec gave him three such strokes that he slaked his sword's thirst in his blood. He severs the shoulder from his body, so that it fell down on the ground. Then, with sword drawn, he attacked the other, as he sought to escape without company or escort. When he sees Erec pursuing him, he is so afraid that he knows not what to do: he does not dare to face him, and cannot turn aside; he has to leave his horse, for he has no more trust in him. He throws away his shield and lance, and slips from his horse to earth. When he saw him on his feet, Erec no longer cared to pursue him, but he stooped over for the lance, not wishing to leave that, because of his own which had been broken. He carries off his lance and goes away, not leaving the horses behind: he catches all five of them and leads them off. Enide had hard work to lead them all; for he hands over all five of them to her with the other three, and commands her to go along smartly, and to keep from addressing him in order that no evil or harm may come to her. So not a word does she reply, but rather keeps silence; and thus they go, leading with them all the eight horses.

They rode till nightfall without coming to any town or shelter. When night came on, they took refuge beneath a tree in an open field. Erec bids his lady sleep, and he will watch. She replies that she will not, for it is not right, and she does not wish to do so. It is for him to sleep who is more weary. Well pleased at this, Erec accedes. Beneath his head he placed his shield, and the lady took her cloak, and stretched it over him from head to foot. Thus, he slept and she kept watch, never dozing the whole night, but holding tight in her hand by the bridle the horses until the morning broke; and much she blamed and reproached herself for the words which she had uttered, and said that she acted badly, and was not half so ill-treated as she deserved to be. "Alas," said she, "in what an evil hour have I witnessed my pride and presumption! I might have known without doubt that there was no knight better than, or so good as, my lord. I knew it well enough before, but now I know it better. For I have seen with my own eyes how he has not quailed before three or even five armed men. A plague for ever upon my tongue for having uttered such pride and insult as now compel me to suffer shame!" All night long she thus lamented until the morning dawned. Erec rises early, and again they take the road, she in front and he behind. At noon a squire met them in a little valley, accompanied by two fellows who were carrying cakes and wine and some rich autumn cheeses to those who were mowing the hay in the meadows belonging to Count Galoain. The squire was a clever fellow, and when he saw Erec and Enide, who were coming from the direction of the woods, he perceived that they must have spent the night in the forest and had had nothing to eat or drink; for within a radius of a day's journey there was no town, city or tower, no strong place or abbey, hospice or place of refuge. So he formed an honest purpose and turned his steps toward them, saluting them politely and saving: "Sire, I presume that you have had a hard experience last night. I am sure you have had no sleep and have spent the night in these woods. I offer you some of this white cake, if it please you to partake of it. I say it not in hope of reward: for I ask and demand nothing of you. The cakes are made of good wheat; I have good wine and rich cheeses, too, a white cloth and fine jugs. If you feel like taking lunch, you need not seek any farther. Beneath these white beeches, here on the greensward, you might lay off your arms and rest yourself a while. My advice is that you dismount." Erec got down from his horse and said: "Fair gentle friend, I thank you kindly: I will eat something, without going farther." The young man knew well what to do: he helped the lady from her horse, and the boys who had come with the squire held the steeds. Then they go and sit down in the shade. The squire relieves Erec of his helmet, unlaces the mouth-piece from before his face; then he spreads out the cloth before them on the thick tuff. He passes them the cake and wine, and prepares and cuts a cheese. Hungry as they were, they helped themselves, and gladly drank of the wine. The squire serves them and omits no attention. When they had eaten and drunk their fill, Erec was courteous and generous. "Friend," says he, "as a reward, I wish to present you with one of my horses. Take the one you like the best. And I pray it may be no hardship for you to return to the town and make ready there a goodly lodging." And he replies that he will gladly do whatever is his will. Then he goes up to the horses and, untying them, chooses the dapple, and speaks his thanks; for this one seems to be the best. Up he springs by the left stirrup, and leaving them both there, he rode off to the town at top speed, where he engaged suitable quarters. Now behold! he is back again: "Now mount, sire, quickly," says he, "for you have a good fine lodging ready." Erec mounted, and then his lady, and, as the town was hard by, they soon had reached their lodging-place. There they were received with joy. The host with kindness welcomed them, and with joy and gladness made generous provision for their needs.

When the squire had done for them all the honour that he could do, he came and mounted his horse again, leading it off in front of the Count's bower to the stable. The Count and three of his vassals were leaning out of the bower, when the Count, seeing his squire mounted on the dappled steed, asked him whose it was. And he replied that it was his. The Count, greatly astonished, says: "How is that? Where didst thou get him?" "A knight whom I esteem highly gave him to me, sire," says he. "I have conducted him within this town, and he is lodged at a burgher's house. He is a very courteous knight and the handsomest man I ever saw. Even if I had given you my word and oath, I could not half tell you how handsome he is." The Count replies: "I suppose and presume that he is not more handsome than I am." "Upon my word, sire," the sergeant says, "you are very handsome and a gentleman. There is not a knight in this country, a native of this land, whom you do not excel in favour. But I dare maintain concerning this one that he is fairer than you, if he were not beaten black and blue beneath his hauberk, and bruised. In the forest he has been fighting single-handed with eight knights, and leads away their eight horses. And there comes with him a lady so fair that never lady was half so fair as she." When the Count hears this news, the desire takes him to go and see if this is true or false. "I never heard such a thing," says he; "take me now to his lodging-place, for certainly I wish to know if thou dost lie or speak the truth." He replies: "Right gladly, sire. This is the way and the path to follow, for it is not far from here." "I am anxious to see them," says the Count. Then he comes down, and the squire gets off his horse, and makes the Count mount in his place. Then he ran ahead to tell Erec that the Count was coming to visit him. Erec's lodging was rich indeed--the kind to which he was accustomed. There were many tapers and candles lighted all about. The Count came attended by only three companions. Erec, who was of gracious manners, rose to meet him, and exclaimed: "Welcome, sire!" And the Count returned his salutation. They both sat down side by side upon a soft white couch, where they chat with each other. The Count makes him an offer and urges him to consent to accept from him a guarantee for the payment of his expenses in the town. But Erec does not deign to accept, saying he is well supplied with money, and has no need to accept aught from him. They speak long of many things, but the Count constantly glances about in the other direction, where he caught sight of the lady. Because of her manifest beauty, he fixed all his thought on her. He looked at her as much as he could; he coveted her, and she pleased him so that her beauty filled him with love. Very craftily he asked Erec for permission to speak with her. "Sire," he says "I ask a favour of you, and may it not displease you. As an act of courtesy and as a pleasure, I would fain sit by yonder lady's side. With good intent I came to see you both, and you should see no harm in that. I wish to present to the lady my service in all respects. Know well that for love of you I would do whatever may please her." Erec was not in the least jealous and suspected no evil or treachery. "Sire," says he, "I have no objection. You may sit down and talk with her. Don't think that I have any objection. I give you permission willingly." The lady was seated about two spearlengths away from him. And the Count took his seat close beside her on a low stool. Prudent and courteous, the lady turned toward him. "Alas," quoth he, "how grieved I am to see you in such humble state! I am sorry and feel great distress. But if you would believe my word, you could have honour and great advantage, and much wealth would accrue to you. Such beauty as yours is entitled to great honour and distinction. I would make you my mistress, if it should please you and be your will; you would be my mistress dear and lady over all my land. When I deign to woo you thus, you ought not to disdain my suit. I know and perceive that your lord does not love and esteem you. If you will remain with me, you would be mated with a worthy lord." "Sire," says Enide, "your proposal is vain. It cannot be. Ah! better that I were yet unborn, or burnt upon a fire of thorns and my ashes scattered abroad than that I should ever in any wise be false to my lord, or conceive any felony or treachery toward him. You have made a great mistake in making such a proposal to me. I shall not agree to it in any wise." The Count's ire began to rise. "You disdain to love me, lady?" says he; "upon my word, you are too proud. Neither for flattery nor for prayer you will do my will? It is surely true that a woman's pride mounts the more one prays and flatters her; but whoever insults and dishonours her will often find her more tractable. I give you my word that if you do not do my will there soon will be some sword-play here. Rightly or wrongly, I will have your lord slain right here before your eyes." "Ah, sire," says Enide, "there is a better way than that you say. You would commit a wicked and treacherous deed if you killed him thus. Calm yourself again, I pray; for I will do your pleasure. You may regard me as all your own, for I am yours and wish to be. I did not speak as I did from pride, but to learn and prove if I could find in you the true love of a sincere heart. But I would not at any price have you commit an act of treason. My lord is not on his guard; and if you should kill him thus, you would do a very ugly deed, and I should have the blame for it. Every one in the land would say that it had been done with my consent. Go and rest until the morrow, when my lord shall be about to rise. Then you can better do him harm without blame and without reproach." With her heart's thoughts her words do not agree. "Sire," says she, "believe me now! Have no anxiety; but send here to-morrow your knights and squires and have me carried away by force. My lord will rush to my defence, for he is proud and bold enough. Either in earnest or in jest, have him seized and treated ill, or strike his head off, if you will. I have led this life now long enough; to tell the truth. I like not the company of this my lord. Rather would I feel your body lying beside me in a bed. And since we have reached this point, of my love you may rest assured." The Count replies: "It is well, my lady! God bless the hour that you were born; in great estate you shall be held." "Sire," says she, "indeed, I believe it. And yet I would fain have your word that you will always hold me dear; I could not believe you otherwise." Glad and merry, the Count replies: "See here, my faith I will pledge to you loyally as a Count, Madame, that I shall do all your behests. Have no further fear of that. All you want you shall always have." Then she took his plighted word; but little she valued or cared for it, except therewith to save her lord. Well she knows how to deceive a fool, when she puts her mind upon it. Better it were to lie to him than that her lord should be cut off. The Count now rose from her side, and commends her to God a hundred times. But of little use to him will be the faith which she has pledged to him. Erec knew nothing at all of this that they were plotting to work his death; but God will be able to lend him aid, and I think He will do so. Now Erec is in great peril, and does not know that he must be on his guard. The Count's intentions are very base in planning to steal away his wife and kill him when he is without defence. In treacherous guise he takes his leave: "To God I commend you," says he, and Erec replies: "And so do I you, sire." Thus they separated. Already a good part of the night was passed. Out of the way, in one of the rooms, two beds were made upon the floor. In one of them Erec lays him down, in the other Enide went to rest. Full of grief and anxiety, she never closed her eyes that night, but remained on watch for her lord's sake; for from what she had seen of the Count, she knew him to be full of wickedness. She knows full well that if he once gets possession of her lord, he will not fail to do him harm. He may be sure of being killed: so for his sake she is in distress. All night she must needs keep her vigil; but before the dawn, if she can bring it about, and if her lord will take her word, they will be ready to depart.

Erec slept all night long securely until daylight. Then Enide realised and suspected that she might hesitate too long. Her heart was tender toward her lord, like a good and loyal lady. Her heart was neither deceitful nor false. So she rises and makes ready, and drew near to her lord to wake him up. "Ah, sire," says she, "I crave your pardon. Rise quickly now, for you are betrayed beyond all doubt, though guiltless and free from any crime. The Count is a proven traitor, and if he can but catch you here, you will never get away without his having cut you in pieces. He hates you because he desires me. But if it please God, who knows all things, you shall be neither slain nor caught. Last evening he would have killed you had I not assured him that I would be his mistress and his wife. You will see him return here soon: he wants to seize me and keep me here and kill you if he can find you." Now Erec learns how loyal his wife is to him. "Lady," says he, "have our horses quickly saddled; then run and call our host, and tell him quickly to come here. Treason has been long abroad." Now the horses are saddled, and the lady summoned the host. Erec has armed and dressed himself, and into his presence came the host. "Sire," said he, "what haste is this, that you are risen at such an hour, before the day and the sun appear?" Erec replies that he has a long road and a full day before him, and therefore he has made ready to set out, having it much upon his mind; and he added: "Sire, you have nor yet handed me any statement of my expenses. You have received me with honour and kindness, and therein great merit redounds to you. Cancel my indebtedness with these seven horses that I brought here with me. Do not disdain them, but keep them for your own. I cannot increase my gift to you by so much as the value of a halter." The burgher was delighted with this gift and bowed low, expressing his thanks and gratitude. Then Erec mounts and takes his leave, and they set out upon their way. As they ride, he frequently warns Enide that if she sees anything she should not be so bold as to speak to him about it. Meanwhile, there entered the house a hundred knights well armed, and very much dismayed they were to find Erec no longer there. Then the Count learned that the lady had deceived him. He discovered the footsteps of the horses, and they all followed the trail, the Count threatening Erec and vowing that, if he can come up with him, nothing can keep him from having his head on the spot. "A curse on him who now hangs back, and does not spur on fast!" quoth he; "he who presents me with the head of the knight whom I hate so bitterly, will have served me to my taste." Then they plunge on at topmost speed, filled with hostility toward him who had never laid eyes on them and had never harmed them by deed or word. They ride ahead until they made him out; at the edge of a forest they catch sight of him before he was hid by the forest trees. Not one of them halted then, but all rushed on in rivalry. Enide hears the clang and noise of their arms and horses, and sees that the valley is full of them. As soon as she saw them, she could not restrain her tongue. "Ah, sire," she cries, "alas, how this Count has attacked you, when he leads against you such a host! Sire, ride faster now, until we be within this wood. I think we can easily distance them, for they are still a long way behind. If you go on at this pace, you can never escape from death, for you are no match for them." Erec replies: "Little esteem you have for me, and lightly you hold my words. It seems I cannot correct you by fair request. But as the Lord have mercy upon me until I escape from here, I swear that you shall pay dearly for this speech of yours; that is, unless my mind should change." Then he straightway turns about, and sees the seneschal drawing near upon a horse both strong and fleet. Before them all he takes his stand at the distance of four cross-bow shots. He had not disposed of his arms, but was thoroughly well equipped. Erec reckons up his opponents' strength, and sees there are fully a hundred of them. Then he who thus is pressing him thinks he had better call a hair. Then they ride to meet each other, and strike upon each other's shield great blows with their sharp and trenchant swords. Erec caused his stout steel sword to pierce his body through and through, so that his shield and hauberk protected him no more than a shred of dark-blue silk. And next the Count comes spurring on, who, as the story tells, was a strong and doughty knight. But the Count in this was ill advised when he came with only shield and lance. He placed such trust in his own prowess that he thought that he needed no other arms. He showed his exceeding boldness by rushing on ahead of all his men more than the space of nine acres. When Erec saw him stand alone, he turned toward him; the Count is not afraid of him, and they come together with clash of arms. First the Count strikes him with such violence upon the breast that he would have lost his stirrups if he had not been well set. He makes the wood of his shield to split so that the iron of his lance protrudes on the other side. But Erec's hauberk was very solid and protected him from death without the tear of a single mesh. The Count was strong and breaks his lance; then Erec strikes him with such force on his yellow painted shield that he ran more than a yard of his lance through his abdomen, knocking him senseless from his steed. Then he turned and rode away without further tarrying on the spot. Straight into the forest he spurs at full speed. Now Erec is in the woods, and the others paused a while over those who lay in the middle of the field. Loudly they swear and vow that they will rather follow after him for two or three days than fail to capture and slaughter him. The Count, though grievously wounded in the abdomen, hears what they say. He draws himself up a little and opens his eyes a tiny bit. Now he realises what an evil deed he had begun to execute. He makes the knights step back, and says: "My lords, I bid you all, both strong and weak, high and low, that none of you be so bold as to dare to advance a single step. All of you return now quickly! I have done a villainous deed, and I repent me of my foul design. The lady who outwitted me is very honourable, prudent, and courteous. Her beauty fired me with love for her; because I desired her, I wished to kill her lord and keep her back with me by force. I well deserved this woe, and now it has come upon me. How abominably disloyal and treacherous I was in my madness! Never was there a better knight born of mother than he. Never shall he receive harm through me if I can in any way prevent it. I command you all to retrace your steps." Back they go disconsolate, carrying the lifeless seneschal on the shield reversed. The Count, whose wound was not mortal, lived on for some time after. Thus was Erec delivered.

Erec goes off at full speed down a road between two hedgerows--he and his wife with him. Both putting spurs to their horses, they rode until they came to a meadow which had been mown. After emerging from the hedged enclosure they came upon a drawbridge before a high tower, which was all closed about with a wall and a broad and deep moat. They quickly pass over the bridge, but had not gone far before the lord of the place espied them from up in his tower. About this man I can tell you the truth: that he was very small of stature, but very courageous of heart. When he sees Erec cross the bridge, he comes down quickly from his tower, and on a great sorrel steed of his he causes a saddle to be placed, which showed portrayed a golden lion. Then he orders to be brought his shield, his stiff, straight lance, a sharp polished sword, his bright shining helmet, his gleaming hauberk, and triple-woven greaves; for he has seen an armed knight pass before his list against whom he wishes to strive in arms, or else this stranger will strive against him until he shall confess defeat. His command was quickly done: behold the horse now led forth; a squire brought him around already bridled and with saddle on. Another fellow brings the arms. The knight passed out through the gate, as quickly as possible, all alone, without companion. Erec is riding along a hill-side, when behold the knight comes tearing down over the top of the hill, mounted upon a powerful steed which tore along at such a pace that he crushed the stones beneath his hoofs finer than a millstone grinds the corn; and bright gleaming sparks flew off in all directions, so that it seemed as if his four feet were all ablaze with fire. Enide heard the noise and commotion, and almost fell from her palfrey, helpless and in a faint. There was no vein in her body in which the blood did not turn, and her face became all pale and white as if she were a corpse. Great is her despair and dismay, for she does not dare to address her lord, who often threatens and chides at her and charges her to hold her peace. She is distracted between two courses to pursue, whether to speak or to hold her peace. She takes counsel with herself, and often she prepares to speak, so that her tongue already moves, but the voice cannot issue forth; for her teeth are clenched with fear, and thus shut up her speech within. Thus she admonishes and reproaches herself, but she closes her mouth and grits her teeth so that her speech cannot issue forth. At strife with herself, she said: "I am sure and certain that I shall incur a grievous loss, if here I lose my lord. Shall I tell him all, then, openly? Not I. Why not? I would not dare, for thus I should enrage my lord. And if my lord's ire is once aroused, he will leave me in this wild place alone, wretched and forlorn. Then I shall be worse off than now. Worse off? What care I? May grief and sorrow always be mine as long as I live, if my lord does not promptly escape from here without being delivered to a violent death. But if I do not quickly inform him, this knight who is spurring hither will have killed him before he is aware; for he seems of very evil intent. I think I have waited too long from fear of his vigorous prohibition. But I will no longer hesitate because of his restraint. I see plainly that my lord is so deep in thought that he forgets himself; so it is right that I should address him." She spoke to him. He threatens her, but has no desire to do her harm, for he realises and knows full well that she loves him above all else, and he loves her, too, to the utmost. He rides toward the knight, who challenges him to battle, and they meet at the foot of the hill, where they attack and defy each other. Both smite each other with their iron-tipped lances with all their strength. The shields that hang about their necks are not worth two coats of bark: the leather tears, and they split the wood, and they shatter the meshes of the hauberks. Both are pierced to the vitals by the lances, and the horses fall to earth. Now, both the warriors were doughty. Grievously, but not mortally, wounded, they quickly got upon their feet and grasped afresh their lances, which were not broken nor the worse for wear. But they cast them away on the ground, and drawing their swords from the scabbard, they attack each other with great fury. Each wounds and injures the other, for there is no mercy on either side. They deal such blows upon the helmets that gleaming sparks fly out when their swords recoil. They split and splinter the shields; they batter and crush the hauberks. In four places the swords are brought down to the bare flesh, so that they are greatly weakened and exhausted. And if both their swords had lasted long without breaking, they would never have retreated, nor would the battle have come to an end before one of them perforce had died. Enide, who was watching them, was almost beside herself with grief. Whoever could have seen her then, as she showed her great woe by wringing her hands, tearing her hair and shedding tears, could have seen a loyal lady. And any man would have been a vulgar wretch who saw and did not pity her. And the knights still fight, knocking the jewels from the helmets and dealing at each other fearful blows. From the third to the ninth hour the battle continued so fierce that no one could in any wise make out which was to have the better of it. Erec exerts himself and strives; he brought his sword down upon his enemy's helmet, cleaving it to the inner lining of mail and making him stagger; but he stood firmly and did not fall. Then he attacked Erec in turn, and dealt him such a blow upon the covering of his shield that his strong and precious sword broke when he tried to pull it out. When he saw that his sword was broken, in a spite he threw as far away as he could the part that remained in his hand. Now he was afraid and must needs draw back; for any knight that lacks his sword cannot do much execution in battle or assault. Erec pursues him until he begs him, for God's sake, not to kill him. "Mercy, noble knight," he cries, "be not so cruel and harsh toward me. Now that I am left without my sword, you have the strength and the power to take my life or make me your prisoner, for I have no means of defence." Erec replies: "When thou thus dost petition me I fain would hear thee admit outright whether thou art defeated and overcome. Thou shalt not again be touched by me if thou dost surrender at my discretion." The knight was slow to make reply. So, when Erec saw him hesitate, in order to further dismay him, he again attacked him, rushing at him with drawn sword; whereupon, thoroughly terrified, he cried: "Mercy, sire! Regard me as your captive, since it cannot be otherwise." Erec answers: "More than that is necessary. You shall not get off so easily as that. Tell me your station and your name, and I in turn will tell you mine." "Sire," says he, "you are right. I am king of this country. My liegemen are Irishmen, and there is none who does not have to pay me rent. My name is Guivret the Little. I am very rich and powerful; for there is no landholder whose lands touch mine in any direction who ever transgresses my command and who does not do my pleasure. I have no neighbour who does not fear me, however proud and bold he may be. But I greatly desire to be your confidant and friend from this time on." Erec replies: "I, too, can boast that I am a noble man. My name is Erec, son of King Lac. My father is king of Farther Wales, and has many a rich city, fine hall, and strong town; no king or emperor has more than he, save only King Arthur. Him, of course, I except; for with him none can compare." Guivret is greatly astonished at this, and says: "Sire, a great marvel is this I hear. I was never so glad of anything as of your acquaintance. You may put full trust in me! And should it please you to abide in my country within my estates, I shall have you treated with great honour. So long as you care to remain here, you shall be recognised as my lord. We both have need of a physician, and I have a castle of mine near here, not eight leagues away, nor even seven. I wish to take you thither with me, and there we shall have our wounds tended." Erec replies: "I thank you for what I have heard you say. However, I will not go, thank you. But only so much I request of you, that if I should be in need, and you should hear that I had need of aid, you would not then forget me." "Sire" says he, "I promise you that never, so long as I am alive, shall you have need of my help but that I shall go at once to aid you with all the assistance I can command." "I have nothing more to ask of you," says Erec; "you have promised me much. You are now my lord and friend, if your deed is as good as your word." Then each kisses and embraces the other. Never was there such an affectionate parting after such a fierce battle; for from very affection and generosity each one cut off long, wide strips from the bottom of his shirt and bound up the other's wounds. When they had thus bandaged each other, they commended each other to God.

So thus they parted. Guivret takes his way back alone, while Erec resumed his road, in dire need of plaster wherewith to heal his wounds. He did not cease to travel until he came to a plain beside a lofty forest all full of stags, hinds, deer, does, and other beasts, and all sorts of game. Now King Arthur and the Queen and the best of his barons had come there that very day. The King wished to spend three or four days in the forest for pleasure and sport, and had commanded tents, pavilions, and canopies to be brought. My lord Gawain had stepped into the King's tent, all tired out by a long ride. In front of the tent a white beech stood, and there he had left a shield of his, together with his ashen lance. He left his steed, all saddled and bridled, fastened to a branch by the rein. There the horse stood until Kay the seneschal came by. He came up quickly and, as if to beguile the time, took the steed and mounted, without the interference of any one. He took the lance and the shield, too, which were close by under the tree. Galloping along on the steed, Kay rode along a valley until it came about by chance that Erec met him. Now Erec recognised the seneschal, and he knew the arms and the horse, but Kay did not recognise him, for he could not be distinguished by his arms. So many blows of sword and lance had he received upon his shield that all the painted design had disappeared from it. And the lady, who did not wish to be seen or recognised by him, shrewdly held her veil before her face, as if she were doing it because of the sun's glare and the dust. Kay approached rapidly and straightway seized Erec's rein, without so much as saluting him. Before he let him move, he presumptuously asked him: "Knight," says he, "I wish to know who you are and whence you come." "You must be mad to stop me thus," says Erec; "you shall not know that just now." And the other replies: "Be not angry; I only ask it for your good. I can see and make out clearly that you are wounded and hurt. If you will come along with me you shall have a good lodging this night; I shall see that you are well cared for, honoured and made comfortable: for you are in need of rest. King Arthur and the Queen are close by here in a wood, lodged in pavilions and tents. In all good faith, I advise you to come with me to see the Queen and King, who will take much pleasure in you and will show you great honour." Erec replies: "You say well; yet will I not go thither for anything. You know not what my business is: I must yet farther pursue my way. Now let me go; too long I stay. There is still some daylight left." Kay makes answer: "You speak madness when you decline to come. I trow you will repent of it. And however much it may be against your will, you shall both go, as the priest goes to the council, willy-nilly. To-night you will be badly served, if, unmindful of my advice, you go there as strangers. Come now quickly, for I will take you." At this word Erec's ire was roused. "Vassal," says he, "you are mad to drag me thus after you by force. You have taken me quite off my guard. I tell you you have committed an offence. For I thought to be quite safe, and was not on my guard against you." Then he lays his hand upon his sword and cries: "Hands off my bridle, vassal! Step aside. I consider you proud and impudent. I shall strike you, be sure of that, if you drag me longer after you. Leave me alone now." Then he lets him go, and draws off across the field more than an acre's width; then turns about and, as a man with evil intent, issues his challenge. Each rushed at the other. But, because Kay was without armour, Erec acted courteously and turned the point of his lance about and presented the butt-end instead. Even so, he gave him such a blow high up on the broad expanse of his shield that he caused it to wound him on the temple, pinning his arm to his breast: all prone he throws him to the earth. Then he went to catch the horse and hands him over by the bridle to Enide. He was about to lead it away, when the wounded man with his wonted flattery begs him to restore it courteously to him. With fair words he flatters and wheedles him. "Vassal," says he, "so help me God, that horse is not mine. Rather does it belong to that knight in whom dwells the greatest prowess in the world, my lord Gawain the Bold. I tell you so much on his behalf, in order that you may send it back to him and thus win honour. So shall you be courteous and wise, and I shall be your messenger." Erec makes answer: "Take the horse, vassal, and lead it away. Since it belongs to my lord Gawain it is not meet that I should appropriate it." Kay takes the horse, remounts, and coming to the royal tent, tells the King the whole truth, keeping nothing back. And the King summoned Gawain, saying: "Fair nephew Gawain, if ever you were true and courteous, go quickly after him and ask him in winsome wise who he is and what his business. And if you can influence him and bring him along with you to us, take care not to fail to do so." Then Gawain mounts his steed, two squires following after him. They soon made Erec out, but did not recognise him. Gawain salutes him, and he Gawain: their greetings were mutual. Then said my lord Gawain with his wonted openness: "Sire," says he, "King Arthur sends me along this way to encounter you. The Queen and King send you their greeting, and beg you urgently to come and spend some time with them (it may benefit you and cannot harm), as they are close by." Erec replies: "I am greatly obliged to the King and Queen and to you who are, it seems, both kind of heart and of gentle mien. I am not in a vigorous state; rather do I bear wounds within my body: yet will I not turn aside from my way to seek a lodging-place. So you need not longer wait: I thank you, but you may be gone." Now Gawain was a man of sense. He draws back and whispers in the ear of one of the squires, bidding him go quickly and tell the King to take measures at once to take down and lower his tents and come and set them up in the middle of the road three or four leagues in advance of where they now are. There the King must lodge to-night, if he wishes to meet and extend hospitality to the best knight in truth whom he can ever hope to see; but who will not go out of his way for a lodging at the bidding of any one. The fellow went and gave his message. The King without delay causes his tents to be taken down. Now they are lowered, the sumpters loaded, and off they set. The King mounted Aubagu, and the Queen afterwards mounted a white Norse palfrey. All this while, my lord Gawain did not cease to detain Erec, until the latter said to him: "Yesterday I covered more ground than I shall do to-day. Sire, you annoy me; let me go. You have already disturbed a good part of my day." And my lord Gawain answers him: "I should like to accompany you a little way, if you do not object; for it is yet a long while until night. They spent so much time in talking that all the tents were set up before them, and Erec sees them, and perceives that his lodging is arranged for him. "Ah! Gawain," he says, "your shrewdness has outwitted me. By your great cunning you have kept me here. Since it has turned out thus, I shall tell you my name at once. Further concealment would be useless. I am Erec, who was formerly your companion and friend." Gawain hears him and straightway embraces him. He raised up his helmet and unlaced his mouthpiece. Joyfully he clasps him in his embrace, while Erec embraces him in turn. Then Gawain leaves him, saying, "Sire, this news will give great pleasure to my lord; he and my lady will both be glad, and I must go before to tell them of it. But first I must embrace and welcome and speak comfortably to my lady Enide, your wife. My lady the Queen has a great desire to see her. I heard her speak of her only yesterday." Then he steps up to Enide and asks her how she is, if she is well and in good case. She makes answer courteously: "Sire, I should have no cause for grief, were I not in great distress for my lord; but as it is, I am in dismay, for he has hardly a limb without a wound." Gawain replies: "This grieves me much. It is perfectly evident from his face, which is all pale and colourless. I could have wept myself when I saw him so pale and wan, but my joy effaced my grief, for at sight of him I felt so glad that I forgot all other pain. Now start and ride along slowly. I shall ride ahead at top-speed to tell the Queen and the King that you are following after me. I am sure that they will both be delighted when they hear it." Then he goes, and comes to the King's tent. "Sire," he cries, "now you and my lady must be glad, for here come Erec and his wife." The King leaps to his feet with joy. "Upon my word!" he says, "right glad I am. I could hear no news which could give me so much happiness." The Queen and all the rest rejoice, and come out from the tents as fast as they may. Even the King comes forth from his pavilion, and they met Erec near at band. When Erec sees the King coming, he quickly dismounts, and Enide too. The King embraces and meets them, and the Queen likewise tenderly kisses and embraces them: there is no one that does not show his joy. Right there, upon the spot, they took off Erec's armour; and when they saw his wounds, their joy turned to sadness. The King draws a deep sigh at the sight of them, and has a plaster brought which Morgan, his sister, had made. This piaster, which Morgan had given to Arthur, was of such sovereign virtue that no wound, whether on nerve or joint, provided it were treated with the piaster once a day, could fail to be completely cured and healed within a week. They brought to the King the piaster which gave Erec great relief. When they had bathed, dried, and bound up his wounds, the King leads him and Enide into his own royal tent, saying that he intends, out of love for Erec, to tarry in the forest a full fortnight, until he be completely restored to health. For this Erec thanks the King, saying: "Fair sire, my wounds are not so painful that I should desire to abandon my journey. No one could detain me; to-morrow, without delay, I shall wish to get off in the morning, as soon as I see the dawn." At this the King shook his head and said: "This is a great mistake for you not to remain with us. I know that you are far from well. Stay here, and you will do the right thing. It will be a great pity and cause for grief if you die in this forest. Fair gentle friend, stay here now until you are quite yourself again." Erec replies: "Enough of this. I have undertaken this journey, and shall not tarry in any wise." The King hears that he would by no means stay for prayer of his; so he says no more about it, and commands the supper to be prepared at once and the tables to be spread. The servants go to make their preparations. It was a Saturday night; so they ate fish and fruit, pike and perch, salmon and trout, and then pears both raw and cooked. Soon after supper they ordered the beds to be made ready. The King, who held Erec dear, had him laid in a bed alone; for he did not wish that any one should lie with him who might touch his wounds. That night he was well lodged. In another bed close by lay Enide with the Queen under a cover of ermine, and they all slept in great repose until the day broke next morning.

Next day, as soon as it is dawn. Erec arises, dresses, commands his horses to be saddled, and orders his arms to be brought to him. The valets run and bring them to him. Again the King and all the knights urge him to remain; but entreaty is of no avail, for he will not stay for anything. Then you might have seen them all weep and show such grief as if they already saw him dead. He puts on his arms, and Enide arises. All the knights are sore distressed, for they think they will never see them more. They follow them out from the tents, and send for their own horses, that they may escort and accompany them. Erec said to them: "Be not angry! but you shall not accompany me a single step. I'll thank you if you'll stay behind!" His horse was brought to him, and he mounts without delay. Taking his shield and lance, he commends them all to God, and they in turn wish Erec well. Then Enide mounts, and they ride away.

Entering a forest, they rode on without halting till hour of prime. While they thus traversed the wood, they heard in the distance the cry of a damsel in great distress. When Erec heard the cry, he felt sure from the sound that it was the voice of one in trouble and in need of help. Straightway calling Enide, he says: "Lady, there is some maiden who goes through the wood calling aloud. I take it that she is in need of aid and succour. I am going to hasten

41

in that direction and see what her trouble is. Do you dismount and await me here, while I go yonder." "Gladly, sire," she says. Leaving her alone, he makes his way until he found the damsel, who was going through the wood, lamenting her lover whom two giants had taken and were leading away with very cruel treatment. The maiden was rending her garments, and tearing her hair and her tender crimson face. Erec sees her and, wondering greatly, begs her to tell him why she cries and weeps so sore. The maiden cries and sighs again, then sobbing, says: "Fair sire, it is no wonder if I grieve, for I wish I were dead. I neither love nor prize my life, for my lover has been led away prisoner by two wicked and cruel giants who are his mortal enemies. God! what shall I do? Woe is me! deprived of the best knight alive, the most noble and the most courteous. And now he is in great peril of death. This very day, and without cause, they will bring him to some vile death. Noble knight, for God's sake, I beg you to succour my lover, if now you can lend him any aid. You will not have to run far, for they must still be close by." "Damsel," says Erec, "I will follow them, since you request it, and rest assured that I shall do all within my power: either I shall be taken prisoner along with him, or I shall restore him to you safe and sound. If the giants let him live until I can find him, I intend to measure my strength with theirs." "Noble knight," the maiden said, "I shall always be your servant if you restore to me my lover. Now go in God's name, and make haste, I beseech you." "Which way lies their path?" "This way, my lord. Here is the path with the footprints." Then Erec started at a gallop, and told her to await him there. The maid commends him to the Lord, and prays God very fervently that He should give him force by His command to discomfit those who intend evil toward her lover.

Erec went off along the trail, spurring his horse in pursuit of the giants. He followed in pursuit of them until he caught sight of them before they emerged from the wood; he saw the knight with bare limbs mounted naked on a nag, his hands and feet bound as if he were arrested for highway robbery. The giants had no lances, shields or whetted swords; but they both had clubs and scourges, with which they were beating him so cruelly that already they had cut the skin on his back to the bone. Down his sides and flanks the blood ran, so that the nag was all covered with blood down to the belly. Erec came along alone after them. He was very sad and distressed about the knight whom he saw them treat so spitefully. Between two woods in an open field he came up with them, and asks: "My lords," says he, "for what crime do you treat this man so ill and lead him along like a common thief? You are treating him too cruelly. You are driving him just as if he had been caught stealing. It is a monstrous insult to strip a knight naked, and then bind him and beat him so shamefully. Hand him over to me, I beg of you with all good-will and courtesy. I have no wish to demand him of you forcibly." "Vassal," they say, "what business is this of yours? You must be mad to make any demand of us. If you do not like it, try and improve matters." Erec replies: "Indeed, I like it not, and you shall not lead him away so easily. Since you have left the matter in my hands, I say whoever can get possession of him let him keep him. Take your positions. I challenge you. You shall not take him any farther before some blows have been dealt." "Vassal," they reply, "you are mad, indeed, to wish to measure your strength with us. If you were four instead of one, you would have no more strength against us than one lamb against two wolves." "I do not know how it will turn out," Erec replies; "if the sky fails and the earth melts, then many a lark will be caught. Many a man boasts loudly who is of little worth. On guard now, for I am going to attack you." The giants were strong and fierce, and held in their clenched hands their big clubs tipped with iron. Erec went at them lance in rest. He fears neither of them, in spite of their menace and their pride, and strikes the foremost of them through the eye so deep into the brain that the blood and brains spurt out at the back of his neck; that one lies dead and his heart stops beating. When the other saw him dead, he had reason to be sorely grieved. Furious, he went to avenge him: with both hands he raised his club on high and thought to strike him squarely upon his unprotected head: but Erec watched the blow, and received it on his shield. Even so, the giant landed such a blow that it quite stunned him, and almost made him fall to earth from his steed. Erec covers himself with his shield and the giant, recovering himself, thinks to strike again quickly upon his head. But Erec had drawn his sword, and attacked him with such fierceness that the giant was severely handled: he strikes him so hard upon the neck that he splits him down to the saddle-bow. He scatters his bowels upon the earth, and the body falls full length, split in two halves. The knight weeps with joy and, worshipping, praises God who has sent him this aid. Then Erec unbound him, made him dress and arm himself, and mount one of the horses; the other he made him lead with his right hand, and asks him who he is. And he replied: "Noble knight, thou art my liege lord. I wish to regard thee as my lord, as by right I ought to do, for thou hast saved my life, which but now would have been cut off from my body with great torment and cruelty. What chance, fair gentle sire, in God's name, guided thee hither to me, to free me by thy courage from the hands of my enemies? Sire, I wish to do thee homage. Henceforth, I shall always accompany thee and serve thee as my lord." Erec sees that he is disposed to serve him gladly, if he may, and says: "Friend, for your service I have no desire; but you must know that I came hither to succour you at the instance of your lady, whom I found sorrowing in this wood. Because of you, she grieves and moans; for full of sorrow is her heart. I wish to present you to her now. As soon as I have reunited you with her, I shall continue my way alone; for you have no call to go with me. I have no need of your company; but I fain would know your name." "Sire," says he, "as you wish. Since you desire to know my name, it must not be kept from you. My name is Cadoc of Tabriol: know that thus I am called. But since I must part from you. I should like to know, if it may be, who you are and of what land, where I may sometime find and search for you, when I shall go away from here." Erec replies: "Friend, that I will never confide to you. Never speak of it again; but if you wish to find it out and do me honour in any wise go quickly now without delay to my lord, King Arthur, who with might and main is hunting the stag in yonder wood, as I take it, not five short leagues from here. Go thither quickly and take him word that you are sent to him as a gift by him whom yesterday within his tent he joyfully received and lodged. And be careful not to conceal from him from what peril I set free both your life and body. I am dearly cherished at the court, and if you present yourself in my name you will do me a service and honour. There you shall ask who I am; but you cannot know it otherwise." "Sire," says Cadoc, "I will follow your bidding in all respects. You need never have any fear that I do not go with a glad heart. I shall tell the King the full truth regarding the battle which you have fought on my behalf." Thus speaking, they continued their way until they came to the maiden where Erec had left her. The damsel's joy knew no bounds when she saw coming her lover whom she never thought to see again. Taking him by the hand, Erec presents him to her with the words: "Grieve no longer, demoiselle! Behold your lover glad and joyous." And she with prudence makes reply: "Sire, by right you have won us both. Yours we should be, to serve and honour. But who could ever repay half the debt we owe you?" Erec makes answer: "My gentle lady, no recompense do I ask of you. To God I now commend you both, for too long, methinks, I have tarried here." Then he turns his horse about, and rides away as fast as he can. Cadoc of Tabriol with his damsel rides off in another direction; and soon he told the news to King Arthur and the Queen.

Erec continues to ride at great speed to the place where Enide was awaiting him in great concern, thinking that surely he had completely deserted her. And he, too, was in great fear lest some one, finding her alone, might have carried her off. So he made all haste to return. But the heat of the day was such, and his arms caused him such distress, that his wounds broke open and burst the bandages. His wounds never stopped bleeding before he came directly to the spot where Enide was waiting for him. She espied him and rejoiced: but she did not realise or know the pain from which he was suffering; for all his body was bathed in blood, and his heart hardly had strength to beat. As he was descending a hill he fell suddenly over upon his horse's neck. As he tried to straighten up, he lost his saddle and stirrups, falling, as if lifeless, in a faint. Then began such heavy grief, when Enide saw him fall to earth. Full of fear at the sight of him, she runs toward him like one who makes no concealment of her grief. Aloud she cries, and wrings her hands: not a shred of her robe remains untorn across her breast. She begins to tear her hair and lacerate her tender face. "Ah God!" she cries, "fair gentle Lord, why dost Thou let me thus live on? Come Death, and kill me hastily!" With these words she faints upon his body. When she recovered, she said to herself reproachfully: "Woe is me, wretched Enide; I am the murderer of my lord, in having killed him by my speech. My lord would still be now alive, if I in my mad presumption had not spoken the word which engaged him in this adventure. Silence never harmed any one, but speech often worketh woe. The truth of this I have tried and proved in more ways than one." Beside her lord she took her seat, holding his head upon her lap. Then she begins her dole anew. "Alas," she says, "my lord, unhappy thou, thou who never hadst a peer; for in thee was beauty seen and prowess was made manifest; wisdom had given thee its heart, and largess set a crown upon thee, without which no one is esteemed. But what did I say? A grievous mistake I made in uttering the word which has killed my lord--that fatal poisoned word for which I must justly be reproached; and I recognise and admit that no one is guilty but myself; I alone must be blamed for this." Then fainting she falls upon the ground, and when she later sat up again, she only moans again the more: "God, what shall I do, and why live on? Why does Death delay and hesitate to come and seize me without respite? Truly, Death holds me in great contempt! Since Death does not deign to take my life, I must myself perforce achieve the vengeance for my sinful deed. Thus shall I die in spite of Death, who will not heed my call for aid. Yet, I cannot die through mere desire, nor would complaining avail me aught. The sword, which my lord had gilded on, ought by right to avenge his death. I will not longer consume myself in distress, in prayer, and vain desire." She draws the sword forth from its sheath and begins to consider it. God, who is full of mercy, caused her to delay a little; and while she passes in review her sorrow and her misfortune, behold there comes riding apace a Count with numerous suite, who from afar had heard the lady's loud outcry. God did not wish to desert her; for now she would have killed herself, had she not been surprised by those who took away from her the sword and thrust it back into its sheath. The Count then dismounted from his horse and began to inquire of her concerning the knight, and whether she was his wife or his lady-love. "Both one and the other, sire," she says, "my sorrow is such as I cannot tell. Woe is me that I am not dead." And the Count begins to comfort her: "Lady," he says, "by the Lord, I pray you, to take some pity on yourself! It is meet that you should mourn, but it is no use to be disconsolate; for you may yet rise to high estate. Do not sink into apathy, but comfort yourself; that will be wise, and God will give you joy again. Your wondrous beauty holds good fortune in store for you; for I will take you as my wife, and make you a countess and dame of rank: this ought to bring you much consolation. And I shall have the body removed and laid away with great honour. Leave off now this grief of yours which in your frenzy you display." And she replies: "Sire, begone! For God's sake, let me be! You can accomplish nothing here. Nothing that one could say or do could ever make me glad again." At this the Count drew back and said: "Let us make a bier, whereon to carry away this body with the lady to the town of Limors. There the body shall be interred. Then will I espouse the lady, whether or not she give consent: for never did I see any one so fair, nor desire any as I do her. Happy I am to have met with her. Now make quickly and without delay a proper bier for this dead knight. Halt not for the trouble, nor from sloth." Then some of his men draw out their swords and soon cut two saplings, upon which they laid branches cross-wise. Upon this litter they laid Erec down; then hitched two horses to it. Enide rides alongside, not ceasing to make lament, and often fainting and falling back; but the horsemen hold her tight, and try to support her with their arms, and raise her up and comfort her. All the way to Limors they escort the body, until they come to the palace of the Count. All the people follow up after them--ladies, knights, and townspeople. In the middle off the hall upon a dais they stretched the body out full length, with his lance and shield alongside. The hall is full, the crowd is dense. Each one is anxious to inquire what is this trouble, what marvel here. Meanwhile the Count takes counsel with his barons privily. "My lords," he says, "upon the spot I wish to espouse this lady here. We can plainly judge by her beauty and prudent mien that she is of very gentle rank. Her beauty and noble bearing show that the honour of a kingdom or empire might well be bestowed upon her. I shall never suffer disgrace through her; rather I think to win more honour. Have my chaplain summoned now, and do you go and fetch the lady. The half of all my land I will give her as her dower if she will comply with my desire." Then they bade the chaplain come, in accordance with the Count's command, and the dame they brought there, too, and made her marry him perforce; for she flatly refused to give consent. But in spite of all, the Count married her in accordance with his wish. And when he had married her, the constable at once had the tables set in the palace, and had the food prepared; for already it was time for the evening meal.

After vespers, that day in May, Enide was in sore distress, nor did her grief cease to trouble her. And the Count urged her mildly by prayer and threat to make her peace and be consoled, and he made her sit down upon a chair, though it was against her will. In spite of her, they made her take a seat and placed the table in front of her. The Count takes his place on the other side, almost beside himself with rage to find that he cannot comfort her. "Lady," he says, "you must now leave off this grief and banish it. You can have full trust in me, that honour and riches will be yours. You must surely realise that mourning will not revive the dead; for no one ever saw such a thing come about. Remember now, though poor you were, that great riches are within your reach. Once you were poor; rich now you will be. Fortune has not been stingy toward you, in bestowing upon you the honour of being henceforth hailed as Countess. It is true that your lord is dead. If you grieve and lament because of this, do you think that I am surprised? Nay. But I am giving you the best advice I know how to give. In that I have married you, you ought to be content. Take care you do not anger me! Eat now, as I bid you do." And she replies: "Not I, my lord. In faith, as long as I live I will neither eat nor drink unless I first see my lord eat who is lying on yonder dais" "Lady, that can never be. People will think that you are mad when you talk such great nonsense. You will receive a poor reward if you give occasion to-day for further reproof." To this she vouchsafed no reply, holding his threats in slight esteem, and the Count strikes her upon the face. At this she shrieks, and the barons present blame the Count. "Hold, sire!" they cry to the Count; "you ought to be ashamed of having struck this lady because she will not eat. You have done a very ugly deed. If this lady is distressed because of her lord whom she now sees dead, no one should say that she is wrong." "Keep silence, all." the Count replies; "the dame is mine and I am hers, and I will do with her as I please." At this she could not hold her peace, but swears she will never be his. And the Count springs up and strikes her again, and she cries out aloud. "Ha! wretch," she says, "I care not what thou say to me, or what thou do! I fear not thy blows, nor yet thy threats. Beat me and strike me, as thou wilt. I shall never heed thy power so much as to do thy bidding more or less, even were thou with thy hands fight now to snatch out my eyes or flay me alive."

In the midst of these words and disputes Erec recovered from his swoon, like a man who awakes from sleep. No wonder that he was amazed at the crowd of people he saw around. But great was his grief and great his woe when he heard the voice of his wife. He stepped to the floor from off the dais and quickly drew his sword. Wrath and the love he bore his wife gave him courage. He runs thither where he sees her, and strikes the Count squarely upon the head, so that he beats out his brains and, knocking in his forehead, leaves him senseless and speechless; his blood and brains flow out. The knights spring from the tables, persuaded that it is the devil who had made his way among them there. Of young or old there none remains, for all were thrown in great dismay. Each one tries to outrun the other in beating a hasty retreat. Soon they were all clear of the palace, and cry aloud, both weak and strong: "Flee, flee, here comes the corpse!" At the door the press is great: each one strives to make his escape, and pushes and shoves as best he may. He who is last in the surging throng would fain get into the foremost line. Thus they make good their escape in flight, for one dares not stand upon another's going. Erec ran to seize his shield, hanging it about his neck by the strap, while Enide lays hands upon the lance. Then they step out into the courtyard. There is no one so bold as to offer resistance; for they did not believe it could be a man who had thus expelled them, but a devil or some enemy who had entered the dead body. Erec pursues them as they flee, and finds outside in the castle-yard a stable-boy in the act of leading his steed to the watering-place, all equipped with bridle and saddle. This chance encounter pleased Erec well: as he steps up quickly to the horse, the boy in fear straightway yields him up. Erec takes his seat between the saddle-bows, while Enide, seizing the stirrup, springs up on to the horse's neck, as Erec, who bade her mount, commanded and instructed her to do. The horse bears them both away; and finding open the town gate, they make their escape without detention. In the town there was great anxiety about the Count who had been killed; but there is no one, however brave, who follows Erec to take revenge. At his table the Count was slain; while Erec, who bears his wife away, embraces and kisses and gives her cheer. In his arms he clasps her against his heart, and says: "Sweet sister mine, my proof of you has been complete! Be no more concerned in any wise, for I love you now more than ever I did before; and I am certain and rest assured that you love me with a perfect love. From this time on for evermore, I offer myself to do your will just as I used to do before. And if you have spoken ill of me, I pardon you and call you quit of both the offence and the word you spoke." Then he kisses her again and clasps her tight. Now Enide is not ill at ease when her lord clasps and kisses her and tells her again that he loves her still. Rapidly through the night they ride, and they are very glad that the moon shines bright.

Meanwhile, the news has travelled fast, and there is nothing else so quick. The news had reached Guivret the Little that a knight wounded with arms had been found dead in the forest, and that with him was a lady making moan, and so wondrous fair that Iseut would have seemed her waiting-maid. Count Oringle of Limors had found them both, and had caused the corpse to be borne away, and wished himself to espouse the lady; but she refused him. When Guivret heard this news, he was by no means pleased; for at once the thought of Erec occurred to him. It came into his heart and mind to go and seek out the lady, and to have the body honourably interred, if it should turn out to be he. He assembled a thousand men-at-arms and knights to take the town. If the Count would not surrender of his own accord the body and the lady, he would put all to fire and flame. In the moonlight shining clear he led his men on toward Limors, with helmets laced, in hauberks clad, and from their necks the shields were hung. Thus, under arms, they all advanced until nearly midnight, when Erec espied them. Now he expects to be ensnared or killed or captured inevitably. He makes Enide dismount beside a thicket-hedge. No wonder if he is dismayed. "Lady, do you stay here," he says, "beside this thicket-hedge a while, until these people shall have passed. I do not wish them to catch sight of you, for I do not know what manner of people they are, nor of what they go in search. I trust we may not attract their attention. But I see nowhere any place where we could take refuge, should they wish to injure us. I know not if any harm may come to me, but not from fear shall I fail to sally out against them. And if any one assails me, I shall not fail to joust with him. Yet, I am so sore and weary that it is no wonder if I grieve. Now to meet them I must go, and do you stay quiet here. Take care that no one see you, until they shall have left you far behind." Behold now Guivret, with lance outstretched, who espied him from afar. They did not recognise each other, for the moon had gone behind the shadow of a dark cloud. Erec was weak and exhausted, and his antagonist was quite recovered from his wounds and blows. Now Erec will be far from wise if he does not promptly make himself known. He steps out from the hedge. And Guivret spurs toward him without speaking to him at all, nor does Erec utter a word to him: he thought he could do more than he could. Whoever tries to run farther than he is able must perforce give up or take a rest. They clash against each other; but the fight was unequal, for one was weak and the other strong. Guivret strikes him with such force that he carries him down to earth from his horse's back. Enide, who was in hiding, when she sees her lord on the ground, expects to be killed and badly used. Springing forth from the hedge, she runs to help her lord. If she grieved before, now her anguish is greater. Coming up to Guivret, she seized his horse's rein, and then said: "Cursed be thou, knight! For thou hast attacked a weak and exhausted man, who is in pain and mortally wounded, with such injustice that thou canst not find reason for thy deed. If thou hadst been alone and helpless, thou wouldst have rued this attack, provided my lord had been in health. Now be generous and courteous, and kindly let cease this battle which thou hast begun. For thy reputation would be no better for having killed or captured a knight who has not the strength to rise, as thou canst see. For he has suffered so many blows of arms that he is all covered with wounds" And he replies: "Fear not, lady! I see that loyally you love your lord, and I commend you for it. Have no fear whatsoever of me or of my company. But tell me now without concealment what is the name of your lord; for only advantage will you get from telling me. Whoever he be, tell me his name; then he shall go safe and unmolested. Neither he nor you have aught to fear, for you are both in safe hands."

Then Enide learns that she is safe, she answers him briefly in a word: "His name is Erec; I ought not to lie, for I see you are honest and of good intent." Guivret, in his delight, dismounts and goes to fall at Erec's feet, where he was lying on the ground. "My lord," he says, "I was going to seek for you, and was on my way to Limors, where I expected to find you dead. It was told and recounted to me as true that Count Oringle had carried off to Limors a knight who was mortally wounded, and that he wickedly intended to marry a lady whom he had found in his company; but that she would have nothing to do with him. And I was coming urgently to aid and deliver her. If he refused to hand over to me both the lady and you without resistance, I should esteem myself of little worth if I left him a foot of earth to stand upon. Be sure that had I not loved you dearly I should never have taken this upon myself. I am Guivret, your friend; but if I have done you any hurt through my failure to recognise you, you surely ought to pardon me." At this Erec sat up, for he could do no more, and said: "Rise up, my friend. Be absolved of the harm you have done me, since you did not recognise me." Guivret gets up, and Erec tells him how he has killed the Count while he sat at meat, and how he had gained possession again of his steed in front of the stable, and how the sergeants and the squires had fled across the yard, crying: "Flee, flee, the corpse is chasing us;" then, how he came near being caught, and how he escaped through the town and down the hill, carrying his wife on his horse's neck: all this adventure of his he told him. Then Guivret said, "Sire, I have a castle here close by, which is well placed in a healthful site. For your comfort and benefit I wish to take you there to-morrow and have your wounds cared for. I have two charming and sprightly sisters who are skilful in the care of wounds: they will soon completely cure you. To-night we shall let our company lodge here in the fields until morning; for I think a little rest to-night will do you much good. My advice is that we spend the night here." Erec replies: "I am in favour of doing so." So there they stayed and spent the night. They were not reluctant to prepare a lodging-place, but they found few accommodations, for the company was quite numerous. They lodge as best they may among the bushes: Guivret had his tent set up, and ordered tinder to be kindled, that they might have light and cheer. He has tapers taken out from the boxes, and they light them within the tent. Now Enide no longer grieves, for all has turned out well. She strips her lord of his arms and clothes, and having washed his wounds, she dried them and bound them up again; for she would let no one else touch him. Now Erec knows no further reason to reproach her, for he has tried her well and found that she bears great love to him. And Guivret, who treats them kindly, had a high, long bed constructed of quilted coverlids, laid upon grass and reed, which they found in abundance. There they laid Erec and covered him up. Then Guivret opened a box and took out two patties. "Friend," says he, "now try a little of these cold patties, and drink some wine mixed with water. I have as much as six barrels of it, but undiluted it is not good for you; for you are injured and covered with wounds. Fair sweet friend, now try to eat; for it will do you good. And my lady will eat some too--

your wife who has been to-day in sore distress on your account. But you have received full satisfaction for all that, and have escaped. So eat now, and I will eat too, fair friend." Then Guivret sat down by Erec's side, and so did Enide who was much pleased by all that Guivret did. Both of them urge him to eat, giving him wine mixed with water'; for unmixed it is too strong and heating. Erec ate as a sick man eats, and drank a little--all he dared. But he rested comfortably and slept all night; for on his account no noise or disturbance was made.

In the early morning they awoke, and prepared again to mount and ride. Erec was so devoted to his own horse that he would ride no other. They gave to Enide a mule, for she had lost her palfrey. But she was not concerned; to judge by her looks, she gave the matter no thought. She had a good mule with an easy gait that bore her very comfortably. And it gave her great satisfaction that Erec was not cast down, but rather assured them that he would recover completely. Before the third hour they reached Penevric, a strong castle, well and handsomely situated. There dwelt the two sisters of Guivret; for the place was agreeable enough. Guivret escorted Erec to a delightful, airy room in a remote part of the castle. His sisters, at his request, exerted themselves to cure Erec; and Erec placed himself in their hands, for they inspired him with perfect confidence. First, they removed the dead flesh, then applied plaster and lint, devoting to his care all their skill, like women who knew their business well. Again and again they washed his wounds and applied the plaster. Four times or more each day they made him eat and drink, allowing him, however, no garlic or pepper. But whoever might go in or out Enide was always with him, being more than any one else concerned. Guivret often came in to ask and inquire if he wanted anything. He was well kept and well served, and everything that he wished was willingly done. But the damsels cheerfully and gladly showed such devotion in caring for him that by the end of a fortnight he felt no hurt or pain. Then, to bring his colour back, they began to give him baths. There was no need to instruct the damsels, for they understood the treatment well. When he was able to walk about. Guivret had two loose gowns made of two different kinds of silk, one trimmed with ermine, the other with vair. One was of a dark purple colour, and the other striped, sent to him as a present by a cousin of his from Scotland. Enide had the purple gown trimmed with ermine, which was very precious, while Erec had the striped stuff with the fur, which was no less valuable. Now Erec was strong and well, cured and recovered. Now that Enide was very happy and had everything she desired, her great beauty returned to her; for her great distress had affected her so much that she was very pale and wan. Now she was embraced and kissed, now she was blessed with all good things, now she had her joy and pleasures; for unadorned they lie in bed and each enfolds and kisses the other; nothing gives them so much joy. They have had so much pain and sorrow, he for her, and she for him, that now they have their satisfaction. Each vies in seeking to please the other. Of their further sport I must not speak. Now they have so welded their love and forgotten their grief that they scarcely remember it any more. But now they must go on their way; so they asked his leave to depart from Guivret, in whom they had found a friend indeed; for he had honoured and served them in every way. When he came to take leave, Erec said: "Sire, I do not wish to delay longer my departure for my own land. Order everything to be prepared and collected, in order that I may have all I need. I shall wish to start to-morrow morning, as soon as it is day. I have stayed so long with you that I feel strong and vigorous. God grant, if it please Him, that I may live to meet you again somewhere, when I may be able in my turn to serve and honour you. Unless I am captured or detained, I do not expect to tarry anywhere until I reach the court of King Arthur, whom I hope to find either at Robais or Carduel." To which Guivret makes prompt reply, "Sire, you shall not go off alone! For I myself shall go with you and shall take companions with us, if it be your pleasure." Erec accedes to this advice, and says that, in accordance with his plans, he wishes the journey to be begun. That night they make preparations for their journey, not wishing to delay there longer. They all make ready and prepare. In the early morning, when they awake, the saddles are placed upon the steeds. Before he leaves, Erec goes to bid farewell to the damsels in their rooms; and Enide (who was glad and full of joy) thither follows him. When their preparations for departure were made, they took their leave of the damsels. Erec, who was very courteous, in taking leave of them, thanks them for his health and life, and pledges to them his service. Then he took one of them by the hand she who was the nearer to him and Enide took the other's hand: hand in hand they came up from the bedroom into the castle hall. Guivret urges them to mount at once without delay. Enide thinks the time will never come for them to mount. They bring around to the block for her a good-tempered palfrey, a soft stepper, handsome and well shaped. The palfrey was of fine appearance and a good mount: it was no less valuable than her own which had stayed behind at Limors. That other one was dappled, this one was sorrel; but the head was of another colour: it was marked in such a way that one cheek was all white, while the other was raven black. Between the two colours there was a line, greener than a grape-vine leaf, which separated the white from the black. Of the bridle, breast-strap, and saddle I can surely say that the workmanship was rich and handsome. All the breast-strap and bridle was of gold set with emeralds. The saddle was decorated in another style, covered with a precious purple cloth. The saddle-bows were of ivory, on which was carved the story of how Aeneas came from Troy, how at Carthage with great joy Dido received him to her bed, how Aeneas deceived her, and how for him she killed herself, how Aeneas conquered Laurentum and all Lombardy, of which he was king all his life. Cunning was the workmanship and well carved, all decorated with fine gold. A skilful craftsman, who made it spent more than seven years in carving it, without touching any other piece of work. I do not know whether he sold it; but he ought to have obtained a good price for it. Now that Enide was presented with this palfrey, she was well compensated for the loss of her own. The palfrey, thus richly apparelled, was given to her and she mounted it gladly; then the gentlemen and squires quickly mounted too. For their pleasure and sport Guivret caused to be taken with them rich falcons, both young and moulted, many a tercel and sparrow-hawk, and many a setter and greyhound.

They rode straight on from morn till eve more than thirty Welsh leagues, and then came to the towers of a stronghold, rich and fair, girt all about with a new wall. And all around, beneath this wall, ran a very deep stream, roaring rushing like a storm. Erec stops to look at it, and ask and find out if any one could truly tell him who was the lord of this town. "Friend," said he to his kind companion, "could you tell me the name of this town, and whose it is? Tell me if it belongs to a count or a king. Since you have brought me here, tell me, if you know." "Sire," he says, "I know very well, and will tell you the truth about it. The name of the town is Brandigant, and it is so strong and fine that it fears neither king nor emperor. If France, and all of England, and all who live from here to Liege were ranged about to lay a siege, they would never take it in their lives; for the isle on which the town stands stretches away four leagues or more, and within the enclosure grows all that a rich town needs: fruit and wheat and wine are found; and of wood and water there is no lack. It fears no assault on any side, nor could anything reduce it to starvation. King Evrain had it fortified, and he has possessed it all his days unmolested, and will possess it all his life. But not because he feared any one did he thus fortify it; but the town is more pleasing so. For if it had no wall or tower, but only the stream that encircles it, it would still be so secure and strong that it would have no fear of the whole world." "God!" said Erec, "what great wealth! Let us go and see the fortress, and we shall take lodging in the town, for I wish to stop here." "Sire," said the other in great distress, "were it not to disappoint you, we should not stop here. In the town there is a dangerous passage." "Dangerous?" says Erec; "do you know about it? Whatever it be, tell us about it; for very gladly would I know." "Sire," says he, "I should fear that you might suffer some harm there. I know there is so much boldness and excellence in your heart that, were I to tell you what I know of the perilous and hard adventure, you would wish to enter in. I have often heard the story, and more than seven years have passed since any one that went in quest of the adventure has come back from the town; yet, proud, bold knights have come hither from many a land. Sire, do not treat this as a jest: for you will never learn the secret from me until you shall have promised me, by the love you have sworn to me, that never by you will be undertaken this adventure, from which no one escapes without receiving shame or death."

Now Erec hears what pleases him, and begs Guivret not to be grieved, saying: "Ah, fair sweet friend, permit that our lodging be made in the town, and do not be disturbed. It is time to halt for the night, and so I trust that it will not displease you; for if any honour comes to us here you ought to be very glad. I appeal to you conceding the adventure that you tell me just the name of it, and I'll not insist upon the rest." "Sire." he says, "I cannot be silent and refuse the information you desire. The name is very fair to say, but the execution is very hard: for no one can come from it alive. The adventure, upon my word, is called 'the Joy of the Court.'" "God! there can be nothing but good in joy," says Erec; "I go to seek it. Don't go now and discourage me about this or anything else, fair gentle friend; but let us have our lodgings taken, for great good may come to us of this. Nothing could restrain me from going to seek the Joy." "Sire," says he, "God grant your prayer, that you may find joy and return without mishap. I clearly see that we must go in. Since otherwise it may not be, let us go in. Our lodging is secured; for no knight of high degree, as I have heard it said and told, can enter this castle with intent to lodge here but that King Evrain offers to shelter him. So gentle and courteous is the King that he has given notice to all his townsmen, appealing to their love for him, that any gentleman from afar should not find lodging in their houses, so that he himself may do honour to all gentlemen who may wish to tarry here."

Thus they proceed toward the castle, passing the list and the drawbridge; and when they passed the listing-place, the people who were gathered in the streets in crowds see Erec in all his beauty, and apparently they think and believe that all the others are in his train. Marvelling much, they stare at him; the whole town was stirred and moved, as they take counsel and discuss about him. Even the maidens at their song leave off their singing and desist, as all together they look at him; and because of his great beauty they cross themselves, and marvellously they pity him. One to another whispers low: "Alas! This knight, who is passing, is on his way to the 'Joy of the Court.' He will be sorry before he returns; no one ever came from another land to claim the 'Joy of the Court' who did not receive shame and harm, and leave his head there as a forfeit." Then, that he may hear their words, they cry-aloud: "God defend thee, knight, from harm; for thou art wondrously handsome, and thy beauty is greatly to be pitied, for to-morrow we shall see it quenched. Tomorrow thy death is come; to-morrow thou shalt surely die if God does not guard and defend thee." Erec hears and understands that they are speaking of him through the lower town: more than two thousand pitied him; but nothing causes him dismay. He passes on without delay, bowing gaily to men and women alike. And they all salute him too; and most of them swear with anxiety, fearing more than he does himself, for his shame and for his hurt. The mere sight of his countenance, his great beauty and his bearing, has so won to him the hearts of all, that knights, ladies, and maids alike fear his harm. King Evrain hears the news that men were arriving at his court who brought with them a numerous train, and by his harness it appeared that their leader was a count or king. King Evrain comes down the street to meet them, and saluting them he cries: "Welcome to this company, both to the master and all his suite. Welcome, gentlemen! Dismount." They dismounted, and there were plenty to receive and take their horses. Nor was King Evrain backward when he saw Enide coming; but he straightway saluted her and ran to help her to dismount. Taking her white and tender hand, he led her up into the palace, as was required by courtesy, and honoured her in every way he could, for he knew right well what he ought to do, without nonsense and without malice. He ordered a chamber to be scented with incense, myrrh, and aloes. When they entered, they all complimented King Evrain on its fine appearance. Hand in hand they enter the room, the King escorting them and taking great pleasure in them. But why should I describe to you the paintings and the silken draperies with which the room was decorated? I should only waste time in folly, and I do not wish to waste it, but rather to hasten on a little; for he who travels the straight road passes him who turns aside; therefore I do not wish to tarry. When the time and hour arrived, the King orders supper to be prepared; but I do not wish to stop over that if I can find some more direct way. That night they had in abundance all that heart desires and craves: birds, venison, and fruit, and wines of different sorts. But better than all is a happy cheer! For of all dishes the sweetest is a joyful countenance and a happy face. They were very richly served until Erec suddenly left off eating and drinking, and began speaking of what rested most upon his heart: he remembered 'the Joy', and began a conversation about it in which King Evrain joined. "Sire" says he, "it is time now to tell you what I intend, and why I have come here. Too long I have refrained from speech, and now can no longer conceal my object. I ask you for 'the Joy' of the Court, for I covet nothing else so much. Grant it to me, whatever it be, if you are in control of it." "In truth, fair friend." the King replies, "I hear you speak great nonsense. This is a very parlous thing, which has caused sorrow to many a worthy man; you yourself will eventually be killed and undone if you will not heed my counsel. But if you were willing to take my word, I should advise you to desist from soliciting so grievous a thing in which you would never succeed. Speak of it no more! Hold your peace! It would be imprudent on your part not to follow my advice. I am not at all surprised that you desire honour and fame; but if I should see you harmed or injured in your body I should be distressed at heart. And know well that I have seen many a man ruined who solicited this joy. They were never any the better for it, but rather did they all die and perish. Before to-morrow's evening come you may expect a like reward. If you wish to strive for the Joy, you shall do so, though it grieve me sore. It is something from which you are free to retreat and draw back if you wish to work your welfare. Therefore I tell you, for I should commit treachery and do you wrong were I not to tell you all the truth." Erec hears him and admits that the King with reason counsels him. But the greater the wonder and the more perilous the adventure, the more he covets it and yearns for it, saying: "Sire, I can tell you that I find you a worthy and a loyal man, and I can put no blame on you. I wish to undertake this boon, however it may fall out with me. The die is cast, for I shall never draw back from anything I have undertaken without exerting all my strength before I quit the field." "I know that well," the King replied; "you are acting against my will. You shall have the Joy which you desire. But I am in great despair; for I greatly fear you will be undone. But now be assured that you shall have what you desire. If you come out of it happily, you will have won such great honour that never did man win greater; and may God, as I desire, grant you a joyous deliverance."

All that night they talked of it, until the beds were prepared and they went to rest. In the morning, when it was daylight, Erec, who was on the watch, saw the clear dawn and the sun, and quickly rising, clothed himself. Enide again is in distress, very sad and ill at ease; all night she is greatly disquieted with the solicitude and fear which she felt for her lord, who is about to expose himself to great peril. But nevertheless he equips himself, for no one can make him change his mind. For his equipment the King sent him, when he arose, arms which he put to good use. Erec did not refuse them, for his own were worn and impaired and in bad state. He gladly accepted the arms and had himself equipped with them in the hall. When he was armed, he descends the steps and finds his horse saddled and the King who had mounted. Every one in the castle and in the houses of the town hastened to mount. In all the town there remained neither man nor woman, erect or deformed, great or small, weak or strong, who is able to go and does not do so. When they start, there is a great noise and clamour in all the streets; for those of high and low degree alike cry out: "Alas, alas! oh knight, the Joy that thou wishest to win has betrayed thee, and thou goest to win but grief and death." And there is not one but says: "God curse this joy! which has been the death of so many gentlemen. To-day it will wreak the worst woe that it has ever yet wrought." Erec hears well and notes that up and down they said of him: "Alas, alas, ill-starred wert thou, fair, gentle, skilful knight! Surely it would not be just that thy life should end so soon, or that harm should come to wound and injure thee." He hears clearly the words and what they said; but notwithstanding, he passes on without lowering his head, and without the bearing of a craven. Whoever may speak, he longs to see and know and understand why they are all in such distress, anxiety, and woe. The King leads him without the town into a garden that stood near by; and all the people follow after, praying that from this trial God may grant him a happy issue. But it is not meet that I should pass on, from weariness and exhaustion of tongue, without telling you the whole truth about the garden, according as the story runs.

The garden had around it no wall or fence except of air: yet, by a spell, the garden was on all sides so shut in by the air that nothing could enter there any more than if the garden were enclosed in iron, unless it flew in over the top. And all through the summer and the winter, too, there were flowers and ripe fruits there; and the fruit was of such a nature that it could be eaten inside; the danger consisted in carrying it out; for whoever should wish to carry out a little would never be able to find the gate, and never could issue from the garden until he had restored the fruit to its place. And there is no flying bird under heaven, pleasing to man, but it sings there to delight and to gladden him, and can be heard there in numbers of every kind. And the earth, however far it stretch, bears no spice or root of use in making medicine, but it had been planted there, and was to be found in abundance. Through a narrow entrance the people entered--King Evrain and all the rest. Erec went riding, lance in rest, into the middle of the garden, greatly delighting in the song of the birds which were singing there; they put him in mind of his Joy the thing he most was longing for. But he saw a wondrous thing, which might arouse fear in the bravest warrior of all whom we know, be it Thiebaut the Esclavon, or Ospinel, or Fernagu. For before them, on sharpened stakes, there stood bright and shining helmets, and each one had beneath the rim a man's head. But at the end there stood a stake where as yet there was nothing but a horn. He knows not what this signifies, yet draws not back a step for that; rather does he ask the King, who was beside him at the right, what this can be. The King speaks and explains to him: "Friend," he says, "do you know the meaning of this thing that you see here? You must be in great terror of it, if you care at all for your own body; for this single stake which stands apart, where you see this horn hung up, has been waiting a very long time, but we know not for whom, whether for you or someone else. Take care lest thy head be set up there; for such is the purpose of the stake. I had warned you well of that before you came here. I do not expect that you will escape hence, but that you will be killed and rent apart. For this much we know, that the stake awaits your head. And if it turns out that it be placed there, as the matter stands agreed, as soon as thy head is fixed upon it another stake will be set up beside it which will await the arrival of some one else--I know not when or whom. I will tell you nothing of the horn; but never has any one been able to blow it. However, he who shall succeed in blowing it his fame and honour will grow until it distance all those of his country, and he shall find such renown that all will come to do him honour, and will hold him to be the best of them all. Now there is no more of this matter. Have your men withdraw; for 'the Joy' will soon arrive, and will make you sorry, I suspect."

Meanwhile King Evrain leaves his side, and Erec stoops over before Enide, whose heart was in great distress, although she held her peace; for grief on lips is of no account unless it also touch the heart. And he who well knew her heart, said to her: "Fair sister dear, gentle, loyal, and prudent lady, I am acquainted with your thoughts. You are in fear, I see that well, and yet you do not know for what; but there is no reason for your dismay until you shall see that my shield is shattered and that my body is wounded, and until you see the meshes of my bright hauberk covered with blood, and my helmet broken and smashed, and me defeated and weary, so that I can no longer defend myself, but must beg and sue for mercy against my will; then you may lament, but now you have begun too soon. Gentle lady, as yet you know not what this is to be; no more do I. You are troubled without cause. But know this truly: if there were in me only so much courage as your love inspires, truly I should not fear to face any man alive. But I am foolish to vaunt myself; yet I say it not from any pride, but because I wish to comfort you. So comfort yourself, and let it be! I cannot longer tarry here, nor can you go along with me; for, as the King has ordered, I must not take you beyond this point." Then he kisses her and commends her to God, and she him. But she is much chagrined that she cannot follow and escort him, until she may learn and see what this adventure is to be, and how he will conduct himself. But since she must stay behind and cannot follow him, she remains sorrowful and grieving. And he went off alone down a path, without companion of any sort, until he came to a silver couch with a cover of gold-embroidered cloth, beneath the shade of a sycamore; and on the bed a maiden of comely body and lovely face, completely endowed with all beauty, was seated all alone. I intended to say no more of her; but whoever could consider well all her attire and her beauty might well say that never did Lavinia of Laurentum, who was so fair and comely, possess the quarter of her beauty. Erec draws near to her, wishing to see her more closely, and the onlookers go and sit down under the trees in the orchard. Then behold, there comes a knight armed with vermilion arms, and he was wondrous tall; and if he were not so immeasurably tall, under the heavens there would be none fairer than he; but, as every one averred, he was a foot taller than any knight he knew. Before Erec caught sight of him, he cried out: "Vassal, vassal! You are mad, upon my life, thus to approach my damsel. I should say you are not worthy to draw near her. You will pay dearly for your presumption, by my head! Stand back!" And Erec stops and looks at him, and the other, too, stood still. Neither made advance until Erec had replied all that he wished to say to him. "Friend," he says, "one can speak folly as well as good sense. Threaten as much as you please, and I will keep silence; for in threatening there is no sense. Do you know why? A man sometimes thinks he has won the game who afterward loses it. So he is manifestly a fool who is too presumptuous and who threatens too much. If there are some who flee there are plenty who chase, but I do not fear you so much that I am going to run away yet. I am ready to make such defence, if there is any who wishes to offer me battle, that he will have to do his uttermost, or otherwise he cannot escape." "Nay," quoth he, "so help me God! know that you shall have the battle, for I defy and challenge you." And you may know, upon my word, that then the reins were not held in. The lances they had were not light, but were big and square; nor were they planed smooth, but were rough and strong. Upon the shields with mighty strength they smote each other with their sharp weapons, so that a fathom of each lance passes through the gleaming shields. But neither touches the other's flesh, nor was either lance cracked; each one, as quickly as he could, draws back his lance, and both rushing together, return to the fray. One against the other rides, and so fiercely they smite each other that both lances break and the horses fall beneath them. But they, being seated on their steeds, sustain no harm; so they quickly rise, for they were strong and lithe. They stand on foot in the middle of the garden, and straightway attack each other with their green swords of German steel, and deal great wicked blows upon their bright and gleaming helmets, so that they hew them into bits, and their eyes shoot out flame. No greater efforts can be made than those they make in striving and toiling to injure and wound each other. Both fiercely smite with the gilded pommel and the cutting edge. Such havoc did they inflict upon each other's teeth, cheeks, nose, hands, arms, and the rest, upon temples, neck, and throat that their bones all ache. They are very sore and very tired; yet they do not desist, but rather only strive the more. Sweat, and the blood which flows down with it, dim their eyes, so that they can hardly see a thing; and very often they missed their blows, like men who did not see to wield their swords upon each other. They can scarcely harm each other now; yet, they do not desist at all from exercising all their strength. Because their eyes are so blinded that they completely lose their sight, they let their shields fall to the ground, and seize each other angrily. Each pulls and drags the other, so that they fall upon their knees. Thus, long they fight until the hour of noon is past, and the big knight is so exhausted that his breath quite fails him. Erec has him at his mercy, and pulls and drags so that he breaks all the lacing of his helmet, and forces him over at his feet. He falls over upon his face against Erec's breast, and has not strength to rise again. Though it distresses him, he has to say and own: "I cannot deny it, you have beaten me; but much it goes against my will. And yet you may be of such degree and fame that only credit will redound to me; and insistently I would request, if it may be in any way, that I might know your name, and he thereby somewhat comforted. If a better man has defeated me, I shall be glad, I promise you; but if it has so fallen out that a baser man than I has worsted me, then I must feel great grief indeed." "Friend, dost thou wish to know my name?" says Erec; "Well, I shall tell thee ere I leave here; but it will be upon condition that thou tell me now why thou art in this garden. Concerning that I will know all what is thy name and what the Joy; for I am very anxious to hear the truth from beginning to end of it." "Sire," says he, "fearlessly I will tell you all you wish to know." Erec no more withholds his name, but says: "Didst thou ever hear of King Lac and of his son Erec?" "Yea, sire, I knew him well; for I was at his father's court for many a day before I was knighted, and, if he had had his will, I should never have left him for anything." "Then thou oughtest to know me well, if thou weft ever with me at the court of my father, the King." "Then, upon my faith, it has turned out well. Now hear who has detained me so long in this garden. I will tell the truth in accordance with your injunction, whatever it may cost me. That damsel who yonder sits, loved me from childhood and I loved her. It pleased us both, and our love grew and increased, until she asked a boon of me, but did not tell me what it was. Who would deny his mistress aught? There is no lover but would surely do all his sweet-heart's pleasure without default or guile, whenever he can in any way. I agreed to her desire; but when I had agreed, she would have it, too, that I should swear. I would have done more than that for her, but she took me at my word. I made her a promise, without knowing what. Time passed until I was made a knight. King Evrain, whose nephew I am, dubbed me a knight in the presence of many honourable men in this very garden where we are. My lady, who is sitting there, at once recalled to me my word, and said that I had promised her that I would never go forth from here until there should come some knight who should conquer me by trial of arms. It was right that I should remain, for rather than break my word, I should never have pledged it. Since I knew the good there was in her, I could nor reveal or show to the one whom I hold most dear that in all this I was displeased; for if she had noticed it, she would have withdrawn her heart, and I would not have had it so for anything that might happen. Thus my lady thought to detain me here for a long stay; she did not think that there would ever enter this garden any vassal who could conquer me. In this way she intended to keep me absolutely shut up with her all the days of my life. And I should have committed an offence if I had had resort to guile and not defeated all those against whom I could prevail; such escape would have been a shame. And I dare to assure you that I have no friend so dear that I would have feigned at all in fighting with him. Never did I weary of arms, nor did I ever refuse to fight. You have surely seen the helmets of those whom I have defeated and put to death; but the guilt of it is not mine, when one considers it aright. I could not help myself, unless I were willing to be false and recreant and disloyal. Now I have told you the truth, and be assured that it is no small honour which you have gained. You have given great joy to the court of my uncle and my friends; for now I shall be released from here; and because all those who are at the court will have joy of it, therefore those who awaited the joy called it 'Joy of the Court'. They have awaited it so long that now it will be granted them by you who have won it by your fight. You have defeated and bewitched my prowess and my chivalry. Now it is right that I tell you my name, if you would know it. I am called Mabonagrain; but I am not remembered by that name in any land where I have been, save only in this region; for never, when I was a squire, did I tell or make known my name. Sire, you knew the truth concerning all that you asked me. But I must still tell you that there is in this garden a horn which I doubt not you have seen. I cannot issue forth from here until you have blown the horn; but then you will have released me, and then the Joy will begin. Whoever shall hear and give it heed no hindrance will detain him, when he shall hear the sound of the horn, from coming straight-way to the court. Rise up, sire! Go quickly now! Go take the horn right joyfully; for you have no further cause to wait; so do that which you must do." Now Erec rose, and the other rises with him, and both approach the horn. Erec takes it and blows it, putting into it all his strength, so that the sound of it reaches far. Greatly did Enide rejoice when she heard the note, and Guivret was greatly delighted too. The King is glad, and so are his people; there is not one who is not well suited and pleased at this. No one ceases or leaves off from making merry and from song. Erec could boast that day, for never was such rejoicing made; it could not be described or related by mouth of man, but I will tell you the sum of it briefly and with few words. The news spreads through the country that thus the affair has turned out. Then there was no holding back from coming to the court. All the people hasten thither in confusion, some on foot and some on horse, without waiting for each other. And those who were in the garden hastened to remove Erec's arms, and in emulation they all sang a song about the Joy; and the ladies made up a lay which they called 'the Lay of Joy', but the lay is not well known. Erec was well sated with joy and well served to his heart's desire; but she who sat on the silver couch was not a bit pleased. The joy which she saw was not at all to her taste. But many people have to keep still and look on at what gives them pain. Enide acted graciously; because she saw her sitting pensive, alone on the couch, she felt moved to go and speak with her and tell her about her affairs and about herself, and to strive, if possible, to make her tell in return about herself, if it did not cause her too great distress. Enide thought to go alone, wishing to take no one with her, but some of the most noble and fairest dames and damsels followed her out of affection to bear her company, and also to comfort her to whom the joy brings great chagrin; for she assumed that now her lover would be no longer with her so much as he had been, inasmuch as he desired to leave the garden. However disappointing it may be, no one can prevent his going away, for the hour and the time have come. Therefore the tears ran down her face from her eyes. Much more than I can say was she grieving and distressed; nevertheless she sat up straight. But she does not care so much for any of those who try to comfort her that she ceases her moan. Enide salutes her kindly; but for a while the other could not reply a word, being prevented by the sighs and sobs which torment and distress her. Some time it was before the damsel returned her salutation, and when she had looked at her and examined her for a while, it seemed that she had seen and known her before. But not being very certain of it, she was not slow to inquire from whence she was, of what country, and where her lord was born; she inquires who they both are. Enide replies briefly and tells her the truth, saying: "I am the niece of the Count who holds sway over Lalut, the daughter of his own sister; at Lalut I was born and brought up." The other cannot help smiling, without hearing more, for she is so delighted that she forgets her sorrow. Her heart leaps with joy which she cannot conceal. She runs and embraces Enide, saying: "I am your cousin! This is the very truth, and you are my father's niece; for he and your father are brothers. But I suspect that you do not know and have never heard how I came into this country. The Count, your uncle, was at war, and to him there came to fight for pay knights of many lands. Thus, fair cousin, it came about, that with these hireling knights there came one who was the nephew of the king of Brandigan. He was with my father almost a year. That was, I think, twelve years ago, and I was still but a little child. He was very handsome and attractive. There we had an understanding between us that pleased us both. I never had any wish but his, until at last he began to love me and promised and swore to me that he would always be my lover, and that he would bring me here; that pleased us both alike. He could not wait, and I was longing to come hither with him; so we both came away, and no one knew of it but ourselves. In those days you and I were both young and little girls. I have told you the truth; so now tell me in turn, as I have told you, all about your lover, and by what adventure he won you." "Fair cousin, he married me in such a way that my father knew all about it, and my mother was greatly pleased. All our relatives knew it and rejoiced over it, as they should do. Even the Count was glad. For he is so good a knight that better cannot be found, and he does not need to prove his honour and knighthood, and he is of very gentle birth: I do not think that any can be his equal. He loves me much, and I love him more, and our love cannot be greater. Never yet could I withhold my love from him, nor should I do so.

For is not my lord the son of a king? For did he not take me when I was poor and naked? Through him has such honour come to me that never was any such vouchsafed to a poor helpless girl. And if it please you, I will tell you without lying how I came to be thus raised up; for never will I be slow to tell the story." Then she told and related to her how Erec came to Lalut; for she had no desire to conceal it. She told her the adventure word for word, without omission. But I pass over it now, because he who tells a story twice makes his tale now tiresome. While they were thus conversing, one lady slipped away alone, who sent and told it all to the gentlemen, in order to increase and heighten their pleasure too. All those who heard it rejoiced at this news. And when Mabonagrain knew it he was delighted for his sweetheart because now she was comforted. And she who bore them quickly the news made them all happy in a short space. Even the King was glad for it; although he was very happy before, yet now he is still happier, and shows Erec great honour. Enide leads away her fair cousin, fairer than Helen, more graceful and charming. Now Erec and Mabonagrain, Guivret and King Evrain, and all the others run to meet them and salute them and do them honour, for no one is grudging or holds back. Mabonagrain makes much of Enide, and she of him. Erec and Guivret, for their part, rejoice over the damsel as they all kiss and embrace each other. They propose to return to the castle, for they have stayed too long in the garden. They are all prepared to go out; so they sally forth joyfully, kissing each other on the way. All go out after the King, but before they reached the castle, the nobles were assembled from all the country around, and all those who knew of the Joy, and who could do so, came hither. Great was the gathering and the press. Every one, high and low, rich and poor, strives to see Erec. Each thrusts himself before the other, and they all salute him and bow before him, saying constantly: "May God save him through whom joy and gladness come to our court! God save the most blessed man whom God has ever brought into being!" Thus they bring him to the court, and strive to show their glee as their hearts dictate. Breton zithers, harps, and viols sound, fiddles, psalteries, and other stringed instruments, and all kinds of music that one could name or mention. But I wish to conclude the matter briefly without too long delay. The King honours him to the extent of his power, as do all the others ungrudgingly. There is no one who does not gladly offer to do his service. Three whole days the Joy lasted, before Erec could get away. On the fourth he would no longer tarry for any reason they could urge. There was a great crowd to accompany him and a very great press when it came to taking leave. If he had wished to reply to each one, he would not have been able in half a day to return the salutations individually. The nobles he salutes and embraces; the others he commends to God in a word, and salutes them. Enide, for her part, is not silent when she takes leave of the nobles. She salutes them all by name, and they in turn do the like. Before she goes, she kisses her cousin very tenderly and embraces her. Then they go and the Joy is over.

They go off and the others return. Erec and Guivret do not tarry, but keep joyfully on their way, until they came in nine days to Robais, where they were told the King was. The day before he had been bled privately in his apartments; with him he had only five hundred nobles of his household. Never before at any time was the King found so alone, and he was much distressed that he had no more numerous suite at his court. At that time a messenger comes running, whom they had sent ahead to apprise the King of their approach. This man came in before the assembly, found the King and all his people, and saluting him correctly, said: "I am a messenger of Erec and of Guivret the Little." Then he told him how they were coming to see him at his court. The King replies: "Let them be welcome, as valiant and gallant gentlemen! Nowhere do I know of any better than they two. By their presence my court will be much enhanced." Then he sent for the Queen and told her the news. The others have their horses saddled to go and meet the gentlemen. In such haste are they to mount that they did not put on their spurs. I ought to state briefly that the crowd of common people, including squires, cooks, and butlers, had already entered the town to prepare for the lodgings. The main party came after, and had already drawn so near that they had entered the town.

Now the two parties have met each other, and salute and kiss each other. They come to the lodgings and make themselves comfortable, removing their hose and making their toilet by donning their rich robes. When they were completely decked out, they took their way to the court. They come to court, where the King sees them, and the Queen, who is beside herself with impatience to see Erec and Enide. The King makes them take seats beside him, kisses Erec and Guivret; about Enide's neck he throws his arms and kisses her repeatedly, in his great joy. Nor is the Queen slow in embracing Erec and Enide. One might well rejoice to see her now so full of joy. Every one enters with spirit into the merry-making. Then the King causes silence to be made, and appeals to Erec and asks news of his adventures. When the noise had ceased, Erec began his story, telling him of his adventures, without forgetting any detail. Do you think now that I shall tell you what motive he had had in starting out? Nay, for you know the whole truth about this and the rest, as I have revealed it to you. To tell the story again would burden me; for the tale is not short, that any one should wish to begin it afresh and re-embellish it, as he told and related it: of the three knights whom he defeated, and then of the five, and then of the Count who strove to do him harm, and then of the two giants--all in order, one after the other, he told him of his adventures up to the point where he met Count Oringle of Limors. "Many a danger have you gone through, fair gentle friend," said the King to him; "now tarry in this country at my court, as you are wont to do." "Sire, since you wish it, I shall remain very gladly three or four years entire. But ask Guivret to remain here too a request in which I would fain join." The King prays him to remain, and he consents to stay. So they both stay: the King kept them with him, and held them dear and honoured them.

Erec stayed at court, together with Guivret and Enide, until the death of his father, the king, who was an old man and full of years. The messengers then started out: the nobles who went to seek him, and who were the greatest men of the land, sought and searched for him until they found him at Tintagel three weeks before Christmas; they told him the truth what had happened to his old, white-haired father, and how he now was dead and gone. This grieved Erec much more than he showed before the people. But sorrow is not seemly in a king, nor does it become a king to mourn. There at Tintagel where he was, he caused vigils for the dead and Masses to be sung; he promised and kept his promises, as he had vowed to the religious houses and churches; he did well all that he ought to do: he chose out more than one hundred and sixty-nine of the wretched poor, and clothed them all in new garments. To the poor clerks and priors he gave, as was right, black copes and warm linings to wear beneath. For God's sake he did great good to all: to those who were in need he distributed more than a barrel of small coins. When he had shared his wealth, he then did a very wise thing in receiving his land from the King's hand; and then he begged the King to crown him at his court. The King bade him quickly be prepared; for they shall both be crowned, he together with his wife, at the approaching Christmastide; and he added: "You must go hence to Nantes in Brittany; there you shall carry a royal ensign with crown on head and sceptre in hand; this gift and privilege I bestow upon you." Erec thanked the King, and said that that was a noble gift. At Christmas the King assembles all his nobles, summoning them individually and commanding them to come to Nantes. He summoned them all, and none stayed behind. Erec, too, sent word to many of his followers, and summoned them to come thither; but more came than he had bidden, to serve him and do him honour. I cannot tell you or relate who each one was, and what his name; but whoever came or did not come, the father and mother of my lady Enide were not forgotten. Her father was sent for first of all, and he came to court in handsome style, like a great lord and a chatelain. There was no great crowd of chaplains or of silly, gaping yokels, but of excellent knights and of people well equipped. Each day they made a long day's journey, and rode on each day with great joy and great display, until on Christmas eve they came to the city of Nantes. They made no halt until they entered the great hall where the King and his courtiers were. Erec and Enide see them, and you may know how glad they were. To meet them they quickly make their way, and salute and embrace them, speaking to them tenderly and showing their delight as they should. When they had rejoiced together, taking each other by the hand, they all four came before the King, saluting him and likewise the Queen, who was sitting by his side. Taking his host by the hand, Erec said: "Sire, behold my good host, my kind friend, who did me such honour that he made me master in his own house. Before he knew anything about me, he lodged me well and handsomely. All that he had he made over to me, and even his daughter he bestowed upon me, without the advice or counsel of any one." "And this lady with him," the King inquires, "who is she?" Erec does not conceal the truth: "Sire," says he, "of this lady I may say that she is the mother of my wife." "Is she her mother?" "Yes, truly, sire." "Certainly, I may then well say that fair and comely should be the flower born of so fair a stem, and better the fruit one picks; for sweet is the smell of what springs from good. Fair is Enide and fair she should be in all reason and by right; for her mother is a very handsome lady, and her father is a goodly knight. Nor does she in aught belie them; for she descends and inherits directly from them both in many respects." Then the King ceases and sits down, bidding them be seated too. They do not disobey his command, but straightway take seats. Now is Enide filled with joy when she sees her father and mother, for a very long time had passed since she had seen them. Her happiness now is greatly increased, for she was delighted and happy, and she showed it all she could, but she could not make such demonstration but that her joy was yet greater. But I wish to say no more of that, for my heart draws me toward the court which was now assembled in force. From many a different country there were counts and dukes and kings, Normans, Bretons. Scotch, and Irish: from England and Cornwall there was a very rich gathering of nobles; for from Wales to Anjou, in Maine and in Poitou, there was no knight of importance, nor lady of quality, but the best and the most elegant were at the court at Nantes, as the King had bidden them. Now hear, if you will, the great joy and grandeur, the display and the wealth, that was exhibited at the court. Before the hour of nones had sounded, King Arthur dubbed four hundred knights or more all sons of counts and of kings. To each one he gave three horses and two pairs of suits, in order that his court may make a better showing. Puissant and lavish was the King; for the mantles he bestowed were not of serge, nor of rabbit-skins, nor of cheap brown fur, but of heavy silk and ermine, of spotted fur and flowered silks, bordered with heavy and stiff gold braid. Alexander, who conquered so much that he subdued the whole world, and who was so lavish and rich, compared with him was poor and mean. Caesar, the Emperor of Rome, and all the kings whose names you hear in stories and in epic songs, did not distribute at any feast so much as Arthur gave on the day that he crowned Erec; nor would Caesar and Alexander dare to spend so much as he spent at the court. The raiment was taken from the chests and spread about freely through the halls; one could take what he would, without restraint. In the midst of the court, upon a rug, stood thirty bushels of bright sterlings; for since the time of Merlin until that day sterlings had currency throughout Britain. There all helped themselves, each one carrying away that night all that he wanted to his lodging-place. At nine o'clock on Christmas day, all came together again at court. The great joy that is drawing near for him had completely filched Erec's heart away. The tongue and the mouth of no man, however skilful, could describe the third, or the fourth, or the fifth part of the display which marked his coronation. So it is a mad enterprise I undertake in wishing to attempt to describe it. But since I must make the effort, come what may, I shall not fail to relate a part of it, as best I may.

The King had two thrones of white ivory, well constructed and new, of one pattern and style. He who made them beyond a doubt was a very skilled and cunning craftsman. For so precisely did he make the two alike in height, in breadth, and in ornamentation, that you could nor look at them from every side to distinguish one from the other and find in one aught that was not in the other. There was no part of wood, but all of gold and fine ivory. Well were they carved with great skill, for the two corresponding sides of each bore the representation of a leopard, and the other two a dragon's shape. A knight named Bruiant of the Isles had made a gift and present of them to King Arthur and the Queen. King Arthur sat upon the one, and upon the other he made Erec sit, who was robed in watered silk. As we read in the story, we find the description of the robe, and in order that no one may say that I lie, I quote as my authority Macrobius, who devoted himself to the description of it. Macrobius instructs me how to describe, according as I have found it in the book, the workmanship and the figures of the cloth. Four fairies had made it with great skill and mastery. One represented there geometry, how it estimates and measures the extent of the heavens and the earth, so that nothing is lacking there; and then the depth and the height, and the width, and the length; then it estimates, besides, how broad and deep the sea is, and thus measures the whole world. Such was the work of the first fairy. And the second devoted her effort to the portrayal of arithmetic, and she strove hard to represent clearly how it wisely enumerates the days and the hours of time, and the water of the sea drop by drop, and then all the sand, and the stars one by one, knowing well how to tell the truth, and how many leaves there are in the woods: such is the skill of arithmetic that numbers have never deceived her, nor will she ever be in error when she wishes to apply her sense to them. The third design was that of music, with which all merriment finds itself in accord, songs and harmonies, and sounds of string: of harp, of Breton violin, and of viol. This piece of work was good and fine; for upon it were portrayed all the instruments and all the pastimes. The fourth, who next performed her task, executed a most excellent work; for the best of the arts she there portrayed. She undertook astronomy, which accomplishes so many marvels and draws inspiration from the stars, the moon, and the sun. Nowhere else does it seek counsel concerning aught which it has to do. They give it good and sure advice. Concerning whatever inquiry it make of them, whether in the past or in the future, they give it information without falsehood and without deception. This work was portrayed on the stuff of which Erec's robe was made, all worked and woven with thread of gold. The fur lining that was sewed within, belonged to some strange beasts whose heads are all white, and whose necks are as black as mulberries, and which have red backs and green bellies, and dark blue tail. These beasts live in India and they are called "barbiolets". They eat nothing but spices, cinnamon, and fresh cloves. What shall I tell you of the mantle? It was very rich and fine and handsome; it had four stones in the tassels--two chrysolites on one side, and two amethysts on the other, which were mounted in gold.

As yet Enide had not come to the palace. When the King sees that she delays, he bids Gawain go quickly to bring her and the Queen. Gawain hastens and was not slow, and with him King Cadoalant and the generous King of Galloway. Guivret the Little accompanies them, followed by Yder the son of Nut. So many of the other nobles ran thither to escort the two ladies that they would have sufficed to overcome a host; for there were more than a thousand of them. The Queen had made her best effort to adorn Enide. Into the palace they brought her the courteous Gawain escorting her on one side, and on the other the generous King of Galloway, who loved her dearly on account of Erec who was his nephew. When they came to the palace, King Arthur came quickly toward them, and courteously seated Enide beside Erec; for he wished to do her great honour. Now he orders to be brought forth from his treasure two massive crowns of fine gold. As soon as he had spoken and given the command, without delay the crowns were brought before him, all sparkling with carbuncles, of which there were four in each. The light of the moon is nothing compared with the light which the least of the carbuncles could shed. Because of the radiance which they shed, all those who were in the palace were so dazzled that for a moment they could see nothing; and even the King was amazed, and yet filled with satisfaction, when he saw them to be so clear and bright. He had one of them held by two damsels, and the other by two gentlemen. Then he bade the bishops and priors and the abbots of the Church step forward and anoint the new King, as the Christian practice is. Now all the prelates, young and old, came forward; for at the court there were a great number of bishops and abbots. The Bishop of Nantes himself, who was a very worthy and saintly man, anointed the new King in a very holy and becoming manner, and placed the crown upon his head. King Arthur had a sceptre brought which was very fine. Listen to the description of the sceptre, which was clearer than a pane of glass, all of one solid emerald, fully as large as your fist. I dare to tell you in very truth that in all the world there is no manner of fish, or of wild beast, or of man, or of flying bird that was not worked and chiselled upon it with its proper figure. The sceptre was handed to the King, who looked at it with amazement; then he put it without delay into King Erec's right hand; and now he was King as he ought to be. Then he crowned Enide in turn. Now the bells ring for Mass, and they go to the main church to hear the Mass and service; they go to pray at the cathedral. You would have seen weeping with joy the father of Queen Enide and her mother, Carsenefide. In truth this was her mother's name, and her father's name was Liconal. Very happy were they both. When they came to the cathedral, the procession came out from the church with relics and treasures to meet them. Crosses and prayerbooks and censers and reliquaries, with all the holy relics, of which there were many in the church, were all brought out to meet them; nor was there any lack of chants made. Never were seen so many kings, counts, dukes, and nobles together at a Mass, and the press was so great and thick that the church was completely filled. No low-born man could enter there, but only ladies and knights. Outside the door of the church a great number still remained, so many were there come together who could not get inside the church. When they had heard all the Mass they returned to the palace. It was all prepared and decorated: tables set and cloths spread five hundred tables and more were there; but I do not wish to make you believe a thing which does not seem true. It would seem too great a lie were I to say that five hundred tables were set in rows in one palace, so I will not say it; rather were there five hails so filled with them that with great difficulty could one make his way among the tables. At each table there was in truth a king or a duke or a count; and full a hundred knights were seated at each table. A thousand knights served the bread, and a thousand served the wine, and a thousand the meat--all of them dressed in fresh fur robes of ermine. All are served with divers dishes. Even if I did not see them, I might still be able to tell you about them; but I must attend to something else than to tell you what they had to eat. They had enough, without wanting more; joyfully and liberally they were served to their heart's desire.

When this celebration was concluded, the King dismissed the assemblage of kings, dukes, and counts, of which the number was immense, and of the other humble folk who had come to the festival. He rewarded them liberally with horses, arms and silver, cloths and brocades of many kinds, because of his generosity, and because of Erec whom he loved so much. Here the story ends at last.

# Cliges

He who wrote of Erec and Enide, and translated into French the commands of Ovid and the Art of Love, and wrote the Shoulder Bite, and about King Mark and the fair Iseut, and about the metamorphosis of the Lapwing, the Swallow, and the Nightingale, will tell another story now about a youth who lived in Greece and was a member of King Arthur's line. But before I tell you aught of him, you shall hear of his father's life, whence he came and of what family. He was so bold and so ambitious that he left Greece and went to England, which was called Britain in those days, in order to win fame and renown. This story, which I intend to relate to you, we find written in one of the books of the library of my lord Saint Peter at Beauvais. From there the material was drawn of which Chretien has made this romance. The book is very old in which the story is told, and this adds to its authority. From such books which have been preserved we learn the deeds of men of old and of the times long since gone by. Our books have informed us that the pre-eminence in chivalry and learning once belonged to Greece. Then chivalry passed to Rome, together with that highest learning which now has come to France. God grant that it may be cherished here, and that it may be made so welcome here that the honour which has taken refuge with us may never depart from France: God had awarded it as another's share, but of Greeks and Romans no more is heard, their fame is passed, and their glowing ash is dead.

Chretien begins his story as we find it in the history, which tells of an emperor powerful in wealth and honour who ruled over Greece and Constantinople. A very noble empress, too, there was, by whom the emperor had two children. But the elder son was already so far advanced before the younger one was born that, if he had wished, he might have become a knight and held all the empire beneath his sway. The name of the elder was Alexander, and the other's name was Alis. Alexander, too, was the father's name, and the mother's name was Tantalis. I shall now say nothing more of the emperor and of Alis; but I shall speak of Alexander, who was so bold and proud that he scorned to become a knight in his own country. He had heard of King Arthur, who reigned in those days, and of the knights whom he always kept about him, thus causing his court to be feared and famed throughout the world. However, the affair may result and whatever fortune may await him, nothing can restrain Alexander from his desire to go into Britain, but he must obtain his father's consent before proceeding to Britain and Cornwall. So Alexander, fair and brave, goes to speak with the emperor in order to ask and obtain his leave. Now he will tell him of his desire and what he wishes to do and undertake. "Fair sire," he says, "in quest of honour and fame and praise I dare to ask you a boon, which I desire you to give me now without delay, if you are willing to grant it to me." The emperor thinks no harm will come from this request: he ought rather to desire and long for his son's honour. "Fair son," he says, "I grant you your desire; so tell me now what you wish me to give you." Now the youth has accomplished his purpose, and is greatly pleased when the boon is granted him which he so greatly desired. "Sire," says he, "do you wish to know what it is that you have promised me? I wish to have a great plenty of gold and silver, and such companions from among your men as I will select; for I wish to go forth from your empire, and to present my service to the king who rules over Britain, in order that he may make me a knight. I promise you never in my life to wear armour on my face or helmet upon my head until King Arthur shall gird on my sword, if he will graciously do so. For from no other than from him will I accept my arms." Without hesitation the emperor replies: "Fair son, for God's sake, speak not so! This country all belongs to you, as well as rich Constantinople. You ought not to think me mean, when I am ready to make you such a gift. I shall be ready soon to have you crowned, and to-morrow you shall be a knight. All Greece will be in your hands, and you shall receive from your nobles, as is right, their homage and oaths of allegiance. Whoever refuses such an offer is not wise."

The youth hears the promise how the next morning after Mass his father is ready to dub him knight; but he says he will seek his fortune for better or worse in another land. "If you are willing in this matter to grant the boon I have asked of you, then give me mottled and grey furs, some good horses and silken stuffs: for before I become a knight I wish to enrol in King Arthur's service. Nor have I yet sufficient strength to bear arms. No one could induce me by prayer or flattery not to go to the foreign land to see his nobles and that king whose fame is so great for courtesy and prowess. Many men of high degree lose through sloth the great renown which they might win, were they to wander about the world. Repose and glory ill agree, as it seems to me; for a man of wealth adds nothing to his reputation if he spends all his days at ease. Prowess is irksome to the ignoble man, and cowardice is a burden to the man of spirit; thus the two are contrary and opposite. He is the slave of his wealth who spends his days in storing and increasing it. Fair father, so long as I have the chance, and so long as my rigour lasts, I wish to devote my effort and energy to the pursuit of fame."

Upon hearing this; the emperor doubtless feels both joy and grief: he is glad that his son's intention is fixed upon honour, and on the other hand he is sorrowful because his son is about to be separated from him. Yet, because of the promise which he made, despite the grief he feels, he must grant his request; for an emperor must keep his word. "Fair son," he says, "I must not fail to do your pleasure, when I see you thus striving for honour. From my treasure you may have two barges full of gold and silver; but take care to be generous and courteous and well-behaved." Now the youth is very happy when his father promises him so much, and places his treasure at his disposal, and bids him urgently to give and spend generously. And his father explains his reason for this: "Fair son," he says, "believe me, that generosity is the dame and queen which sheds glory upon all the other virtues. And the proof of this is not far to seek. For where could you find a man, be he never so rich and powerful, who is not blamed if he is mean? Nor could you find one, however ungracious he may be, whom generosity will not bring into fair repute? Thus largess makes the gentleman, which result can be accomplished neither by high birth, courtesy, knowledge, gentility, money, strength, chivalry, boldness, dominion, beauty, or anything else. But just as the rose is fairer than any other flower when it is fresh and newly blown, so there, where largess dwells, it takes its place above all other virtues, and increases five hundred fold the value of other good traits which it finds in the man who acquits himself well. So great is the merit of generosity that I could not tell you the half of it." The young man has now successfully concluded the negotiations for what he wished; for his father has acceded to all his desires. But the empress was sorely grieved when she heard of the journey which her son was about to take. Yet, whoever may grieve or sorrow, and whoever may attribute his intention to youthful folly, and ever may blame and seek to dissuade him, the youth ordered his ships to be made ready as soon as possible, desiring to tarry no longer in his native land. At his command the ships were freighted that very night with wine, meat, and biscuit.

The ships were loaded in the port, and the next morning Alexander came to the strand in high spirits, accompanied by his companions, who were happy over the prospective voyage. They were escorted by the emperor and the empress in her grief. At the port they find the sailors in the ships drawn up beside the cliff. The sea was calm and smooth, the wind was light, and the weather clear. When he had taken leave of his father, and bidden farewell to the empress, whose heart was heavy in her bosom, Alexander first stepped from the small boat into the skip; then all his companions hastened by fours, threes, and twos to embark without delay. Soon the sail was spread and the anchor raised. Those on shore whose heart is heavy because of the men whom they watch depart, follow them with their gaze as long as they can: and in order to watch them longer, they all climb a high hill behind the beach. From there they sadly gaze, as long as their eyes can follow them. With sorrow, indeed, they watch them go, being solicitous for the youths, that God may bring them to their haven without accident and without peril. All of April and part of May they spent at sea. Without any great danger or mishap they came to port at Southampton. One day, between three o'clock and vespers, they cast anchor and went ashore. The young men, who had never been accustomed to endure discomfort or pain, had suffered so long from their life at sea that they had all lost their colour, and even the strongest and most vigorous were weak and faint. In spite of that, they rejoice to have escaped from the sea and to have arrived where they wished to be. Because of their depleted state, they spend the night at Southampton in happy frame, and make inquiries whether the King is in England. They are told that he is at Winchester, and that they can reach there in a very short time if they will start early in the morning and keep to the straight road. At this news they are greatly pleased, and the next morning at daybreak the youths wake early, and prepare and equip themselves. And when they were ready, they left Southampton, and kept to the direct road until they reached Winchester, where the King was. Before six o'clock in the morning the Greeks had arrived at the court. The squires with the horses remain below in the yard, while the youths go up into the presence of the King, who was the best that ever was or ever will be in the world. And when the King sees them coming, they please him greatly, and meet with his favour. But before approaching the King's presence, they remove the cloaks from about their necks, lest they should be considered ill-bred. Thus, all unmantled, they came before the King, while all the nobles present held their peace, greatly pleased at the sight of these handsome and well-behaved young men. They suppose that of course they are all sons of counts or kings; and, to be sure, so they were, and of a very charming age, with graceful and shapely forms. And the clothes they wore were all of the same stuff and cut of the same appearance and colour. There were twelve of them beside their lord, of whom I need tell you no more than that there was none better than he. With modesty and orderly mien, he was handsome and shapely as he stood uncovered before the King. Then he kneeled before him, and all the others, for honour's sake, did the same beside their lord.

Alexander, with his tongue well skilled in speaking fair and wisely, salutes the King. "King," he says, "unless the report is false that spreads abroad your fame, since God created the first man there was never born a God-fearing man of such puissance as yours. King, your widespread renown has drawn me to serve and honour you in your court, and if you will accept my service, I would fain remain here until I be dubbed a knight by your hand and by no one else. For unless I receive this honour from your hand, I shall renounce all intention of being knighted. If you will accept my service until you are willing to dub me a knight, retain me now, oh gentle King, and my companions gathered here." To which at once the King replies: "Friend, I refuse neither you nor your companions. Be welcome all. For surely you seem, and I doubt it not, to be sons of high-born men. Whence do you come?" "From Greece." "From Greece?" "Yes." "Who is thy father?" "Upon my word, sire, the emperor." "And what is thy name, fair friend?" "Alexander is the name that was given me when I received the salt and holy oil, and Christianity and baptism." "Alexander, my dear, fair friend. I will keep you with me very gladly, with great pleasure and delight. For you have done me signal honour in thus coming to my court. I wish you to be honoured here, as free vassals who are wise and gentle. You have been too long upon your knees; now, at my command, and henceforth make your home with man and in my court; it is well that you have come to us."

Then the Greeks rise up, joyful that the King has so kindly invited them to stay. Alexander did well to come; for he lacks nothing that he desires, and there is no noble at the court who does not address him kindly and welcome him. He is not so foolish as to be puffed up, nor does he vaunt himself nor boast. He makes acquaintance with my lord Gawain and with the others, one by one. He gains the good graces of them all, but my lord Gawain grows so fond of him that he chooses him as his friend and companion. The Greeks took the best lodgings to be had, with a citizen of the town. Alexander had brought great possessions with him from Constantinople, intending to give heed above all to the advice and counsel of the Emperor, that his heart should be ever ready to give and dispense his riches well. To this end he devotes his efforts, living well in his lodgings, and giving and spending liberally, as is fitting in one so rich, and as his heart dictates. The entire court wonders where he got all the wealth that he bestows; for on all sides he presents the valuable horses which he had brought from his own land. So much did Alexander do, in the performance of his service, that the King, the Queen, and the nobles bear him great affection. King Arthur about this time desired to cross over into Brittany. So he summons all his barons together to take counsel and inquire to whom he may entrust England to be kept in peace and safety until his return. By common consent, it seems, the trust was assigned to Count Angres of Windsor, for it was their judgement that there was no more trustworthy lord in all the King's realm. When this man had received the land, King Arthur set out the next day accompanied by the Queen and her damsels. The Bretons make great rejoicing upon hearing the news in Brittany that the King and his barons are on the way.

Into the ship in which the King sailed there entered no youth or maiden save only Alexander and Soredamors, whom the Queen brought with her. This maiden was scornful of love, for she had never heard of any man whom she would deign to love, whatever might be his beauty, prowess, lordship, or birth. And yet the damsel was so charming and fair that she might fitly have learned of love, if it had pleased her to lend a willing ear; but she would never give a thought to love. Now Love will make her grieve, and will avenge himself for all the pride and scorn with which she has always treated him. Carefully Love has aimed his dart with which he pierced her to the heart. Now she grows pale and trembles, and in spite of herself must succumb to Love. Only with great difficulty can she restrain herself from casting a glance toward Alexander; but she must be on her guard against her brother, my lord Gawain. Dearly she pays and atones for her great pride and disdain. Love has heated for her a bath which heats and burns her painfully. At first it is grateful to her, and then it hurts; one moment she likes it, and the next she will have none of it. She accuses her eyes of treason, and says: "My eyes, you have betrayed me now! My heart, usually so faithful, now bears me ill-will because of you. Now what I see distresses me. Distresses? Nay, verily, rather do I like it well. And if I actually see something that distresses me, can I not control my eyes? My strength must indeed have failed, and little should I esteem myself, if I cannot control my eyes and make them turn their glance elsewhere. Thus, I shall be able to baffle Love in his efforts to get control of me. The heart feels no pain when the eye does not see; so, if I do not look at him, no harm will come to me. He addresses me no request or prayer, as he would do were he in love with me. And since he neither loves nor esteems me, shall I love him without return? If his beauty allures my eyes, and my eyes listen to the call, shall I say that I love him just for that? Nay, for that would be a lie. Therefore, he has no ground for complaint, nor can I make any claim against him. One cannot love with the eyes alone. What crime, then, have my eyes committed, if their glance but follows my desire? What is their fault and what their sin? Ought I to blame them, then? Nay, verily. Who, then, should be blamed? Surely myself, who have them in control. My eye glances at nothing unless it gives my heart delight. My heart ought not to have any desire which would give me pain. Yet its desire causes me pain. Pain? Upon my faith, I must be mad, if to please my heart I wish for something which troubles me. If I can, I ought to banish any wish that distresses me. If I can? Mad one, what have I said? I must, indeed, have little power if I have no control over myself. Does Love think to set me in the same path which is wont to lead others astray? Others he may lead astray, but not me who care not for him. Never shall I be his, nor ever was, and I shall never seek his friendship." Thus she argues with herself, one moment loving, and hating the next. She is in such doubt that she does not know which course she had better adopt. She thinks to be on the defence against Love, but defence is not what she wants. God! She does not know that Alexander is thinking of her too! Love bestows upon them equally such a share as is their due. He treats them very fairly and justly, for each one loves and desires the other. And this love would be true and right if only each one knew what was the other's wish. But he does not know what her desire is, and she knows not the cause of his distress.

The Queen takes note of them and sees them often blanch and pale and heave deep sighs and tremble. But she knows no reason why they should do so, unless it be because of the sea where they are. I think she would have divined the cause had the sea not thrown her off her guard, but the sea deceives and tricks her, so that she does not discover love because of the sea; and it is from love that comes the bitter pain that distresses them. But of the three concerned, the Queen puts all the blame upon the sea; for the other two accuse the third to her, and hold it alone responsible for their guilt. Some one who is not at fault is often blamed for another's wrong. Thus, the Queen lays all the blame and guilt upon the sea, but it is unfair to put the blame upon the sea, for it is guilty of no misdeed. Soredamors' deep distress continued until the vessel came to port. As for the King, it is well known that the Bretons were greatly pleased, and served him gladly as their liege lord. But of King Arthur I will not longer speak in this place; rather shall you hear me tell how Love distresses these two lovers whom he has attacked.

Alexander loves and desires her; and she, too, pines for the love of him, but he knows it not, nor will he know it until he has suffered many a pain and many a grief. It is for her sake that he renders to the Queen loving service, as well as to her maids-in-waiting; but to her on whom his thoughts are fixed, he dares not speak or address a word. If she but dared to assert to him the right which she thinks she has, she would gladly inform him of the truth; but she does not dare, and cannot do it. They dare neither speak nor act in accordance with what each sees in the other--which works a great hardship to them both, and their love but grows and flames the more. However, it is the custom of all lovers to feast their eyes gladly with gazing, if they can do no more; and they assume that, because they find pleasure in that which causes their love to be born and grow, therefore it must be to their advantage; whereas it only harms them more, just as he who approaches and draws close beside the fire burns himself more than he who holds aloof. Their love waxes and grows anon; but each is abashed before the other, and so much is hidden and concealed that no flame or smoke arises from the coals beneath the ashes. The heat is no less on this account, but rather is better sustained beneath the ashes than above. Both of them are in great torment; for, in order that none may perceive their trouble, they are forced to deceive people by a feigned bearing; but at night comes the bitter moan, which each one makes within his breast. Of Alexander I will tell you first how he complains and vents his grief. Love presents before his mind her for whom he is in such distress; it is she who has filched his heart away, and grants him no rest upon his bed, because, forsooth, he delights to recall the beauty and the grace of her who, he has no hope, will ever bring him any joy. "I may as well hold myself a madman." he exclaims. "A madman? Truly, I am beside myself, when I dare not speak what I have in mind; for it would speedily fare worse with me (if I held my peace). I have engaged my thoughts in a mad emprise. But is it not better to keep my thoughts to myself than to be called a fool? My wish will never then be known. Shall I then conceal the cause of my distress, and not dare to seek aid and healing for my wound? He is mad who feels himself afflicted, and seeks not what will bring him health, if perchance he may find it anywhere; but many a one seeks his welfare by striving for his heart's desire, who pursues only that which brings him woe instead. And why should one ask for advice, who does not expect to gain his health? He would only exert himself in vain. I feel my own illness to be so grievous that I shall never be healed by any medicine or draught, by any herb or root. For some ills there is no remedy, and mine lies so deep within that it is beyond the reach of medicine. Is there no help, then? Methinks I have lied. When first I felt this malady, if I had dared to make mention of it. I might have spoken with a physician who could have completely cured me. But I like not to discuss such matters; I think he would pay me no heed and would not consent to accept a fee. No wonder, then, if I am terrified; for I am very ill, yet I do not know what disease this is which has me in its grip, and I know not whence this pain has come. I do not know? I know full well that it is Love who does me this injury. How is that? Can Love do harm? Is he not gentle and well-bred? I used to think that there was naught but good in Love; but I have found him full of enmity. He who has not had experience of him does not know what tricks Love plays. He is a fool who joins his ranks; for he always seeks to harm his followers. Upon my faith, his tricks are bad. It is poor sport to play with him, for his game will only do me harm. What shall I do, then? Shall I retreat? I think it would be wise to do so, but I know not how to do it. If Love chastens and threatens me in order to teach and instruct me, ought I to disdain my teacher? He is a fool who scorns his master. I ought to keep and cherish the lesson which Love teaches me, for great good may soon come of it. But I am frightened because he beats me so. And dost thou complain, when no sign of blow or wound appears? Art thou not mistaken? Nay, for he has wounded me so deep that he has shot his dart to my very heart, and has not yet drawn it out again. How has he pierced thy body with it, when no wound appears without? Tell me that, for I wish to know. How did he make it enter in? Through the eye. Through the eye? But he has not put it out? He did not harm the eye at all, but all the pain is in the heart. Then tell me, if the dart passed through the eye, how is it that the eye itself is not injured or put out. If the dart entered through the eye, why does the heart in the breast complain, when the eye, which received the first effect, makes no complaint of it at all? I can readily account for that: the eye is not concerned with the understanding, nor has it any part in it; but it is the mirror of the heart, and through this mirror passes, without doing harm or injury, the flame which sets the heart on fire. For is not the heart placed in the breast just like a lighted candle which is set in a lantern? If you take the candle away no light will shine from the lantern; but so long as the candle lasts the lantern is not dark at all, and the flame which shines within does it no harm or injury. Likewise with a pane of glass, which might be very strong and solid, and yet a ray of the sun could pass through it without cracking it at all; yet a piece of glass will never be so bright as to enable one to see, unless a stronger light strikes its surface. Know that the same thing is true of the eyes as of the glass and the lantern; for the light strikes the eyes in which the heart is accustomed to see itself reflected, and lo! it sees some light outside, and many other things, some green, some purple, others red or blue; and some it dislikes, and some it likes, scorning some and prizing others. But many an object seems fair to it when it looks at it in the glass, which will deceive it if it is not on its guard. My mirror has greatly deceived me; for in it my heart saw a ray of light with which I am afflicted, and which has penetrated deep within me, causing me to lose my wits. I am ill-treated by my friend, who deserts me for my enemy. I may well accuse him of felony for the wrong he has done to me. I thought I had three friends, my heart and my two eyes together; but it seems that they hate me. Where shall I ever find a friend, when these three are my enemies, belonging to me, yet putting me to death? My servants mock at my authority, in doing what they please without consulting my desire. After my experience with these who have done me wrong, I know full well that a good man's love may be befouled by wicked servants in his employ. He who is attended by a wicked servant will surely have cause to rue it, sooner or later. Now I will tell you how the arrow, which has come into my keeping and possession, is made and fashioned; but I fear greatly that I shall fail in the attempt; for the fashion of it is so fine that it will be no wonder if I fail. Yet I shall devote all my effort to telling you how it seems to me. The notch and the feathers are so close together, when carefully examined, that the line of separation is as fine as a hair's breadth; but the notch is so smooth and straight that in it surely no improvement could be made. The feathers are coloured as if they were of gold or gilt; but gilt is here beside the mark, for I know these feathers were more brilliant than any gilt. This dart is barbed with the golden tresses that I saw the other day at sea. That is the dart which awakes my love. God! What a treasure to possess! Would he who could gain such a prize crave other riches his whole life long? For my part I could swear that I should desire nothing else; I would not give up even the barb and the notch for all the gold of Antioch. And if I prize so highly these two things, who could estimate the value of what remains? That is so fair and full of charm, so dear and precious, that I yearn and long to gaze again upon her brow, which God's hand has made so clear that it were vain to compare with it any mirror, emerald, or topaz. But all this is of little worth to him who sees her flashing eyes; to all who gaze on them they seem like twin candles burning. And whose tongue is so expert as to describe the fashion of her well-shaped nose and radiant face, in which the rose suffuses the lily so as to efface it somewhat, and thus enhance the glory of her visage? And who shall speak of her laughing mouth, which God shaped with such great skill that none might see it and not suppose that she was laughing? And what about her teeth? They are so close to one another that it seems they are all of one solid piece, and in order that the effect might still be enhanced Nature added her handiwork; for any one, to see her part her lips, would suppose that the teeth were of ivory or of silver. There is so much to be said were I to portray each detailed charm of chin and ears, that it would not be strange were I to pass over some little thing. Of her throat I shall only say that crystal beside it looks opaque. And her neck beneath her hair is four times as white as ivory. Between the border of her gown and the buckle at the parted throat, I saw her bosom left exposed and whiter than new-fallen snow. My pain would be indeed assuaged, if I had seen the dart entire. Gladly would I tell, if I but knew, what was the nature of the shaft. But I did nor see it, and it is not my fault if I do not attempt to describe something I have never seen. At that time Love showed me only the notch and the barb; for the shaft was hidden in the quiver, to wit, in the robe and shift in which the damsel was arrayed. Upon my faith, malady which tortures me is the arrow--it is the dart at which I am a wretch to be enraged. I am ungrateful to be incensed. Never shall a straw be broken because of any distrust or quarrel that may arise between Love and me. Now let Love do what he will with me as with one who belongs to him; for I wish it, and so it pleases me. I hope that this malady may never leave me, but that it may thus always maintain its hold, and that health may never come to me except from the source of my illness."

Alexander's complaint is long enough; but that of the maiden is nothing less. All night she lies in such distress that she cannot sleep or get repose. Love has confined within her heart a struggle and conflict which disturbs her breast, and which causes her such pain and anguish that she weeps and moans all night, and tosses about with sudden starts, so that she is almost beside herself. And when she has tossed and sobbed and groaned and started up and sighed again then she looked within her heart to see who and what manner of man it was for whom Love was tormenting her. And when she has refreshed herself somewhat with thinking to her heart's content, she stretches and tosses about again, and ridicules all the thoughts she has had. Then she takes another course, and says: "Silly one, what matters it to me if this youth is of good birth and wise and courteous and valorous? All this is simply to his honour and credit. And as for his beauty, what care I? Let his beauty be gone with him! But if so, it will be against my will, for it is not my wish to deprive him of anything. Deprive? No, indeed! That I surely will not do. If he had the wisdom of Solomon, and if Nature had bestowed on him all the beauty she can place in human form, and if God had put in my power to undo it all, yet would I not injure him; but I would gladly, if I could, make him still more wise and fair. In faith, then, I do not hate him! And am I for that reason his friend? Nay, I am not his any more than any other man's. Then what do I think of him so much, if he pleases me no more than other men? I do not know; I am all confused; for I never thought so much about any man in the world, and if I had my will, I should see him all the time, and never take my eyes from him. I feel such joy at the sight of him! Is this love? Yes, I believe it is. I should not appeal to him so often, if I did not love him above all others. So I love him, then, let it be agreed. Then shall I not do what I please? Yes, provided he does not refuse. This intention of mine is wrong; but Love has so filled my heart that I am mad and beside myself, nor will any defence avail me now, if I must endure the assault of Love. I have demeaned myself prudently toward Love so long, and would never accede to his will; but now I am more than kindly disposed toward him. And what thanks will he owe to me, if he cannot have my loving service and good-will? By force he has humbled my pride, and now I must follow his pleasure. Now I am ready to love, and I have a master, and Love will teach me--but what? How I am to serve his will. But of that I am very well informed, and am so expert in serving him that no one could find fault with me. I need learn no more of that. Love would have it, and so would I, that I should be sensible and modest and kind and approachable to all for the sake of one I love. Shall I love all men, then, for the sake of one? I should be pleasant to every one, but Love does not bid me be the true friend of every one. Love's lessons are only good. It is not without significance that I am called by the name of Soredamors. I am destined to love and be loved in turn, and I intend to prove it by my name, if I can find the explanation there. There is some significance in the fact that the first part of my name is of golden colour; for what is golden is the best. For this reason I highly esteem my name, because it begins with that colour with which the purest gold harmonises. And the end of the name calls Love to my mind; for whoever calls me by my right name always refreshes me with love. And one half gilds the other with a bright coat of yellow gold; for Soredamors has the meaning of 'one gilded over with Love.' Love has highly honoured me in gilding me over with himself. A gilding of real gold is not so fine as that which makes me radiant. And I shall henceforth do my best to be his gilding, and shall never again complain of it. Now I love and ever more shall love. Whom? Truly, that is a fine question! Him whom Love bids me love, for no other shall ever have my love. What will he care in his ignorance, unless I tell him of it myself? What shall I do, if I do not make to him my prayer? Whoever desires anything ought to ask for it and make request. What? Shall I beseech him, then? Nay. Why? Did ever such a thing come about that a woman should be so forward as to make love to any man; unless she were clean beside herself. I should be mad beyond question if I uttered anything for which I might be reproached. If he should know the truth through word of mine I think he would hold me in slight esteem, and would often reproach me with having solicited his love. May love never be so base that I should be the first to prefer a request which would lower me in his eyes! Alas, God! How will he ever know the truth, since I shall not tell him of it? As yet I have very little cause to complain. I will wait until his attention is aroused, if ever it is to be aroused. He will surely guess the truth, I think, if ever he has had commerce with Love, or has heard of it by word of mouth. Heard of it? That is a foolish thing to say. Love is not of such easy access that any one may claim acquaintance by hear-say only and without personal experience. I have come to know that well enough myself; for I could never learn anything of love through flattery and wooing words, though I have often been in the school of experience, and have been flattered many a time. But I have always stood aloof, and now he makes me pay a heavy penalty: now I know more about it than does the ox of ploughing. But one thing causes me despair: I fear he has never been in love. And if he is not in love, and never has been so, then I have sowed in the sea where no seed can take root. So there is nothing to do but wait and suffer, until I see whether I can lead him on by hints and covered words. I shall continue this until he is sure of my love and dares to ask me for it. So there is nothing more about the matter, but that I love him and am his. If he loves me not, yet will I love him."

Thus he and she utter their complaint, unhappy at night and worse by day, each hiding the truth from the other's eyes. In such distress they remained a long time in Brittany, I believe, until the end of the summer came. At the beginning of October there came messengers by Dover from London and Canterbury, bearing to the King news which troubled him. The messengers told him that he might be tarrying too long in Brittany; for, he to whom he had entrusted the kingdom was intending to withstand him, and had already summoned a great army of his vassals and friends, and had established himself in London for the purpose of defending the city against Arthur when he should return.

When the King heard this news, angry and sore displeased he summons all his knights. In order the better to spur them on to punish the traitor, he tells them that they are entirely to blame for his trouble and strife; for on their advice he entrusted his land to the hands of the traitor, who is worse than Ganelon. There is not a single one who does not agree that the King is right, for he had only followed their advice; but now this man is to be outlawed, and you may be sure that no town or city will avail to save his body from being dragged out by force. Thus they all assure the King, giving him their word upon oath, that they will deliver the traitor to him, or never again claim their fiefs. And the King proclaims throughout Brittany that no one who can bear arms shall refuse to follow him at once.

All Brittany is now astir. Never was such an army seen as King Arthur brought together. When the ships came to set sail, it seemed that the whole world was putting out to sea; for even the water was hid from view, being covered with the multitude of ships. It is certainly true that, to judge by the commotion, all Brittany is under way. Now the ships have crossed the Channel, and the assembled host is quartered on the shore. Alexander bethought himself to go and pray the King to make him a knight, for if ever he should win renown it will be in this war. Prompted by his desire, he takes his companions with him to accomplish what he has in mind. On reaching the King's quarters, they found him seated before his tent. When he saw the Greeks approaching, he summoned them to him, saying: "Gentlemen, do not conceal what business has brought you here." Alexander replied on behalf of all, and told him his desire: "I have come," he says, "to request of you, as I ought to do of my liege lord, on behalf of my companions and myself, that you should make us knights." The King replies: "Very gladly; nor shall there be any delay about it, since you have preferred your request." Then the King commands that equipment shall be furnished for twelve knights. Straightway the King's command is done. As each one asks for his equipment, it is handed to him--rich arms and a good horse: thus each one received his outfit. The arms and robes and horse were of equal value for each of the twelve; but the harness for Alexander s body, if it should be valued or sold, was alone worth as much as that of all the other twelve. At the water's edge they stripped, and then washed and bathed themselves. Not wishing that any other bath should be heated for them, they washed in the sea and used it as their tub.

All this is known to the Queen, who bears Alexander no ill will, but rather loves, esteems, and values him. She wishes to make Alexander a gift, but it is far more precious than she thinks. She seeks and delves in all her boxes until she finds a white silk shirt, well made of delicate texture, and very soft. Every thread in the stitching of it was of gold, or of silver at least. Soredamors had taken a hand in the stitching of it here and there, and at intervals, in the sleeves and neck, she had inserted beside the gold a strand of her own hair, to see if any man could be found who, by close examination, could detect the difference. For the hair was quite as bright and golden as the thread of gold itself. The Queen takes the shirt and presents it to Alexander. Ah, God! What joy would Alexander have felt had he known what the Queen was giving him! And how glad would she, too, have been, who had inserted her own hair, if she had known that her lover was to own and wear it! She could then have taken great comfort; for she would not have cared so much for all the hair she still possessed as for the little that Alexander had. But, more is the pity, neither of them knew the truth. The Queen's messenger finds the youths on the shore where they are bathing, and gives the shirt to Alexander. He is greatly pleased with it, esteeming the present all the more because it was given him by the Queen. But if he had known the rest, he would have valued it still more; in exchange for it he would not have taken the whole world, but rather would have made a shrine of it and worshipped it, doubtless, day and night.

Alexander delays no longer, but dresses himself at once. When he was dressed and ready, he returned to the King's tent with all his companions. The Queen, it seems, had come there, too, wishing to see the new knights present themselves. They might all be called handsome, but Alexander with his shapely body was the fairest of them all. Well, now that they are knights I will say no more of them for the present, but will tell of the King and of his host which came to London. Most of the people remained faithful to him, though many allied themselves with the opposition. Count Angres assembled his forces, consisting of all those whose influence could be gained by promises or gifts. When he had gathered all his strength, he slipped away quietly at night, fearing to be betrayed by the many who hated him. But before he made off, he sacked London as completely as possible of provisions, gold and silver, which he divided among his followers. This news was told to the King, how the traitor had escaped with all his forces, and that he had carried off from the city so many supplies that the distressed citizens were impoverished and destitute. Then the King replied that he would not take a ransom for the traitor, but rather hang him, if he could catch him or lay hands on him. Thereupon, all the army proceeded to Windsor. However it may be now, in those days the castle was not easy to take when any one chose to defend it. The traitor made it secure, as soon as he planned his treacherous deed, with a triple line of walls and moats, and had so braced the walls inside with sharpened stakes that catapults could not throw them down. They had taken great pains with the fortifications, spending all of June, July, and August in building walls and barricades, making moats and drawbridges, ditches, obstructions, and barriers, and iron portcullises and a great square tower of stone. The gate was never closed from fear or against assault. The castle stood upon a high hill, and around beneath it flows the Thames. The host encamped on the river bank, and that day they have time only to pitch camp and set up the tents.

The army is in camp beside the Thames, and all the meadow is filled with green and red tents. The sun, striking on the colours, causes the river to flash for more than a league around. Those in the town had come down to disport themselves upon the river bank with only their lances in their hands and their shields grasped before their breasts, and carrying no other arms at all. In coming thus, they showed those without the walls that they stood in no fear of them. Alexander stood aloof and watched the knights disporting themselves at feats of arms. He yearns to attack them, and summons his companions one by one by name. First Cornix, whom he dearly loved, then the doughty Licorides, then Nabunal of Mycene, and Acorionde of Athens, and Ferolin of Salonica, and Calcedor from Africa, Parmenides and Francagel, mighty Torin and Pinabel, Nerius and Neriolis. "My lords," he says, "I feel the call to go with shield and lance to make the acquaintance of those who disport themselves yonder before our eyes. I see they scorn us and hold us in slight esteem, when they come thus without their arms to exercise before our very eyes. We have just been knighted, and have not yet given an account of ourselves against any knight or manikin. We have kept our first lances too long intact. And for what were our shields intended? As yet, they have not a hole or crack to show. There is no use in having them except in a combat or a fight. Let's cross the ford and rush at them!" "We shall not fail you," all reply; and each one adds: "So help me God, who fails you now is no friend of yours." Then they fasten on their swords, tighten their saddles and girths, and mount their steeds with shields in hand. When they had hung the shields about their necks, and taken their lances with the gaily coloured ensigns, they all proceed to the ford at once. Those on the farther side lower their lances, and quickly ride to strike at them. But they (on the hither bank) knew how to pay them back, not sparing nor avoiding them, nor yielding to them a foot of ground. Rather, each man struck his opponent so fiercely that there is no knight so brave but is compelled to leave the saddle. They did not underestimate the experience, skill, and bravery of their antagonists, but made their first blows count, and unhorsed thirteen of them. The report spread to the camp of the fight and of the blows that were being struck. There would soon have been a merry strife if the others had dared to stand their ground. All through the camp they run to arms, and raising a shout they cross the ford. And those on the farther bank take to flight, seeing no advantage in staying where they are. And the Greeks pursue them with blows of lance and sword. Though they struck off many a head they themselves did not receive a wound, and gave a good account of themselves that day. But Alexander distinguished himself, who by his own efforts led off four captive knights in bonds. The sands are strewn with headless dead, while many others lie wounded and injured.

Alexander courteously presents the victims of his first conquest to the Queen, not wishing them to fall into the hands of the King, who would have had them all hanged. The Queen, however, had them seized and safely kept under guard, as being charged with treason. Throughout the camp they talk of the Greeks, and all maintain that Alexander acted very courteously and wisely in not surrendering the knights whom he had captured to the King, who would surely have had them burned or hanged. But the King is not so well satisfied, and sending promptly to the Queen he bids her come into his presence and not detain those who have proved treacherous towards him, for either she must give them up or offend him by keeping them. While the Queen was in conference with the King, as was necessary, about the traitors, the Greeks remained in the Queen's tent with her maids-in-waiting. While his twelve companions conversed with them, Alexander uttered not a word. Soredamors took note of this, seated as she was close by his side. Her head resting upon her hand, it was plain that she was lost in thought. Thus they sat a long time, until Soredamors saw on his sleeve and about his neck the hair which she had stitched into the shirt. Then she drew a little closer thinking now to find an excuse for speaking a word to him. She considers how she can address him first, and what the first word is to be--whether she should address him by his name; and thus she takes counsel with herself: "What shall I say first?" she says; "shall I address him by his name, or shall I call him 'friend'? Friend? Not I. How then? Shall I call him by his name? God! The name of 'friend' is fair and sweet to take upon the lips. If I should dare to call him 'friend'! Should I dare? What forbids me to do so? The fact that that implies a lie. A lie? I know not what the result will be, but I shall be sorry if I do not speak the truth. Therefore, it is best to admit that I should not like to speak a lie. God! yet he would not speak a lie were he to call me his sweet friend! And should I lie in thus addressing him? We ought both to tell the truth. But if I lie the fault is his. But why does his name seem so hard to me that I should wish to replace it by a surname? I think it is because it is so long that I should stop in the middle. But if I simply called him 'friend', I could soon utter so short a name. Fearing lest I should break down in uttering his proper name, I would fain shed my blood if his name were simply 'my sweet friend.'"

She turns this thought over in her mind until the Queen returns from the King who had summoned her. Alexander, seeing her come, goes to meet her, and inquires what is the King's command concerning the prisoners, and what is to be their fate. "Friend," says she, "he requires of me to surrender them at his discretion, and to let his justice be carried out. Indeed, he is much incensed that I have not already handed them over. So I must needs send them to him, since I see no help for it." Thus they passed that day; and the next day there was a great assembly of all the good and loyal knights before the royal tent to sit in judgment and decide by what punishment and torture the four traitors should die. Some hold that they should be flayed alive, and others that they should be hanged or burned. And the King, for his part, maintains that traitors ought to be torn asunder. Then he commands them to be brought in. When they are brought, he orders them to be bound, and says that they shall not be torn asunder until they are taken beneath the town, so that those within may see the sight.

When this sentence was pronounced, the King addresses Alexander, calling him his dear friend. "My friend," he says, "yesterday I saw you attack and defend yourself with great bravery. I wish now to reward your action! I will add to your company five hundred Welsh knights and one thousand troopers from that land. In addition to what I have given you, when the war is over I will crown you king of the best kingdom in Wales. Towns and castles, cities and halls will I give you until the time you receive the land which your father holds, and of which you are to be emperor." Alexander's companions join him in thanking the King kindly for this boon, and all the nobles of the court say that the honour which the King has bestowed upon Alexander is well deserved.

As soon as Alexander sees his force, consisting of the companions and the men-at-arms whom it had pleased the King to give him, straightway they begin to sound the horns and trumpets throughout the camp. Men of Wales and Britain, of Scotland and Cornwall, both good and bad without exception--all take arms, for the forces of the host were recruited from all quarters. The Thames was low because of the drought resulting from a summer without rain, so that all the fish were dead, and the ships were stranded upon the shore, and it was possible to ford the stream even in the widest part.

After fording the Thames, the army divided, some taking possession of the valley, and others occupying the high ground. Those in the town take notice of them, and when they see approaching the wonderful array, bent upon reducing and taking the town, they prepare on their side to defend it. But before any assault is made, the King has the traitors drawn by four horses through the valleys and over the hills and unploughed fields. At this Count Angres is much distressed, when he sees those whom he held dear dragged around outside the town. And his people, too, are much dismayed, but in spite of the anxiety which they feel, they have no mind to yield the place. They must needs defend themselves, for the King makes it plain to all that he is angry, and ill-disposed, and they see that if he should lay hands upon them he would make them die a shameful death.

When the four had been torn asunder and their limbs lay strewn upon the field, then the assault begins. But all their labour is in vain, for no matter how much they cast and shoot, their efforts are of no effect. Yet they strive to do their utmost, hurling their javelins amain, and shooting darts and bolts. On all sides is heard the din of cross-bows and slings as the arrows and the round stones fly thick, like rain mixed with hail. Thus all day long the struggle of attack and defence continues, until the night separates them. And the King causes to be proclaimed what gift he will bestow upon him who shall effect the surrender of the town: a cup of great price weighing fifteen marks of gold, the richest in his treasure, shall be his reward. The cup will be very fine and rich, and, to tell the truth, the cup is to be esteemed for the workmanship rather than for the material of which it is made. But good as the workmanship may be, and fine though the gold, if the truth be told, the precious stones set in the outside of the cup were of most value. He through whose efforts the town shall be taken is to have the cup, if he be only a foot soldier; and if the town is taken by a knight, with the cup in his possession he shall never seek his fortune in vain, if there is any to be found in the world.

When this news was announced, Alexander had not forgotten his custom of going to see the Queen each evening. That night, too, he had gone thither and was seated beside the Queen. Soredamors was sitting alone close by them, looking at him with such satisfaction that she would not have exchanged her lot for Paradise. The Queen took Alexander by the hand, and examined the golden thread which was showing the effects of wear; but the strand of hair was becoming more lustrous, while the golden thread was tarnishing. And she laughed as she happened to recall that the embroidery was the work of Soredamors. Alexander noticed this, and begged her to tell him, if suitable, why she laughed. The Queen was slow to make reply, and looking toward Soredamors, bade her come to her. Gladly she went and knelt before her. Alexander was overjoyed when he saw her draw so near that he could have touched her. But he is not so bold as even to look at her; but rather does he so lose his senses that he is well-nigh speechless. And she, for her part, is so overcome that she has not the use of her eyes; but she casts her glance upon the ground without fastening it upon anything. The Queen marvels greatly at seeing her now pale, now crimson, and she notes well in her heart the bearing and expression of each of them. She notices and thinks she sees that these changes of colour are the fruit of love. But not wishing to embarrass them, she pretends to understand nothing of what she sees. In this she did well, for she gave no evidence of what was in her mind beyond saying: "Look here, damsel, and tell us truly where the shirt was sewed that this knight has on, and if you had any hand in it or worked anything of yours into it." Though the maiden feels some shame, yet she tells the story gladly; for she wishes the truth to be known by him, who, when he hears her tell of how the shirt was made, can hardly restrain himself for joy from worshipping and adoring the golden hair. His companions and the Queen, who were with him, annoy him and embarrass him; for their presence prevents him from raising the hair to his eyes and mouth, as he would fain have done, had he not thought that it would be remarked. He is glad to have so much of his lady, but he does not hope or expect ever to receive more from her: his very desire makes him dubious. Yet, when he has left the Queen and is by himself, he kisses it more than a hundred thousand times, feeling how fortunate he is. All night long he makes much of it, but is careful that no one shall see him. As he lies upon his bed, he finds a vain delight and solace in what can give him no satisfaction. All night he presses the shirt in his arms, and when he looks at the golden hair, he feels like the lord of the whole wide world. Thus Love makes a fool of this sensible man, who finds his delight in a single hair and is in ecstasy over its possession. But this charm will come to an end for him before the sun's bright dawn. For the traitors are met in council to discuss what they can do; and what their prospects are. To be sure they will be able to make a long defence of the town if they determine so to do; but they know the King's purpose to be so firm that he will not give up his efforts to take the town so long as he lives, and when that time comes they needs must die. And if they should surrender the town, they need expect no mercy for doing so. Thus either outcome looks dark indeed, for they see no help, but only death in either case. But this decision at last is reached, that the next morning, before dawn appears, they shall issue secretly from the town and find the camp disarmed, and the knights still sleeping in their beds. Before they wake and get their armour on there will have been such slaughter done that posterity will always speak of the battle of that night. Having no further confidence in life, the traitors as a last resort all subscribe to this design. Despair emboldened them to fight, whatever the result might be; for they see nothing sure in store for them save death or imprisonment. Such an outcome is not attractive; nor do they see any use in flight, for they see no place where they could find refuge should they betake themselves to flight, being completely surrounded by the water and their enemies. So they spend no more time in talk, but arm and equip themselves and make a sally by an old postern gate toward the north-west, that being the side where they thought the camp would least expect attack. In serried ranks they sallied forth, and divided their force into five companies, each consisting of two thousand well armed foot, in addition to a thousand knights. That night neither star nor moon had shed a ray across the sky. But before they reached the tents, the moon began to show itself, and I think it was to work them woe that it rose sooner than was its wont. Thus God, who opposed their enterprise, illumined the darkness of the night, having no love for these evil men, but rather hating them for their sin. For God hates traitors and treachery more than any other sin. So the moon began to shine in order to hamper their enterprise.

They are much hampered by the moon, as it shines upon their shields, and they are handicapped by their helmets, too, as they glitter in the moonlight. They are detected by the pickets keeping watch over the host, who now shout throughout the camp: "Up, knights, up! Rise quickly, take your arms and arm yourselves! The traitors are upon us." Through all the camp they run to arms, and hastily strive to equip themselves in the urgent need; but not a single one of them left his place until they were all comfortably armed and mounted upon their steeds. While they are arming themselves, the attacking forces are eager for battle and press forward, hoping to catch them off their guard and find them disarmed. They bring up from different directions the five companies into which they had divided their troops: some hug the woods, others follow the river, the third company deploys upon the plain, while the fourth enters a valley, and the fifth proceeds beside a rocky cliff. For they planned to fall upon the tents suddenly with great fury. But they did not find the path clear. For the King's men resist them, defying them courageously and reproaching them for their treason. Their iron lance-tips are splintered and shattered as they meet; they come together with swords drawn, striking each other and casting each other down upon the face. They rush upon each other with the fury of lions, which devour whatever they capture. In this first rush there was heavy slaughter on both sides. When they can no longer maintain themselves, help comes to the traitors, who are defending themselves bravely and selling their lives dearly. They see their troops from four sides arrive to succour them. And the King's men ride hard with spur to attack them. They deal such blows upon their shields that, beside the wounded, they unhorse more than five hundred of them. Alexander, with his Greeks, has no thought of sparing them, making every effort to prevail into the thickest of the fight he goes to strike a knave whose shield and hauberk are of no avail to keep him from falling to the earth. When he has finished with him, he offers his service to another freely and without stint, and serves him, too, so savagely that he drives the soul from his body quite, and leaves the apartment without a tenant. After these two, he addresses himself to another, piercing a noble and courteous knight clean through and through, so that the blood spurts out on the other side, and his expiring soul takes leave of the body. Many he killed and many stunned, for like a flying thunderbolt he blasts all those whom he seeks out. Neither coat of mail nor shield can protect him whom he strikes with lance or sword. His companions, too, are generous in the spilling of blood and brains, for they, too, know well how to deal their blows. And the royal troops butcher so many of them that they break them up and scatter them like low-born folk who have lost their heads. So many dead lay about the fields, and so long did the battle rage, that long before the day dawned the ranks were so cut in pieces that the rows of dead stretched for five leagues along the stream. Count Angres leaves his banner on the field and steals away, accompanied by only seven of his men. Towards his town he made his way by a secret path, thinking that no one could see him. But Alexander notices this, and sees them escaping from the troops, and he thinks that if he can slip away without the knowledge of any one, he will go to catch up with them. But before he got down into the valley, he saw thirty knights following him down the path, of whom six were Greeks, and twenty-four were men of Wales. These intended to follow him at a distance until he should stand in need of them. When Alexander saw them coming, he stopped to wait for them, without failing to observe what course was taken by those who were making their way back to the town. Finally, he saw them enter it. Then he began to plan a very daring deed and a very marvellous design. And when he had made up his mind, he turned toward his companions and thus addressed them: "My lords," says he, "whether it be folly or wisdom, frankly grant me my desire if you care for my good-will." And they promised him never to oppose his will in aught. Then he says: "Let us change our outer gear, by taking the shields and lances from the traitors whom we have killed. Thus, when we approach the town, the traitors within will suppose that we are of their party, and regardless of the fate in store for them, they will throw open the gates for us. And do you know what reward we shall offer them? If God so will we shall take them all dead or alive. Now, if any of you repents of his promise, be sure that, so long as I live, I shall never hold him dear."

All the others grant his boon, and, despoiling the corpses of their shields, they arm themselves with them instead. The men within the town had mounted to the battlements, and, recognising the shields, suppose that they belong to their party, never dreaming of the ruse hidden beneath the shields. The gatekeeper opens the gate for them and admits them to the town. He is beguiled and deceived in not addressing them a word; for no one of them speaks to him, but silently and mute they pass, making such a show of grief that they trail their lances after them and support themselves upon their shields. Thus it seems that they are in great distress, as they pass on at their own sweet will until they are within the triple walls. Inside they find a number of men-at-arms and knights with the Count. I cannot tell you just how many; but they were unarmed, except eight of them who had just returned from the fight, and even they were preparing to remove their arms. But their haste was ill considered; for now the other party make no further pretence, but without any challenge by way of warning, they brace themselves in the stirrups, and let their horses charge straight at them, attacking them with such rigour that they lay low more than thirty-one of them. The traitors in great dismay shout out: "We are betrayed, betrayed!" But the assailants take no heed of this, and let those whom they find unarmed feel the temper of their swords. Indeed, three of those whom they found still armed were so roughly handled that but five remained alive. Count Angres rushed at Calcedor, and in the sight of all struck him upon his golden shield with such violence that he stretched him dead upon the ground. Alexander is greatly troubled, and is almost beside himself with rage when he sees his companion dead; his blood boils with anger, but his strength and courage are doubled as he strikes the Count with such fury that he breaks his lance. If possible, he would avenge his friend. But the Count was a powerful man and a good and hardy knight, whose match it would have been hard to find, had he not been a base traitor. He now returns the blow, making his lance double up so that it splits and breaks; but the other's shield holds firm, and neither gives way before the other any more than a rock would do, for both men were passing strong. But the fact that the Count was in the wrong disturbs him greatly and troubles him. The anger of each rises higher as they both draw their swords after their lances had been broken. No escape would have been possible if these two swordsmen had persisted in continuing the fight. But at last one or the other must die. The Count dares not longer hold his ground, when he sees lying dead about him his men who had been caught unarmed. Meanwhile the others press them hard, cutting, slashing, and carving them, spilling their brains, and reproaching the Count for his treachery. When he hears himself accused of treason, he flees for safety to his tower, followed by his men. And their enemies follow after them, fiercely charging them from the rear, and not letting a single one escape of all upon whom they lay their hands. They kill and slay so many of them that I guess not more than seven made good their escape.

When they had got inside the tower, they made a stand at the gate; for those who were coming close behind had followed so closely after them that they too would have pressed in had the gateway been left exposed. The traitors make a brave defence, waiting for succour from their friends, who were arming themselves down in the town. But upon the advice of Nabunal, who was a Greek of great wisdom, the approach was blocked so that relief could not arrive in time; for those below had tarried too long, either from cowardice or sloth. Now there was only one entrance to the stronghold; so that, if they stop that entrance-way, they need have no fear that any force shall approach to do them harm. Nabunal bids and exhorts twenty of them to hold the gate; for soon such a company might arrive with force as would do them harm by their assault and attack. While these twenty hold the gate, the remaining ten should attack the tower and prevent the Count from barricading himself inside. Nabunal's advice is taken: ten remain to continue the assault at the entrance of the tower, while twenty go to defend the gate. In doing so, they delay almost too long; for they see approaching, furious and keen for the fight, a company containing many cross-bow men and foot soldiers of different grades who carried arms of divers sorts. Some carried light missiles, and others Danish axes, lances and Turkish swords, bolts for cross-bows, arrows and javelins. The Greeks would have had to pay a heavy score, if this crowd had actually fallen upon them; but they did not reach the place in time. Nabunal by his foresight and counsel had blocked their plans, and they were forced to remain outside. When they see that they are shut out, they pause in their advance, as it is evident they can gain nothing by making an assault. Then there begins such weeping and wailing of women and young children, of old men and youths, that those in the town could not have heard a thunder-clap from heaven. At this the Greeks are overjoyed; for now they know of a certainty that the Count by no good luck can escape capture. Four of them mount the walls to keep watch lest those outside by any means or ruse should enter the stronghold and fall upon them. The remaining sixteen returned to where the ten were fighting. The day was already breaking, and the ten had fought so well that they had forced their way within the tower. The Count took his stand against a post, and, armed with a battleaxe, defended himself with great bravery. Those whom he reaches, he splits in half. And his men line up about him, and are not slow to avenge themselves in this last stand of the day, Alexander's men have reason to complain, for of the original sixteen there remain now but thirteen. Alexander is almost beside himself when he sees the havoc wrought among his dead or exhausted followers. Yet his thoughts are fixed on vengeance: finding at hand a long heavy club, he struck one of the rascals with it so fiercely that neither shield nor hauberk was worth a button in preventing him from failing to the ground. After finishing with him, he pursues the Count, and raising his club to strike him he deals him such a blow with his square club that the axe falls from his hands; and he was so stunned and bewildered that he could not have stood up unless he had leaned against the wall.

After this blow the battle ceases. Alexander leaps at the Count and holds him so that he cannot move. Of the others nothing need be said, for they were easily mastered when they saw the capture of their lord. All are made prisoners with the Count and led away in disgrace, in accordance with their deserts. Of all this the men outside knew nothing. But when morning came they found their companions shields lying among the slain when the battle was over. Then the Greeks, misled, made a great lament for their lord. Recognising his shield, all are in an agony of grief, swooning at sight of his shield and saying that now they have lived too long. Cornix and Nerius first swoon, then, recovering their senses, wish they were dead. So do Torin and Acorionde. The tears run down in floods from their eyes upon their breasts. Life and joy seem hateful now. And Parmenides more than the rest tore his hair in dire distress. No greater grief could be shown than that of these five for their lord. Yet, their dismay is groundless, for it is another's body which they bear away when they think to have their lord. Their distress is further increased by the sight of the other shields, which cause them to mistake these corpses for their companions. So over them they lament and swoon. But they are deceived by all these shields, for of their men only one was killed, whose name was Neriolis. Him, indeed, they would have borne away had they known the truth. But they are in as great anxiety for the others as for him; so they bore them all away. In every case but one they were misled. But like the man who dreams and takes a fiction for the truth, so the shields cause them to suppose this illusion to be a reality. It is the shields, then, that cause this mistake. Carrying the corpses, they move away and come to their tents, where there was a sorrowing troop. Upon hearing the lament raised by the Greeks, soon all the others gathered, until there was but one great outcry. Now Saredamors thinks of her wretched estate when she hears the cry and lament over her lover. Their anguish and distress cause her to lose her senses and her colour, and her grief and sorrow are increased because she dares not openly show a trace of her distress. She shut up her grief within her heart. Had any one looked at her, he could have seen by the expression of her face what agony she was in; but every one was so engrossed with his own sorrow that he had no care for another's grief. Each one lamented his own loss. For they find the river bank covered with their relatives and friends, who had been wounded or roughly treated. Each one wept for his own heavy and bitter loss: here is a son weeping for a father, there a father for a son; one swoons at the sight of his cousin, another over his nephew. Thus fathers, brothers, and relatives bemoan their loss on every side. But above all is noticeable the sorrow of the Greeks; and yet they might have anticipated great joy, for the deepest grief of all the camp will soon be changed into rejoicing.

The Greeks outside continue their lament, while those inside strive to let them know the news which will cause them to rejoice. They disarm and bind their prisoners, who pray and beg of them to strike off their heads straightway. But the Greeks are unwilling, and disdain their entreaties, saying that them will keep then under guard and hand them over to the King, who will grant them such recompense as shall require their services. When they had disarmed them all they made them go up on the wall that they might be seen by the troops below. This privilege is not to their liking, and when they saw their lord bound as a prisoner, they were unhappy men. Alexander upon the walls swears to God and all the saints that he will not let one of them live, but will kill them all speedily, unless they will go to surrender to the King before he can seize them. "Go," says he, "confidently to the King at my command, and cast yourselves upon his mercy. None of you, except the Count, has deserved to die. You shall not lose either life or limb if you surrender to the King. If you do not deliver yourselves from death by crying for mercy, you need have little hope of saving your lives or bodies. Go forth disarmed to meet the King, and tell him from me that Alexander sends you to him. Your action will not be in vain; for my lord the King is so gentle and courteous that he will lay aside his wrath and anger. But if you wish to act otherwise, you must expect to die, for his heart will be closed to pity." All agree in accepting this advice, and do not hesitate until they come to the King's tent, where they all fall at his feet. The story they told was soon known throughout the camp. The King and all his men mounted and spurred their horses to the town without delay.

Alexander goes out from the town to meet the King, who was greatly pleased, and to surrender to him the Count. The King did not delay in fitly punishing him. But Alexander is congratulated and praised by the King and all the others who esteem him highly. Their joy drives away the grief which they had felt not long before. But no joy of the others can compare with the exultation of the Greeks. The King presents him with the precious cup, weighing fifteen marks, and tells him confidently that there is nothing in his possession so valuable that he would not place it in his hands upon request--save only the crown and the Queen. Alexander dares not mention his heart's desire, though he knows well that he would not be refused in asking for his sweetheart's hand. But he fears so much lest he might displease her, whose heart would have been made glad, that he prefers to suffer without her rather than to win her against her will. Therefore, he asks for a little time, not wishing to prefer his request until he is sure of her pleasure. But he asked for no respite or delay in accepting the cup of gold. He takes the cup, and courteously begs my lord Gawain to accept this cup as a gift from him, which Gawain did most reluctantly. When Soredamors learned the truth about Alexander she was greatly pleased and delighted. When she heard that he was alive, she was so happy that it seemed to her as though she could never be sad again. But she reflects that he is slower in coming than is his wont. Yet in good time she will have her wish, for both of them in rivalry are occupied with one common thought.

It seemed to Alexander an age before he could feast his eyes with even one soft glance from her. Long ago he would fain have gone to the Queen's tent, if he had not been detained elsewhere. He was much put out by this delay, and as soon as he could, he betook himself to the Queen in her tent. The Queen went to greet him, and, without his having confided in her, she had already read his thoughts, and knew what was passing in his mind. She greets him at the entrance of the tent, and strives to make him welcome, well knowing for what purpose he has come. Desirous of according him a favour, she beckons Soredamors to join them, and they three engage in conversation at some distance from the rest. The Queen first speaks, in whose mind there was no doubt that this couple were in love. Of this fact she is quite sure, and is persuaded moreover that Soredamors could not have a better lover. She took her place between the two and began to say what was appropriate.

"Alexander," says the Queen, "any love is worse than hate, when it torments and distresses its devotee. Lovers know not what they do when they conceal their passion from one another. Love is a serious business, and whoever does not boldly lay its foundation firm can hardly succeed in completing the edifice. They say there is nothing so hard to cross as the threshold. Now I wish to instruct you in the lore of love; for I know well that Love is tormenting you. Therefore, I have undertaken to instruct you; and do you take good care not to keep anything back from me, for I have plainly seen in the faces of you both that of two hearts you have made but one. So beware, and conceal nothing from me! You are acting very foolishly in not speaking out your mind; for concealment will be the death of you; thus you will be the murderers of Love. Now I counsel you to exercise no tyranny, and to seek no passing gratification in your love; but to be honourably joined together in marriage. So, I believe, your love shall long endure. I can assure you that, if you agree to this, I will arrange the marriage."

When the Queen had spoken her mind, Alexander thus made reply: "Lady," he says, "I enter no defence against the charge you make, but rather admit the truth of all you say. I wish never to be deserted by love, but always to fix my thoughts on it. I am pleased and delighted by what you have so kindly said. Since you know what my wishes are, I see no reason why I should conceal them from you. Long ago, if I had dared I would have confessed them openly; for the silence has been hard. But it may well be that for some reason this maiden may not wish that I be hers and she mine. But even if she grant me no rights over her, yet will I place myself in her hands." At these words she trembled, having no desire to refuse the gift. Her heart's desire betrays itself in her words and her countenance. Falteringly she gives herself to him, and says that without exception her will, her heart, and her body all is at the disposal of the Queen, to do with her as she may please. The Queen clasps them both in her arms, and presents one to the other. Then laughingly she adds: "I give over to thee, Alexander, thy sweetheart's body, and I know that thy heart does not draw back. Whoever may like it or like it not, I give each of you to the other. Do thou, Soredamors, take what is thine, and thou, Alexander, take what is thine!" Now she has her own entire, and he has his without lack. At Windsor that day, with the approval and permission of my lord Gawain and the King, the marriage was celebrated. No one could tell, I am sure, so much of the magnificence and the food, of the pleasure and entertainment, at this wedding without falling short of the truth. Inasmuch as it would be distasteful to some, I do not care to waste further words upon the matter, but am anxious to turn to another subject.

That day at Windsor Alexander had all the honour and happiness that he could desire. Three different joys and honours were his: one was the town which he captured; another was the present of the best kingdom in Wales, which King Arthur had promised to give him when the war was over; that very day he made him king in his hall. But the greatest joy of all was the third--that his sweetheart was queen of the chess-board where he was king. Before five months had passed, Soredamors found herself with child, and carried it until the time was fulfilled. The seed remained in germ until the fruit was fully matured. No more beautiful child was ever born before or since than he whom they now called Cliges.

So Cliges was born, in whose honour this story has been put in the Romance tongue. You shall hear me tell of him and of his valorous deeds, when he shall have grown to manhood and obtained a good report. But meanwhile in Greece it came about that he who ruled over Constantinople drew near his end. He died, as indeed he must, not being able to outlive his time. But before he died he assembled all the nobles of his land to send and seek for his son Alexander, who was happily detained in Britain. The messengers start out from Greece, and begin their voyage over the seas; but a tempest catches them in its grasp, and damages their ship and company. They were all drowned at sea, except one unfaithful wretch, who was more devoted to Alis the younger son than to Alexander the elder. When he escaped from the sea, he returned to Greece with the story that they had all been lost at sea as they were conducting their lord back from Britain, and that he was the only survivor of the tragedy. They believed this lie of his, and, taking Alis without objection or dissent, they crowned him emperor of Greece. But it was not long before Alexander learned that Alis was emperor. Then he took leave of King Arthur, unwilling to let his brother usurp his land without protest. The King makes no opposition to his plan, but bids him take with him so great a company of Welshmen, Scots, and Cornishmen that his brother will not dare to withstand him when he sees him come with such a host. Alexander, had he pleased, might have led a mighty force; but he has no desire to harm his own people, if his brother will consent to do his will. He took with him forty knights besides Soredamors and his son; these two persons, who were so dear to him, he did not wish to leave behind. Escorted as far as Shoreham by the entire court, they there embarked, and with fair winds their ship made way more quickly than a fleeing stag. Within a month, I think, they arrived in port before Athens, a rich and powerful city. Indeed, the emperor was residing there, and had convoked, a great assembly of his noblemen. As soon as they arrived Alexander sent a privy messenger into the city to learn whether they would receive him, or whether they would resist his claim to be their only lawful lord.

He who was chosen for this mission was a courteous knight with good judgment, named Acorionde, a rich man and eloquent; he was a native of the country, too, having been born in Athens. His ancestors for generations had always exercised lordship in the city. When he had learned that the emperor was in the city he went and challenged the crown on behalf of his brother Alexander, accusing him openly of having usurped it unlawfully. Arriving at the palace, he finds plenty of people who welcome him; but he says nothing to any of those who greet him until he learns what is their attitude and disposition toward their lawful lord. Coming into the presence of the emperor he neither greets him nor bows before him nor calls him emperor. "Alis," he says, "I bring thee tidings of Alexander, who is out yonder in the harbour. Listen to thy brother's message: he asks thee for what belongs to him, nor does he demand what is unjust. Constantinople, which thou dost hold, should be his and shall be his. It would be neither just nor right that discord should arise between you two. So give him the crown without contest, for it is right that thou shouldst surrender it."

Alis replies: "Fair gentle friend, thou hast undertaken a mad enterprise in bearing this message. There is little comfort in thy speech, for well I know that my brother is dead. I should rejoice, indeed, to learn that he was still alive. But I shall not believe the news until I have seen him with my eyes. He died some time ago, alas! What thou sayest is not credible. And if he lives, why does he not come? He need never fear that I will not bestow on him some lands. He is a fool to hold aloof from me, for in serving me he will find profit. But no one shall possess the crown and empire beside me." He liked not the speech of the emperor, and did not fail to speak his mind in the reply he made. "Alis," he says, "may God confound me if the matter is thus allowed to stand. I defy thee in thy brother's name, and dutifully speaking in his name, I summon all those whom I see here to renounce thee and to join his cause. It is right that they should side with him and recognise him as their lord. Let him who is loyal now stand forth."

Upon saying this he leaves the court, and the emperor summons those in whom he has most confidence. He requests their advice concerning this defiance upon his brother's part, and wishes to learn if he can trust them to lend no support or help to his brother's claim. Thus he tries to test the loyalty of each; but he finds not one who sides with him in the dispute, rather do they all bid him remember the war which Eteocles undertook against his own brother Polynices, and how each one died by the other's hand. "So, too, it may happen to you, if you undertake a war, and all the land will be distressed." Therefore, they advise that such a peace be sought as shall be both reasonable and just, and that neither one make excessive demands. Thus Alis understands that if he does not make an equitable agreement with his brother all his vassals will desert him; so he says that he will respect their wishes in making any suitable contract, provided that however the affair may rum out the crown shall remain in his possession.

In order to secure a firm and stable peace Alis sends one of his officers to Alexander, bidding him come to him in person and receive the government of the land, but stipulating that he should leave to him the honour of emperor in name and of wearing the crown: thus, if Alexander is willing, peace may be established between them. When this news was brought to Alexander his men made ready with him and came to Athens, where they were received with joy. But Alexander is not willing that his brother should have the sovereignty of the empire and of the crown unless he will pledge his word never to take a wife, and that after him Cliges shall be emperor of Constantinople. Upon this the brothers both agreed. Alexander dictated the terms of the oath, and his brother agreed and gave his word that he would never in his life take a wife in marriage. So peace is made, and they are friends again, to the great satisfaction of the lords. They hold Alis as their emperor, but all business is referred to Alexander. What he commands is done, and little is done except through him. Alis has nothing but the name of emperor; but Alexander is served and loved; and he who does not serve him for love must needs do so from fear. Through the effect of one or the other of these two motives he has all the land within his power. But he whom they call Death spares neither the strong man nor the weak, but kills and slays them all. So Alexander had to die; for a disease caught him in its grip from which he could obtain no relief. But before he was surprised by death he summoned his son and said to him: "Fair son Cliges, thou canst never know that prowess and valour are thine unless thou go first to make test of them with the Bretons and French at King Arthur's court. If adventure takes thee thither, so conduct and demean thyself that thy identity be not known until thou hast tried thy strength with the most excellent knights of that court. I beg thee to heed my counsel in this matter, and if the occasion arises have no fear to measure thy skill with thy uncle, my lord Gawain. Do not forget this advice, I pray."

After he had thus exhorted him, he did not live long. Soredamors' grief was such that she could not survive him, but died after him of a broken heart. Alis and Cliges both mourned him becomingly, but finally they ceased their grief, for sorrow, like everything else, must be outlived. To continue in sorrow is wrong, for no good can come from it. So the mourning was ended, and the emperor refrained for a long time from taking a wife, being careful of his word. But there is no court in all the world which is free from evil counsel. Great men often go astray, and do not observe loyalty because of the bad advice they take. Thus, the emperor hears his men giving him advice and counselling him to take a wife; and daily they so exhort and urge him that by their very insistence they persuade him to break his oath, and to accede to their desire. But he insists that she who is to be mistress of Constantinople must be gentle, fair, wise, rich, and noble. Then his counsellors say that they wish to prepare to go away to the German land, and seek the daughter of the emperor. She is the choice they propose to him; for the emperor of Germany is very rich and powerful, and his daughter is so charming that never was there a maid of her beauty in Christendom. The emperor grants them full authority, and they set out upon the journey well provided with all they need. They proceeded on their way until they found the emperor at Regensburg, when they asked him to give them his oldest daughter at the instance of their lord.

The emperor was pleased with this request, and gladly gave them his daughter; for in doing so, he does not debase himself, nor diminish his honour in any way. But he says that he had promised her to the Duke of Saxony, and that they would not be able to lead her away unless the emperor should come with a great army, so that the duke would be unable to do him any harm or injury while homeward bound.

When the messengers heard the emperor's reply, they took leave and departed. They returned to their lord, and bore him the answer. And the emperor selected a chosen company of the most experienced knights whom he could find, and took with him his nephew, in whose interests he had vowed never to marry a wife, but he will not respect this vow if he can once reach Cologne. Upon a certain day he leaves Greece and draws near to Germany, intending to take a wife despite all blame and reproach; but his honour will be smirched. Upon reaching Cologne, he found that the emperor had assembled all his court for a festival. When the company of the Greeks reached Cologne, there was such a great number of Greeks and Germans that it was necessary to lodge more than sixty thousand of them outside the city.

Great was the crowd of people, and great the joy of the two emperors when they met. When the barons had gathered in the vast palace, the emperor summoned his charming daughter. The maiden made no delay in coming straightway into the palace. She had been made very fair and shapely by the Creator, whose pleasure it had been to arouse the people's admiration. God, who had fashioned her, never gave man a word which could adequately express such beauty as she possessed.

Fenice was the maiden's name, and for this there was good reason: for if the Phoenix bird is unique as the most beautiful of all the birds, so Fenice, it seems to me, had no equal in beauty. She was such a miracle and marvel that Nature was never able to make her like again. In order to be more brief, I will not describe in words her arms, her body, her head and hands; for if I should live a thousand years, and if my skill were to double every day, yet should I waste all my time in trying to tell the truth about her. I know very well, if I should undertake it, that I would exhaust my brain and waste my pains: it would be but misspent energy. The damsel hastened until she came into the palace, with head uncovered and face unveiled; and the radiance of her beauty lighted the palace more brightly than four carbuncles would have done. Cliges stood, his over-cloak removed, in his uncle's presence. The day outside was somewhat dark, but he and the maiden were both so fair that a ray shone forth from their beauty which illumined the palace, just as the morning sun shines clear and red.

I wish to attempt in a very few words to describe the beauty of Cliges. He was in his flower, being now almost fifteen years of age. He was more comely and charming than Narcissus who saw his reflection in the spring beneath the elm-tree, and, when he saw it, he loved it so that he died, they say, because he could not get it. Narcissus was fair, but had little sense; but as fine gold surpasses copper, so was Cliges better endowed with wisdom, and even then I have not said all. His locks seemed made of fine gold, and his face was of a fresh rosy colour. He had a well-formed nose and shapely mouth, and in stature he was built upon Nature's best pattern; for in him she had united gifts which she is wont to scatter wide. Nature was so lavish with him that she gave him all she could, and placed all in one receptacle. Such was Cliges, who combined good sense and beauty, generosity and strength. He possessed the wood as well as the bark; he knew more of fencing and of the bow than did Tristan, King Mark's nephew, and more about birds and hounds than he. In Cliges there lacked no good thing.

Cliges stood in all his beauty before his uncle, and those who did not know who he was looked at him with eager curiosity. And on the other hand, the interest was aroused of those who did not know the maiden: wonderingly they gaze upon her. But Cliges, under the sway of love, let his eyes rest on her covertly, and withdrew them again so discreetly that in their passage to and fro no one could blame his lack of skill. Blithely he looks upon the maid, but does not note that she repays him in kind. Not flattering him, but in sincere love, she gives him her eyes, and takes back his. This exchange seems good to her, and would have seemed to her better still had she known something of who he was. But she knows nothing except that he is fair, and that, if she is ever to love any one for beauty's sake, she need not seek elsewhere to bestow her heart. She handed over to him the possession of her eyes and heart, and he pledged his in turn to her. Pledged? Rather gave outright. Gave? Nay, upon my faith, I lie; for no one can give away his heart. I must express it some other way. I will not say it, as some have done who make two hearts dwell in one body, for it bears not even the semblance of truth that there should be in one body two hearts; and even if they could be so united, it would never seem true. But if it please you to heed my words, I shall be able explain how two hearts form but one without coming to be identified. Only so far are they merged in one as the desire of each passes from one to the other, thus joining in one common desire; and because of this harmony of desire, there are some who are wont to say that each one has both hearts; but one heart cannot be in two places. Each one always keeps his own heart, though the desire be shared by both, just as many different men may sing a song or tune in unison. By this comparison I prove that for one body to contain two hearts it is not enough to know each other's wish, nor yet for one to know what the other loves and what he hates; just as voices which are heard together seem to be merged in one, and yet do not all come from one mouth, so it is with a body which can contain but one heart. But there is no need of further argument, for other matters press upon me. I must speak now of the damsel and of Cliges, and you shall hear of the Duke of Saxony, who has sent to Cologne a young nephew of his. This youth informs the emperor that his uncle, the duke, sends word that he need expect no peace or trace with him, unless he sends to him his daughter, and that the one who is intending to carry her away with him had better not start home, for he will find the road occupied and well defended unless the maiden be surrendered.

The youth spoke his message well, without pride and without insult. But he found neither knight nor emperor who would answer him. When he saw that they all held their peace and treated him with scorn, he left the court in defiant mood. But youth and thirst for daring deeds made Cliges defy him in combat as he left. For the contest they mount their steeds, three hundred of them on either side, exactly equal thus in strength. All the palace is quite emptied of knights and ladies, who mount to the balconies, battlements, and windows to see and watch those who were about to fight. Even the maiden, whose will Love had subdued beneath his sway, sought for a point from which to see. She took her place at a window, where she sat with great delight, because from there she could get a view of him whom she holds secretly in her heart with no desire to remove him thence; for she will never love any other man. But she does not know his name, nor who he is, nor of what race; for it is not proper to ask questions; but she yearns to hear tidings which will bring joy to her heart. She looks out of the window at the shields with their gleaming gold, and she gazes at those who wear the shields about their necks, as they prepare for the trial at arms. But all her thoughts and glances soon rest upon one object, and to all others she is indifferent. Whereever Cliges goes, she seeks to follow him with her eyes. And he in turn does his best for her, and battles openly, in order that she at least may hear it said that he is bold and very skilled: thus she will be compelled to prize him for his prowess. He attacks the duke's nephew, who was breaking many a lance and sorely discomfiting the Greeks. But Cliges, who is displeased at this, braces himself firmly in his stirrups, and goes to strike him so speedily that in spite of himself he had to vacate the saddle-bows. When he got up, the uproar was great; for the youth arose and mounted, thinking to avenge his shame. But many a man only falls into deeper disgrace who thinks to avenge his shame when he has the chance. The young man rushes at Cliges, who lowers his lance to meet him, and thrusts at him with such force that he carries him to earth again. Now his shame is doubled, and all his followers are in dismay, seeing that they can never leave the field with honour; for not one of them is so valiant that he can keep his seat in the saddle when Cliges thrust reaches him. But those of Germany and the Greeks are overjoyed when they see their party drive off the Saxons, who retreat discomfited. With mockery they pursue them until they come up with them at a stream, into which they drive them for a plunge. In the deepest part of the ford Cliges unhorsed the duke's nephew and so many of his men that they escaped grieving and sad in their shame and confusion. But Cliges, twice victor, returned in glee, and entered a gate which was near the apartment where the maiden was; and as he passed through the gate she exacted as toll a tender glance, which he paid her as their eyes met. Thus was the maiden subdued by the man. But there is not a German of the lowland or highland, possessing the power of speech who does not cry: "God! who is this in whom such beauty is radiant? God! how has it happened that so suddenly he has attained such great success?" Thus one man and another asks: "Who is this youth, who is he, I say?" Thus, soon throughout the city it is known what his name is, and who is his father, and what pledge that was which had been made to him by the emperor. So much was said and noised about that the news reached the ears of her who in her heart rejoiced because she could no more say that Love had made sport of her, nor had she any ground for complaint. For Love has made her give her heart to the fairest, most courteous, and valiant man that could anywhere be found. But some force must be employed, if she would gain possession of him who is not free do her will. This makes her anxious and distraught. For she has no one with whom to take counsel concerning him for whom she pines, but must waste herself in thought and vigils. She becomes so affected by these cares that she loses her colour and grows wan, and it becomes plain to all that her loss of colour betokens an unfulfilled desire. She plays less now than she used to do, and laughs less and loses her gaiety. But she conceals her trouble and passes it off, if any one asks what her ailment is. Her old nurse's name was Thessala, who was skilled in necromancy, having been born in Thessaly, where devilish charms are taught and wrought; for the women of that country perform many a charm and mystic rite.

Thessala saw pale and wan her whom Love holds in his bonds, and thus she addressed her with advice: "God!" she said, "are you bewitched, my lady dear, that your face should be so pale? I wonder what your trouble is. Tell me, if you can, where this pain attacks you most, for if any one can cure you, you may safely trust me to give you back your health again. I can cure the dropsy, gout, quinsy, and asthma; I am so expert in examining the urine and the pulse that you need consult no other physician. And I dare say that I know more than ever Medea knew of enchantments and of charms which tests have proven to be true. I have never spoken to you of this, though I have cared for you all your life; and now I should not mention it did I not plainly see that you are so afflicted as to need my ministrations. My lady, you will do well to tell me what your sickness is before its hold becomes more severe. The emperor has committed you to me in order that I may care for you, and my devotion has been such that I have kept you safe and sound. Now all my pains will come to naught if I do not relieve this malady. Take care not to conceal from me whether this is sickness or something else." The damsel dares not openly expose her desire in all its fullness for she is in fear lest she be disapproved and blamed. And when she hears and understands how Thessala boasts and highly rates herself as being expert in enchantments, charms, and potions, she decides to tell her what is the cause of her pale and colourless face; but first she makes her promise to keep her secret and never to oppose her will.

"Nurse," she said, "I truly thought I felt no pain, but I shall soon feel differently. For as soon as I begin to think about it, I feel great pain, and am dismayed. But when one has no experience, how can one tell what is sickness and what is health? My illness is different from all others; for when I wish to speak of it, it causes me both joy and pain, so happy I am in my distress. And if it can be that sickness brings delight, then my trouble and joy are one, and in my illness consists my health. So I do not know why I complain, for I know not whence my trouble comes, unless it is caused by my desire. Perchance my desire is my disease, but I find so much joy in it that the suffering it causes me is grateful, and there is so much contentment in my pain that it is sweet to suffer so. Nurse Thessala, now tell me true, is not this a deceitful ill, to charm and torment me both at once? I do not see how I can tell whether this is a disease or not. Nurse, tell me now its name, nature, and character. But understand well that I have no desire to be cured of it, for my distress is very dear to me." Thessala, who was very wise about love and its symptoms knows full well from what she hears that it is love which is tormenting her; the tender, endearing terms she uses are certain proof that she is in love, for all other woes are hard to bear, except that alone which comes from love; but love transforms its bitterness into sweetness and joy, then often transforms them back again. The nurse, who was expert in this matter, thus replies to her: "Have no fear, for I will tell you at once the name of your malady. You told me, I believe, that the pain which you feel seems rather to be joy and health: now of such a nature is love-sickness, for in it, too, there is joy and bliss. You are in love, then, as I can prove to you, for I find no pleasure in any malady save only in love. All other sickness is always bad and horrible, but love is sweet and peaceable. You are in love; of that I am sure, nor do I see any wrong in that. But I shall consider it very wrong, if through some childish folly you conceal from me your heart." "Nurse, there is no need of your speaking so. But first I must be sure and certain that under no circumstances will you speak of it to any living soul." "My lady, surely the winds will speak of it before I do without your leave, and I will give you my word so to favour your desires that you may safely trust in having your joy fulfilled through my services." "In that case, Nurse, I shall be cured. But the emperor is giving me in marriage, wherefore I grieve and am sorrowful; for he who has won my heart is the nephew of him whom I must take. And though he may find joy in me, yet is my joy forever lost, and no respite is possible. I would rather be torn limb from limb than that men should speak of us as they speak of the loves of Iseut and Tristan, of so many unseemly stories are told that I should be ashamed to mention them. I could never bring myself to lead the life that Iseut led. Such love as hers was far too base; for her body belonged to two, whereas her heart was possessed by one. Thus all her life was spent, refusing her favours to neither one. But mine is fixed on one object, and under no circumstances will there be any sharing of my body and heart. Never will my body be portioned out between two shareholders. Who has the heart has the body, too, and may bid all others stand aside. But I cannot clearly see how he whom I love can have my body when my father gives me to another, and his will I do not dare resist. And when this other is lord of my body, and does something which displeases me, it is not right for me to summon another to my aid. Nor can this man marry a wife without breaking his plighted word; for, unless injustice be done, Cliges is to have the empire after his uncle's death. But I should be well served by you, if you were so skilful as to present him, to whom I am pledged and engaged, from having any claim upon me. O Nurse, exert yourself to the end that he may not break the pledge which he gave to the father of Cliges, when he promised him solemnly never to take a wife in marriage. For now, if he should marry me his promise would be broken. But Cliges is so dear to me that I would rather be under ground than that he should ever lose through me a penny of the fortune which should be his. May never a child be born to me to cause his disinheritance! Nurse, now do your best, and I will always be your slave." Then the nurse tells her and assures her that she will cast so many charms, and prepare so many potions and enchantments that she need never have any worry or fear concerning the emperor after he shall have drunk of the potion which she will give him; even when they shall lie together and she be at his side, she may be as secure as if there were a wall between them. "But do not be alarmed, if, in his sleep, he sports with you, for when he is plunged in sleep he will have his sport with you, and he will be convinced that he has had you when wide awake, nor will he think it is all a dream, a fiction, and illusion. Thus he will have his sport with you when asleep, he will think he is awake."

The maiden is highly pleased and delighted by the nurse's kindness and offer of help. Her nurse inspires good hope in her by the promise which she makes, and which she binds herself to keep; with this hope she expects to obtain her desire, in spite of wearisome delay, for if Cliges' nature is as noble as she takes it to be he cannot fail to take pity upon her when he learns that she loves him, and that she has imposed virginity upon herself in order to insure his inheritance. So the maiden believes her nurse, and puts full confidence in her. One promises to the other, and gives her word, that this plot shall be kept so secret as never to be revealed. At this point their conversation ceases, and the next morning the emperor summons his daughter. At his command she goes to him. But why should I weary you with details? The two emperors have so settled the matter that the marriage is solemnised, and joy reigns in the palace. But I do not wish to stop to describe all this in detail. Rather will I address myself to Thessala, as she diligently prepares and tempers her potions.

Thessala steeps her drink, putting in spices in abundance to sweeten and temper it. After having well beaten and mixed it, she strains it clear, with no sharp or bitter taste, for the spices she puts in give it a sweet and pleasant fragrance. When the potion was prepared, the day had drawn to a close, the tables were set for supper, and the cloths were spread. But Thessala delays the supper, because she must discover by what device and what agent she can have the potion served. At supper, finally, all were seated, and more than six dishes had been passed, and Cliges served behind his uncle's place. Thessala, as she watches him, thinks how ill he serves his own interests, and how he is assisting in his own disinheritance, and the thought torments and worries her. Then in her kindness she conceives the plan of having the potion served by him to whom it will bring both joy and honour. So Thessala summoned Cliges; and when he had come to her, he asked her why she had sent for him. "Friend," said she, "I wish to present the emperor at this meal with a beverage which he will esteem highly, and I want him to taste no other to-night, either at supper or when he goes to bed. I think he cannot fail to relish it, for he never has tasted a better drink or one that has cost so much. And I warn you, take good care to let no one else drink of it, for there is but a little of it. And this, too, I beg of you, not to let him know whence it came; but tell him it came about by chance that you found it among the presents, and tasted it yourself, and detected the aroma of the sweet spices in the air; then, seeing the wine to be all clear you poured it into his cup. If by chance he should inquire, you can satisfy him with this reply. But have no suspicion yourself, after what I have said, for the drink is pure and healthful, full excellent spices, and I think it may some day bring you joy." When he heard that advantage would come to him, he took the potion and went away, for he did not know there was any harm in it. He set it in a crystal cup before the emperor, who took it without question, trusting in his nephew. After taking a long draught of the beverage, he straightway feels its strength, as it descends from head to heart, and rises again from heart to head, and penetrates every part of him without doing the slightest harm. And by the time they left the tables, the emperor had drunk so much of the pleasing drink that he can never escape it influence. Every night he will sleep under its influence, and its effects will be such that he will think he is awake when sound asleep.

Now the emperor has been deceived. Many bishops and abbots were present to bless and hallow the marriage-bed. When the time came to retire, the emperor, as was his right, lay beside his wife that night. "As was his right;" but the statement is inexact, for he neither kissed nor fondled her, yet they lay together in one bed. At first the maiden trembled with fear and anxiety lest the potion should not act. But it has so mastered him that he will never desire her or any other woman except in his sleep. But when asleep he will have such sport with her as one may have in dreams, and he will think the dream is true. Nevertheless, she is on her guard, and at first, holds aloof from him, so that he cannot approach her. But now he must needs fall asleep; then he sleeps and dreams, though, the senses are awake, and he exerts himself to win the favours of the maid, while she, realising the danger, defends her virginity. He woos her and calls her gently his sweetheart, and thinks he possesses her, but in vain. But he is gratified by this vain semblance, embracing, kissing, and fondling an empty thing, seeing and speaking to no purpose, struggling and striving without effect. Surely the potion was effective in thus possessing and mastering him. All his pains are of no avail, as he thinks and is persuaded that the fortress is won. Thus he thinks and is convinced, when he desists after his vain efforts. But now I may say once for all that his satisfaction was never more than this. To such relations with her he will for ever be condemned if indeed he can lead her to his own land; but before he can get her to safety, I judge that there is trouble in store for him. For while he is on his journey home, the duke, to whom his bride had been betrothed, will appear upon the scene. The duke gathered a numerous force, and garrisoned the frontiers, while at court he had his spies to inform him each day of the emperor's doings and preparations, and how long they are going to stay, and by what route they intend to return. The emperor did not tarry long after the marriage, but left Cologne in high spirits. The German emperor escorted him with a numerous company, fearing and dreading the force of the Duke of Saxony.

The two emperors pursued their journey until they were beyond Regensburg, where one evening they were encamped in a meadow by the Danube. The Greeks were in their tents in the fields bordering upon the Black Forest. Opposite to them the Saxons were lodged, spying upon them. The duke's nephew stood alone upon a hill, whence he could reconnoitre for a chance to inflict some loss or harm on the enemy. From that point of vantage he espied Cliges with three of his young men disporting themselves with lances and shields, eager for a conflict and shock of arms. If he could get the chance the duke's nephew would gladly attack them and do them harm. Starting out with five companions he concealed them in a valley close by a wood, so that the Greeks never saw them until they emerged from the valley; then the duke's nephew made an attack, and striking Cliges, wounded him slightly in the back. Cliges, bending over, avoids the lance which passed him, inflicting only a slight hurt.

When Cliges felt himself wounded, he charged the youth, and struck him with such force that he drove his lance quite through his heart, and stretched him dead. Then all the Saxons in fear of him betook themselves to flight through the woods. And Cliges, ignorant of the ambuscade, courageously but imprudently leaving his companions behind, pursues them to the place where the duke's troops were in force preparing to attack the Greeks. Alone he goes in hot pursuit after the youths, who, in despair over their lord whom they had lost, come running to the duke and tell him weeping of his nephew's death. The duke saw no joke in this affair; and, swearing by God and all His saints that he will take no joy or pride in life so long as the slayer of his nephew remains alive, he adds that whoever will bring him his head will be his friend and will serve him well. Then a knight made boast that if he can find the guilty man, he will present him with Cliges' head. Cliges follows the young men until he falls among the Saxons, when he is seen by him who had undertaken to carry off his head, and who starts after him without delay. But Cliges haste had turned back to escape from his enemies and came in to where he had left his companions; he found none there, for they had returned to camp to relate their adventure. And the emperor ordered to horse the Greeks and Germans in one band. Soon all through the camp the knights are arming and mounting. Meanwhile Cliges is hotly pursued by his enemy, all armed and with helmet closed. Cliges, who never wished to be numbered among the coward and craven-hearted, notices that he comes alone. First, the knight challenged him, calling him "fellow," unable to conceal his rage: "Young fellow," he cried, "thou shalt leave me here a pledge for my lord whom thou hast killed. If I do not carry away thy head with me, I am not worth a counterfeit besant. I must make of it a present to the duke, and will accept no other forfeit. In return for his nephew, I shall make such restitution that he will profit by the exchange." Cliges hears him reproaching him thus boldly and with impudence. "Vassal," he says, "be on your guard! For I will defend my head, and you shall not get it without my leave." Then the attack begins. The other missed his blow, while Cliges struck him with such force that horse and rider went down together in one heap. The horse fell upon him so heavily that he shattered completely one of his legs. Cliges dismounted on the greensward and disarmed him. When he had disarmed him, he appropriated his weapons, and cut off his enemy's head with the sword which had just now been his. After severing his head he fixed it firmly on the point of his lance, thinking to offer it to the duke, to whom his nephew had promised to present his own if he could meet him in the strife. Cliges had no sooner put on the dead man's helmet and taken his shield and mounted his steed, letting his own stray at large to terrify the Greeks, than he saw advancing with more than a hundred banners flying several full squadrons of Greeks and Germans. Now the fierce and cruel struggles will soon begin between the Saxons and the Greeks. As soon as Cliges sees his men advancing, he betakes himself toward the Saxons, his own men hotly pursuing him, and not knowing him in his disguise. It is no wonder that his uncle is in despair and fear, when he sees the head he is carrying off. So all the host pursue him fast, while Cliges leads them on to provoke a fight, until the Saxons see him drawing near. But they, too, are quite misled by the arms with which he has armed and equipped himself. He succeeds in deceiving and mocking them; for the duke and all the rest, when they saw him approaching lance in rest, cried out: "Here comes our knight! On the point of his lance he carries Cliges' head, and the Greeks are hotly pursuing him!" Then, as they give their horses rein, Cliges spurs to meet the Saxons, crouching low beneath his shield, the lance out straight with the head affixed. Now, though he was braver than a lion, he was no stronger than any other man. Both parties think that he is dead, and while the Saxons rejoice, the Greeks and Germans grieve. But before long the truth will out. For Cliges no longer held his peace: but, rushing fiercely at a Saxon, he struck him with his ashen lance upon the head and in the breast, so that he made him lose his stirrups, and at the same time he cried aloud: "Strike gentlemen, for I am Cliges whom you seek. Come on, my bold and hardy knights! Let none hold back, for the first joust is already won! He is a coward who does not relish such a dish."

The emperor's joy was great when he heard the voice of his nephew Cliges summoning and exhorting them; he was greatly pleased and comforted. But the duke is greatly chagrined now when he sees he is betrayed, unless his force should prove the stronger. While he draws together his troops in serried lines, the Greeks do the same, and pressing them close, attack and rush upon them. On both sides lances are lowered as they meet for the proper reception of a hostile host. At the first shock shields are pierced and lances shattered, girths are cut and stirrups broken, while the horses of those who fall to earth are left without a rider. But regardless of what any other does, Cliges and the duke meet in the fray; holding their lances low, they strike one another upon the shield with such violence that the strong and well-made lances fly into splinters. Cliges was skilful on horseback, and sits straight in his saddle without shaking or losing his balance. But the duke has lost his seat, and in spite of himself quits the saddle-bows. Cliges struggled and strove to capture him and carry him away, but his strength did not suffice, for the Saxons were around about fighting to rescue him. Nevertheless, Cliges escapes from the conflict without receiving harm and with a precious prize; for he makes off with the duke's steed, which was whiter than wool, and was worth more to a gentleman than the fortune of Octavian at Rome. The steed was an Arabian. The Greeks and Germans are overjoyed to see Cliges on such a mount, for they had already remarked the excellence and beauty of the Arab steed. But they were not on their guard against an ambuscade; and before they are aware of it great damage will be done.

A spy came to the duke, bringing him welcome news. "Duke," says the spy, "not a man remains in all the encampment of the Greeks who is able to defend himself. If thou wilt take my word for it, now is the time to have the emperor's daughter seized, while the Greeks are seen intent upon the battle and the strife. Lend me a hundred of thy knights, and I will put the lady in their hands. By an old and secluded path I will lead them so carefully that they will not be seen or met by any man of Germany, until they can seize the damsel in her tent and carry her off so handily that no resistance will be made." At this the duke is highly pleased. He sent a hundred and more tried knights with the spy, who so successfully conducted them that they carried the maiden away captive without exerting any force; for they could abduct her easily. After carrying her some distance from the tents, they send her on under escort of twelve of their number whom they accompany but a short distance. While the twelve led the damsel on, the others went to tell the duke how successful they had been. The duke's desire being now satisfied, he at once makes a truce with the Greeks until next day. The truce was sworn by both parties. The duke's men then turned back, while the Greeks without delay repaired each man to his own tent. But Cliges stays behind alone, stationed upon a little hill where no one caught sight of him, until he saw the twelve pass by with her whom they were carrying off at topmost speed. Cliges, in his thirst for glory, rides at them without delay; for he thinks within himself, and his heart tells him, that it is not for nothing that they flee. So, as soon as he espied them, he spurred after them; and when they saw him coming on, a foolish thought occurred to them: "It is the duke," they said, "who comes. Let us rein in a little; for he has left the troops and is riding hard after us alone." Every man thinks that so it is. They all want to turn back to meet him, but each one wishes to go alone. Meanwhile, Cliges must needs descend a deep valley between two mountains. He would never have recognised their blazons, if they had not come to meet him, or if they had not awaited him. Six of the twelve come to meet him in an encounter they will soon regret. The other six stay with the damsel, leading her gently at a walk and easy jog. And the six ride quickly on, spurring up the valley, until he who had the swiftest horse reached him first and cried aloud: "Hail, Duke of Saxony! God bless thee! Duke, we have recovered thy lady. The Greeks shall not get her now, for she shall be placed in thy hands." When Cliges heard the words this fellow shouts, his heart is not gay; rather is it strange that he does not lose his wits. Never was any wild beast--leopard, tiger, or lion--upon seeing its young captured, so fierce and furious as Cliges, who sets no value upon his life if he deserts his sweetheart now. He would rather die than not win her back. In his trouble he feels great wrath, which gives him the courage he requires. He urges and spurs the Arab steed, and rushes to give the Saxon such a blow upon his painted shield that without exaggeration, he makes his heart feel the lance. This gives Cliges confidence. He drove and spurred the Arab charger on for more than the space of an acre before he came upon the next Saxon, for they came up singly, each fearless of his predecessor's fare, for Cliges fights them one by one. As he takes them thus individually, no one receives another's aid. He makes a rush at the second one, who, like the first, thought to give him joy by telling him of his own evil fate. But Cliges has no concern to heed his talk and idle charter. Thrusting his lance into his body so that the blood spurts out when it is withdrawn, he deprives him of life and the gift of speech. After these two he meets the third, who expects to find him in good humour and to make him rejoice over his own mischance. Spurring eagerly he came up to him; but before he has time to say a word, Cliges ran a fathom of his lance through the middle of his body, leaving him senseless on the ground. To the fourth he gives such a blow that he leaves him fainting on the field. After the fourth he goes at the fifth, and after him he attacks the sixth. None of them could defend himself, but each was left silent and mute. He stood in less fear of the others now, and more hardily pressed after them, taking no further thought of the six dead men.

Feeling no further care for them, he starts to present a debt of shame and woe to the others who are leading the maid away. He caught up with them, and made such an onslaught upon them as a hungry and ravenous wolf makes when leaping upon its prey. Now he feels his luck has come, when he can display his chivalry and bravery openly before her who is his very life. Now may he die, if he does not rescue her! And she, too, is at death's door from anxiety for his sake, though she does not know that he is no near. Lance in rest, Cliges made an attack which pleased him well; for he struck first one Saxon and then another, so that with a single rush he carried them both to earth, though it cost him his ashen lance. And they both fall in such distress, being wounded in the body, that they have no power to rise again and do him any harm or ill. The other four in bitter rage join in an attack upon Cliges; but he neither quails nor trembles, and they are unable to dislodge him from his seat. Quickly drawing his keen sword from its sheath, in order to please her who awaits his love, he rode hard at a Saxon and, striking him with his whetted blade, he severed his head and half his neck from the body: such was the limit of his pity. Fenice, who witnesses what transpires, does not know yet that this is Cliges. She wishes that it were he, indeed, but because of the present danger she says to herself that she would not have him there. Thus, doubly she shows the devotion of a sweetheart, fearing at once his death, and desiring that honour may be his. And Cliges sword in hand attacks the other three, who face him bravely and puncture and split his shield. But they are unable to lay hands upon him, or to pierce the meshes of his hauberk. And whatever Cliges reaches cannot stand against his blow, but must needs be split and torn apart; for he turns faster than a top driven and lashed by the whip. Boldness and love, which holds him enthralled, make him eager for the fray. He pressed the Saxons so hard that he left them all dead and defeated, some only wounded, and others dead--except one whom he let escape, disdaining to kill him when left alone at his mercy; besides, he wished him to tell the duke of the loss and injury he had sustained. But before this fellow left Cliges, he begged him to tell him his name, which later he repeated to the duke, thus rousing his bitter ire.

Now bad luck had fallen to the duke, who was in great distress and grief. And Cliges takes back Fenice, whose love torments and troubles him. If he does not confess to her now, love will long be his enemy, and hers too, if she holds her peace and speaks not the word which will bring him joy; for now each can tell the other privily the thoughts that lie within the heart. But they so fear to be refused that they dare not reveal their hearts. For his part, he fears lest she will not accept his love, whereas she, too, would have spoken out had she not feared to be rejected. In spite of this, the eyes of each reveal the hidden thought, if only they had heeded this evidence. They converse by glance of eye, but their tongues are so cowardly that they dare not speak in any wise of the love which possesses them. No wonder if she hesitates to begin, for a maid must be a simple and shrinking thing; but he--why does he wait and hold back who was so bold for her just now, but now in her presence is cowardly? God! whence comes this fear, that he should shrink from a lonely girl, feeble and timid, simple and mild? It is as if I should see the dog flee before the hare, and the fish chase the beaver, the lamb the wolf, and the dove the eagle. In the same fashion the labourer would forsake his pick with which he strives to earn a livelihood, and the falcon would flee from the duck, and the gerfalcon from the heron, and the pike from the minnow, and the stag would chase the lion, and everything would be reversed. Now I feel within me the desire to give some reason why it should happen to true lovers that they lose their sense and boldness to say what they have in mind when they have leisure and place and time.

Ye who are interested in the art of Love, who do faithfully maintain the customs and usage of his court, who never failed to obey his law, whatever the result might be, tell me if there is anything that pleases because of love without causing us to tremble and grow pale. If any one oppose me in this, I can at once refute his argument; for whoever does not grow pale and tremble, whoever does not lose his senses and memory, is trying to filch and get by stealth what does not by right belong to him. The servant who does not fear his master ought not to remain in his employ nor do his service. He who does not esteem his lord does not fear him, and whoever does not esteem him does not hold him dear, but rather tries to deceive him and to steal from him what is his. The servant ought to tremble with fear when his master calls or summons him. And whoever commits himself to Love owns him as his lord and master, and is bound to do him reverence and fear him much and honour him, if he wishes to be numbered in his court. Love without alarm or fear is like a fire without flame or heat, day without sun, comb without honey, summer without flowers, winter without frost, sky without moon, and a book without letters. Such is my argument in refutation, for where fear is absent love is not to be mentioned. Whoever would love must needs feel fear, for otherwise he cannot be in love. But let him fear only her whom he loves, and for her sake be brave against all others. Then if he stands in awe of his lady-love Cliges is guilty of nothing wrong. Even so, he would not have failed to speak straightway with her of love, whatever the outcome might have been, had it not been that she was his uncle's wife. This causes the festering of his wound, and it torments and pains him the more because he dares not utter what he fain would say.

Thus they make their way back to their own people, and if they speak of anything it is nothing of much concern. Each seated on a white horse, they rode rapidly toward the camp, which was plunged in great sorrow. The whole army is beside itself with grief, but they are altogether wrong in supposing Cliges to be dead: hence their bitter and poignant grief. And for Fenice, too, they are in dismay, thinking never to win her back again. Thus, for her and him the whole army is in great distress. But soon upon their return the whole affair will change its aspect; for now they have reached the camp again, and have quickly changed the grief to joy. Joy returns and sorrow flees. All the troops come together and sally forth to welcome them. The two emperors, upon hearing the report about Cliges and the damsel, go to meet them with joyful hearts, and each can hardly wait to hear how Cliges found and recovered the empress. Cliges tells them, and, as they listen, they are amazed and are loud in their praises of his courage and devotion. But, for his part, the duke is furious, swearing and proclaiming his determination to fight Cliges, if he dares, in single combat; and it shall be agreed that if Cliges wins the battle the emperor shall proceed unchallenged, and freely take the maiden with him, and if he should kill or defeat Cliges, who had done him such injury, then let there be no truce or stay to prevent each party from doing its best. This is what the duke desires, and by an interpreter of his, who knew both the Greek and the German tongues, he announces to the two emperors his desire thus to arrange the battle.

The messenger delivered his message so well in both languages that all could understand it. The entire army was in an uproar, saying that may God forbid that Cliges ever engage in the battle. Both emperors are in a fright, but Cliges throws himself at their feet and begs them not to grieve, but if ever he did them any favour, he prays them to grant him this battle as a guerdon and reward. And if the right to fight should be denied him, then he will never again serve for a single day his uncle's cause and honour. The emperor, who loved his nephew as he should, raised him by the hand and said: "Fair nephew, I am deeply grieved to know you are so keen to fight; for after joy, sorrow is to be expected. You have made me glad, I cannot deny it; but it is hard for me to yield the point and send you forth to this battle, when I see you still so young. And yet I know you to be so confident of yourself that I dare not ever refuse anything that you choose to ask of me. Be assured that, merely to gratify you, it should be done; but if my request has any power, you would never assume this task." "My lord, there is no need of further speech," said Cliges; "may God damn me, if I would take the whole world, and miss this battle! I do not know why I should seek from you any postponement or long delay." The emperor weeps with pity, while Cliges sheds tears of joy when the permission to fight is granted him. Many a tear was shed that day, and no respite or delay was asked. Before the hour of prime, by the duke's own messenger the challenge to battle was sent back to him accepted as he had proposed.

The duke, who thinks and confidently trusts that Cliges will be unable to stave off death and defeat at his hands, has himself quickly armed. Cliges, who is anxious for the fight, feels no concern as to how he shall defend himself. He asks the emperor for his arms, and desires him to dub him a knight. So the emperor generously gives him his arms, and he takes them, his heart being keen for the battle which he anticipates with joy and eagerness. No time is lost in arming him. And when he was armed from head to foot, the emperor, all sorrowing, girds the sword upon his side. Thus Cliges completely armed mounts his white Arab steed; from his neck he hangs by the straps an ivory shield, such as will never break or split; and upon it there was neither colour nor design. All his armour was white, and the steed, and the harness, too, was all whiter than any snow.

Cliges and the duke, now being armed, summon each other to meet half way, and they stipulate that their men shall take their stand on either side, but without their swords and lances, under oath and pledge that not a man will be so rash, so long as the battle lasts, as to dare to move for any reason, any more than he would dare to pluck out his own eye. When this had been agreed upon, they came together, each yearning ardently for the glory he hopes to win and for the joy of victory. But before a single blow was dealt, the empress has herself borne thither, solicitous for Cliges' fate. It seems to her that if he dies, she, too, must needs do so. No comfort can avail to keep her from joining him in death, for, without him, life has no joys for her. When all were gathered on the field--high and low, young and old--and the guards had taken their place, then both seized their lances and rushed together so savagely that they both broke their lances and fell to the ground, unable to keep their saddles. But not being wounded, they quickly get upon their feet and attack each other without delay. Upon their resonant helmets they play such a tune with swords that it seems to those who are looking on that the helmets are on fire and send forth sparks. And when the swords rebound in air, gleaming sparks fly off from them as from a smoking piece of iron which the smith beats upon his anvil after, drawing it from the forge. Both of the vassals are generous in dealing blows in great plenty, and each has the best of intentions to repay quickly what he borrows; neither one holds back from repaying promptly capital and interest, without accounting and without measure. But the duke is much chagrined with anger and discomfiture when he fails to defeat and slay Cliges in the first assault. Such a marvellously great and mighty blow he deals him that he falls at his feet upon his knee.

When this blow brought Cliges down, the emperor was struck with fear, and would have been no more dismayed had he himself been beneath the shield. Nor could Fenice in her fear longer contain herself, whatever the effect might be, from crying: "God help him!" as loud as she could. But that was the only word she uttered, for straightway her voice failed her, and she fell forward upon her face, which was somewhat wounded by the fall. Two high nobles raised her up and supported her upon her feet until she returned to consciousness. But in spite of her countenance, none who saw her guessed why she had swooned. Not a man there blamed her, but rather praised her for her act, for each one supposes that she would have done the same thing for him, if he had been in Cliges' place, but in all this they are quite astray. Cliges heard, and well understood, the sound of Fenice's cry. Her voice restored his strength and courage, as he leaped up quickly, and came with fury, toward the duke, so charging and attacking him that the duke in turn was now dismayed. For now he found him more fierce for the fray, stronger and more agile and energetic than when at first they came together. And because he feared his onslaught, he cried: "Young man, so help me God, I see thou art brave and very bold. If it were not for my nephew now, whom I shall never more forget, I would gladly make peace with thee, and leave thy quarrel without interfering in it more."

"Duke," says Cliges, "what is your pleasure now? Must one not surrender his right when he is unable to recover it? When one of two evils must be faced, one should choose the lesser one. Your nephew was not wise to become angrily embroiled with me. You may be sure that I shall treat you in like fashion, if I get the chance, unless you agree to my terms of peace." The duke, to whom it seems that Cliges' vigour is steadily growing, thinks that he had better desist in mid-career before he is utterly undone. Nevertheless, he does not openly give in, but says: "Young man, I see thou art skilful and alert and not lacking in courage. But thou art yet too young; therefore I feel assured that if I defeat and kill thee I shall gain no praise or fame, and I should never like to confess in the hearing of a man of honour that I had fought with thee, for I should but do thee honour, and myself win shame. But if thou art aware of honour's worth, it will always be a glorious thing for thee to have withstood me for two rounds at arms. So now my heart and feeling bid me let thee have thy way, and no longer fight with thee." "Duke," says Cliges, "that will not do. In the hearing of all you must repeat those words, for it shall never be said and noised abroad that you let me off and had mercy on me. In the hearing of all those who are gathered here, you must repeat your words, if you wish to be reconciled with me." So the duke repeats his words in the hearing of all. Then they make peace and are reconciled. But however the matter be regarded Cliges had all the honour and glory of it, and the Greeks were greatly pleased. For their part, the Saxons could not laugh, all of them having plainly seen that their lord was worn out and exhausted just now; but there is no doubt at all that, if he could have helped himself, this peace would never have been made, and that Cliges' soul would have been drawn from his body had it proven possible. The duke goes back to Saxony sorrowing, downcast, and filled with shame; for of his men there are not even two who do not regard him as worsted, defeated, and disgraced. The Saxons with all their shame have now returned to Saxony, while the Greeks without delay make their way with joy and gladness toward Constantinople, for Cliges by his prowess has opened the way for them. The emperor of Germany no longer follows and convoys them. Taking leave of the Greek troops and of his daughter and Cliges, and finally of the emperor, he stayed behind in Germany. And the emperor of the Greeks goes off happily and in joyous mood. Cliges, brave and courteous, calls to mind his sire's command. If his uncle, the emperor, will give him his permission, he will go and ask him for leave to return to Britain and there converse with his great-uncle, the King; for he is desirous of seeing and knowing him. So he presents himself before the emperor, and requests that he consent to let him go to Britain to see his uncle and his friends. Gently he proffered his request. But his uncle refused, when he had listened to the request he made. "Fair nephew," he said, "it is not my will that you should wish to leave me. I shall never give you without regret this permission to go away. For it is my pleasure and desire that you should be my companion and lord, with me, of all my empire."

Now Cliges hears something that does not suit him when his uncle refuses the prayer and request he made. "Fair sire," said he, "I am not brave and wise enough, nor would it be seemly for me to join myself with you or any one else in the duty of governing this empire; I am too young and inexperienced. They put gold to the test when they wish to learn if it is fine. And so it is my wish, in brief, to try to prove myself, wherever I can find the test. In Britain, if I am brave, I can apply myself to the whetstone and to the real true test, whereby my prowess shall be proved. In Britain are the gentlemen whom honour and prowess distinguish. And he who wishes to win honour should associate himself with them, for honour is won and gained by him who associates with gentlemen. And so I ask you for leave to go, and you may be very sure that if you do not grant me the boon and send me thither I shall go without your leave." "Fair nephew, I will give you leave, seeing you are so disposed that I cannot keep you back either by force or prayer of mine. Now since prayer, prohibition, and force do not avail, may God give you the desire and inclination promptly to return. I wish you to take with you more than a bushel of gold and silver, and I will give for your pleasure such horses as you may choose." He had no sooner spoken than Cliges bowed before him. All that the emperor, mentioned and promised him was straightway brought thither.

Cliges took all the money and companions that he wished and needed. For his personal use he took four horses of different colours: one white, one sorrel, one fallow red, and one black. But I must have passed over something which it is not proper to omit. Cliges goes to ask and obtain leave to depart from his sweetheart Fenice; for he wishes to commend her to God's safe keeping. Coming before her, he throws himself upon his knees, weeping so bitterly that the tears moisten his tunic and ermine, the while keeping his eyes upon the ground; for he dares not raise his eyes to her, as if he were guilty of some crime and misdeed toward her, for which he seems overcome with shame. And Fenice, who timidly and fearfully looks at him, does not know the occasion of his coming, and speaks to him with difficulty. "Rise, friend and fair sir! Sit here beside me, and weep no more, and tell me what your pleasure is." "Lady, what shall I say, and what leave unsaid? I come to ask your leave." "Leave? To do what?" "Lady, I must go off to Britain." "Then tell me what your business is, before I give you leave to go." "Lady, my father, before he departed this life and died, begged me not to fail to go to Britain as soon as I should be made a knight. I should not wish for any reason to disregard his command. I must not falter until I have accomplished the journey. It is a long road from here to Greece, and if I should go thither, the journey would be too long from Constantinople to Britain. But it is right that I should ask leave from you to whom I altogether belong." Many a covert sigh and sob marked the separation. But the eyes of none were keen enough, nor the ears of any sharp enough, to learn from what he saw and heard that there was any love between these two. Cliges, in spite of the grief he felt, took his leave at the first opportunity. He is full of thought as he goes away, and so are the emperor and many others who stay behind. But more than all the others, Fenice is pensive: she finds no bottom or bound to the reflections which occupy her, so abundantly are her cares multiplied. She was still oppressed with thought when she arrived in Greece. There she was held in great honour as mistress and empress; but her heart and mind belong to Cliges, wherever he goes, and she wishes her heart never to return to her, unless it is brought back to her by him who is perishing of the same disease with which he has smitten her. If he should get well, she would recover too, but he will never be its victim without her being so as well. Her trouble appears in her pale and changed colour; for the fresh, clear, and radiant colour which Nature had given her is now a stranger to her face. She often weeps and often sighs. Little she cares for her empire and for the riches that are hers. She always cherishes in her remembrance the hour when Cliges went away, and the leave he took of her, how he changed colour and grew pale, and how tearful his expression was, for he came to weep in her presence humbly and simply upon his knees, as if constrained to worship her. All this is sweet and pleasant for her to remember and think about. And afterward, as a little treat, she takes on her tongue instead of spice a sweet word which for all Greece she would not wish him to have used contrary to the sense she had understood when he first had uttered it; for she lives upon no other dainty, and there is nothing else that pleases her. This word alone sustains and nourishes her, and assuages all her pain. She cares to eat and drink of no other dish or beverage, for when the two lovers came to part, Cliges had said he was "altogether hers." This word is so sweet and tastes so good that from the tongue it stirs her heart, and she takes it into her mouth and heart to be all the more sure of it. Under any other lock she would not dare to store this treasure. Nowhere could it be lodged so well as in her own bosom. She will never leave it exposed at any price, being in such fear of robbers and thieves. But there is no ground for her anxiety, and she need have no fear of the birds of prey, for her treasure is not movable, but is rather like a house which cannot be destroyed by fire or flood, but will always stay fixed in a single place. But she feels no confidence in the matter, so she worries and strives to find and hold some ground on which to stand, interpreting the situation in divers ways. She both opposes and defends her position, and engages in the following argument: "With what intention should Cliges say 'I am altogether yours' unless it was love that prompted him? What power can I have over him that he should esteem me so highly as to make me the mistress of his heart? Is he not more fair than I, and of higher rank than I? I see in it naught but love, which could vouchsafe me such a boon. I, who cannot escape its power, will prove by my own case that unless he loved me he would never say that he was mine; unless love holds him in its toils, Cliges could never say that he was mine any more than I could say that I was altogether his unless love had put me in his hands. For if he loves me not, at least he does not fear me. I hope that love which gives me to him will in return give him to me. But now I am sore dismayed because it is so trite a word, and I may simply be deceived, for many there be who in flattering terms will say even to a total stranger, 'I and all that I have are yours,' and they are more idle chatterers than the jays. So I do not know what to think, for it might well turn out that he said it just to flatter me. Yet I saw his colour change, and I saw him weeping piteously. In my judgment, the tears and his face confused and pale were not produced by treachery, nor were they the fruits of trickery. Those eyes from which I saw tears roll down were not guilty of falsehood. Signs enough of love I saw, if I know anything about it. Yes, in an evil hour I thought of love; woe is me that I ever learned it, for the experience has been bitter. Has it indeed? Yes, verily. I am dead when I cannot see him who has stolen my heart away by his cajoling flattery, because of which my heart leaves its dwelling, and will not abide with me, hating my home and establishment. In truth I have been ill treated by him who has my heart in his keeping. He who robs me and takes what is mine cannot love me, of that I am sure. But am I sure? Why then did he weep? Why? It was not in vain, for there was cause enough. I must not assume that I was the cause of it, for one is always loath to leave people whom one loves and knows. So it is not strange if he was sorry and grieved and if he wept when he left some one whom he knew. But he who gave him this advice to go and dwell in Britain could not have smitten me more effectively. He is cut to the quick who loses his heart. He who deserves it, should be treated ill; but I have never deserved such treatment. Alas, unhappy one, why has Cliges killed me when I am innocent? But I am unjust to accuse him thus without cause. Surely Cliges would never have deserted me if his heart were like mine. I am sure his heart is not like mine. And if my heart is lodged in his it will never draw away, and his will never part from mine, for my heart follows him secretly: they have formed such a goodly company. But, after all, to tell the truth, they are very different and contrary. How are they different and contrary? Why, his is the master and mine the slave; and the slave can have no will of his own, but only do his master's will and forsake all other affairs. But what reference has that to me? My heart and service are no concern to him. This arrangement distresses me, that one is master of us both. Why is not my heart as independent as his? Then their power would be equalised. My heart is now a prisoner, unable to move itself unless his moves as well. And whether his heart wanders or stays still, mine must needs prepare to follow him in his train. God! why are our bodies not so near one another that I could in some way bring back my heart! Bring back? Foolish one, if I should remove it from its joy I should be the death of it. Let it stay there! I have no desire to dislodge it, but rather wish that it tarry with its lord until he feel some pity for it. For rather over there than here ought he to have mercy on his servant, because they are both in a foreign land. If my heart knows well the language of flattery, as is necessary for the courtier, it will be rich ere it comes back. Whoever wishes to stand in the good graces of his lord and sit beside him on his right, to be in the fashion now-a-days, must remove the feather from his head, even when there is none there. But there is one bad feature of this practice: while he is smoothing down his master, who is filled with evil and villainy, he will never be so courteous as to tell him the truth; rather he makes him think and believe that no one could compare with him in prowess and in knowledge, and the master thinks that he is speaking the truth. That man does not know himself who takes another's word about qualities which he does not possess. For even if he is a wicked and insolent wretch, and as cowardly as a hare, mean, crazy, and misshapen, and a villain both in word and deed--yet some man will praise him to his face who behind his back will mock at him. But when in his hearing he speaks of him to some other, he praises him, while his lord pretends not to hear what they say between themselves; if, however, he thought that he would not be heard, he would say something his master would not like. And if his master is pleased to lie, the servant is all ready with his consent, and will never be backward in averring that all his master says is true. He who frequents courts and lords must ever be ready with a lie. So, too, must my heart do if it would find favour with its lord. Let it flatter and be obsequious. But Cliges is such a knight, so fair, so open, and so loyal, that my heart, in praising him, need never be false or perfidious, for in him there is nothing to be improved. Therefore I wish my heart to serve him, for, as the people's proverb runs, 'He who serves a noble man is bad indeed if he does not improve in his company.'"

Thus love harrows Fenice. But this torment is her delight, of which she can never grow weary. And Cliges now has crossed the sea and come to Wallingford. There he took expensive quarters in great state. But his thoughts are always of Fenice, not forgetting her for a single hour. While he delays and tarries there, his men, acting under his instructions, made diligent inquiries. They were informed that King Arthur's barons and the King in person had appointed a tourney to be held in the plain before Oxford, which lies close to Wallingford. There the struggle was arranged, and it was to last four days. But Cliges will have abundant time to prepare himself if in the meantime he needs anything, for more than a fortnight must elapse before the tournament begins. He orders three of his squires to go quickly to London and there buy three different sets of arms, one black, another red, the third green, and that on the way back each shall be kept covered with new cloth, so that if any one should meet them on the road he may not know the colour of the arms they carry. The squires start at once and come to London, where they find available everything they need. Having finished this errand, they return at once without losing any time. When the arms they had brought were shown to Cliges he was well pleased with them. He ordered them to be set away and concealed, together with those which the emperor had given him by the Danube, when he knighted him. I do not choose to tell you now why he had them stored away; but it will be explained to you when all the high barons of the land are mounted on their steeds and assemble in search of fame.

On the day which had been agreed upon, the nobles of renown came together. King Arthur, with all his men whom he had selected from among the best, took up his position at Oxford, while most of the knights ranged themselves near Wallingford. Do not expect me to delay the story and tell you that such and such kings and counts were there, and that this, that, and the other were of the number. When the time came for the knights to gather, in accordance with the custom of those days, there came forth alone between two lines one of King Arthur's most valiant knights to announce that the tourney should begin. But in this case no one dares to advance and confront him for the joust. There is none who does not hold back. And there are some who ask: "Why do these knights of ours delay, without stepping forward from the ranks? Some one will surely soon begin." And the others make reply: "Don't you see, then, what an adversary yonder party has sent against us? Any one who does not know should learn that he is a pillar, able to stand beside the best three in the world." "Who is he, then?" "Why, don't you see? It is Sagremor the Wild." "Is it he?" "It surely is." Cliges listens and hears what they say, as he sits on his horse Morel, clad in armour blacker than a mulberry: for all his armour was black. As he emerges from the ranks and spurs Morel free of the crowd, there is not one, upon seeing him, but exclaims to his neighbour: "That fellow rides well lance in rest; he is a very, skilful knight and carries his arms right handily; his shield fits well about his neck. But he must be a fool to undertake of his own free will to joust with one of the most valiant knights to be found in all the land. Who can he be? Where was he born? Who knows him here?" "Not I." "Nor I." "There is not a flake of snow on him; but all his armour is blacker far than the cloak of any monk or prior." While thus they talk, the two contestants give their horses rein without delay, for they are very eager and keen to come together in the fight. Cliges strikes him so that he crushes the shield against his arm, and the arm against his body, whereupon Sagremor falls full length. Cliges goes unerringly and bids him declare himself his prisoner, which Sagremor does at once. Now the tourney is fairly begun, and adversaries meet in rivalry. Cliges rushes about the field, seeking adversaries with whom to joust, but not a knight presents himself whom he does not cast down or take prisoner. He excels in glory, all the knights on either side, for wherever he goes to battle, there the fight is quickly ended. That man may be considered brave who holds his ground to joust with him, for it is more credit to dare face him than it is to defeat another knight. And if Cliges leads him away prisoner, for this at least he gains renown that he dared to wait and fight with him. Cliges wins the fame and glory of all the tournament. When evening came, he secretly repaired to his lodging-place in order that none might have any words with him. And lest any one should seek the house where the black arms are displayed, he puts them away in a room in order that no one may find them or see them, and he hangs up his green arms at the street-door, where they will be in evidence, and where passers-by will see them. And if any one asks and inquires where his lodging is, he cannot learn when he sees no sign of the black shield for which he seeks.

By this ruse Cliges remains hidden in the town. And those who were his prisoners went from one end of the town to the other asking for the black knight, but none could give them any information. Even King Arthur himself has search made up and down for him; but there is only one answer: "We have not seen him since we left the lists, and do not know what became of him." More than twenty young men seek him, whom the King sent out; but Cliges so successfully concealed himself that they cannot find a trace of him. King Arthur is filled with astonishment when he is informed that no one of high or low degree can point out his lodging-place, any more than if he were in Caesarea, Toledo, or Crete. "Upon my word," he says, "I know not what they may say, but to me this seems a marvellous thing. Perchance it was a phantom that appeared in our midst. Many a knight has been unhorsed, and noble men have pledged faith to one whose house they cannot find, or even his country or locality; each of these men perforce must fail to keep his pledge." Thus the King spoke his mind, but he might as well have held his peace.

That evening among all the barons there was much talk of the black knight, for indeed they spoke of nothing else. The next day they armed themselves again without summons and without request. Lancelot of the Lake, in whom there is no lack of courage, rides forth with lance upright to await a contestant in the first joust. Here comes Cliges tiding fast, greener than the grass of the field, and mounted on a fallow red steed, carrying its mane on the right-hand side. Wherever Cliges spurs the horse, there is no one, either with hair or without, who does not look at him amazed and exclaim to his neighbour on either side: "This knight is in all respects more graceful and skilful than the one who yesterday wore the black arms, just as a pine is more beautiful than a white beech, and the laurel than the elder-bush. As yet we know not who yesterday's victor was; but we shall know to-night who this man is." Each one makes reply: "I don't know him, nor did I ever see him, that I am aware. But he is fairer than he who fought yesterday, and fairer than Lancelot of the Lake. If this man rode armed in a bag and Lancelot in silver and gold, this man would still be fairer than he." Thus they all take Cliges' part. And the two champions drive their steeds together with all the force of spur. Cliges gives him such a blow upon the golden shield with the lion portrayed thereon that he knocks him down from his saddle and stands over him to receive his surrender. For Lancelot there was no help; so he admitted himself his prisoner. Then the noise began afresh with the shock of breaking lances. Those who are on Cliges' side place all their confidence in him. For of those whom he challenges and strikes, there is none so strong but must fall from his horse to earth. That day Cliges did so well, and unhorsed and took captive so many knights, that he gave double the satisfaction to his side, and won for himself twice the glory that he had gained on the preceding day. When evening came, he betook himself as fast as he could to his lodging-place, and quickly ordered out the vermilion shield and his other arms, while he ordered the arms which he had worn that day to be laid away: the host carefully put them aside. Again that evening the knights whom he had captured sought for him, but without hearing any news of him. In their lodging-places, most of those who speak of him do so with praise and admiration. The next day the gay and doughty knights return to the contest. From the Oxford side comes forth a vassal of great renown--his name was Perceval of Wales. As soon as Cliges saw him start, and learned certainly who it was, when he had heard the name of Perceval he was very anxious to contest with him. He issued straightway from the ranks upon a Spanish sorrel steed, and completely clad in vermilion armour. Then all gaze at him, wondering more than ever before, and saying that they had never seen so perfect a knight. And the contestants without delay spur forward until their mighty blows land upon their shields. The lances, though they were short and stout, bend until they look like hoops. In the sight of all who were looking on, Cliges struck Perceval so hard that he knocked him from his horse and made him surrender without a long struggle or much ado. When Perceval had pledged his word then the joust began again, and the engagement became general. Every knight whom Cliges meets he forces to earth. He did not quit the lists that day even for a single hour, while all the others struck at him as at a tower--individually, of course, and not in groups of two or three, for such was not the custom then. Upon his shield, as upon an anvil, the others strike and pound, splitting and hewing it to bits. But every one who strikes him there, he pays back by casting him from his stirrups and saddle; and no one, unless he wished to lie, could fail to say when the jousting ceased that the knight with the red shield had won all the glory on that day. And all the best and most courtly knights would fain have made his acquaintance. But their desire was not felt before he had departed secretly, seeing the sun already set; and he had his vermilion shield and all his other harness removed, and ordered his white arms to be brought out, in which he had first been dubbed a knight, while the other arms and the steeds were fastened outside by the door. Those who notice this realise and exclaim that they have all been defeated and undone by one single man; for each day he has disguised himself with a different horse and set of armour, thus seeming to change his identity; for the first time now they noticed this. And my lord Gawain proclaimed that he never saw such a champion, and therefore he wished to make his acquaintance and learn his name, announcing that on the morrow he himself will be the first at the rally of the knights. Yet, withal, he makes no boast; on the other hand, he says that he fully expects the stranger knight will have all the advantage with the lance; but it may be that with the sword he will not be his superior (for with the sword Gawain had no master). Now it is Gawain's desire to measure his strength on the morrow with this strange knight who changes every day his arms, as well as his horse and harness. His moultings will soon be numerous if he continues thus each day, as is his custom, to discard his old and assume new plumage. Thus, when he thought of the sword and the lance respectively. Gawain disparaged and esteemed highly the prowess of his foe. The next day he sees Cliges come back whiter than the fleur-delis, his shield grasped tight by the inside straps and seated on his white Arab steed, as he had planned the night before. Gawain, brave and illustrious, seeks no repose on the battleground, but spurs and rides forward, endeavouring as best he may to win honour in the fray, if he can find an opponent. In a moment they will both be on the field. For Cliges had no desire to hold back when he overheard the words of the men who said: "There goes Gawain, who is no weakling either on foot or ahorse. He is a man whom no one will attack." When Cliges hears these words, he rushes toward him in mid-field; they both advance and come together with a swifter leap than that of the stag who hears the sound of the dogs as they come baying after him. The lances are thrust at the shields, and the blows produce such havoc that the lances split, crack and break clear down to the butt-end, and the saddle-bows behind give away, and the girths and breast-straps snap. Both come to earth at once and draw their naked swords, while the others gather round to watch the battle. Then King Arthur stepped forward to separate them and establish peace. But before the truce was sworn, the white hauberks were badly torn and rent apart, the shields were cracked and hewed to bits, and the helmets crushed.

The King viewed them with pleasure for a while, as did many others who said that they esteemed the white knight's deeds of arms no less than those of my lord Gawain, and they were not ready yet to say which was the better and which the worse, nor which was likely to win, if they had been allowed to fight to a finish; but it did not please the King to let them do more than they had done. So he stepped forward to separate them, saying: "Stop now! Woe if another blow be struck! Make peace now, and be good friends. Fair nephew Gawain, I make this request of you; for without resentment and hate it is not becoming for a gentleman to continue to fight and defy his foe. But if this knight would consent to come to my court and join our sport it would not be to his sorrow or hurt. Nephew, make this request of him." "Gladly, my lord." Cliges has no desire to refuse, and gladly consents to go when the tourney is concluded. For now he has more than sufficiently carried out the injunction of his father. And the King says he has no desire that the tournament shall last too long, and that they can afford to stop at once. So the knights drew off, according to the wish and order of the King. Now that he is to follow in the royal suite, Cliges sends for all his armour. As soon as he can, he comes to court; but first, he completely changed his gear, and came dressed in the style of the French. As soon as he arrived at court, all ran to meet him without delay, making such joy and festival that never was there greater seen, and all those call him lord whom he had captured in the joust; but he would hear none of this, and said they might all go free, if they were quite sure and satisfied that it was he who had captured them. And there was not one who did not cry: "You were the man; we are sure of that! We value highly your acquaintance, and we ought to love and esteem you and call you our lord, for none of us can equal you. Just as the sun outshines the little stars, so that their light cannot be seen in the sky when the sun's rays appear, so is our prowess extinguished and abased in the presence of yours, though ours too was once famous in the world." Cliges knows not what to reply, for in his opinion they all praise him more than he deserves; it pleases him, but he feels ashamed, and the blood rises in his face, revealing to all his modesty. Escorting him into the middle of the hall, they led him to the King, where all ceased their words of compliment and praise. The time for the meal had come, and those whose duty it was hastened to set the tables. The tables in the hall were quickly spread, then while some took the towels, and others held the basins, they offered water to all who came. When all had washed, they took their seats. And the King, taking Cliges by the hand, made him sit down in front of him, for he wished to learn this very day, if possible, who he was. Of the meal I need not further speak, for the courses were as well supplied as if beef were selling at a penny.

When all the courses had been served, the King no longer held his peace. "My friend," he says, "I wish to learn if it was from pride that you did not deign to come to court as soon as you arrived in this country, and why you kept aloof from people, and why you changed your arms; and tell me what your name is, too, and from what race you spring." Cliges replies: "It shall not be hid." He told and related to the King everything he wished to know. And when the King had heard it all, he embraced him, and made much of him, while all joined in greeting him. And when my lord Gawain learned the truth, he, more than the others, cordially welcomed him. Thus, all unite in saluting him, saying that he is very fair and brave. The King loves and honours him above all his nephews. Cliges tarries with the King until the summer comes around, in the meantime visiting all Brittany, France, and Normandy, where he did so many knightly deeds that he thoroughly proved his worth. But the love whose wound he bears gives him no peace or relief. The inclination of his heart keeps him fixed upon a single thought. To Fenice his thought harks back, who from afar afflicts his heart. The desire takes him to go back; for he has been deprived too long of the sight of the most desired lady who was ever desired by any one. He will not prolong this privation, but prepares to return to Greece, and sets out, after taking leave. The King and my lord Gawain were grieved, I can well believe, when they could no longer detain him. But he is anxious to return to her whom he loves and so covets that the way seems long to him as he passes over land and sea: so ardently he longs for the sight of her who has stolen and filched Iris heart away. But she makes him recompense in full; for she pays him, as it were rent, the coin of her own heart, which is no less dear to her. But he is by no means sure of that, having no contract or agreement to show; wherefore his anxiety is great. And she is in just as great distress, harried and tormented by love, taking no pleasure in aught she sees since that moment when she saw him last. The fact that she does not even know whether he be alive or not fills her heart with anguish. But Cliges draws nearer day by day, being fortunate in having favourable winds, until he joyfully comes to port before Constantinople. When the news reached the city, none need ask if the emperor was glad; but a hundred times greater was the empress's joy.

Cliges, with his company, having landed at Constantinople, has now returned to Greece. The richest and most noble men all come to meet him at the port. And when the emperor encounters him, who before all others had gone to meet him with the empress by his side, he runs to embrace and greet him in the presence of them all. And when Fenice welcomes him, each changes colour in the other's presence, and it is indeed a marvel, when they are so close together, how they keep from embracing each other and bestowing such kisses as love would have; but that would have been folly and madness. The people come together from all sides with the desire to see him, and conduct him through the city, some on foot and some on horseback, until they bring him to the imperial palace. No words can ever tell the joy and honour and courteous service that were there displayed. But each one strove as best he might to do everything which he thought would please and gratify Cliges. And his uncle hands over to him all his possessions, except the crown: he wishes him to gratify his pleasure fully, and to take all he desires of his wealth, either in the form of land or treasure. But he has no care for silver or gold, so long as he dares not reveal his thoughts to her because of whom he can find no repose; and yet he has plenty of time and opportunity to speak, if he were not afraid of being repelled; for now he can see her every day, and sit beside her "tete-a-tete" without opposition or hindrance, for no one sees any harm in that.

Some time after his return, he came alone one day to the room of her who was not his enemy, and you may be sure that the door was not barred at his approach. By her side he took his seat, while the others moved away, so that no one might be seated near them and hear their words. First, Fenice spoke of Britain, and asked him about the character and appearance of my lord Gawain, until her words finally hit upon the subject which filled her with dread. She asked him if he had given his love to any dame or damsel in that land. Cliges was not obstinate or slow to respond to this demand, but he knew at once what reply to make as soon as she had put the question. "Lady," he says, "I was in love while there, but not with any one of that land. In Britain my body was without my heart, as a piece of bark without the wood. Since leaving Germany I have not known what became of my heart, except that it came here after you. My heart was here, and my body was there. I was not really away from Greece; for hither my heart had come, for which I now have come back again; yet, it does not return to its lodging-place, nor can I draw it back to me, nor do I wish to do so, if I could. And you--how has it fared with you, since you came to this country? What joy have you had here? Do you like the people, do you like the land? I ought not to ask you any other question than whether the country pleases you." "It has not pleased me until now; but at present I feel a certain joy and satisfaction, which, you may be sure, I would not lose for Pavia or Piacenza. From this joy I cannot wrest my heart, nor shall I ever use force in the attempt. Nothing but the bark is left in me, for I live and exist without a heart. I have never been in Britain, and yet without me my heart has been engaged in business there I know not what." "Lady, when was it that your heart was there? Tell me when it went thither--the time and season--if it be a thing that you can fairly tell me or any one else. Was it there while I was there?" "Yes, but you were not aware of it. It was there as long as you were, and came away again with you." "God! I never saw it, nor knew it was there. God! why did I not know it? If I had been informed of this, surely, my lady, I would have borne it pleasant company." "You would have repaid me with the consolation which you really owed to me, for I should have been very gracious to your heart if it had been pleased to come where it might have known I was." "Lady, surely it came to you." "To me? Then it came to no strange place, for mine also went to you." "Then, lady, according to what you say, our hearts are here with us now, for my heart is altogether in your hands." "You in turn have mine, my friend; so we are in perfect accord. And you may be sure, so help me God, that your uncle has never shared in me, for it was not my pleasure, and he could not. Never has he yet known me as Adam knew his wife. In error I am called a wife; but I am sure that whoever calls me wife does not know that I am still a maid. Even your uncle is not aware of it, for, having drunk of the sleeping potion, he thinks he is awake when he is asleep, and he fancies he has his sport with me while I lie in his embrace. But his exclusion has been complete. My heart is yours, and my body too, and from me no one shall ever learn how to practise villainy. For when my heart went over to you it presented you with the body too, and it made a pledge that none other should ever share in it. Love for you has wounded me so deep that I should never recover from it, any more than the sea can dry up. If I love you, and you love me, you shall never be called Tristan, nor I Iseut; for then our love would not be honourable. But I make you this promise, that you shall never have other joy of me than that you now have, unless you can devise some means whereby I can be removed from your uncle and his society without his finding me again, or being able to blame either you or me, or having any ground for accusation. And to-morrow you shall tell me of the best plan you have devised, and I, too, will think of it. To-morrow, as soon as I arise, come and speak with me; then each of us will speak his mind, and we shall proceed to execute whatever seems best."

As soon as Cliges heard her will be fully agreed with her, and said that would be the best thing to do. He leaves her happy, and goes off with a light heart himself. That night each one lies awake thinking over, with great delight, what the best plan will be. The next morning, as soon as they had arisen, they meet again to take counsel privately, as indeed they must. Cliges speaks first and says what he had thought of in the night: "My lady," says he, "I think, and am of the opinion, that we could not do better than go to Britain; I thought I might take you there; now do not refuse, for never was Helen so joyfully received at Troy when Paris took her thither but that still greater joy would be felt over you and me in the land of the King, my uncle. And if this plan does not meet with your favour, tell me what you think, for I am ready, whatever may happen, to abide by your decision." And she replies: "This is my answer: I will never go off with you thus; for after we had gone away, every one would speak of us as they do of Iseut the Blond and of Tristan. And everywhere all men and women would speak evil of our love. No one would believe, nor is it natural that they should do so, the truth of the matter. Who would believe that I have thus, all to no purpose, evaded and escaped from your uncle still a maid? I should be regarded simply as wanton and dissolute, and you would be thought mad. It is well to remember and observe the injunction of St. Paul: if any one is unwilling to live chaste, St. Paul counsels him to act so that he shall receive no criticism, or blame, or reproach. It is well to stop evil mouths, and therefore, if you agree, I have a proposal to make: it seems best to me to consent to feign that I am dead. I shall fall sick in a little while. And you in the meantime may plan some preparations for a place of burial. Put all your wits to work to the end that a sepulchre and bier be so constructed that I shall not die in it, or be stifled, and that no one shall mount guard over it at night when you come to take me out. So now seek such a retreat for me, where no one may see me excepting you; and let no one provide for any need of mine except you, to whom I surrender and give myself. Never, my whole life long, do I wish to be served by other man than you. My lord and my servant you shall be; whatever you do shall seem good to me; and never shall I be mistress of any empire unless you are its master. Any wretched place, however dark and foul, will seem brighter to me than all these halls if you are with me. If I have you where I can see you, I shall be mistress of boundless treasure, and the world will belong to me. And if the business is carefully managed, no harm will come of it, and no one will ever be able to speak ill of it, for it will be believed throughout the empire that I am mouldering in the ground. My maid, Thessala, who has been my nurse, and in whom I have great confidence, will give me faithful aid, for she is very clever, and I trust her fully." And Cliges, when he heard his sweetheart, replies: "My lady, if this is feasible, and if you think your nurse's advice reliable, we have nothing to do but make our preparations without delay; but if we commit any imprudence, we are lost without escape. In this city there is an artisan who cuts and carves wonderful images: there is no land where he is not known for the figures which he has shapen and carved and made. John is his name, and he is a serf of mine. No one could cope with John's best efforts in any art, however varied it might be. For, compared with him, they are all novices, and like a child with nurse. By imitating his handiwork the artisans of Antioch and Rome have learned all they know how to do--and besides there is no more loyal man. Now I want to make a test, and if I can put trust in him I will set him and all his descendants free; and I shall not fail to tell him of all our plan if he will swear and give his word to me that he will aid me loyally, and will never divulge my secret."

And she replies: "So let it be." With her permission Cliges left the room and went away. And she sends for Thessala, her maid, whom she brought with her from her native land. Thessala came at once without delay, yet not knowing why she was summoned. When she asked Fenice privately what was her desire and pleasure, she concealed none of her intentions from her. "Nurse," she said, "I know full well that anything I tell you will go no further, for I have tried you thoroughly and have found you very prudent. I love you for all you have done for me. In all my troubles I appeal to you without seeking counsel elsewhere. You know why I lie awake, and what my thoughts and wishes are. My eyes behold only one object which pleases me, but I can have no pleasure or joy in it if I do not first buy it with a heavy price. For I have now found my peer; and if I love him he loves me in return, and if I grieve he grieves too for my pain and sorrow. Now I must acquaint you with a plan and project upon which we two have privately agreed." Then she told and explained to her how she was willing to feign illness, and would complain so bitterly that at last she would pretend to be dead, and how Cliges would steal her away at night, and then they would be together all their days. She thinks that in no other way she could longer bear to live. But if she was sure that she would consent to lend her aid, the matter would be arranged in accordance with their wishes. "But I am tired of waiting for my joy and luck." Then her nurse assured her that she would help her in every way, telling her to have no further fear. She said that as soon as she set to work she would bring it about that there would be no man, upon seeing her, who would not certainly believe that the soul had left the body after she had drunk of a potion which would leave her cold, colourless, pale, and stiff, without power of speech and deprived of health; yet she would be alive and well, and would have no sensations of any kind, and would be none the worse for a day and a night entire spent in the sepulchre and bier.

When Fenice heard these words, she thus spoke in reply: "Nurse, I commit myself to you, and, with full confidence in you, will take no steps in my own behalf. I am in your hands; so think of my interests, and tell all the people who are here to betake themselves away, for I am ill, and they bother me." So, like a prudent woman, she said to them: "My lords, my lady is not well, and desires you all to go away. You are talking loud and making a noise, and the noise is disagreeable to her. She can get no rest or repose so long as you are in the room. I never remember her to have complained of such a sickness as this so violent and serious does it seem. So go away, and don't feel hurt." As soon as she had issued this command, they all quickly go away. And Cliges sent for John to come quickly, and thus in private spoke to him: "John, dost thou know what I am about to say? Thou art my slave and I thy master, and I can give away or sell thy body like a thing which is my own. But if I could trust thee in an affair I meditate, thou wouldst go for ever free, as well as the heirs which may be born of thee." John, in his desire for freedom, replies at once: "My lord, there is nothing I would not gladly do to see myself, my wife, and children free. Tell me what your orders are, for nothing can be so hard as to cause me any work or pain or be hard for me to execute. For that matter, even were it against my will, I must needs obey your commands and give up my own affairs." "True, John; but this is a matter of which I hardly dare to speak, unless thou wilt assure me upon thy oath thou wilt faithfully give me aid and never betray me." "Willingly, sire," John makes reply: "have never a fear on that account! For I will swear and pledge my word that, so long as I live, I will never say a word which I think will grieve you or cause you harm." "Ah John, even were I to die for it, there is no man to whom I would dare mention the matter in which I desire thy counsel; I would rather have my eye plucked out; I would rather be put to death by thee than that thou shouldst speak of it to another man. But I hold thee to be so loyal and prudent that I will reveal to thee all my thought. I am sure thou wilt observe my wishes, both by aiding me and holding thy peace." "Truly, sire so, help me God!" Then Cliges speaks and explains to him openly the adventurous plan. And when he had revealed the project--as you have heard me set it forth--then John said that he would promise to construct the sepulchre in accordance with his best skill, and said that he would take him to see a certain house of his which no one yet had ever seen--not even his wife or any child of his. This house, which he had built, he would show him, if he cared to go with him to the place where in absolute privacy he works and paints and carves. He would show him the finest and prettiest place that he had ever seen. Cliges replies: "Let us go thither then."

Below the city, in a remote spot, John had expended much labour in the construction of a tower. Thither he conducted Cliges, leading him through the different storeys, which were decorated with fine painted pictures. He shows him the rooms and the fire-places, taking him everywhere up and down. Cliges examines this lonely house where no one lives or has access. He passes from one room to another, until he thinks he has seen it all, and he is much pleased with the tower and says he thinks it is very fine. The lady will be comfortable there as long as she lives, for no one will know of her dwelling place. "No sire, you are right; she will never be discovered here. But do you think you have seen all of my tower and fair retreat? There still remain rooms so concealed that no man could ever find them out. And if you choose to test the truth of this by investigating as thoroughly as you can, you can never be so shrewd and clever in your search as to find another story here, unless I show you and point it out. You must know that baths are not lacking here, nor anything else which a lady needs, and which I can think of or recall. The lady will be here at her ease. Below the level of the ground the tower widens out, as you will see, and you cannot anywhere find any entrance-door. The door is made of hard stone with such skill and art that you cannot find the crack." Cliges says: "These are wonderful things I hear. Lead on and I will follow you, for I am anxious to see all this." Then John started on, taking Cliges by the hand, until he came to a smooth and polished door, all coloured and painted over. When John came to the wall, he stopped, holding Cliges by the right hand. "Sire," he says, "there is no one who could see a window or a door in this wall; and do you think that any one could pass through it without using violence and breaking it down?" And Cliges replies that he does not think so, and that he will never think so, unless he sees it first. Then John says that he shall see it at once, and that he will open a door in the wall for him. John, who constructed this piece of work, unfastens the door in the wall and opens it for him, so that he has to use no strength or violence to force it; then, one stepping before the other, they descend by a winding-stair to a vaulted apartment where John used to do his work, when it pleased him to labour at anything. "Sire," he says, "of all the men God ever made, no one but us two has ever been where we are now. And you shall see presently how convenient the place is. My advice is that you choose this as your retreat, and that your sweetheart be lodged here. These quarters are good enough for such a guest; for there are bedrooms, and bathrooms with hot water in the tubs, which comes through pipes under the ground. Whoever is looking for a comfortable place in which to establish and conceal his lady, would have to go a long way before he would find anything so charming. When you shall have explored it thoroughly you will find this place very suitable." Then John showed him everything, fine chambers and painted vaults, pointing out many examples of his work which pleased Cliges much. When they had examined the whole tower, Cliges said: "John, my friend, I set you free and all your descendants, and my life is absolutely in your hands. I desire that my sweetheart be here all alone, and that no one shall know of it excepting me and you and her." John makes answer: "I thank you, sire. Now we have been here long enough, and as we have nothing more to do, let us return." "That is right," says Cliges, "let us be gone." Then they go away, and leave the tower. Upon their return they hear every one in the city saying to his neighbour: "Don't you know the marvellous news about my lady, the empress? May the Holy Spirit give her health--the gentle and prudent lady; for she lies sick of a grievous malady."

When Cliges heard this talk he went in haste to the court. But there was no joy or gladness there: for all the people were sad and prostrated because of the empress, who is only feigning to be ill; for the illness of which she complains causes her no grief or pain. But she has told them all that she wishes no one to enter her room so long as her sickness maintains its grip with its accompanying pains in her heart and head. She makes an exception, however, in favour of the emperor and his nephew, not wishing to place a ban upon them; but she will not care if the emperor, her lord, does not come. For Cliges' sake she is compelled to pass through great pain and peril. It distresses her that he does not come, for she has no desire to see any one but him. Cliges, however, will soon be there, to tell her of what he has seen and found. He came into the room and spoke to her, but stayed only a moment, for Fenice, in order that they might think she was annoyed by what pleased her so, cried out aloud: "Be gone, be gone! You disturb and bother me too much, for I am so seriously ill that I shall never rise up again." Cliges, though pleased with this, goes away with a sad face: you would never see so woeful a countenance. To judge from his appearance he is very sad; but within his heart is gay in anticipation of its joy.

The empress, without being really ill, complains and pretends that she is sick. And the emperor, who has faith in her, ceases not to grieve, and summons a physician. But she will not allow any one to see her or touch her. The emperor may well feel chagrined when she says that she will never have but one doctor, who can easily restore her to health whenever it pleases him to do so. He can cause her to die or to live, and to him she trusts her health and life. They think that she refers to God; but her meaning is very different, for she is thinking of no one but Cliges. He is her god who can bring her health, or who can cause her death.

Thus the empress takes care that no physician shall examine her; and more completely to deceive the emperor she refuses to eat or drink, until she grows all pale and blue. Meanwhile her nurse keeps busy about her, and with great shrewdness sought privily all through the city, without the knowledge of any one, until she found a woman who was hopelessly ill with a mortal disease. In order to perfect her ruse she used to go to see her often and promised to cure her of her illness; so each day she used to take a urinal in which to examine the urine, until she saw one day that no medicine could ever be of any help, and that she would die that very day. This urine Thessala carried off and kept until the emperor arose, when she went to him and said: "If now it be your will, my lord, send for all your physicians; for my mistress has passed some water; she is very ill with this disease, and she desires the doctors to see it, but she does not wish them to come where she is." The doctors came into the hall and found upon examination that the urine was very bad and colourless, and each one said what he thought about it. Finally, they all agreed that she would never recover, and that she would scarcely live till three o'clock, when, at the latest, God would take her soul to Himself. This conclusion they reached privately, when the emperor asked and conjured them to tell him the truth. They reply that they have no confidence in her recovery, and that she cannot live past three o'clock but will yield up her soul before that time. When the emperor heard this, he almost fell unconscious to the floor, as well as many others who heard the news. Never did any people make such moan as there was then throughout the palace. However, I will speak no further of their grief; but you shall hear of Thessala's activities--how she mixes and brews the potion. She mixed and stirred it up, for she had provided herself a long time in advance with everything which she would need for the potion. A little before three o'clock she gives her the potion to drink. At once her sight became dimmed, her face grew as pale and white as if she had lost her blood: she could not have moved a foot or hand, if they had flayed her alive, and she does not stir or say a word, although she perceives and hears the emperor's grief and the cries which fill the hall. The weeping crowds lament through all the city, saying: "God! what woe and misfortune has been brought upon us by wicked death! O covetous and voracious death! Death is worse than a she-wolf which always remains insatiable. Such a cruel bite thou hast never inflicted upon the world! Death, what hast thou done? May God confound thee for having put out the light of perfect beauty! Thou hast done to death the fairest and most lovely creature, had she but lived, whom God has ever sought to form. God's patience surely is too great when He suffers thee to have the power to break in pieces what belongs to Him. Now God ought to be wroth with thee, and cast thee out of thy bailiwick; for thy impudence has been too great, as well as thy pride and disrespect." Thus the people storm about and wring their arms and beat their hands; while the priests read their psalms, making prayers for the good lady, that God may have mercy on her soul.

In the midst of the tears and cries, as the story runs, there arrived aged physicians from Salerno, where they had long sojourned. At the sight of the great mourning they stopped to ask and inquire the cause of the cries and tears--why all the people are in such sorrow and distress. And this is the answer they receive: "God! gentlemen, don't you know? The whole world would be beside itself as we are, if it but knew of the great sorrow and grief and woe and loss which has come to us this day. God! where have you come from, then, that you do not know what has happened just now in this city? We will tell you the truth, for we wish you to join with us in the grief we feel. Do you not know about grim Death, who desires and covets all things, and everywhere lies in wait for what is best, do you not know what mad act she has committed to-day, as it is her wont to do? God has illuminated the world with one great radiance, with one bright light. But Death cannot restrain herself from acting as her custom is. Every day, to the extent of her power, she blots out the best creature she can find. So she wishes to try her power, and in one body she has carried off more excellence than she has left behind. She would have done better to take the whole world, and leave alive and sound this prey which now she has carried off. Beauty, courtesy, and knowledge, and all that a lady can possess of goodness has been taken and filched from us by Death, who has destroyed all goodness in the person of our lady, the empress. Thus Death has deprived us all of life." "Ah, God!" the doctors say, "we know that Thou art wroth with this city because we did not reach here sooner. If we had arrived here yesterday, Death might have boasted of her strength if she could wrest her prey from us." "Gentlemen, madame would not have allowed you at any price to see her or to exercise your skill. Of good physicians there was no lack, but madame would not permit any one of them to see her or to investigate her malady." "No?" "Truly, sirs, that she would not." Then they recalled the case of Solomon, who was so hated by his wife that she deceived him by feigning death. They think this woman has done the same. But if they could in any way bring about her cure, no one could make them lie or keep them from exposing the truth, if they discovered any trickery. So to the court they take their way, where there was such a noise and cry that you could not have heard God's thunder crash. The chief of these three doctors, who knew the most, drew near the bier. No one says to him "Keep hands off," and no one tries to hold him back. He places his hand on her breast and side, and surely feels that life is still in the body: he perceives and knows that well enough. He sees the emperor standing by, mad and tormented by his grief. Seeing him, he calls aloud: "Emperor, console thyself! I am sure and plainly see that this lady is not dead. Leave off thy grief, and be comforted! If I do not restore her alive to thee, thou mayst kill me or string me up."

At once throughout the palace the noise is quieted and hushed. And the emperor bade the doctor tell him fully his orders and wishes, whatever they might be. If he can restore life in the empress he will be sire and lord over the emperor himself; but if he has in any respect lied to him he will be hanged like a common thief. And the doctor said: "I consent to that, and may you never have mercy upon me if I do not cause her to speak to you here! Without tarrying and without delay have the palace cleared at once, and let not a single soul remain. I must examine in private the illness which afflicts the lady. These two doctors, who are my friends, will remain with me alone in the room, and let every one else go out." This order would have been opposed by Cliges, John, and Thessala; but all the others who were there might have turned against them if they had tried to oppose his order. So they hold their peace and approve what they hear approved by the others, and leave the palace. After the three doctors had forcibly tipped apart the lady's winding-sheer, without using any knife or scissors, they said to her: "Lady, don't be frightened, have no fear, but speak to us with confidence! We know well enough that you are perfectly sound and in good state. Be sensible and obliging now, and do not despair of anything, for if you have any need of us we will all three assure you of our aid, whether for good or ill. We shall be very loyal to you, both in keeping our counsel and in helping you. Do not keep us talking here! Since we put at your disposal our skill and service, you should surely not refuse." Thus they think to hoodwink and deceive her, but they have no success; for she has no need or care for the service which they promise her; so they are wasting their time in a vain effort. When the three physicians see that they will make nothing out of her either by prayer or flattery, then they take her from her bier, and begin to beat and belabour her. But their efforts are foolish, for not a word can they extract from her. Then they threaten and try to terrify her by saying that if she does not speak she will soon have reason to repent of her folly, for they are going to do such a wonderful thing to her that such a thing was never done to the body of any wretched woman. "We know that you are alive, and will not deign to speak to us. We know that you are feigning death, and would thus deceive the emperor. Have no fear of us! If any of us has angered you, before we do you further harm, cease your mad behaviour now, for you are acting wickedly; and we will lend you our aid in any enterprise--wise or mad." But it cannot be; they have no success. Then they renew their attack, striking her with thongs upon the back, so that the welts are plainly seen, and they combine to tear her tender flesh until they cause the blood to flow.

When they had beaten her with the thongs until they had slashed her flesh, and when the blood is dropping down, as it trickles from among the wounds, even then their efforts are of no avail to extract from her a sigh or word, nor to make her stir or move. Then they say that they must procure fire and lead, which they will melt and lay upon her hands, rather than fail in their efforts to make her speak. After securing a light and some lead they kindle a fire and melt the lead. Thus the miserable villains torment and afflict the lady, by taking the lead all boiling hot from the fire and pouring it into the palms of her hands. Not satisfied with pouring the lead clean through her palms, the cowardly rascals say that, if she does not speak at once they will straightway stretch her on the grate until she is completely grilled. Yet, she holds her peace, and does not refuse to have her body beaten and maltreated by them. Now they were on the point of placing her upon the fire to be roasted and grilled when more than a thousand ladies, who were stationed before the palace, come to the door and through a little crack catch sight of the torture and anguish which they were inflicting upon the lady, as with coal and flame they accomplished her martyrdom. They bring clubs and hammers to smash and break down the door. Great was the noise and uproar as they battered and broke in the door. If now they can lay hands on the doctors, the latter will not have long to wait before they receive their full deserts. With a single rush the ladies enter the palace, and in the press is Thessala, who has no other aim than to reach her mistress.

Beside the fire she finds her stripped, severely wounded and injured. She puts her back in the bier again, and over her she spreads a cloth, while the ladies go to give their reward to the three doctors, without wishing to wait for the emperor or his seneschal. Out of the windows they threw them down into the court-yard, breaking the necks, ribs, arms, and legs of all: no better piece of work was ever done by any ladies.

Now the three doctors have received their gruesome reward at the hands of the ladies. But Cliges is terror-stricken and filled with grief upon hearing of the pain and martyrdom which his sweetheart has endured for him. He is almost beside himself, fearing greatly, and with good reason, that she may be dead or badly injured by the torture inflicted upon her by the three physicians who now are dead. So he is in despair and despondency when Thessala comes, bringing with her a very precious ointment with which she has already gently rubbed the body and wounds of her mistress. When they laid her back in her bier the ladies wrapped her again in a cloth of Syrian stuff, leaving her face uncovered. All that night there is no abatement of the cries they raise unceasingly. Throughout the city, high and low, poor and rich, are beside themselves with grief, and it seems as if each one boasts that he will outdo all others in his woe, and would fain never be comforted. All that night the grief continues. The next morning John came to the court; and the emperor sends for him and issues to him this command: "John, if ever thou wroughtest a fine piece of work, now put forth and show all thy skill in constructing such a sepulchre as for beauty and workmanship shall have no match." And John, who had already performed the task, says that he has already completed one which is very fine and cleverly wrought; but when he began the work he had no thought that other than a holy body should be laid in it. "Now let the empress be laid in it and buried in some sacred place, for she, I think, is sanctified." "You have spoken well," says the emperor; "she shall be buried yonder in my lord Saint Peter's Church, where bodies are wont to be interred. For before her death she made this request of me, that I should have her buried there. Now go about your task, and place your sepulchre in the best position in the cemetery, where it ought rightfully to be." John replies: "Very well, my lord." John at once takes his leave, and prepares the sepulchre with great skill; a feather-bed he placed inside, because the stone was hard and cold; and in order that the odour may be sweet, he spreads flowers and leaves about. Another reason for doing this was that no one might perceive the mattress he had laid within the grave. Already Mass had been said for the dead in the churches and parishes, and the bells were tolling continuously as is proper for the dead. Orders are given to bring the body to be laid in the sepulchre, which John with all his skill has constructed so richly and handsomely. In all Constantinople none remains, whether small or great, who does not follow the body in tears, cursing and reproaching Death. Knights and youths alike grow faint, while the ladies and damsels beat their breasts as they thus find fault with Death: "O Death," cries each, "why didst thou not take ransom for my lady? Surely, thy gain was slight enough, whereas the loss to us is great." And in this grief Cliges surely bears his part, as he suffers and laments more than all the others do, and it is strange he does not kill himself. But still he decides to put this off until the hour and the time shall come for him to disinter her and get possession of her and see whether she be alive or not. Over the gave stand the men who let down the body into its place; but, with John there, they do not meddle with the adjustment of the sarcophagus, and since they were so prostrated that they could not see, John had plenty of time to perform his special task. When the coffin was in its place, and nothing else was in the grave, he sealed up tightly all the joints. When this was done, any one would have been skilful who, except by force or violence, could take away or loosen anything which John had put inside.

Fenice lies in the sepulchre until the darkness of night came on. But thirty knights mount guard over her, and there are ten tapers burning there, which light up the place all about. The knights were weary and exhausted by the strain they had undergone; so they ate and drank that night until they all fell sound asleep. When night came on, Cliges steals away from the court and from all his followers, so that there was not a single knight or servant who knew what had become of him. He did not stop until he found John, who advises him as best he can. He furnishes him with arms, but he will never have any need of them. Once armed, they both spur to the cemetery. The cemetery was enclosed all about with a high wall, so that the knights, who had gone asleep after making the gate fast within, could rest assured that no one would enter there. Cliges does not see how he can get in, for there is no passing through the gate. And yet, somehow he must pass through, for love bids him and drives him on. He tries the wall and climbs up, being strong and agile. Inside was a garden planted with trees, one of which stood so near the wall that it touched it. Now Cliges had what he needed, and after letting himself down by the tree, the first thing he did was to go to open the gate for John. Seeing the knights asleep, they extinguished all the lights, so that the place remained in darkness. And John now uncovers the grave and opens the coffin, taking care to do it no harm. Cliges steps into the grave and lifts out his Sweetheart, all weak and prostrate, whom he fondles, kisses, and embraces. He does not know whether to rejoice or regret that she does not stir or move. And John, as quickly as he could, closed up the sepulchre again, so that it was not apparent that any one had tampered with it. Then they betook themselves as fast as they could to the tower. When they had set her in the tower, in the rooms which were beneath the level of the ground, they took off her grave clothes; and Cliges, who knew nothing of the potion which she had taken, which made her dumb and kept her motionless, thinks that she is dead, and is in despair with anxiety as he heavily sighs and weeps. But soon the time will come for the potion to lose its force. And Fenice, who hears his grief, struggles and strives for strength to comfort him by word or glance. Her heart almost bursts because of the sorrow which he shows. "Ah Death!" he says, "how mean thou art, to spare and reprieve all things despicable and vile--to let them live on and endure. Death! art thou beside thyself or drunk, who hast killed my lady without me? This is a marvellous thing I see: my lady is dead, and I still live on! Ah, precious one, why does your lover live to see you dead? One now could rightly say that you have died in my service, and that it is I who have killed and murdered you. Sweetheart, then I am the death that has smitten you. Is not that wrong? For it is my own life I have lost in you, and have preserved your life in me. For did not your health and life belong to me, sweet one? And did not mine belong to you? For I loved nothing excepting you, and our double existence was as one. So now I have done what was right in keeping your soul in my body while mine has escaped from your body, and one ought to go to seek the company of the other, wherever it may be, and nothing ought to separate them." At this she heaves a gentle sigh and whispers faintly: "Lover mine, I am not altogether dead, but very near it. I value my life but little now. I thought it a jest and a mere pretence; but now I am indeed to be pitied, for death has not treated this as a jest. It will be a marvel if I escape alive. For the doctors have seriously wounded me, and broken my flesh and disfigured me. And yet, if it was possible for my nurse to come here, and if efforts were of any avail, she would restore me to health again." "Do not worry, dear, about that," says Cliges, "for this very night I will bring her here." "Dear, let John go for her now." So John departed and looked for her until he found her, and told her how he wished her to come along and to let no other cause detain her; for Fenice and Cliges have sent for her to come to a tower where they are awaiting her; and that Fenice is in a grievous state, so that she must come provided with ointments and remedies, and to bear in mind that she will not live long, if she does not quickly come to bear her aid. Thessala runs at once and, taking ointments, plaster, and remedies which she has prepared, she meets John again. Secretly they go out from the city, until they come straight to the tower. When Fenice sees her nurse, she feels already cured, because of the loving faith and trust she places in her. And Cliges greets her affectionately, and says: "Welcome, nurse, whom I love and prize. Nurse, for God's sake, what do you think of this young lady's malady? What is your opinion? Will she recover?" "Yes, my lord, have no fear but that I shall restore her completely. A fortnight will not pass before I make her so well that she was never before so lively and strong."

While Thessala is busy with her remedies, John goes to provide the tower with everything that is necessary. Cliges goes to the tower and comes away bravely and openly, for he has lodged a moulting falcon there, and he says that he goes to visit it; thus no one can guess that he goes there for any other reason than for the falcon. He makes long stays there night and day. He orders John to guard the tower, so that no one shall enter against his will. Fenice now has no further cause to complain, for Thessala has completely cured her. If Cliges were Duke of Almeria, Morocco, or Tudela, he would not consider it all worth a holly-berry compared with the joy which he now feels. Certainly Love did not debase itself when it joined these two, for it seems to them, when they embrace and kiss each other, that all the world must be better for their joy and happiness. Now ask me no more of this, for one can have no wish in which the other does not acquiesce. Thus they have but one desire, as if they two themselves were one.

Fenice was in the tower, I believe, all that year and full two months of the next, until summer came again. When the trees bring forth their flowers and leaves, and the little birds rejoice, singing gaily their litanies, it came about that Fenice one morning heard the song of the nightingale. Cliges was holding her tightly clasped with his arms about her waist and neck, and she held him in a like embrace, as she said: "Dear fair lover mine. A garden would do me good, in which I could disport myself. For more than fifteen months I have not seen the light of moon or sun. If possible, I would fain go out yonder into the daylight, for here in this tower I am confined. If there was a garden near, where I could go and amuse myself, it would often do me good." Then Cliges promises her to consult with John about it as soon as he can see him. At that very moment John came in, as he was often wont to do, and Cliges spoke to him of what Fenice desired. John replies: "All that she asks for is already provided and supplied. This tower is well equipped with what she wishes and requires." Then Fenice was very glad, and asked John to take her there, which he said he would very gladly do. Then John goes and opens a door, constructed in a fashion which I cannot properly describe. No one but John could have made it, and no one could have asserted that there was any door or window there--so perfectly was it concealed.

When Fenice saw the door open, and the sun come streaming in, as she had not seen it for many a day, her heart beat high with joy; she said that now there was nothing lacking, since she could leave her dungeon-tower, and that she wished for no other lodging-place. She passed out through the door into the garden, with its pleasures and delights. In the middle of the garden stood a grafted tree loaded with blooming flowers and leaves, and with a wide-spreading top. The branches of it were so trained that they all hung downwards until they almost touched the ground; the main trunk, however, from which they sprang, rose straight into the air. Fenice desires no other place. Beneath the tree the turf is very pleasant and fine, and at noon, when it is hot, the sun will never be high enough for its rays to penetrate there. John had shown his skill in arranging and training the branches thus. There Fenice goes to enjoy herself, where they set up a bed for her by day. There they taste of joy and delight. And the garden is enclosed about with a high wall connected with the tower, so that nothing can enter there without first passing through the tower.

Fenice now is very happy: there is nothing to cause her displeasure, and nothing is lacking which she desires, when her lover is at liberty to embrace her beneath the blossoms and the leaves. At the season when people take the sparrow-hawk and setter and hunt the lark and brown-thrush or stalk the quail and partridge, it chanced that a knight of Thrace, who was young and alert and inclined to knightly sport, came one day close by the tower in his search for game. The hawk of Bertrand (for such was his name) having missed a lark, had flown away, and Bertrand thought how great his loss would be if he should lose his hunting-bird. When he saw it come down and light in a garden beneath the tower he was glad, for he thought he could not lose it now. At once he goes and clambers up the wall until he succeeds in getting over it, when beneath the tree he sees Fenice and Cliges lying asleep and naked in close embrace. "God!" said he, "what has happened to me now? What marvel is this I see? Is that not Cliges? It surely is. Is not that the empress with him there? Nay, but it looks like her. Never did one thing so resemble another. Her nose, her mouth, and brow are like those of my lady the empress. Never did Nature make two creatures of such similitude. There is no feature in this woman here which I have not seen in my lady. If she were alive, I should say that it was certainly she herself." Just then a pear falls down and strikes close by Fenice's ear. She jumps and awakes and, seeing Bertrand, cries out aloud: "My dear, my dear, we are lost. Yonder is Bertrand. If he escapes you, we are caught in a bad trap, for he will tell that he has seen us." Then Bertrand realised that it was the empress beyond any doubt. He sees the necessity of leaving at once, for Cliges had brought with him his sword into the garden, and had laid it down beside the bed. He jumped up now and grasped his sword, while Bertrand hastily took his leave. As fast as he could he scaled the wall, and was almost safely over when Cliges coming after him raised his sword and struck him with such violence that he severed his leg below the knee, as if it had been a fennel stalk. In spite of this, Bertrand got away, though badly wounded and maimed. Beside themselves with grief and wrath at the sight of his sorry state, his men on the other side picked him up, and insistently inquired who it was who had used him thus. "Don't speak to me now," he says, "but help me to mount my horse. No mention shall be made of this excepting to the emperor. He who thus has treated me must be, and doubtless is, in great terror; for he is in great danger of his life." Then they set him upon his palfrey and lead him through the city, sorely grieved in their fright the while. After them more than twenty thousand others come, following them to the court. And all the people run together, each striving to be there first. Bertrand made his complaint aloud, in the hearing of all, to the emperor: but they took him for an idle chatterer when he said that he had seen the empress all exposed. The city is in a ferment of excitement: some regard the news they hear as simple nonsense, others advise and urge the emperor to visit the tower himself. Great is the noise and confusion of the people who prepare to accompany him. But they find nothing in the tower, for Fenice and Cliges make their escape, taking with them Thessala, who comforts them and declares to them that, if perchance they see people coming after them to arrest them, they need have no fear; that they would never approach to do them harm within the range of a strong cross-bow. And the emperor within the tower has John sought for and brought. He orders him to be bound and tied saying that he will have him hanged or burnt, and will have his ashes scattered wide. He shall receive his due reward for the shame he has caused the emperor; but this reward will not be agreeable, because John has hidden in the tower his nephew with his wife. "Upon my word, you tell the truth," says John; "I will not lie, but will go still further and declare the truth, and if I have done any wrong it is right that I should be seized. But I offer this as my excuse: that a servant ought to refuse nothing when his lawful lord commands. Now, every one knows forsooth that I am his, and this tower is too." "It is not, John. Rather is it thine." "Mine, sire? Yes, after him: but neither do I belong to myself, nor have I anything which is mine, except what he pleased to bestow on me. And if you should think to say that my lord is guilty of having done you wrong, I am ready to take up his defence without any command from him. But I feel emboldened to proclaim openly what is on my mind, just as I have thought it out, for I know full well that I must die. So I will speak regardless of results. For if I die for my lord's sake, I shall not die an ignoble death, for the facts are generally known about that oath and pledge which you gave to your brother, that after you Cliges should be emperor, who now is banished as a wanderer. But if God will, he shall yet be emperor! Hence you are open to reproach, for you ought not to have taken a wife; yet you married her and did Cliges a wrong, and he has done you no wrong at all. And if I am punished with death by you, and if I die wrongfully for his sake, and if he is still alive, he will avenge my death on you. Now go and do the best you can, for if I die you shall also die."

The emperor trembles with wrath upon hearing the mocking words addressed to him by John. "John," he says, "thou shalt have so much respite, until we find thy lord, who has done such wrong to me, though I loved him dearly and had no thought of defrauding him.

Meanwhile, thou shalt stay in prison. If thou knowest what has become of him, tell me at once, I order thee." "I tell you? How can I commit such treachery? Were the life to be drawn from my body I would not reveal my lord to you, even if I knew his whereabouts. As a matter of fact, I do not know any more than you where they have gone, so help me God! But there is no need for your jealousy. I do not so much fear your wrath that I should not say, so that all can hear, how you have been deceived, even my words are not believed. You were deceived and tricked by potion you drank on your wedding night. Unless it happened in dream, when you were asleep, you have never had your pleasure with her; but the night made you dream, and the dream gave you as much satisfaction as if it had happened in your waking hours that she had held you in her arms: that was the sum of your satisfaction. Her heart was so devoted to Cliges that she feigned death for his sake; and he had such confidence in me that he explained it all to me and established her in my house, which rightfully belongs to him. You ought not to find fault with me. I ought, indeed, to be burnt or hanged, were I to betray my lord or refuse to do his will."

When the emperor's attention is recalled to the potion which he had been pleased to drink, and with which Thessala had deceived him, then he realised for the first time that he had never had pleasure with his wife, unless it had happened in a dream: thus it was but an illusory joy. And he says that if he does not take vengeance for the shame and disgrace inflicted upon him by the traitor who has seduced his wife, he will never again be happy. "Now quick!" he says, "as far as Pavia, and from here to Germany, let no castle, town, or city remain in which search is not made. I will hold that man above all others dear who will bring to me captive the two of them. Now up and down, near and far, go diligently and search!" Then they started out with zeal and spent all that day in the search. But in the number Cliges had some friends, who, if they found them, would have led them to some hiding-place rather than hale them back again. All that fortnight they exhausted themselves in a fruitless search. For Thessala, who is acting as their guide, conducts them by her arts and charms in such security that they feel no dread or fear of all the strength of the emperor. They seek repose in no town or city; yet they have all they wish or desire, even more so than is usually the case. For all they need is procured for them by Thessala, who searches and scours and purveys for them. Nor is there any who hunts them now, for all have returned to their homes again. Meanwhile Cliges is not idle, but starts to find his uncle, King Arthur. He continued his search until he found him, and to him he made his claim and protest about his uncle, the emperor, who, in order to disinherit him, had disloyally taken a wife, which it was not right for him to do; for he had sworn to his father that he would never marry in his life. And the King says that with a fleet he will proceed to Constantinople, and that he will fill a thousand ships with knights, and three thousand more with men-at-arms, until no city or burg, town or castle, however strong or however high, will be able to withstand their assault. Then Cliges did not forget to thank the King for the aid he offered him. The King sends out to seek and summon all the high barons of the land, and causes to be requisitioned and equipped ships, war vessels, boats, and barks. He has a hundred ships loaded and filled with shields, lances, bucklers, and armour fit for knights. The King makes such great preparations for the war that never did Caesar or Alexander make the like. He orders to assemble at his summons all England, and all Flanders, Normandy, France, and Brittany, and all the men as far as the Pyrenees. Already they were about to set sail, when messengers arrived from Greece who delayed the embarkation and kept the King and his people back. Among the messengers who came was John, that trusty man, for he would never be a witness or messenger of any news which was not true, and which he did not know for a certainty. The messengers were high born men of Greece, who came in search for Cliges. They made inquiry and asked for him, until they found him at the King's court, when they said to him: "God save you, sire! Greece is made over to you, and Constantinople is given to you by all those of your empire, because of the right you have to them. Your uncle (but you know it not) is dead of the grief he felt because he could not discover you. His grief was such that he lost his mind;

he would neither drink nor eat, but died like a man beside himself. Fair sire, now come back again! For all your lords have sent for you. Greatly they desire and long for you, wishing to make you their emperor." Some there were that rejoiced at this; and others there were who would have gladly seen their guests elsewhere, and the fleet make sail for Greece. But the expedition is given up, and the King dismisses his men, and the hosts depart to their homes again. And Cliges hurriedly makes haste in his desire to return to Greece. He has no wish to tarry. His preparations made, he took his leave of the King, and then of all his friends, and taking Fenice with him, he goes away. They travel until they arrive in Greece, where they receive him with the jubilation which they ought to show to their rightful lord, and they give him his sweetheart to be his wife. Both of them are crowned at once. His mistress he has made his wife, but he still calls her his mistress and sweetheart, and she can complain of no loss of affection, for he loves her still as his mistress, and she loves him, too, as a lady ought to love her lover. And each day saw their love grow stronger: he never doubted her, nor did she blame him for anything. She was never kept confined, as so many women have been who have lived since her time. For never since has there been an emperor who did not stand in fear of his wife, lest he should be deceived by her, upon his hearing the story of how Fenice deceived Alis, first with the potion which he drank, and then later by that other ruse. Therefore, every empress, however rich and noble she may be, is guarded in Constantinople as in a prison, for the emperor has no confidence in her when he remembers the story of Fenice. He keeps her constantly guarded in her room, nor is there ever allowed any man in her presence, unless he be a eunuch from his youth; in the case of such there is no fear or doubt that Love will ensnare them in his bonds. Here ends the work of Chretien.

# Yvain: The Knight with the Lion

Arthur, the good King of Britain, whose prowess teaches us that we, too, should be brave and courteous, held a rich and royal court upon that precious feast-day which is always known by the name of Pentecost. The court was at Carduel in Wales. When the meal was finished, the knights betook themselves whither they were summoned by the ladies, damsels, and maidens. Some told stories; others spoke of love, of the trials and sorrows, as well as of the great blessings, which often fall to the members of its order, which was rich and flourishing in those days of old. But now its followers are few, having deserted it almost to a man, so that love is much abased. For lovers used to deserve to be considered courteous, brave, generous, and honourable. But now love is a laughing-stock, for those who have no intelligence of it assert that they love, and in that they lie. Thus they utter a mockery and lie by boasting where they have no right. But let us leave those who are still alive, to speak of those of former time. For, I take it, a courteous man, though dead, is worth more than a living knave. So it is my pleasure to relate a matter quite worthy of heed concerning the King whose fame was such that men still speak of him far and near; and I agree with the opinion of the Bretons that his name will live on for evermore. And in connection with him we call to mind those goodly chosen knights who spent themselves for honour's sake. But upon this day of which I speak, great was their astonishment at seeing the King quit their presence; and there were some who felt chagrined, and who did not mince their words, never before having seen the King, on the occasion of such a feast, enter his own chamber either to sleep or to seek repose. But this day it came about that the Queen detained him, and he remained so long at her side that he forgot himself and fell asleep. Outside the chamber door were Dodinel, Sagremor, and Kay, my lord Gawain, my lord Yvain, and with them Calogrenant, a very comely knight, who had begun to tell them a tale, though it was not to his credit, but rather to his shame. The Queen could hear him as he told his tale, and rising from beside the King, she came upon them so stealthily that before any caught sight of her, she had fallen, as it were, right in their midst. Calogrenant alone jumped up quickly when he saw her come. Then Kay, who was very quarrelsome, mean, sarcastic, and abusive, said to him: "By the Lord, Calogrenant, I see you are very bold and forward now, and certainly it pleases me to see you the most courteous of us all. And I know that you are quite persuaded of your own excellence, for that is in keeping with your little sense. And of course it is natural that my lady should suppose that you surpass us all in courtesy and bravery. We failed to rise through sloth, forsooth, or because we did not care! Upon my word, it is not so, my lord; but we did not see my lady until you had risen first." "Really, Kay," the Queen then says, "I think you would burst if you could not pour out the poison of which you are so full. You are troublesome and mean thus to annoy your companions." "Lady," says Kay, "if we are not better for your company, at least let us not lose by it. I am not aware that I said anything for which I ought to be accused, and so I pray you say no more. It is impolite and foolish to keep up a vain dispute. This argument should go no further, nor should any one try to make more of it. But since there must be no more high words, command him to continue the tale he had begun." Thereupon Calogrenant prepares to reply in this fashion: "My lord, little do I care about the quarrel, which matters little and affects me not. If you have vented your scorn on me, I shall never be harmed by it. You have often spoken insultingly, my lord Kay, to braver and better men than I, for you are given to this kind of thing. The manure-pile will always stink, and gadflies sting, and bees will hum, and so a bore will torment and make a nuisance of himself. However, with my lady's leave, I'll not continue my tale to-day, and I beg her to say no more about it, and kindly not give me any unwelcome command." "Lady," says Kay, "all those who are here will be in your debt, for they are desirous to hear it out. Don't do it as a favour to me! But by the faith you owe the King, your lord and mine, command him to continue, and you will do well." "Calogrenant," the Queen then says, "do not mind the attack of my lord Kay the seneschal. He is so accustomed to evil speech that one cannot punish him for it. I command and request you not to be angered because of him, nor should you fail on his account to say something which it will please us all to hear; if you wish to preserve my good-will, pray begin the tale anew." "Surely, lady, it is a very unwelcome command you lay upon me. Rather than tell any more of my tale to-day, I would have one eye plucked out, if I did not fear your displeasure. Yet will I perform your behest, however distasteful it may be. Then since you will have it so, give heed. Let your heart and ears be mine. For words, though heard, are lost unless understood within the heart. Some men there are who give consent to what they hear but do not understand: these men have the hearing alone. For the moment the heart fails to understand, the word falls upon the ears simply as the wind that blows, without stopping to tarry there; rather it quickly passes on if the heart is not so awake as to be ready to receive it. For the heart alone can receive it when it comes along, and shut it up within. The ears are the path and channel by which the voice can reach the heart, while the heart receives within the bosom the voice which enters through the ear. Now, whoever will heed my words, must surrender to me his heart and ears, for I am not going to speak of a dream, an idle tale, or lie, with which many another has regaled you, but rather shall I speak of what I saw."

"It happened seven years ago that, lonely as a countryman, I was making my way in search of adventures, fully armed as a knight should be, when I came upon a road leading off to the right into a thick forest. The road there was very bad, full of briars and thorns. In spite of the trouble and inconvenience, I followed the road and path. Almost the entire day I went thus riding until I emerged from the forest of Broceliande. Out from the forest I passed into the open country where I saw a wooden tower at the distance of half a Welsh league: it may have been so far, but it was not anymore. Proceeding faster than a walk, I drew near and saw the palisade and moat all round it, deep and wide, and standing upon the bridge, with a moulted falcon upon his wrist, I saw the master of the castle. I had no sooner saluted him than he came forward to hold my stirrup and invited me to dismount. I did so, for it was useless to deny that I was in need of a lodging-place. Then he told me more than a hundred times at once that blessed was the road by which I had come thither. Meanwhile, we crossed the bridge, and passing through the gate, found ourselves in the courtyard. In the middle of the courtyard of this vavasor, to whom may God repay such joy and honour as he bestowed upon me that night, there hung a gong not of iron or wood, I trow, but all of copper. Upon this gong the vavasor struck three times with a hammer which hung on a post close by. Those who were upstairs in the house, upon hearing his voice and the sound, came out into the yard below. Some took my horse which the good vavasor was holding; and I saw coming toward me a very fair and gentle maid. On looking at her narrowly I saw she was tall and slim and straight. Skilful she was in disarming me, which she did gently and with address; then, when she had robed me in a short mantle of scarlet stuff spotted with a peacock's plumes, all the others left us there, so that she and I remained alone. This pleased me well, for I needed naught else to look upon. Then she took me to sit down in the prettiest little field, shut in by a wall all round about. There I found her so elegant, so fair of speech and so well informed, of such pleasing manners and character, that it was a delight to be there, and I could have wished never to be compelled to move. But as ill luck would have it, when night came on, and the time for supper had arrived. The vavasor came to look for me. No more delay was possible, so I complied with his request. Of the supper I will only say that it was all after my heart, seeing that the damsel took her seat at the table just in front of me. After the supper the vavasor admitted to me that, though he had lodged many an errant knight, he knew not how long it had been since he had welcomed one in search of adventure. Then, as a favour, he begged of me to return by way of his residence, if I could make it possible. So I said to him: 'Right gladly, sire!' for a refusal would have been impolite, and that was the least I could do for such a host."

"That night, indeed, I was well lodged, and as soon as the morning light appeared, I found my steed ready saddled, as I had requested the night before; thus my request was carried out. My kind host and his dear daughter I commended to the Holy Spirit, and, after taking leave of all, I got away as soon as possible. I had not proceeded far from my stopping-place when I came to a clearing, where there were some wild bulls at large; they were fighting among themselves and making such a dreadful and horrible noise that if the truth be known, I drew back in fear, for there is no beast so fierce and dangerous as a bull. I saw sitting upon a stump, with a great club in his hand, a rustic lout, as black as a mulberry, indescribably big and hideous; indeed, so passing ugly was the creature that no word of mouth could do him justice. On drawing near to this fellow, I saw that his head was bigger than that of a horse or of any other beast; that his hair was in tufts, leaving his forehead bare for a width of more than two spans; that his ears were big and mossy, just like those of an elephant; his eyebrows were heavy and his face was flat; his eyes were those of an owl, and his nose was like a cat's; his jowls were split like a wolf, and his teeth were sharp and yellow like a wild boar's; his beard was black and his whiskers twisted; his chin merged into his chest and his backbone was long, but twisted and hunched. There he stood, leaning upon his club and accoutred in a strange garb, consisting not of cotton or wool, but rather of the hides recently flayed from two bulls or two beeves: these he wore hanging from his neck. The fellow leaped up straightway when he saw me drawing near. I do not know whether he was going to strike me or what he intended to do, but I was prepared to stand him off, until I saw him stop and stand stock-still upon a tree trunk, where he stood full seventeen feet in height. Then he gazed at me but spoke not a word, any more than a beast would have done. And I supposed that he had not his senses or was drunk. However, I made bold to say to him: 'Come, let me know whether thou art a creature of good or not.' And he replied: 'I am a man.' 'What kind of a man art thou?' 'Such as thou seest me to be: I am by no means otherwise.' 'What dost thou here?' 'I was here, tending these cattle in this wood.' 'Wert thou really tending them? By Saint Peter of Rome! They know not the command of any man. I guess one cannot possibly guard wild beasts in a plain or wood or anywhere else unless they are tied or confined inside.' 'Well, I tend and have control of these beasts so that they will never leave this neighbourhood.' 'How dost thou do that? Come, tell me now!' 'There is not one of them that dares to move when they see me coming. For when I can get hold of one I give its two horns such a wrench with my hard, strong hands that the others tremble with fear, and gather at once round about me as if to ask for mercy. No one could venture here but me, for if he should go among them he would be straightway done to death. In this way I am master of my beasts. And now thou must tell me in turn what kind of a man thou art, and what thou seekest here.' 'I am, as thou seest, a knight seeking for what I cannot find; long have I sought without success.' 'And what is this thou fain wouldst find?' 'Some adventure whereby to test my prowess and my bravery. Now I beg and urgently request thee to give me some counsel, if possible, concerning some adventure or marvellous thing.' Says he: 'Thou wilt have to do without, for I know nothing of adventure, nor did I ever hear tell of such. But if thou wouldst go to a certain spring here hard by and shouldst comply with the practice there, thou wouldst not easily come back again. Close by here thou canst easily find a path which will lead thee thither. If thou wouldst go aright, follow the straight path, otherwise thou mayst easily go astray among the many other paths. Thou shalt see the spring which boils, though the water is colder than marble. It is shadowed by the fairest tree that ever Nature formed, for its foliage is evergreen, regardless of the winter's cold, and an iron basin is hanging there by a chain long enough to reach the spring. And beside the spring thou shalt find a massive stone, as thou shalt see, but whose nature I cannot explain, never having seen its like. On the other side a chapel stands, small, but very beautiful. If thou wilt take of the water in the basin and spill it upon the stone, thou shalt see such a storm come up that not a beast will remain within this wood; every doe, star, deer, boar, and bird will issue forth. For thou shalt see such lightning-bolts descend, such blowing of gales and crashing of trees, such torrents fail, such thunder and lightning, that, if thou canst escape from them without trouble and mischance, thou wilt be more fortunate than ever any knight was yet.' I left the fellow then, after he had pointed our the way. It must have been after nine o'clock and might have been drawing on toward noon, when I espied the tree and the chapel. I can truly say that this tree was the finest pine that ever grew on earth. I do not believe that it ever rained so hard that a drop of water could penetrate it, but would rather drip from the outer branches. From the tree I saw the basin hanging, of the finest gold that was ever for sale in any fair. As for the spring, you may take my word that it was boiling like hot water. The stone was of emerald, with holes in it like a cask, and there were four rubies underneath, more radiant and red than is the morning sun when it rises in the east. Now not one word will I say which is not true. I wished to see the marvellous appearing of the tempest and the storm; but therein I was not wise, for I would gladly have repented, if I could, when I had sprinkled the perforated stone with the water from the basin. But I fear I poured too much, for straightway I saw the heavens so break loose that from more than fourteen directions the lightning blinded my eyes, and all at once the clouds let fall snow and rain and hail. The storm was so fierce and terrible that a hundred times I thought I should be killed by the bolts which fell about me and by the trees which were rent apart. Know that I was in great distress until the uproar was appeased. But God gave me such comfort that the storm did not continue long, and all the winds died down again. The winds dared not blow against God's will. And when I saw the air clear and serene I was filled with joy again. For I have observed that joy quickly causes trouble to be forgot. As soon as the storm was completely past, I saw so many birds gathered in the pine tree (if any one will believe my words) that not a branch or twig was to be seen which was not entirely covered with birds. The tree was all the more lovely then, for all the birds sang in harmony, yet the note of each was different, so that I never heard one singing another's note. I, too, rejoiced in their joyousness, and listened to them until they had sung their service through, for I have never heard such happy song, nor do I think any one else will hear it, unless he goes to listen to what filled me with such joy and bliss that I was lost in rapture. I stayed there until I heard some knights coming, as I thought it seemed that there must be ten of them. But all the noise and commotion was made by the approach of a single knight. When I saw him coming on alone I quickly caught my steed and made no delay in mounting him. And the knight, as if with evil intent, came on swifter than an eagle, looking as fierce as a lion. From as far as his voice could reach he began to challenge me, and said: 'Vassal, without provocation you have caused me shame and harm. If there was any quarrel between us you should first have challenged me, or at least sought justice before attacking me. But, sir vassal, if it be within my power, upon you shall fall the punishment for the damage which is evident. About me here lies the evidence of my woods destroyed. He who has suffered has the right to complain. And I have good reason to complain that you have driven me from my house with lightning-bolt and rain. You have made trouble for me, and cursed be he who thinks it fair. For within my own woods and town you have made such an attack upon me that resources of men of arms and of fortifications would have been of no avail to me; no man could have been secure, even if he had been in a fortress of solid stone and wood. But be assured that from this moment there shall be neither truce nor peace between us.' At these words we rushed together, each one holding his shield well gripped and covering himself with it. The knight had a good horse and a stout lance, and was doubtless a whole head taller than I. Thus, I was altogether at a disadvantage, being shorter than he, while his horse was stronger than mine. You may be sure that I will tell the facts, in order to cover up my shame. With intent to do my best, I dealt him as hard a blow as I could give, striking the top of his shield, and I put all my strength into it with such effect that my lance flew all to splinters. His lance remained entire, being very heavy and bigger than any knight's lance I ever saw. And the knight struck me with it so heavily that he knocked me over my horse's crupper and laid me flat upon the ground, where he left me ashamed and exhausted, without bestowing another glance upon me. He took my horse, but me he left, and started back by the way he came. And I, who knew not what to do, remained there in pain and with troubled thoughts. Seating myself beside the spring I rested there awhile, not daring to follow after the knight for fear of committing some rash act of madness. And, indeed, had I had the courage, I knew not what had become of him. Finally, it occurred to me that I would keep my promise to my host and would return by way of his dwelling. This idea pleased me, and so I did. I laid off all my arms in order to proceed more easily, and thus with shame I retraced my steps. When I reached his home that night, I found my host to be the same good-natured and courteous man as I had before discovered him to be. I could not observe that either his daughter or he himself welcomed me any less gladly, or did me any less honour than they had done the night before. I am indebted to them for the great honour they all did me in that house; and they even said that, so far as they knew or had heard tell, no one had ever escaped, without being killed or kept a prisoner, from the place whence I returned. Thus I went and thus I returned, feeling, as I did so, deeply ashamed. So I have foolishly told you the story which I never wished to tell again."

"By my head," cries my lord Yvain, "you are my own cousin-german, and we ought to love each other well. But I must consider you as mad to have concealed this from me so long. If I call you mad, I beg you not to be incensed. For if I can, and if I obtain the leave, I shall go to avenge your shame." "It is evident that we have dined," says Kay, with his ever-ready speech; "there are more words in a pot full of wine than in a whole barrel of beer. They say that a cat is merry when full. After dinner no one stirs, but each one is ready to slay Noradin, and you will take vengeance on Forre! Are your saddle-cloths ready stuffed, and your iron greaves polished, and your banners unfurled? Come now, in God's name, my lord Yvain, is it to-night or to-morrow that you start? Tell us, fair sire, when you will start for this rude test, for we would fain convoy you thither. There will be no provost or constable who will not gladly escort you. And however it may be, I beg that you will not go without taking leave of us; and if you have a bad dream to-night, by all means stay at home!" "The devil, Sir Kay," the Queen replies, "are you beside yourself that your tongue always runs on so? Cursed be your tongue which is so full of bitterness! Surely your tongue must hate you, for it says the worst it knows to every man. Damned be any tongue that never ceases to speak ill! As for your tongue, it babbles so that it makes you hated everywhere. It cannot do you greater treachery. See here: if it were mine, I would accuse it of treason. Any man that cannot be cured by punishment ought to be tied like a madman in front of the chancel in the church." "Really, madame," says my lord Yvain, "his impudence matters not to me. In every court my lord Kay has so much ability, knowledge, and worth that he will never be deaf or dumb. He has the wit to reply wisely and courteously to all that is mean, and this he has always done. You well know if I lie in saying so. But I have no desire to dispute or to begin our foolishness again. For he who deals the first blow does not always win the fight, but rather he who gains revenge. He who fights with his companion had better fight against some stranger. I do not wish to be like the hound that stiffens up and growls when another dog yaps at him."

While they were talking thus, the King came out of his room where he had been all this time asleep. And when the knights saw him they all sprang to their feet before him, but he made them at once sit down again. He took his place beside the Queen, who repeated to him word for word, with her customary skill, the story of Calogrenant. The King listened eagerly to it, and then he swore three mighty oaths by the soul of his father Utherpendragon, and by the soul of his son, and of his mother too, that he would go to see that spring before a fortnight should have passed; and he would see the storm and the marvels there by reaching it on the eve of my lord Saint John the Baptist's feast; there he would spend the night, and all who wished might accompany him. All the court thought well of this, for the knights and the young bachelors were very eager to make the expedition. But despite the general joy and satisfaction my lord Yvain was much chagrined, for he intended to go there all alone; so he was grieved and much put out because of the King who planned to go. The chief cause of his displeasure was that he knew that my lord Kay, to whom the favour would not be refused if he should solicit it, would secure the battle rather than he himself, or else perchance my lord Gawain would first ask for it. If either one of these two should make request, the favour would never be refused him. But, having no desire for their company, he resolves not to wait for them, but to go off alone, if possible, whether it be to his gain or hurt. And whoever may stay behind, he intends to be on the third day in the forest of Broceliande, and there to seek if possibly he may find the narrow wooded path for which he yearns eagerly, and the plain with the strong castle, and the pleasure and delight of the courteous damsel, who is so charming and fair, and with the damsel her worthy sire, who is so honourable and nobly born that he strives to dispense honour. Then he will see the bulls in the clearing, with the giant boor who watches them. Great is his desire to see this fellow, who is so stout and big and ugly and deformed, and as black as a smith. Then, too, he will see, if possible, the stone and the spring itself, and the basin and the birds in the pine-tree, and he will make it rain and blow. But of all this he will not boast, nor, if he can help it, shall any one know of his purpose until he shall have received from it either great humiliation or great renown: then let the facts be known.

My lord Yvain gets away from the court without any one meeting him, and proceeds alone to his lodging place. There he found all his household, and gave orders to have his horse saddled; then, calling one of his squires who was privy to his every thought, he says: "Come now, follow me outside yonder, and bring me my arms. I shall go out at once through yonder gate upon my palfrey. For thy part, do not delay, for I have a long road to travel. Have my steed well shod, and bring him quickly where I am; then shalt thou lead back my palfrey. But take good care, I adjure thee, if any one questions thee about me, to give him no satisfaction. Otherwise, whatever thy confidence in me, thou need never again count on my goodwill." "Sire," he says, "all will be well, for no one shall learn anything from me. Proceed, and I shall follow you."

My lord Yvain mounts at once, intending to avenge, if possible, his cousin's disgrace before he returns. The squire ran for the arms and steed; he mounted at once without delay, since he was already equipped with shoes and nails. Then he followed his master's track until he saw him standing mounted, waiting to one side of the road in a place apart. He brought him his harness and equipment, and then accoutred him. My lord Yvain made no delay after putting on his arms, but hastily made his way each day over the mountains and through the valleys, through the forests long and wide, through strange and wild country, passing through many gruesome spots, many a danger and many a strait, until he came directly to the path, which was full of brambles and dark enough; then he felt he was safe at last, and could not now lose his way. Whoever may have to pay the cost, he will not stop until he sees the pine which shades the spring and stone, and the tempest of hail and rain and thunder and wind. That night, you may be sure, he had such lodging as he desired, for he found the vavasor to be even more polite and courteous than he had been told, and in the damsel he perceived a hundred times more sense and beauty than Calogrenant had spoken of, for one cannot rehearse the sum of a lady's or a good man's qualities. The moment such a man devotes himself to virtue, his story cannot be summed up or told, for no tongue could estimate the honourable deeds of such a gentleman. My lord Yvain was well content with the excellent lodging he had that night, and when he entered the clearing the next day, he met the bulls and the rustic boor who showed him the way to take. But more than a hundred times he crossed himself at sight of the monster before him--how Nature had ever been able to form such a hideous, ugly creature. Then to the spring he made his way, and found there all that he wished to see. Without hesitation and without sitting down he poured the basin full of water upon the stone, when straightway it began to blow and rain, and such a storm was caused as had been foretold. And when God had appeased the storm, the birds came to perch upon the pine, and sang their joyous songs up above the perilous spring. But before their jubilee had ceased there came the knight, more blazing with wrath than a burning log, and making as much noise as if he were chasing a lusty stag. As soon as they espied each other they rushed together and displayed the mortal hate they bore. Each one carried a stiff, stout lance, with which they dealt such mighty blows that they pierced the shields about their necks, and cut the meshes of their hauberks; their lances are splintered and sprung, while the fragments are cast high in air. Then each attacks the other with his sword, and in the strife they cut the straps of the shields away, and cut the shields all to bits from end to end, so that the shreds hang down, no longer serving as covering or defence; for they have so split them up that they bring down the gleaming blades upon their sides, their arms, and hips. Fierce, indeed, is their assault; yet they do not budge from their standing-place any more than would two blocks of stone. Never were there two knights so intent upon each other's death. They are careful not to waste their blows, but lay them on as best they may; they strike and bend their helmets, and they send the meshes of their hauberks flying so, that they draw not a little blood, for the hauberks are so hot with their body's heat that they hardly serve as more protection than a coat. As they drive the sword-point at the face, it is marvellous that so fierce and bitter a strife should last so long. But both are possessed of such courage that one would not for aught retreat a foot before his adversary until he had wounded him to death. Yet, in this respect they were very honourable in not trying or deigning to strike or harm their steeds in any way; but they sat astride their steeds without putting foot to earth, which made the fight more elegant. At last my lord Yvain crushed the helmet of the knight, whom the blow stunned and made so faint that he swooned away, never having received such a cruel blow before. Beneath his kerchief his head was split to the very brains, so that the meshes of his bright hauberk were stained with the brains and blood, all of which caused him such intense pain that his heart almost ceased to beat. He had good reason then to flee, for he felt that he had a mortal wound, and that further resistance would not avail. With this thought in mind he quickly made his escape toward his town, where the bridge was lowered and the gate quickly opened for him; meanwhile my lord Yvain at once spurs after him at topmost speed. As a gerfalcon swoops upon a crane when he sees him rising from afar, and then draws so near to him that he is about to seize him, yet misses him, so flees the knight, with Yvain pressing him so close that he can almost throw his arm about him, and yet cannot quite come up with him, though he is so close that he can hear him groan for the pain he feels. While the one exerts himself in flight the other strives in pursuit of him, fearing to have wasted his effort unless he takes him alive or dead; for he still recalls the mocking words which my lord Kay had addressed to him. He had not yet carried out the pledge which he had given to his cousin; nor will they believe his word unless he returns with the evidence. The knight led him a rapid chase to the gate of his town, where they entered in; but finding no man or woman in the streets through which they passed, they both rode swiftly on till they came to the palace-gate.

The gate was very high and wide, yet it had such a narrow entrance-way that two men or two horses could scarcely enter abreast or pass without interference or great difficulty; for it was constructed just like a trap which is set for the rat on mischief bent, and which has a blade above ready to fall and strike and catch, and which is suddenly released whenever anything, however gently, comes in contact with the spring. In like fashion, beneath the gate there were two springs connected with a portcullis up above, edged with iron and very sharp. If anything stepped upon this contrivance the gate descended from above, and whoever below was struck by the gate was caught and mangled. Precisely in the middle the passage lay as narrow as if it were a beaten track. Straight through it exactly the knight rushed on, with my lord Yvain madly following him apace, and so close to him that he held him by the saddle-bow behind. It was well for him that he was stretched forward, for had it not been for this piece of luck he would have been cut quite through; for his horse stepped upon the wooden spring which kept the portcullis in place. Like a hellish devil the gate dropped down, catching the saddle and the horse's haunches, which it cut off clean. But, thank God, my lord Yvain was only slightly touched when it grazed his back so closely that it cut both his spurs off even with his heels. And while he thus fell in dismay, the other with his mortal wound escaped him, as you now shall see. Farther on there was another gate just like the one they had just passed; through this the knight made his escape, and the gate descended behind him. Thus my lord Yvain was caught, very much concerned and discomfited as he finds himself shut in this hallway, which was all studded with gilded nails, and whose walls were cunningly decorated with precious paints. But about nothing was he so worried as not to know what had become of the knight. While he was in this narrow place, he heard open the door of a little adjoining room, and there came forth alone a fair and charming maiden who closed the door again after her. When she found my lord Yvain, at first she was sore dismayed. "Surely, sir knight," she says, "I fear you have come in an evil hour. If you are seen here, you will be all cut to pieces. For my lord is mortally wounded, and I know it is you who have been the death of him. My lady is in such a state of grief, and her people about her are crying so that they are ready to die with rage; and, moreover, they know you to be inside. But as yet their grief is such that they are unable to attend to you. The moment they come to attack you, they cannot fail to kill or capture you, as they may choose." And my lord Yvain replies to her: "If God will they shall never kill me, nor shall I fall into their hands." "No," she says, "for I shall do my utmost to assist you. It is not manly to cherish fear. So I hold you to be a man of courage, when you are not dismayed. And rest assured that if I could I would help you and treat you honourably, as you in turn would do for me. Once my lady sent me on an errand to the King's court, and I suppose I was not so experienced or courteous or so well behaved as a maiden ought to be; at any rate, there was not a knight there who deigned to say a word to me except you alone who stand here now; but you, in your kindness, honoured and aided me. For the honour you did me then I shall now reward you. I know full well what your name is, and I recognised you at once: your name is my lord Yvain. You may be sure and certain that if you take my advice you will never be caught or treated ill. Please take this little ring of mine, which you will return when I shall have delivered you." Then she handed him the little ring and told him that its effect was like that of the bark which covers the wood so that it cannot be seen; but it must be worn so that the stone is within the palm; then he who wears the ring upon his finger need have no concern for anything; for no one, however sharp his eyes may be, will be able to see him any more than the wood which is covered by the outside bark. All this is pleasing to my lord Yvain. And when she had told him this, she led him to a seat upon a couch covered with a quilt so rich that the Duke of Austria had none such, and she told him that if he cared for something to eat she would fetch it for him; and he replied that he would gladly do so. Running quickly into the chamber, she presently returned, bringing a roasted fowl and a cake, a cloth, a full pot of good grape-wine covered with a white drinking-cup; all this she offered to him to eat. And he, who stood in need of food, very gladly ate and drank.

By the time he had finished his meal the knights were astir inside looking for him and eager to avenge their lord, who was already stretched upon his bier. Then the damsel said to Yvain: "Friend, do you hear them all seeking you? There is a great noise and uproar brewing. But whoever may come or go, do not stir for any noise of theirs, for they can never discover you if you do not move from this couch. Presently you will see this room all full of ill-disposed and hostile people, who will think to find you here; and I make no doubt that they will bring the body here before interment, and they will begin to search for you under the seats and the beds. It will be amusing for a man who is not afraid when he sees people searching so fruitlessly, for they will all be so blind, so undone, and so misguided that they will be beside themselves with rage. I cannot tell you more just now, for I dare no longer tarry here. But I may thank God for giving me the chance and the opportunity to do some service to please you, as I yearned to do." Then she turned away, and when she was gone all the crowd with one accord had come from both sides to the gates, armed with clubs and swords. There was a mighty crowd and press of hostile people surging about, when they espied in front of the gate the half of the horse which had been cut down. Then they felt very sure that when the gates were opened they would find inside him whose life they wished to take. Then they caused to be drawn up those gates which had been the death of many men. But since no spring or trap was laid for their passage they all came through abreast. Then they found at the threshold the other half of the horse that had been killed; but none of them had sharp enough eyes to see my lord Yvain, whom they would gladly have killed; and he saw them beside themselves with rage and fury, as they said: "How can this be? For there is no door or window here through which anything could escape, unless it be a bird, a squirrel, or marmot, or some other even smaller animal; for the windows are barred, and the gates were closed as soon as my lord passed through. The body is in here, dead or alive, since there is no sign of it outside there; we can see more than half of the saddle in here, but of him we see nothing, except the spurs which fell down severed from his feet. Now let us cease this idle talk, and search in all these comers, for he is surely in here still, or else we are all enchanted, or the evil spirits have filched him away from us." Thus they all, aflame with rage, sought him about the room, beating upon the walls, and beds, and seats. But the couch upon which he lay was spared and missed the blows, so that he was not struck or touched. But all about they thrashed enough, and raised an uproar in the room with their clubs, like a blind man who pounds as he goes about his search. While they were poking about under the beds and the stools, there entered one of the most beautiful ladies that any earthly creature ever saw. Word or mention was never made of such a fair Christian dame, and yet she was so crazed with grief that she was on the point of taking her life. All at once she cried out at the top of her voice, and then fell prostrate in a swoon. And when she had been picked up she began to claw herself and tear her hair, like a woman who had lost her mind. She tears her hair and rips her dress, and faints at every step she takes; nor can anything comfort her when she sees her husband borne along lifeless in the bier; for her happiness is at an end, and so she made her loud lament. The holy water and the cross and the tapers were borne in advance by the nuns from a convent; then came missals and censers and the priests, who pronounce the final absolution required for the wretched soul.

My lord Yvain heard the cries and the grief that can never be described, for no one could describe it, nor was such ever set down in a book. The procession passed, but in the middle of the room a great crowd gathered about the bier, for the fresh warm blood trickled out again from the dead man's wound, and this betokened certainly that the man was still surely present who had fought the battle and had killed and defeated him. Then they sought and searched everywhere, and turned and stirred up everything, until they were all in a sweat with the trouble and the press which had been caused by the sight of the trickling crimson blood. Then my lord Yvain was well struck and beaten where he lay, but not for that did he stir at all. And the people became more and more distraught because of the wounds which burst open, and they marvelled why they bled, without knowing whose fault it was. And each one to his neighbour said: "The murderer is among us here, and yet we do not see him, which is passing strange and mysterious." At this the lady showed such grief that she made an attempt upon her life, and cried as if beside herself: "Ah God, then will the murderer not be found, the traitor who took my good lord's life? Good? Aye, the best of the good, indeed! True God, Thine will be the fault if Thou dost let him thus escape. No other man than Thou should I blame for it who dost hide him from my sight. Such a wonder was never seen, nor such injustice, as Thou dost to me in not allowing me even to see the man who must be so close to me. When I cannot see him, I may well say that some demon or spirit has interposed himself between us, so that I am under a spell. Or else he is a coward and is afraid of me: he must be a craven to stand in awe of me, and it is an act of cowardice not to show himself before me. Ah, thou spirit, craven thing! Why art thou so in fear of me, when before my lord thou weft so brave? O empty and elusive thing, why cannot I have thee in my power? Why cannot I lay hands upon thee now? But how could it ever come about that thou didst kill my lord, unless it was done by treachery? Surely my lord would never have met defeat at thy hands had he seen thee face to face. For neither God nor man ever knew of his like, nor is there any like him now. Surely, hadst thou been a mortal man, thou wouldst never have dared to withstand my lord, for no one could compare with him." Thus the lady struggles with herself, and thus she contends and exhausts herself. And her people with her, for their part, show the greatest possible grief as they carry off the body to burial. After their long efforts and search they are completely exhausted by the quest, and give it up from weariness, inasmuch as they can find no one who is in any way guilty. The nuns and priests, having already finished the service, had returned from the church and were gone to the burial. But to all this the damsel in her chamber paid no heed. Her thoughts are with my lord Yvain, and, coming quickly, she said to him: "Fair sir, these people have been seeking you in force. They have raised a great tumult here, and have poked about in all the corners more diligently than a hunting-dog goes ferreting a partridge or a quail. Doubtless you have been afraid." "Upon my word, you are right," says he: "I never thought to be so afraid. And yet, if it were possible I should gladly look out through some window or aperture at the procession and the corpse." Yet he had no interest in either the corpse or the procession, for he would gladly have seen them all burned, even had it cost him a thousand marks. A thousand marks? Three thousand, verily, upon my word. But he said it because of the lady of the town, of whom he wished to catch a glimpse. So the damsel placed him at a little window, and repaid him as well as she could for the honour which he had done her. From this window my lord Yvain espies the fair lady, as she says: "Sire, may God have mercy upon your soul! For never, I verily believe, did any knight ever sit in saddle who was your equal in any respect. No other knight, my fair sweet lord, ever possessed your honour or courtesy. Generosity was your friend and boldness your companion. May your soul rest among the saints, my fair dear lord." Then she strikes and tears whatever she can lay her hands upon. Whatever the outcome may be, it is hard for my lord Yvain to restrain himself from running forward to seize her hands. But the damsel begs and advises him, and even urgently commands him, though with courtesy and graciousness, not to commit any rash deed, saying: "You are well off here. Do not stir for any cause until this grief shall be assuaged; let these people all depart, as they will do presently. If you act as I advise, in accordance with my views, great advantage may come to you. It will be best for you to remain seated here, and watch the people inside and out as they pass along the way without their seeing you. But take care not to speak violently, for I hold that man to be rather imprudent than brave who goes too far and loses his self-restraint and commits some deed of violence the moment he has the time and chance. So if you cherish some rash thought be careful not to utter it. The wise man conceals his imprudent thought and works out righteousness if he can. So wisely take good care not to risk your head, for which they would accept no ransom. Be considerate of yourself and remember my advice. Rest assured until I return, for I dare not stay longer now. I might stay so long, I fear, that they would suspect me when they did not see me in the crowd, and then I should suffer for it."

Then she goes off, and he remains, not knowing how to comport himself. He is loath to see them bury the corpse without his securing anything to take back as evidence that he has defeated and killed him. If he has no proof or evidence he will be held in contempt, for Kay is so mean and obstinate, so given to mockery, and so annoying, that he could never succeed in convincing him. He would go about for ever insulting him, flinging his mockery and taunts as he did the other day. These taunts are still fresh and rankling in his heart. But with her sugar and honey a new Love now softened him; he had been to hunt upon his lands and had gathered in his prey. His enemy carries off his heart, and he loves the creature who hates him most. The lady, all unaware, has well avenged her lord's death. She has secured greater revenge than she could ever have done unless she had been aided by Love, who attacks him so gently that he wounds his heart through his eyes. And this wound is more enduring than any inflicted by lance or sword. A sword-blow is cured and healed at once as soon as a doctor attends to it, but the wound of love is worst when it is nearest to its physician. This is the wound of my lord Yvain, from which he will never more recover, for Love has installed himself with him. He deserts and goes away from the places he was wont to frequent. He cares for no lodging or landlord save this one, and he is very wise in leaving a poor lodging-place in order to betake himself to him. In order to devote himself completely to him, he will have no other lodging-place, though often he is wont to seek out lowly hostelries. It is a shame that Love should ever so basely conduct himself as to select the meanest lodging-place quite as readily as the best. But now he has come where he is welcome, and where he will be treated honourably, and where he will do well to stay. This is the way Love ought to act, being such a noble creature that it is marvellous how he dares shamefully to descend to such low estate. He is like him who spreads his balm upon the ashes and dust, who mingles sugar with gall, and suet with honey. However, he did not act so this time, but rather lodged in a noble place, for which no one can reproach him. When the dead man had been buried, all the people dispersed, leaving no clerks or knights or ladies, excepting only her who makes no secret of her grief. She alone remains behind, often clutching at her throat, wringing her hands, and beating her palms, as she reads her psalms in her gilt lettered psalter. All this while my lord Yvain is at the window gazing at her, and the more he looks at her the more he loves her and is enthralled by her. He would have wished that she should cease her weeping and reading, and that she should feel inclined to converse with him. Love, who caught him at the window, filled him with this desire. But he despairs of realising his wish, for he cannot imagine or believe that his desire can be gratified. So he says: "I may consider myself a fool to wish for what I cannot have. Her lord it was whom I wounded mortally, and yet do I think I can be reconciled with her? Upon my word, such thoughts are folly, for at present she has good reason to hate me more bitterly than anything. I am right in saying 'at present', for a woman has more than one mind. That mind in which she is just now I trust she will soon change; indeed, she will change it certainly, and I am mad thus to despair. God grant that she change it soon! For I am doomed to be her slave, since such is the will of Love. Whoever does not welcome Love gladly, when he comes to him, commits treason and a felony. I admit (and let whosoever will, heed what I say) that such an one deserves no happiness or joy. But if I lose, it will not be for such a reason; rather will I love my enemy. For I ought not to feel any hate for her unless I wish to betray Love. I must love in accordance with Love's desire. And ought she to regard me as a friend? Yes, surely, since it is she whom I love. And I call her my enemy, for she hates me, though with good reason, for I killed the object of her love. So, then, am I her enemy? Surely no, but her true friend, for I never so loved any one before. I grieve for her fair tresses, surpassing gold in their radiance; I feel the pangs of anguish and torment when I see her tear and cut them, nor can her tears e'er be dried which I see falling from her eyes; by all these things I am distressed. Although they are full of ceaseless, ever-flowing tears, yet never were there such lovely eyes. The sight of her weeping causes me agony, but nothing pains me so much as the sight of her face, which she lacerates without its having merited such treatment. I never saw such a face so perfectly formed, nor so fresh and delicately coloured. And then it has pierced my heart to see her clutch her throat. Surely, it is all too true that she is doing the worst she can. And yet no crystal nor any mirror is so bright and smooth. God! why is she thus possessed, and why does she not spare herself? Why does she wring her lovely hands and beat and tear her breast? Would she not be marvellously fair to look upon when in happy mood, seeing that she is so fair in her displeasure? Surely yes, I can take my oath on that. Never before in a work of beauty was Nature thus able to outdo herself, for I am sure she has gone beyond the limits of any previous attempt. How could it ever have happened then? Whence came beauty so marvellous? God must have made her with His naked hand that Nature might rest from further toil. If she should try to make a replica, she might spend her time in vain without succeeding in her task. Even God Himself, were He to try, could not succeed, I guess, in ever making such another, whatever effort He might put forth."

Thus my lord Yvain considers her who is broken with her grief, and I suppose it would never happen again that any man in prison, like my lord Yvain in fear for his life, would ever be so madly in love as to make no request on his own behalf, when perhaps no one else will speak for him. He stayed at the window until he saw the lady go away, and both the portcullises were lowered again. Another might have grieved at this, who would prefer a free escape to tarrying longer where he was. But to him it is quite indifferent whether they be shut or opened. If they were open he surely would not go away, no, even were the lady to give him leave and pardon him freely for the death of her lord. For he is detained by Love and Shame which rise up before him on either hand: he is ashamed to go away, for no one would believe in the success of his exploit; on the other hand, he has such a strong desire to see the lady at least, if he cannot obtain any other favour, that he feels little concern about his imprisonment. He would rather die than go away. And now the damsel returns, wishing to bear him company with her solace and gaiety, and to go and fetch for him whatever he may desire. But she found him pensive and quite worn out with the love which had laid hold of him; whereupon she addressed him thus: "My lord Yvain, what sort of a time have you had to-day?" "I have been pleasantly occupied," was his reply. "Pleasantly? In God's name, is that the truth? What? How can one enjoy himself seeing that he is hunted to death, unless he courts and wishes it?" "Of a truth," he says, "my gentle friend, I should by no means wish to die; and yet, as God beholds me, I was pleased, am pleased now, and always shall be pleased by what I saw." "Well, let us say no more of that," she makes reply, "for I can understand well enough what is the meaning of such words. I am not so foolish or inexperienced that I cannot understand such words as those; but come now after me, for I shall find some speedy means to release you from your confinement. I shall surely set you free to-night or to-morrow, if you please. Come now, I will lead you away." And he thus makes reply: "You may be sure that I will never escape secretly and like a thief. When the people are all gathered out there in the streets, I can go forth more honourably than if I did so surreptitiously." Then he followed her into the little room. The damsel, who was kind, secured and bestowed upon him all that he desired. And when the opportunity arose, she remembered what he had said to her how he had been pleased by what he saw when they were seeking him in the room with intent to kill him.

The damsel stood in such favour with her lady that she had no fear of telling her anything, regardless of the consequences, for she was her confidante and companion. Then, why should she be backward in comforting her lady and in giving her advice which should redound to her honour? The first time she said to her privily: "My lady, I greatly marvel to see you act so extravagantly. Do you think you can recover your lord by giving away thus to your grief?" "Nay, rather, if I had my wish," says she, "I would now be dead of grief." "And why?" "In order to follow after him." "After him? God forbid, and give you again as good a lord, as is consistent with His might." "Thou didst never speak such a lie as that, for He could never give me so good a lord again." "He will give you a better one, if you will accept him, and I can prove it." "Begone! Peace! I shall never find such a one." "Indeed you shall, my lady, if you will consent. Just tell me, if you will, who is going to defend your land when King Arthur comes next week to the margin of the spring? You have already been apprised of this by letters sent you by the Dameisele Sauvage. Alas, what a kind service she did for you! you ought to be considering how you will defend your spring, and yet you cease not to weep! If it please you, my dear lady, you ought not to delay. For surely, all the knights you have are not worth, as you well know, so much as a single chamber-maid. Neither shield nor lance will ever be taken in hand by the best of them. You have plenty of craven servants, but there is not one of them brave enough to dare to mount a steed. And the King is coming with such a host that his victory will be inevitable." The lady, upon reflection, knows very well that she is giving her sincere advice, but she is unreasonable in one respect, as also are other women who are, almost without exception, guilty of their own folly, and refuse to accept what they really wish. "Begone," she says; "leave me alone. If I ever hear thee speak of this again it will go hard with thee, unless thou flee. Thou weariest me with thy idle words." "Very well, my lady," she says; "that you are a woman is evident, for woman will grow irate when she hears any one give her good advice."

Then she went away and left her alone. And the lady reflected that she had been in the wrong. She would have been very glad to know how the damsel could ever prove that it would be possible to find a better knight than her lord had ever been. She would be very glad to hear her speak, but now she has forbidden her. With this desire in mind, she waited until she returned. But the warning was of no avail, for she began to say to her at once: "My lady, is it seemly that you should thus torment yourself with grief? For God's sake now control yourself, and for shame, at least, cease your lament. It is not fitting that so great a lady should keep up her grief so long. Remember your honourable estate and your very gentle birth! Think you that all virtue ceased with the death of your lord? There are in the world a hundred as good or better men." "May God confound me, if thou dost not lie! Just name to me a single one who is reputed to be so excellent as my lord was all his life." "If I did so you would be angry with me, and would fly into a passion and you would esteem me less." "No, I will not, I assure thee." "Then may it all be for your future welfare if you would but consent, and may God so incline your will! I see no reason for holding my peace, for no one hears or heeds what we say. Doubtless you will think I am impudent, but I shall freely speak my mind. When two knights have met in an affray of arms and when one has beaten the other, which of the two do you think is the better? For my part I award the prize to the victor. Now what do you think?" "It seems to me you are laying a trap for me and intend to catch me in my words." "Upon my faith, you may rest assured that I am in the right, and I can irrefutably prove to you that he who defeated your lord is better than he was himself. He beat him and pursued him valiantly until he imprisoned him in his house." "Now," she replies, "I hear the greatest nonsense that was ever uttered. Begone, thou spirit charged with evil! Begone, thou foolish and tiresome girl! Never again utter such idle words, and never come again into my presence to speak a word on his behalf!" "Indeed, my lady, I knew full well that I should receive no thanks from you, and I said so before I spoke. But you promised me you would not be displeased, and that you would not be angry with me for it. But you have failed to keep your promise, and now, as it has turned out, you have discharged your wrath on me, and I have lost by not holding my peace."

Thereupon she goes back to the room where my lord Yvain is waiting, comfortably guarded by her vigilance. But he is ill at ease when he cannot see the lady, and he pays no attention, and hears no word of the report which the damsel brings to him. The lady, too, is in great perplexity all night, being worried about how she should defend the spring; and she begins to repent of her action to the damsel, whom she had blamed and insulted and treated with contempt. She feels very sure and certain that not for any reward or bribe, nor for any affection which she may bear him, would the maiden ever have mentioned him; and that she must love her more than him, and that she would never give her advice which would bring her shame or embarrassment: the maid is too loyal a friend for that. Thus, lo! the lady is completely changed: she fears now that she to whom she had spoken harshly will never love her again devotedly; and him whom she had repulsed, she now loyally and with good reason pardons, seeing that he had done her no wrong. So she argues as if he were in her presence there, and thus she begins her argument: "Come," she says, "canst thou deny that my lord was killed by thee?" "That," says he, "I cannot deny. Indeed, I fully admit it." "Tell me, then, the reason of thy deed. Didst thou do it to injure me, prompted by hatred or by spite?" "May death not spare me now, if I did it to injure you." "In that case, thou hast done me no wrong, nor art thou guilty of aught toward him. For he would have killed thee, if he could. So it seems to me that I have decided well and righteously." Thus, by her own arguments she succeeds in discovering justice, reason, and common sense, how that there is no cause for hating him; thus she frames the matter to conform with her desire, and by her own efforts she kindles her love, as a bush which only smokes with the flame beneath, until some one blows it or stirs it up. If the damsel should come in now, she would win the quarrel for which she had been so reproached, and by which she had been so hurt. And next morning, in fact, she appeared again, taking the subject up where she had let it drop. Meanwhile, the lady bowed her head, knowing she had done wrong in attacking her. But now she is anxious to make amends, and to inquire concerning the name, character, and lineage of the knight: so she wisely humbles herself, and says: "I wish to beg your pardon for the insulting words of pride which in my rage I spoke to you: I will follow your advice. So tell me now, if possible, about the knight of whom you have spoken so much to me: what sort of a man is he, and of what parentage? If he is suited to become my mate, and provided he be so disposed, I promise you to make him my husband and lord of my domain. But he will have to act in such a way that no one can reproach me by saying: 'This is she who took him who killed her lord.'" "In God's name, lady, so shall it be. You will have the gentlest, noblest, and fairest lord who ever belonged to Abel's line." "What is his name?" "My lord Yvain." "Upon my word, if he is King Urien's son he is of no mean birth, but very noble, as I well know." "Indeed, my lady, you say the truth." "And when shall we be able to see him?" "In five days' time." "That would be too long; for I wish he were already come. Let him come to-night, or to-morrow, at the latest." "My lady, I think no one could fly so far in one day. But I shall send one of my squires who can run fast, and who will reach King Arthur's court at least by to-morrow night, I think; that is the place we must seek for him." "That is a very long time. The days are long. But tell him that to-morrow night he must be back here, and that he must make greater haste than usual. If he will only do his best, he can do two days' journey in one. Moreover, to-night the moon will shine; so let him turn night into day. And when he returns I will give him whatever he wishes me to give." "Leave all care of that to me; for you shall have him in your hands the day after to-morrow at the very latest. Meanwhile you shall summon your men and confer with them about the approaching visit of the King. In order to make the customary defence of your spring it behoves you to consult with them. None of them will be so hardy as to dare to boast that he will present himself. In that case you will have a good excuse for saying that it behoves you to marry again. A certain knight, highly qualified, seeks your hand; but you do not presume to accept him without their unanimous consent. And I warrant what the outcome will be: I know them all to be such cowards that in order to put on some one else the burden which would be too heavy for them, they will fall at your feet and speak their gratitude; for thus their responsibility will be at an end. For, whoever is afraid of his own shadow willingly avoids, if possible, any meeting with lance or spear; for such games a coward has no use." "Upon my word," the lady replies, "so I would have it, and so I consent, having already conceived the plan which you have expressed; so that is what we shall do. But why do you tarry here? Go, without delay, and take measures to bring him here, while I shall summon my liege-men." Thus concluded their conference. And the damsel pretends to send to search for my lord Yvain in his country; while every day she has him bathed, and washed, and groomed. And besides this she prepares for him a robe of red scarlet stuff, brand new and lined with spotted fur. There is nothing necessary for his equipment which she does not lend to him: a golden buckle for his neck, ornamented with precious stones which make people look well, a girdle, and a wallet made of rich gold brocade. She fitted him out perfectly, then informed her lady that the messenger had returned, having done his errand well. "How is that?" she says, "is he here? Then let him come at once, secretly and privily, while no one is here with me. See to it that no one else come in, for I should hate to see a fourth person here." At this the damsel went away, and returned to her guest again. However, her face did not reveal the joy that was in her heart; indeed, she said that her lady knew that she had been sheltering him, and was very much incensed at her. "Further concealment is useless now. The news about you has been so divulged that my lady knows the whole story and is very angry with me, heaping me with blame and reproaches. But she has given me her word that I may take you into her presence without any harm or danger. I take it that you will have no objection to this, except for one condition (for I must not disguise the truth, or I should be unjust to you): she wishes to have you in her control, and she desires such complete possession of your body that even your heart shall not be at large." "Certainly," he said, "I readily consent to what will be no hardship to me. I am willing to be her prisoner." "So shall you be: I swear it by this right hand laid upon you!. Now come and, upon my advice, demean yourself so humbly in her presence that your imprisonment may not be grievous. Otherwise feel no concern. I do not think that your restraint will be irksome." Then the damsel leads him off, now alarming, now reassuring him, and speaking to him mysteriously about the confinement in which he is to find himself; for every lover is a prisoner. She is right in calling him a prisoner; for surely any one who loves is no longer free.

Taking my lord Yvain by the hand, the damsel leads him where he will be dearly loved; but expecting to be ill received, it is not strange if he is afraid. They found the lady seated upon a red cushion. I assure you my lord Yvain was terrified upon entering the room, where he found the lady who spoke not a word to him. At this he was still more afraid, being overcome with fear at the thought that he had been betrayed. He stood there to one side so long that the damsel at last spoke up and said: "Five hundred curses upon the head of him who takes into a fair lady's chamber a knight who will not draw near, and who has neither tongue nor mouth nor sense to introduce himself." Thereupon, taking him by the arm, she thrust him forward with the words: "Come, step forward, knight, and have no fear that my lady is going to snap at you; but seek her good-will and give her yours. I will join you in your prayer that she pardon you for the death of her lord, Esclados the Red." Then my lord Yvain clasped his hands, and failing upon his knees, spoke like a lover with these words: "I will not crave your pardon, lady, but rather thank you for any treatment you may inflict on me, knowing that no act of yours could ever be distasteful to me." "Is that so, sir? And what if I think to kill you now?" "My lady, if it please you, you will never hear me speak otherwise." "I never heard of such a thing as this: that you put yourself voluntarily and absolutely within my power, without the coercion of any one." "My lady, there is no force so strong, in truth, as that which commands me to conform absolutely to your desire. I do not fear to carry out any order you may be pleased to give. And if I could atone for the death, which came through no fault of mine, I would do so cheerfully." "What?" says she, "come tell me now and be forgiven, if you did no wrong in killing my lord?" "Lady," he says, "if I may say it, when your lord attacked me, why was I wrong to defend myself? When a man in self-defence kills another who is trying to kill or capture him, tell me if in any way he is to blame." "No, if one looks at it aright. And I suppose it would have been no use, if I had had you put to death. But I should be glad to learn whence you derive the force that bids you to consent unquestioningly to whatever my will may dictate. I pardon you all your misdeeds and crimes. But be seated, and tell us now what is the cause of your docility?" "My lady," he says, "the impelling force comes from my heart, which is inclined toward you. My heart has fixed me in this desire." "And what prompted your heart, my fair sweet friend?" "Lady, my eyes." "And what the eyes?" "The great beauty that I see in you." "And where is beauty's fault in that?" "Lady, in this: that it makes me love." "Love? And whom?" "You, my lady dear." "I?" "Yes, truly." "Really? And how is that?" "To such an extent that my heart will not stir from you, nor is it elsewhere to be found; to such an extent that I cannot think of anything else, and I surrender myself altogether to you, whom I love more than I love myself, and for whom, if you will, I am equally ready to die or live." "And would you dare to undertake the defence of my spring for love of me?" "Yes, my lady, against the world." "Then you may know that our peace is made."

Thus they are quickly reconciled. And the lady, having previously consulted her lords, says: "We shall proceed from here to the hall where my men are assembled, who, in view of the evident need, have advised and counselled me to take a husband at their request. And I shall do so, in view of the urgent need: here and now I give myself to you; for I should not refuse to accept as lord, such a good knight and a king's son."

Now the damsel has brought about exactly what she had desired. And my lord Yvain's mastery is more complete than could be told or described; for the lady leads him away to the hall, which was full of her knights and men-at-arms. And my lord Yvain was so handsome that they all marvelled to look at him, and all, rising to their feet, salute and bow to my lord Yvain, guessing well as they did so: "This is he whom my lady will select. Cursed be he who opposes him! For he seems a wonderfully fine man. Surely, the empress of Rome would be well married with such a man. Would now that he had given his word to her, and she to him, with clasped hand, and that the wedding might take place to-day or tomorrow." Thus they spoke among themselves. At the end of the hall there was a seat, and there in the sight of all the lady took her place. And my lord Yvain made as if he intended to seat himself at her feet; but she raised him up, and ordered the seneschal to speak aloud, so that his speech might be heard by all. Then the seneschal began, being neither stubborn nor slow of speech: "My lords," he said, "we are confronted by war. Every day the King is preparing with all the haste he can command to come to ravage our lands. Before a fortnight shall have passed, all will have been laid waste, unless some valiant defender shall appear. When my lady married first, not quite seven years ago, she did it on your advice. Now her husband is dead, and she is grieved. Six feet of earth is all he has, who formerly owned all this land, and who was indeed its ornament. It is a pity he lived so short a while. A woman cannot bear a shield, nor does she know how to fight with lance. It would exalt and dignify her again if she should marry some worthy lord. Never was there greater need than now; do all of you recommend that she take a spouse, before the custom shall lapse which has been observed in this town for more than the past sixty years." At this, all at once proclaim that it seems to them the right thing to do, and they all throw themselves at her feet. They strengthen her desire by their consent; yet she hesitates to assert her wishes until, as if against her will, she finally speaks to the same intent as she would have done, indeed, if every one had opposed her wish: "My lords, since it is your wish, this knight who is seated beside me has wooed me and ardently sought my hand. He wishes to engage himself in the defence of my rights and in my service, for which I thank him heartily, as you do also. It is true I have never known him in person, but I have often heard his name. Know that he is no less a man than the son of King Urien. Beside his illustrious lineage, he is so brave, courteous, and wise that no one has cause to disparage him. You have all already heard, I suppose, of my lord Yvain, and it is he who seeks my hand. When the marriage is consummated, I shall have a more noble lord than I deserve." They all say: "If you are prudent, this very day shall not go by without the marriage being solemnised. For it is folly to postpone for a single hour an advantageous act." They beseech her so insistently that she consents to what she would have done in any case. For Love bids her do that for which she asks counsel and advice; but there is more honour for him in being accepted with the approval of her men. To her their prayers are not unwelcome; rather do they stir and incite her heart to have its way. The horse, already under speed, goes faster yet when it is spurred. In the presence of all her lords, the lady gives herself to my lord Yvain. From the hand of her chaplain he received the lady, Laudine de Landuc, daughter of Duke Laudunet, of whom they sing a lay. That very day without delay he married her, and the wedding was celebrated. There were plenty of mitres and croziers there, for the lady had summoned her bishops and abbots. Great was the joy and rejoicing, there were many people, and much wealth was displayed--more than I could tell you of, were I to devote much thought to it. It is better to keep silent than to be inadequate. So my lord Yvain is master now, and the dead man is quite forgot. He who killed him is now married to his wife, and they enjoy the marriage rights. The people love and esteem their living lord more than they ever did the dead. They served him well at his marriage-feast, until the eve before the day when the King came to visit the marvellous spring and its stone, bringing with him upon this expedition his companions and all those of his household; not one was left behind. And my lord Kay remarked: "Ah, what now has become of Yvain, who after his dinner made the boast that he would avenge his cousin's shame? Evidently he spoke in his cups. I believe that he has run away. He would not dare to come back for anything. He was very presumptuous to make such a boast. He is a bold man who dares to boast of what no one would praise him for, and who has no proof of his great feats except the words of some false flatterer. There is a great difference between a coward and a hero; for the coward seated beside the fire talks loudly about himself, holding all the rest as fools, and thinking that no one knows his real character. A hero would be distressed at hearing his prowess related by some one else. And yet I maintain that the coward is not wrong to praise and vaunt himself, for he will find no one else to lie for him. If he does not boast of his deeds, who will? All pass over him in silence, even the heralds, who proclaim the brave, but discard the cowards." When my lord Kay had spoken thus, my lord Gawain made this reply: "My lord Kay, have some mercy now! Since my lord Yvain is not here, you do not know what business occupies him. Indeed, he never so debased himself as to speak any ill of you compared with the gracious things he has said." "Sire," says Kay, "I'll hold my peace. I'll not say another word to-day, since I see you are offended by my speech." Then the King, in order to see the rain, poured a whole basin full of water upon the stone beneath the pine, and at once the rain began to pour. It was not long before my lord Yvain without delay entered the forest fully armed, tiding faster than a gallop on a large, sleek steed, strong, intrepid, and fleet of foot. And it was my lord Kay's desire to request the first encounter. For, whatever the outcome might be, he always wished to begin the fight and joust the first, or else he would be much incensed. Before all the rest, he requested the King to allow him to do battle first. The King says: "Kay, since it is your wish, and since you are the first to make the request, the favour ought not to be denied." Kay thanks him first, then mounts his steed. If now my lord Yvain can inflict a mild disgrace upon him, he will be very glad to do so; for he recognises him by his arms. Each grasping his shield by the straps, they rush together. Spurring their steeds, they lower the lances, which they hold tightly gripped. Then they thrust them forward a little, so that they grasped them by the leather-wrapped handles, and so that when they came together they were able to deal such cruel blows that both lances broke in splinters clear to the handle of the shaft. My lord Yvain gave him such a mighty blow that Kay took a summersault from out of his saddle and struck with his helmet on the ground. My lord Yvain has no desire to inflict upon him further harm, but simply dismounts and takes his horse. This pleased them all, and many said: "Ah, ah, see how you prostrate lie, who but now held others up to scorn! And yet it is only right to pardon you this time; for it never happened to you before." Thereupon my lord Yvain approached the King, leading the horse in his hand by the bridle, and wishing to make it over to him. "Sire," says he, "now take this steed, for I should do wrong to keep back anything of yours." "And who are you?" the King replies; "I should never know you, unless I heard your name, or saw you without your arms." Then my lord told him who he was, and Kay was overcome with shame, mortified, humbled, and discomfited, for having said that he had run away. But the others were greatly pleased, and made much of the honour he had won. Even the King was greatly gratified, and my lord Gawain a hundred times more than any one else. For he loved his company more than that of any other knight he knew. And the King requested him urgently to tell him, if it be his will, how he had fared; for he was very curious to learn all about his adventure; so the King begs him to tell the truth. And he soon told him all about the service and kindness of the damsel, not passing over a single word, not forgetting to mention anything. And after this he invited the King and all his knights to come to lodge with him, saying they would be doing him great honour in accepting his hospitality. And the King said that for an entire week he would gladly do him the honour and pleasure, and would bear him

127

company. And when my lord Yvain had thanked him, they tarry no longer there, but mount and take the most direct road to the town. My lord Yvain sends in advance of the company a squire beating a crane-falcon, in order that they might not take the lady by surprise, and that her people might decorate the streets against the arrival of the King. When the lady heard the news of the King's visit she was greatly pleased; nor was there any one who, upon hearing the news, was not happy and elated. And the lady summons them all and requests them to go to meet him, to which they make no objection or remonstrance, all being anxious to do her will.

Mounted on great Spanish steeds, they all go to meet the King of Britain, saluting King Arthur first with great courtesy and then all his company. "Welcome," they say, "to this company, so full of honourable men! Blessed be he who brings them hither and presents us with such fair guests!" At the King's arrival the town resounds with the joyous welcome which they give. Silken stuffs are taken out and hung aloft as decorations, and they spread tapestries to walk upon and drape the streets with them, while they wait for the King's approach. And they make still another preparation, in covering the streets with awnings against the hot rays of the sun. Bells, horns, and trumpets cause the town to ring so that God's thunder could not have been heard. The maidens dance before him, flutes and pipes are played, kettle-drums, drums, and cymbals are beaten. On their part the nimble youths leap, and all strive to show their delight. With such evidence of their joy, they welcome the King fittingly. And the Lady came forth, dressed in imperial garb a robe of fresh ermine-- and upon her head she wore a diadem all ornamented with rubies. No cloud was there upon her face, but it was so gay and full of joy that she was more beautiful, I think, than any goddess. Around her the crowd pressed close, as they cried with one accord: "Welcome to the King of kings and lord of lords!" The King could not reply to all before he saw the lady coming toward him to hold his stirrup. However, he would not wait for this, but hastened to dismount himself as soon as he caught sight of her. Then she salutes him with these words: "Welcome a hundred thousand times to the King, my lord, and blessed be his nephew, my lord Gawain!" The King replies: "I wish all happiness and good luck to your fair body and your face, lovely creature!" Then clasping her around the waist, the King embraced her gaily and heartily as she did him, throwing her arms about him. I will say no more of how gladly she welcomed them, but no one ever heard of any people who were so honourably received and served. I might tell you much of the joy should I not be wasting words, but I wish to make brief mention of an acquaintance which was made in private between the moon and the sun. Do you know of whom I mean to speak? He who was lord of the knights, and who was renowned above them all, ought surely to be called the sun. I refer, of course, to my lord Gawain, for chivalry is enhanced by him just as when the morning sun sheds its rays abroad and lights all places where it shines. And I call her the moon, who cannot be otherwise because of her sense and courtesy. However, I call her so not only because of her good repute, but because her name is, in fact, Lunete.

The damsel's name was Lunete, and she was a charming brunette, prudent, clever, and polite. As her acquaintance grows with my lord Gawain, he values her highly and gives her his love as to his sweetheart, because she had saved from death his companion and friend; he places himself freely at her service. On her part she describes and relates to him with what difficulty she persuaded her mistress to take my lord Yvain as her husband, and how she protected him from the hands of those who were seeking him; how he was in their midst but they did not see him. My lord Gawain laughed aloud at this story of hers, and then he said: "Mademoiselle, when you need me and when you don't, such as I am, I place myself at your disposal. Never throw me off for some one else when you think you can improve your lot. I am yours, and do you be from now on my demoiselle!" "I thank you kindly, sire," she said. While the acquaintance of these two was ripening thus, the others, too, were engaged in flirting. For there were perhaps ninety ladies there, each of whom was fair and charming, noble and polite, virtuous and prudent, and a lady of exalted birth, so the men could agreeably employ themselves in caressing and kissing them, and in talking to them and in gazing at them while they were seated by their side; that much satisfaction they had at least. My lord Yvain is in high feather because the King is lodged with him. And the lady bestows such attention upon them all, as individuals and collectively, that some foolish person might suppose that the charming attentions which she showed them were dictated by love. But such persons may properly be rated as fools for thinking that a lady is in love with them just because she is courteous and speaks to some unfortunate fellow, and makes him happy and caresses him. A fool is made happy by fair words, and is very easily taken in. That entire week they spent in gaiety; forest and stream offered plenty of sport for any one who desired it. And whoever wished to see the land which had come into the hands of my lord Yvain with the lady whom he had married, could go to enjoy himself at one of the castles which stood within a radius of two, three, or four leagues. When the King had stayed as long as he chose, he made ready to depart. But during the week they had all begged urgently, and with all the insistence at their command, that they might take away my lord Yvain with them. "What? Will you be one of those." said my lord Gawain to him, "who degenerate after marriage?  Cursed be he by Saint Mary who marries and then degenerates! Whoever has a fair lady as his mistress or his wife should be the better for it, and it is not right that her affection should be bestowed on him after his worth and reputation are gone. Surely you, too, would have cause to regret her love if you grew soft, for a woman quickly withdraws her love, and rightly so, and despises him who degenerates in any way when he has become lord of the realm. Now ought your fame to be increased! Slip off the bridle and halter and come to the tournament with me, that no one may say that you are jealous. Now you must no longer hesitate to frequent the lists, to share in the onslaught, and to contend with force, whatever effort it may cost! Inaction produces indifference. But, really, you must come, for I shall be in your company. Have a care that our comradeship shall not fail through any fault of yours, fair companion; for my part, you may count on me. It is strange how a man sets store by the life of ease which has no end. Pleasures grow sweeter through postponement; and a little pleasure, when delayed, is much sweeter to the taste than great pleasure enjoyed at once. The sweets of a love which develops late are like a fire in a green bush; for the longer one delays in lighting it the greater will be the heat it yields, and the longer will its force endure. One may easily fall into habits which it is very difficult to shake off, for when one desires to do so, he finds he has lost the power. Don't misunderstand my words, my friend: if I had such a fair mistress as you have, I call God and His saints to witness, I should leave her most reluctantly; indeed, I should doubtless be infatuated. But a man may give another counsel, which he would not take himself, just as the preachers, who are deceitful rascals, and preach and proclaim the right but who do not follow it themselves."

My lord Gawain spoke at such length and so urgently that he promised him that he would go; but he said that he must consult his lady and ask for her consent. Whether it be a foolish or a prudent thing to do, he will not fail to ask her leave to return to Britain. Then he took counsel with his wife, who had no inkling of the permission he desired, as he addressed her with these words: "My beloved lady, my heart and soul, my treasure, joy, and happiness, grant me now a favour which will redound to your honour and to mine." The lady at once gives her consent, not knowing what his desire is, and says: "Fair lord, you may command me your pleasure, whatever it be." Then my lord Yvain at once asks her for permission to escort the King and to attend at tournaments, that no one may reproach his indolence. And she replies: "I grant you leave until a certain date; but be sure that my love will change to hate if you stay beyond the term that I shall fix. Remember that I shall keep my word; if you break your word I will keep mine. If you wish to possess my love, and if you have any regard for me, remember to come back again at the latest a year from the present date a week after St. John's day; for to-day is the eighth day since that feast. You will be checkmated of my love if you are not restored to me on that day."

My lord Yvain weeps and sighs so bitterly that he can hardly find words to say: "My lady, this date is indeed a long way off. If I could be a dove, whenever the fancy came to me, I should often rejoin you here. And I pray God that in His pleasure He may not detain me so long away. But sometimes a man intends speedily to return who knows not what the future has in store for him. And I know not what will be my fate--perhaps some urgency of sickness or imprisonment may keep me back: you are unjust in not making an exception at least of actual hindrance." "My lord," says she, "I will make that exception. And yet I dare to promise you that, if God deliver you from death, no hindrance will stand in your way so long as you remember me. So put on your finger now this ring of mine, which I lend to you. And I will tell you all about the stone: no true and loyal lover can be imprisoned or lose any blood, nor can any harm befall him, provided he carry it and hold it dear, and keep his sweetheart in mind. You will become as hard as iron, and it will serve you as shield and hauberk. I have never before been willing to lend or entrust it to any knight, but to you I give it because of my affection for you." Now my lord Yvain is free to go, but he weeps bitterly on taking leave. The King, however, would not tarry longer for anything that might be said: rather was he anxious to have the palfreys brought all equipped and bridled. They acceded at once to his desire, bringing the palfreys forth, so that it remained only to mount. I do not know whether I ought to tell you how my lord Yvain took his leave, and of the kisses bestowed on him, mingled with tears and steeped in sweetness. And what shall I tell you about the King how the lady escorts him, accompanied by her damsels and seneschal? All this would require too much time. When he sees the lady's tears, the King implores her to come no farther, but to return to her abode. He begged her with such urgency that, heavy at heart, she turned about followed by her company.

My lord Yvain is so distressed to leave his lady that his heart remains behind. The King may take his body off, but he cannot lead his heart away. She who stays behind clings so tightly to his heart that the King has not the power to take it away with him. When the body is left without the heart it cannot possibly live on. For such a marvel was never seen as the body alive without the heart. Yet this marvel now came about: for he kept his body without the heart, which was wont to be enclosed in it, but which would not follow the body now. The heart has a good abiding-place, while the body, hoping for a safe return to its heart, in strange fashion takes a new heart of hope, which is so often deceitful and treacherous. He will never know in advance, I think, the hour when this hope will play him false, for if he overstays by single day the term which he has agreed upon, it will be hard for him to gain again his lady's pardon and goodwill. Yet I think he will overstay the term, for my lord Gawain will not allow him to part from him, as together they go to joust wherever tournaments are held. And as the year passes by my lord Yvain had such success that my lord Gawain strove to honour him, and caused him to delay so long that all the first year slipped by, and it came to the middle of August of the ensuing year, when the King held court at Chester, whither they had returned the day before from a tournament where my lord Yvain had been and where he had won the glory and the story tells how the two companions were unwilling to lodge in the town, but had their tents set up outside the city, and held court there. For they never went to the royal court, but the King came rather to join in theirs, for they had the best knights, and the greatest number, in their company. Now King Arthur was seated in their midst, when Yvain suddenly had a thought which surprised him more than any that had occurred to him since he had taken leave of his lady, for he realised that he had broken his word, and that the limit of his leave was already exceeded. He could hardly keep back his tears, but he succeeded in doing so from shame. He was still deep in thought when he saw a damsel approaching rapidly upon a black palfrey with white forefeet. As she got down before the tent no one helped her to dismount, and no one went to take her horse. As soon as she made out the King, she let her mantle fall, and thus displayed she entered the tent and came before the King, announcing that her mistress sent greetings to the King, and to my lord Gawain and all the other knights, except Yvain, that disloyal traitor, liar, hypocrite, who had deserted her deceitfully. "She has seen clearly the treachery of him who pretended he was a faithful lover while he was a false and treacherous thief. This thief has traduced my lady, who was all unprepared for any evil, and to whom it never occurred that he would steal her heart away. Those who love truly do not steal hearts away; there are, however, some men, by whom these former are called thieves, who themselves go about deceitfully making love, but in whom there is no real knowledge of the matter. The lover takes his lady's heart, of course, but he does not run away with it; rather does he treasure it against those thieves who, in the guise of honourable men, would steal it from him. But those are deceitful and treacherous thieves who vie with one another in stealing hearts for which they care nothing. The true lover, wherever he may go, holds the heart dear and brings it back again. But Yvain has caused my lady's death, for she supposed that he would guard her heart for her, and would bring it back again before the year elapsed. Yvain, thou wast of short memory when thou couldst not remember to return to thy mistress within a year. She gave thee thy liberty until St. John's day, and thou settest so little store by her that never since has a thought of her crossed thy mind. My lady had marked every day in her chamber, as the seasons passed: for when one is in love, one is ill at ease and cannot get any restful sleep, but all night long must needs count and reckon up the days as they come and go. Dost thou know how lovers spend their time? They keep count of the time and the season. Her complaint is not presented prematurely or without cause, and I am not accusing him in any way, but I simply say that we have been betrayed by him who married my lady. Yvain, my mistress has no further care for thee, but sends thee word by me never to come back to her, and no longer to keep her ring. She bids thee send it back to her by me, whom thou seest present here. Surrender it now, as thou art bound to do."

Senseless and deprived of speech, Yvain is unable to reply. And the damsel steps forth and takes the ring from his finger, commending to God the King and all the others except him, whom she leaves in deep distress. And his sorrow grows on him: he feels oppressed by what he hears, and is tormented by what he sees. He would rather be banished alone in some wild land, where no one would know where to seek for him, and where no man or woman would know of his whereabouts any more than if he were in some deep abyss. He hates nothing so much as he hates himself, nor does he know to whom to go for comfort in the death he has brought upon himself. But he would rather go insane than not take vengeance upon himself, deprived, as he is, of joy through his own fault. He rises from his place among the knights, fearing he will lose his mind if he stays longer in their midst. On their part, they pay no heed to him, but let him take his departure alone. They know well enough that he cares nothing for their talk or their society. And he goes away until he is far from the tents and pavilions. Then such a storm broke loose in his brain that he loses his senses; he tears his flesh and, stripping off his clothes, he flees across the meadows and fields, leaving his men quite at a loss, and wondering what has become of him. They go in search of him through all the country around--in the lodgings of the knights, by the hedgerows, and in the gardens--but they seek him where he is not to be found. Still fleeing, he rapidly pursued his way until he met close by a park a lad who had in his hand a bow and five barbed arrows, which were very sharp and broad. He had sense enough to go and take the bow and arrows which he held. However, he had no recollection of anything that he had done. He lies in wait for the beasts in the woods, killing them, and then eating the venison raw. Thus he dwelt in the forest like a madman or a savage, until he came upon a little, low-lying house belonging to a hermit, who was at work clearing his ground. When he saw him coming with nothing on, he could easily perceive that he was not in his right mind; and such was the case, as the hermit very well knew. So, in fear, he shut himself up in his little house, and taking some bread and fresh water, he charitably set it outside the house on a narrow window-ledge. And thither the other comes, hungry for the bread which he takes and eats. I do not believe that he ever before had tasted such hard and bitter bread. The measure of barley kneaded with the straw, of which the bread, sourer than yeast, was made, had not cost more than five sous; and the bread was musty and as dry as bark. But hunger torments and whets his appetite, so that the bread tasted to him like sauce. For hunger is itself a well mixed and concocted sauce for any food. My lord Yvain soon ate the hermit's bread, which tasted good to him, and drank the cool water from the jar. When he had eaten, he betook himself again to the woods in search of stags and does. And when he sees him going away, the good man beneath his roof prays God to defend him and guard him lest he ever pass that way again. But there is no creature, with howsoever little sense, that will not gladly return to a place where he is kindly treated. So, not a day passed while he was in this mad fit that he did not bring to his door some wild game. Such was the life he led; and the good man took it upon himself to remove the skin and set a good quantity of the venison to cook; and the bread and the water in the jug was always standing on the window-ledge for the madman to make a meal. Thus he had something to eat and drink: venison without salt or pepper, and good cool water from the spring. And the good man exerted himself to sell the hide and buy bread made of barley, or oats, or of some other grain; so, after that, Yvain had a plentiful supply of bread and venison, which sufficed him for a long time, until one day he was found asleep in the forest by two damsels and their mistress, in whose service they were. When they saw the naked man, one of the three ran and dismounted and examined him closely, before she saw anything about him which would serve to identify him. If he had only been richly attired, as he had been many a time, and if she could have seen him then she would have known him quickly enough. But she was slow to recognise him, and continued to look at him until at last she noticed a scar which he had on his face, and she recollected that my lord Yvain's face was scarred in this same way; she was sure of it, for she had often seen it. Because of the scar she saw that it was he beyond any doubt; but she marvelled greatly how it came about that she found him thus poor and stripped. Often she crosses herself in amazement, but she does not touch him or wake him up; rather does she mount her horse again, and going back to the others, tells them tearfully of her adventure. I do not know if I ought to delay to tell you of the grief she showed; but thus she spoke weeping to her mistress: "My lady, I have found Yvain, who has proved himself to be the best knight in the world, and the most virtuous. I cannot imagine what sin has reduced the gentleman to such a plight. I think he must have had some misfortune, which causes him thus to demean himself, for one may lose his wits through grief. And any one can see that he is not in his right mind, for it would surely never be like him to conduct himself thus indecently unless he had lost his mind. Would that God had restored to him the best sense he ever had, and would that he might then consent to render assistance to your cause! For Count Alier, who is at war with you, has made upon you a fierce attack. I should see the strife between you two quickly settled in your favour if God favoured your fortunes so that he should return to his senses and undertake to aid you in this stress." To this the lady made reply: "Take care now! For surely, if he does not escape, with God's help I think we can clear his head of all the madness and insanity. But we must be on our way at once! For I recall a certain ointment with which Morgan the Wise presented me, saying there was no delirium of the head which it would not cure." Thereupon, they go off at once toward the town, which was hard by, for it was not any more than half a league of the kind they have in that country; and, as compared with ours, two of their leagues make one and four make two. And he remains sleeping all alone, while the lady goes to fetch the ointment. The lady opens a case of hers, and, taking out a box, gives it to the damsel, and charges her not to be too prodigal in its use: she should rub only his temples with it, for there is no use of applying it elsewhere; she should anoint only his temples with it, and the remainder she should carefully keep, for there is nothing the matter with him except in his brain. She sends him also a robe of spotted fur, a coat, and a mantle of scarlet silk. The damsel takes them, and leads in her right hand an excellent palfrey. And she added to these, of her own store, a shirt, some soft hose, and some new drawers of proper cut. With all these things she quickly set out, and found him still asleep where she had left him. After putting her horse in an enclosure where she tied him fast, she came with the clothes and the ointment to the place where he was asleep. Then she made so bold as to approach the madman, so that she could touch and handle him: then taking the ointment she rubbed him with it until none remained in the box, being so solicitous for his recovery that she proceeded to anoint him all over with it; and she used it so freely that she heeded not the warning of her mistress, nor indeed did she remember it. She put more on than was needed, but in her opinion it was well employed. She rubbed his temples and forehead, and his whole body down to the ankles. She rubbed his temples and his whole body so much there in the hot sunshine that the madness and the depressing gloom passed completely out of his brain. But she was foolish to anoint his body, for of that there was no need. If she had had five measures of it she would doubtless have done the same thing. She carries off the box, and takes hidden refuge by her horse. But she leaves the robe behind, wishing that, if God calls him back to life, he may see it all laid out, and may take it and put it on. She posts herself behind an oak tree until he had slept enough, and was cured and quite restored, having regained his wits and memory. Then he sees that he is as naked as ivory, and feels much ashamed; but he would have been yet more ashamed had he known what had happened. As it is, he knows nothing but that he is naked. He sees the new robe lying before him, and marvels greatly how and by what adventure it had come there. But he is ashamed and concerned, because of his nakedness, and says that he is dead and utterly undone if any one has come upon him there and recognised him. Meanwhile, he clothes himself and looks out into the forest to see if any one was approaching. He tries to stand up and support himself, but cannot summon the strength to walk away, for his sickness has so affected him that he can scarcely stand upon his feet. Thereupon, the damsel resolves to wait no longer, but, mounting, she passed close by him, as if unaware of his presence. Quite indifferent as to whence might come the help, which he needed so much to lead him away to some lodging-place, where he might recruit his strength, he calls out to her with all his might. And the damsel, for her part, looks about her as if not knowing what the trouble is. Confused, she goes hither and thither, not wishing to go straight up to him. Then he begins to call again: "Damsel, come this way, here!" And the damsel guided toward him her soft-stepping palfrey. By this ruse she made him think that she knew nothing of him and had never seen him before; in so doing she was wise and courteous. When she had come before him, she said: "Sir knight, what do you desire that you call me so insistently?" "Ah," said he, "prudent damsel, I have found myself in this wood by some mishap--I know not what. For God's sake and your belief in Him, I pray you to lend me, taking my word as pledge, or else to give me outright, that palfrey you are leading in your hand." "Gladly, sire: but you must accompany me whither I am going." "Which way?" says he. "To a town that stands near by, beyond the forest." "Tell me, damsel, if you stand in need of me." "Yes," she says, "I do; but I think you are not very well. For the next two weeks at least you ought to rest. Take this horse, which I hold in my right hand, and we shall go to our lodging-place." And he, who had no other desire, takes it and mounts, and they proceed until they come to a bridge over a swift and turbulent stream. And the damsel throws into the water the empty box she is carrying, thinking to excuse herself to her mistress for her ointment by saying that she was so unlucky as to let the box fall into the water for, when her palfrey stumbled under her, the box slipped from her gasp, and she came near falling in too, which would have been still worse luck. It is her intention to invent this story when she comes into her mistress' presence. Together they held their way until they came to the town, where the lady detained my lord Yvain and asked her damsel in private for her box and ointment: and the damsel repeated to her the lie as she had invented it, not daring to tell her the truth. Then the lady was greatly enraged, and said: "This is certainly a very serious loss, and I am sure and certain that the box will never be found again. But since it has happened so, there is nothing more to be done about it. One often desires a blessing which turns out to be a curse; thus I, who looked for a blessing and joy from this knight, have lost the dearest and most precious of my possessions. However, I beg you to serve him in all respects." "Ah, lady, how wisely now you speak! For it would be too bad to convert one misfortune into two."

Then they say no more about the box, but minister in every way they can to the comfort of my lord Yvain, bathing him and washing his hair, having him shaved and clipped, for one could have taken up a fist full of hair upon his face. His every want is satisfied: if he asks for arms, they are furnished him: if he wants a horse, they provide him with one that is large and handsome, strong and spirited. He stayed there until, upon a Tuesday, Count Alier came to the town with his men and knights, who started fires and took plunder. Those in the town at once rose up and equipped themselves with arms. Some armed and some unarmed, they issued forth to meet the plunderers, who did not deign to retreat before them, but awaited them in a narrow pass. My lord Yvain struck at the crowd; he had had so long a rest that his strength was quite restored, and he struck a knight upon his shield with such force that he sent down in a heap, I think, the knight together with his horse. The knight never rose again, for his backbone was broken and his heart burst within his breast. My lord Yvain drew back a little to recover. Then protecting himself completely with his shield, he spurred forward to clear the pass. One could not have counted up to four before one would have seen him cast down speedily four knights. Whereupon, those who were with him waxed more brave, for many a man of poor and timid heart, at the sight of some brave man who attacks a dangerous task before his eyes, will be overwhelmed by confusion and shame, which will drive out the poor heart in his body and give him another like to a hero's for courage. So these men grew brave and each stood his ground in the fight and attack. And the lady was up in the tower, whence she saw the fighting and the rush to win and gain possession of the pass, and she saw lying upon the ground many who were wounded and many killed, both of her own party and of the enemy, but more of the enemy than of her own. For my courteous, bold, and excellent lord Yvain made them yield just as a falcon does the teal. And the men and women who had remained within the town declared as they watched the strife: "Ah, what a valiant knight! How he makes his enemies yield, and how fierce is his attack! He was about him as a lion among the fallow deer, when he is impelled by need and hunger. Then, too, all our other knights are more brave and daring because of him, for, were it not for him alone, not a lance would have been splintered nor a sword drawn to strike. When such an excellent man is found he ought to be loved and dearly prized. See now how he proves himself, see how he maintains his place, see how he stains with blood his lance and bare sword, see how he presses the enemy and follows them up, how he comes boldly to attack them, then gives away and turns about; but he spends little time in giving away, and soon returns to the attack. See him in the fray again, how lightly he esteems his shield, which he allows to be cut in pieces mercilessly. Just see how keen he is to avenge the blows which are dealt at him. For, if some one should use all the forest of Argone to make lances for him, I guess he would have none left by night. For he breaks all the lances that they place in his socket, and calls for more. And see how he wields the sword when he draws it! Roland never wrought such havoc with Durendal against the Turks at Ronceval or in Spain! If he had in his company some good companions like himself, the traitor, whose attack we are suffering, would retreat today discomfited, or would stand his ground only to find defeat." Then they say that the woman would be blessed who should be loved by one who is so powerful in arms, and who above all others may be recognised as a taper among candles, as a moon among the stars, and as the sun above the moon. He so won the hearts of all that the prowess which they see in him made them wish that he had taken their lady to wife, and that he were master of the land.

Thus men and women alike praised him, and in doing so they but told the truth. For his attack on his adversaries was such that they vie with one another in flight. But he presses hard upon their heels, and all his companions follow him, for by his side they feel as safe as if they were enclosed in a high and thick stone wall. The pursuit continues until those who flee become exhausted, and the pursuers slash at them and disembowel their steeds.

The living roll over upon the dead as they wound and kill each other. They work dreadful destruction upon each other; and meanwhile the Count flees with my lord Yvain after him, until he comes up with him at the foot of a steep ascent, near the entrance of a strong place which belonged to the Count. There the Count was stopped, with no one near to lend him aid; and without any excessive parley my lord Yvain received his surrender. For as soon as he held him in his hands, and they were left just man to man, there was no further possibility of escape, or of yielding, or of self-defence; so the Count pledged his word to go to surrender to the lady of Noroison as her prisoner, and to make such peace as she might dictate. And when he had accepted his word he made him disarm his head and remove the shield from about his neck, and the Count surrendered to him his sword. Thus he won the honour of leading off the Count as his prisoner, and of giving him over to his enemies, who make no secret of their joy. But the news was carried to the town before they themselves arrived. While all come forth to meet them, the lady herself leads the way. My lord Yvain holds his prisoner by the hand, and presents him to her. The Count gladly acceded to her wishes and demands, and secured her by his word, oath, and pledges. Giving her pledges, he swears to her that he will always live on peaceful terms with her, and will make good to her all the loss which she can prove, and will build up again the houses which he had destroyed. When these things were agreed upon in accordance with the lady's wish, my lord Yvain asked leave to depart. But she would not have granted him this permission had he been willing to take her as his mistress, or to marry her. But he would not allow himself to be followed or escorted a single step, but rather departed hastily: in this case entreaty was of no avail. So he started out to retrace his path, leaving the lady much chagrined, whose joy he had caused a while before. When he will not tarry longer she is the more distressed and ill at ease in proportion to the happiness he had brought to her, for she would have wished to honour him, and would have made him, with his consent, lord of all her possessions, or else she would have paid him for his services whatever sum he might have named. But he would not heed any word of man or woman. Despite their grief he left the knights and the lady who vainly tried to detain him longer.

Pensively my lord Yvain proceeded through a deep wood, until he heard among the trees a very loud and dismal cry, and he turned in the direction whence it seemed to come. And when he had arrived upon the spot he saw in a cleared space a lion, and a serpent which held him by the tail, burning his hind-quarters with flames of fire. My lord Yvain did not gape at this strange spectacle, but took counsel with himself as to which of the two he should aid. Then he says that he will succour the lion, for a treacherous and venomous creature deserves to be harmed. Now the serpent is poisonous, and fire bursts forth from its mouth--so full of wickedness is the creature. So my lord Yvain decides that he will kill the serpent first. Drawing his sword he steps forward, holding the shield before his face in order not to be harmed by the flame emerging from the creature's throat, which was larger than a pot. If the lion attacks him next, he too shall have all the fight he wishes; but whatever may happen afterwards he makes up his mind to help him now. For pity urges him and makes request that he should bear succour and aid to the gentle and noble beast. With his sword, which cuts so clean, he attacks the wicked serpent, first cleaving him through to the earth and cutting him in two, then continuing his blows until he reduces him to tiny bits. But he had to cut off a piece of the lion's tail to get at the serpent's head, which held the lion by the tail. He cut off only so much as was necessary and unavoidable. When he had set the lion free, he supposed that he would have to fight with him, and that the lion would come at him; but the lion was not minded so. Just hear now what the lion did! He acted nobly and as one well-bred; for he began to make it evident that he yielded himself to him, by standing upon his two hind-feet and bowing his face to the earth, with his fore-feet joined and stretched out toward him. Then he fell on his knees again, and all his face was wet with the tears of humility. My lord Yvain knows for a truth that the lion is thanking him and doing him homage because of the serpent which he had killed, thereby delivering him from death. He was greatly pleased by this episode. He cleaned his sword of the serpent's poison and filth; then he replaced it in its scabbard, and resumed his way. And the lion walks close by his side, unwilling henceforth to part from him: he will always in future accompany him, eager to serve and protect him. He goes ahead until he scents in the wind upon his way some wild beasts feeding; then hunger and his nature prompt him to seek his prey and to secure his sustenance. It is his nature so to do. He started ahead a little on the trail, thus showing his master that he had come upon and detected the odour and scent of some wild game. Then he looks at him and halts, wishing to serve his every wish, and unwilling to proceed against his will. Yvain understands by his attitude that he is showing that he awaits his pleasure. He perceives this and understands that if he holds back he will hold back too, and that if he follows him he will seize the game which he has scented. Then he incites and cries to him, as he would do to hunting-dogs. At once the lion directed his nose to the scent which he had detected, and by which he was not deceived, for he had not gone a bow-shot when he saw in a valley a deer grazing all alone. This deer he will seize, if he has his way. And so he did, at the first spring, and then drank its blood still warm. When he had killed it he laid it upon his back and carried it back to his master, who thereupon conceived a greater affection for him, and chose him as a companion for all his life, because of the great devotion he found in him. It was near nightfall now, and it seemed good to him to spend the night there, and strip from the deer as much as he cared to eat. Beginning to carve it he splits the skin along the rib, and taking a steak from the loin he strikes from a flint a spark, which he catches in some dry brush-wood; then he quickly puts his steak upon a roasting spit to cook before the fire, and roasts it until it is quite cooked through. But there was no pleasure in the meal, for there was no bread, or wine, or salt, or cloth, or knife, or anything else. While he was eating, the lion lay at his feet; nor a movement did he make, but watched him steadily until he had eaten all that he could eat of the steak. What remained of the deer the lion devoured, even to the bones. And while all night his master laid his head upon his shield to gain such rest as that afforded, the lion showed such intelligence that he kept awake, and was careful to guard the horse as it fed upon the grass, which yielded some slight nourishment.

In the morning they go off together, and the same sort of existence, it seems, as they had led that night, they two continued to lead all the ensuing week, until chance brought them to the spring beneath the pine-tree. There my lord Yvain almost lost his wits a second time, as he approached the spring, with its stone and the chapel that stood close by. So great was his distress that a thousand times he sighed "alas!" and grieving fell in a swoon; and the point of his sharp sword, falling from its scabbard, pierced the meshes of his hauberk right in the neck beside the cheek. There is not a mesh that does not spread, and the sword cuts the flesh of his neck beneath the shining mail, so that it causes the blood to start. Then the lion thinks that he sees his master and companion dead. You never heard greater grief narrated or told about anything than he now began to show. He casts himself about, and scratches and cries, and has the wish to kill himself with the sword with which he thinks his master has killed himself. Taking the sword from him with his teeth he lays it on a fallen tree, and steadies it on a trunk behind, so that it will not slip or give way, when he hurls his breast against it, His intention was nearly accomplished when his master recovered from his swoon, and the lion restrained himself as he was blindly rushing upon death, like a wild boar heedless of where he wounds himself. Thus my lord Yvain lies in a swoon beside the stone, but, on recovering, he violently reproached himself for the year during which he had overstayed his leave, and for which he had incurred his lady's hate, and he said: "Why does this wretch not kill himself who has thus deprived himself of joy? Alas! why do I not take my life? How can I stay here and look upon what belongs to my lady? Why does the soul still tarry in my body? What is the soul doing in so miserable a frame? If it had already escaped away it would not be in such torment. It is fitting to hate and blame and despise myself, even as in fact I do. Whoever loses his bliss and contentment through fault or error of his own ought to hate himself mortally. He ought to hate and kill himself. And now, when no one is looking on, why do I thus spare myself? Why do I not take my life? Have I not seen this lion a prey to such grief on my behalf that he was on the point just now of thrusting my sword through his breast? And ought I to fear death who have changed happiness into grief? Joy is now a stranger to me. Joy? What joy is that? I shall say no more of that, for no one could speak of such a thing; and I have asked a foolish question. That was the greatest joy of all which was assured as my possession, but it endured for but a little while. Whoever loses such joy through his own misdeed is undeserving of happiness."

While he thus bemoaned his fate, a lorn damsel in sorry plight, who was in the chapel, saw him and heard his words through a crack in the wall. As soon as he was recovered from his swoon, she called to him: "God," said she, "who is that I hear? Who is it that thus complains?" And he replied: "And who are you?" "I am a wretched one," she said, "the most miserable thing alive." And he replied: "Be silent, foolish one! Thy grief is joy and thy sorrow is bliss compared with that in which I am cast down. In proportion as a man becomes more accustomed to happiness and joy, so is he more distracted and stunned than any other man by sorrow when it comes. A man of little strength can carry, through custom and habit, a weight which another man of greater strength could not carry for anything." "Upon my word," she said, "I know the truth of that remark; but that is no reason to believe that your misfortune is worse than mine. Indeed, I do not believe it at all, for it seems to me that you can go anywhere you choose to go, whereas I am imprisoned here, and such a fate is my portion that to-morrow I shall be seized and delivered to mortal judgment." "Ah, God!" said he, "and for what crime?" "Sir knight, may God never have mercy upon my soul, if I have merited such a fate! Nevertheless, I shall tell you truly, without deception, why I am here in prison: I am charged with treason, and I cannot find any one to defend me from being burned or hanged to-morrow." "In the first place," he replied, "I may say that my grief and woe are greater than yours, for you may yet be delivered by some one from the peril in which you are. Is that not true?" "Yes, but I know not yet by whom. There are only two men in the world who would dare on my behalf to face three men in battle." "What? In God's name, are there three of them?" "Yes, sire, upon my word. There are three who accuse me of treachery." "And who are they who are so devoted to you that either one of them would be bold enough to fight against three in your defence?" "I will answer your question truthfully: one of them is my lord Gawain, and the other is my lord Yvain, because of whom I shall to-morrow be handed over unjustly to the martyrdom of death." "Because of whom?" he asked, "what did you say?" "Sire, so help me God, because of the son of King Urien." "Now I understand your words, but you shall not die, without he dies too. I myself am that Yvain, because of whom you are in such distress. And you, I take it, are she who once guarded me safely in the hall, and saved my life and my body between the two portcullises, when I was troubled and distressed, and alarmed at being trapped. I should have been killed or seized, had it not been for your kind aid. Now tell me, my gentle friend, who are those who now accuse you of treachery, and have confined you in this lonely place?" "Sire, I shall not conceal it from you, since you desire me to tell you all. It is a fact that I was not slow in honestly aiding you. Upon my advice my lady received you, after heeding my opinion and my counsel. And by the Holy Paternoster, more for her welfare than for your own I thought I was doing it, and I think so still. So much now I confess to you: it was her honour and your desire that I sought to serve, so help me God! But when it became evident that you had overstayed the year when you should return to my mistress, then she became enraged at me, and thought that she had been deceived by putting trust in my advice. And when this was discovered by the seneschal--a rascally, underhanded, disloyal wretch, who was jealous of me because in many matters my lady trusted me more than she trusted him, he saw that he could now stir up great enmity between me and her. In full court and in the presence of all he accused me of having betrayed her in your favour. And I had no counsel or aid except my own; but I knew that I had never done or conceived any treacherous act toward my lady, so I cried out, as one beside herself, and without the advice of any one, that I would present in my own defence one knight who should fight against three. The fellow was not courteous enough to scorn to accept such odds, nor was I at liberty to retreat or withdraw for anything that might happen. So he took me at my word, and I was compelled to furnish bail that I would present within forty days a knight to do battle against three knights. Since then I have visited many courts; I was at King Arthur's court, but found no help from any there, nor did I find any one who could tell me any good news of you, for they knew nothing of your affairs." "Pray tell me. Where then was my good and gentle lord Gawain? No damsel in distress ever needed his aid without its being extended to her." "If I had found him at court, I could not have asked him for anything which would have been refused me; but a certain knight has carried off the Queen, so they told me; surely the King was mad to send her off in his company. I believe it was Kay who escorted her to meet the knight who has taken her away; and my lord Gawain in great distress has gone in search for her. He will never have any rest until he finds her. Now I have told you the whole truth of my adventure. Tomorrow I shall be put to a shameful death, and shall be burnt inevitably, a victim of your criminal neglect." And he replies: "May God forbid that you should be harmed because of me! So long as I live you shall not die! You may expect me tomorrow, prepared to the extent of my power to present my body in your cause, as it is proper that I should do. But have no concern to tell the people who I am! However the battle may turn out, take care that I be not recognised!" "Surely, sire, no pressure could make me reveal your name. I would sooner suffer death, since you will have it so. Yet, after all, I beg you not to return for my sake. I would not have you undertake a battle which will be so desperate. I thank you for your promised word that you would gladly undertake it, but consider yourself now released, for it is better that I should die alone than that I should see them rejoice over your death as well as mine; they would not spare my life after they had put you to death. So it is better for you to remain alive than that we both should meet death." "That is very ungrateful remark, my dear," says my lord Yvain; "I suppose that either you do not wish to be delivered from death, or else that you scorn the comfort I bring you with my aid. I will not discuss the matter more, for you have surely done so much for me that I cannot fail you in any need. I know that you are in great distress; but, if it be God's will, in whom I trust, they shall all three be discomfited. So no more upon that score: I am going off now to find some shelter in this wood, for there is no dwelling near at hand." "Sire," she says, "may God give you both good shelter and good night, and protect you as I desire from everything that might do you harm!" Then my lord Yvain departs, and the lion as usual after him. They journeyed until they came to a baron's fortified place, which was completely surrounded by a massive, strong, and high wall. The castle, being extraordinarily well protected, feared no assault of catapult or storming-machine; but outside the walls the ground was so completely cleared that not a single hut or dwelling remained standing. You will learn the cause of this a little later, when the time comes. My lord Yvain made his way directly toward the fortified place, and seven varlets came out who lowered the bridge and advanced to meet him. But they were terrified at sight of the lion, which they saw with him, and asked him kindly to leave the lion at the gate lest he should wound or kill them. And he replies: "Say no more of that! For I shall not enter without him. Either we shall both find shelter here or else I shall stay outside; he is as dear to me as I am myself. Yet you need have no fear of him! For I shall keep him so well in hand that you may be quite confident." They made answer: "Very well!" Then they entered the town, and passed on until they met knights and ladies and charming damsels coming down the street, who salute him and wait to remove his armour as they say: "Welcome to our midst, fair sire! And may God grant that you tarry here until you may leave with great honour and satisfaction!" High and low alike extend to him a glad welcome, and do all they can for him, as they joyfully escort him into the town. But after they had expressed their gladness they are overwhelmed by grief, which makes them quickly forget their joy, as they begin to lament and weep and beat themselves. Thus, for a long space of time, they cease not to rejoice or make lament: it is to honour their guest that they rejoice, but their heart is not in what they do, for they are greatly worried over an event which they expect to take place on the following day, and they feel very sure and certain that it will come to pass before midday. My lord Yvain was so surprised that they so often changed their mood, and mingled grief with their happiness, that he addressed the lord of the place on the subject. "For God's sake," he said, "fair gentle sir, will you kindly inform me why you have thus honoured me, and shown at once such joy and such heaviness?" "Yes, if you desire to know, but it would be better for you to desire ignorance and silence. I will never tell you willingly anything to cause you grief. Allow us to continue to lament, and do you pay no attention to what we do!" "It would be quite impossible for me to see you sad and nor take it upon my heart, so I desire to know the truth, whatever chagrin may result to me." "Well, then," he said, "I will tell you all. I have suffered much from a giant, who has insisted that I should give him my daughter, who surpasses in beauty all the maidens in the world. This evil giant, whom may God confound, is named Harpin of the Mountain. Not a day passes without his taking all of my possessions upon which he can lay his hands. No one has a better right than I to complain, and to be sorrowful, and to make lament. I might well lose my senses from very grief, for I had six sons who were knights, fairer than any I knew in the world, and the giant has taken all six of them. Before my eyes he killed two of them, and to-morrow he will kill the other four, unless I find some one who will dare to fight him for the deliverance of my sons, or unless I consent to surrender my daughter to him; and he says that when he has her in his possession he will give her over to be the sport of the vilest and lewdest fellows in his house, for he would scorn to take her now for himself. That is the disaster which awaits me to-morrow, unless the Lord God grant me His aid. So it is no wonder, fair sir, if we are all in tears. But for your sake we strive for the moment to assume as cheerful a countenance as we can. For he is a fool who attracts a gentleman to his presence and then does not honour him; and you seem to be a very perfect gentleman. Now I have told you the entire story of our great distress. Neither in town nor in fortress has the giant left us anything, except what we have here. If you had noticed, you must have seen this evening that he has not left us so much as an egg, except these walls which are new; for he has razed the entire town. When he had plundered all he wished, he set fire to what remained. In this way he has done me many an evil turn."

My lord Yvain listened to all that his host told him, and when he had heard it all he was pleased to answer him: "Sire, I am sorry and distressed about this trouble of yours; but I marvel greatly that you have not asked assistance at good King Arthur's court. There is no man so mighty that he could not find at his court some who would be glad to try their strength with his." Then the wealthy man reveals and explains to him that he would have had efficient help if he had known where to find my lord Gawain. "He would not have failed me upon this occasion, for my wife is his own sister; but a knight from a strange land, who went to court to seek the King's wife, has led her away. However, he could not have gotten possession of her by any means of his own invention, had it not been for Kay, who so befooled the King that he gave the Queen into his charge and placed her under his protection. He was a fool, and she imprudent to entrust herself to his escort. And I am the one who suffers and loses in all this; for it is certain that my excellent lord Gawain would have made haste to come here, had he known the facts, for the sake of his nephews and his niece. But he knows nothing of it, wherefore I am so distressed that my heart is almost breaking, for he is gone in pursuit of him, to whom may God bring shame and woe for having led the Queen away." While listening to this recital my lord Yvain does not cease to sigh. Inspired by the pity which he feels, he makes this reply: "Fair gentle sire, I would gladly undertake this perilous adventure, if the giant and your sons should arrive to-morrow in time to cause me no delay, for tomorrow at noon I shall be somewhere else, in accordance with a promise I have made." "Once for all, fair sire," the good man said, "I thank you a hundred thousand times for your willingness." And all the people of the house likewise expressed their gratitude.

Just then the damsel came out of a room, with her graceful body and her face so fair and pleasing to look upon. She was very simple and sad and quiet as she came, for there was no end to the grief she felt: she walked with her head bowed to the ground. And her mother, too, came in from an adjoining room, for the gentleman had sent for them to meet his guest. They entered with their mantles wrapped about them to conceal their tears; and he bid them throw back their mantles, and hold up their heads, saying: "You ought not to hesitate to obey my behests, for God and good fortune have given us here a very well-born gentleman who assures me that he will fight against the giant. Delay no longer now to throw yourselves at his feet!" "May God never let me see that!" my lord Yvain hastens to exclaim; "surely it would not be proper under any circumstances for the sister and the niece of my lord Gawain to prostrate themselves at my feet. May God defend me from ever giving place to such pride as to let them fall at my feet! Indeed, I should never forget the shame which I should feel; but I should be very glad if they would take comfort until to-morrow, when they may see whether God will consent to aid them. I have no other request to make, except that the giant may come in such good time that I be not compelled to break my engagement elsewhere; for I would not fail for anything to be present to-morrow noon at the greatest business I could ever undertake." Thus he is unwilling to reassure them completely, for he fears that the giant may not come early enough to allow him to reach in time the damsel who is imprisoned in the chapel. Nevertheless, he promises them enough to arouse good hope in them. They all alike join in thanking him, for they place great confidence in his prowess, and they think he must be a very good man, when they see the lion by his side as confident as a lamb would be. They take comfort and rejoice because of the hope they stake on him, and they indulge their grief no more. When the time came they led him off to bed in a brightly lighted room; both the damsel and her mother escorted him, for they prized him dearly, and would have done so a hundred thousand times more had they been informed of his prowess and courtesy. He and the lion together lay down there and took their rest. The others dared not sleep in the room; but they closed the door so tight that they could not come out until the next day at dawn. When the room was thrown open he got up and heard Mass, and then, because of the promise he had made, he waited until the hour of prime. Then in the hearing of all he summoned the lord of the town and said: "My lord, I have no more time to wait, but must ask your permission to leave at once; I cannot tarry longer here. But believe truly that I would gladly and willingly stay here yet awhile for the sake of the nephews and the niece of my beloved lord Gawain, if I did not have a great business on hand, and if it were not so far away." At this the damsel's blood quivered and boiled with fear, as well as the lady's and the lord's. They were so afraid he would go away that they were on the point of humbling themselves and casting themselves at his feet, when they recalled that he would not approve or permit their action. Then the lord makes him an offer of all he will take of his lands or wealth, if only he will wait a little longer. And he replied: "God forbid that ever I should take anything of yours!" Then the damsel, who is in dismay, begins to weep aloud, and beseeches him to stay. Like one distracted and prey to dread, she begs him by the glorious queen of heaven and of the angels, and by the Lord, not to go but to wait a little while; and then, too, for her uncle's sake, whom he says he knows, and loves, and esteems. Then his heart is touched with deep pity when he hears her adjuring him in the name of him whom he loves the most, and by the mistress of heaven, and by the Lord, who is the very honey and sweet savour of pity. Filled with anguish he heaved a sigh, for were the kingdom of Tarsus at stake he would not see her burned to whom he had pledged his aid. If he could not reach her in time, he would be unable to endure his life, or would live on without his wits on the other hand, the kindness of his friend, my lord Gawain, only increased his distress; his heart almost bursts in half at the thought that he cannot delay. Nevertheless, he does not stir, but delays and waits so long that the giant came suddenly, bringing with him the knights: and hanging from his neck he carried a big square stake with a pointed end, and with this he frequently spurred them on. For their part they had no clothing on that was worth a straw, except some soiled and filthy shirts: and their feet and hands were bound with cords, as they came riding upon four limping jades, which were weak, and thin, and miserable. As they came riding along beside a wood, a dwarf, who was puffed up like a toad, had tied the horses' tails together, and walked beside them, beating them remorselessly with a four-knotted scourge until they bled, thinking thereby to be doing something wonderful. Thus they were brought along in shame by the giant and the dwarf. Stopping in the plain in front of the city gate, the giant shouts out to the noble lord that he will kill his sons unless he delivers to him his daughter, whom he will surrender to his vile fellows to become their sport. For he no longer loves her nor esteems her, that he should deign to abase himself to her. She shall be constantly beset by a thousand lousy and ragged knaves, vacant wretches, and scullery boys, who all shall lay hands on her. The worthy man is well-nigh beside himself when he hears how his daughter will be made a bawd, or else, before his very eyes, his four sons will be put to a speedy death. His agony is like that of one who would rather be dead than alive. Again and again he bemoans his fate, and weeps aloud and sighs. Then my frank and gentle lord Yvain thus began to speak to him: "Sire, very vile and impudent is that giant who vaunts himself out there. But may God never grant that he should have your daughter in his power! He despises her and insults her openly. It would be too great a calamity if so lovely a creature of such high birth were handed over to become the sport of boys. Give me now my arms and horse! Have the drawbridge lowered, and let me pass. One or the other must be cast down, either I or he, I know not which. If I could only humiliate the cruel wretch who is thus oppressing you, so that he would release your sons and should come and make amends for the insulting words he has spoken to you, then I would commend you to God and go about my business." Then they go to get his horse, and hand over to him his arms, striving so expeditiously that they soon have him quite equipped. They delayed as little as they could in arming him. When his equipment was complete, there remained nothing but to lower the bridge and let him go. They lowered it for him, and he went out. But the lion would by no means stay behind. All those who were left behind commended the knight to the Saviour, for they fear exceedingly lest their devilish enemy, who already had slain so many good men on the same field before their eyes, would do the same with him. So they pray God to defend him from death, and return him to them safe and sound, and that He may give him strength to slay the giant. Each one softly prays to God in accordance with his wish. And the giant fiercely came at him, and with threatening words thus spake to him: "By my eyes, the man who sent thee here surely had no love for thee! No better way could he have taken to avenge himself on thee. He has chosen well his vengeance for whatever wrong thou hast done to him." But the other, fearing naught, replies: "Thou treatest of what matters not. Now do thy best, and I'll do mine. Idle parley wearies me." Thereupon my lord Yvain, who was anxious to depart, rides at him. He goes to strike him on the breast, which was protected by a bear's skin, and the giant runs at him with his stake raised in air. My lord Yvain deals him such a blow upon the chest that he thrusts through the skin and wets the tip of his lance in his body's blood by way of sauce. And the giant belabours him with the stake, and makes him bend beneath the blows. My lord Yvain then draws the sword with which he knew how to deal fierce blows. He found the giant unprotected, for he trusted in his strength so much that he disdained to arm himself. And he who had drawn his blade gave him such a slash with the cutting edge, and not with the flat side, that he cut from his cheek a slice fit to roast. Then the other in turn gave him such a blow with the stake that it made him sing in a heap upon his horse's neck. Thereupon the lion bristles up, ready to lend his master aid, and leaps up in his anger and strength, and strikes and tears like so much bark the heavy bearskin the giant wore, and he tore away beneath the skin a large piece of his thigh, together with the nerves and flesh. The giant escaped his clutches, roaring and bellowing like a bull, for the lion had badly wounded him. Then raising his stake in both hands, he thought to strike him, but missed his aim, when the lion leaded backward so he missed his blow, and fell exhausted beside my lord Yvain, but without either of them touching the other. Then my lord Yvain took aim and landed two blows on him. Before he could recover himself he had severed with the edge of his sword the giant's shoulder from his body. With the next blow he ran the whole blade of his sword through his liver beneath his chest; the giant falls in death's embrace. And if a great oak tree should fall, I think it would make no greater noise than the giant made when he tumbled down. All those who were on the wall would fain have witnessed such a blow. Then it became evident who was the most fleet of foot, for all ran to see the game, just like hounds which have followed the beast until they finally come up with him. So men and women in rivalry ran forward without delay to where the giant lay face downward. The daughter comes running, and her mother too. And the four brothers rejoice after the woes they have endured. As for my lord Yvain they are very sure that they could not detain him for any reason they might allege, but they beseech him to return and stay to enjoy himself as soon as he shall have completed the business which calls him away. And he replies that he cannot promise them anything, for as yet he cannot guess whether it will fare well or ill with him. But thus much did he say to his host: that he wished that his four sons and his daughter should take the dwarf and go to my lord Gawain when they hear of his return, and should tell and relate to him how he has conducted himself. For kind actions are of no use if you are not willing that they be known. And they reply: "It is not right that such kindness as this should be kept hid: we shall do whatever you desire. But tell us what we can say when we come before him. Whose praises can we speak, when we know not what your name may be?" And he answers them: "When you come before him, you may say thus much: that I told you 'The Knight with the Lion' was my name. And at the same time I must beg you to tell him from me that, if he does not recognise who I am, yet he knows me well and I know him. Now I must be gone from here, and the thing which most alarms me is that I may too long have tarried here, for before the hour of noon be passed I shall have plenty to do elsewhere, if indeed I can arrive there in time." Then, without further delay, he starts. But first his host begged him insistently that he would take with him his four sons: for there was none of them who would not strive to serve him, if he would allow it. But it did not please or suit him that any one should accompany him; so he left the place to them, and went away alone. And as soon as he starts, riding as fast as his steed can carry him, he heads toward the chapel. The path was good and straight, and he knew well how to keep the road. But before he could reach the chapel, the damsel had been dragged out and the pyre prepared upon which she was to be placed. Clad only in a shift, she was held bound before the fire by those who wrongly attributed to her an intention she had never had. My lord Yvain arrived, and, seeing her beside the fire into which she was about to be cast, he was naturally incensed. He would be neither courteous nor sensible who had any doubt about that fact. So it is true that he was much incensed; but he cherishes within himself the hope that God and the Right will be on his side. In such helpers he confides; nor does he scorn his lion's aid. Rushing quickly toward the crowd, he shouts: "Let the damsel be, you wicked folk! Having committed no crime, it is not right that she should be cast upon a pyre or into a furnace." And they draw off on either side, leaving a passage-way for him. But he yearns to see with his own eyes her whom his heart beholds in whatever place she may be. His eyes seek her until he finds her, while he subdues and holds in check his heart, just as one holds in check with a strong curb a horse that pulls. Nevertheless, he gladly gazes at her, and sighs the while; but he does not sigh so openly that his action is detected; rather does he stifle his sighs, though with difficulty. And he is seized with pity at hearing, seeing, and perceiving the grief of the poor ladies, who cried: "Ah, God, how hast Thou forgotten us! How desolate we shall now remain when we lose so kind a friend, who gave us such counsel and such aid, and interceded for us at court! It was she who prompted madame to clothe us with her clothes of vair. Henceforth the situation will change, for there will be no one to speak for us! Cursed be he who is the cause of our loss! For we shall fare badly in all this. There will be no one to utter such advice as this: 'My lady, give this vair mantle, this cloak, and this garment to such and such an honest dame!

Truly, such charity will be well employed, for she is in very dire need of them.' No such words as these shall be uttered henceforth, for there is no one else who is frank and courteous; but every one solicits for himself rather than for some one else, even though he have no need."

Thus they were bemoaning their fate; and my lord Yvain who was in their midst, heard their complaints, which were neither groundless nor assumed. He saw Lunete on her knees and stripped to her shift, having already made confession, and besought God's mercy for her sins. Then he who had loved her deeply once came to her and raised her up, saying: "My damsel, where are those who blame and accuse you? Upon the spot, unless they refuse, battle will be offered them." And she, who had neither seen nor looked at him before, said: "Sire, you come from God in this time of my great need! The men who falsely accuse me are all ready before me here; if you had been a little later I should soon have been reduced to fuel and ashes. You have come here in my defence, and may God give you the power to accomplish it in proportion as I am guiltless of the accusation which is made against me!" The seneschal and his two brothers heard these words. "Ah!" they exclaim, "woman, chary of uttering truth but generous with lies! He indeed is mad who for thy words assumes so great a task. The knight must be simple-minded who has come here to die for thee, for he is alone and there are three of us. My advice to him is that he turn back before any harm shall come to him." Then he replies, as one impatient to begin: "Whoever is afraid, let him run away! I am not so afraid of your three shields that I should go off defeated without a blow. I should be indeed discourteous, if, while yet unscathed and in perfect case, I should leave the place and field to you. Never, so long as I am alive and sound, will I run away before such threats. But I advise thee to set free the damsel whom thou hast unjustly accused; for she tells me, and I believe her word, and she has assured me upon the salvation of her soul, that she never committed, or spoke, or conceived any treason against her mistress. I believe implicitly what she has told me, and will defend her as best I can, for I consider the righteousness of her cause to be in my favour. For, if the truth be known, God always sides with the righteous cause, for God and the Right are one; and if they are both upon my side, then I have better company and better aid than thou." Then the other responds imprudently that he may make every effort that pleases him and is convenient to do him injury, provided that his lion shall not do him harm. And he replies that he never brought the lion to champion his cause, nor does he wish any but himself to take a hand: but if the lion attacks him, let him defend himself against him as best he can, for concerning him he will give no guarantee. Then the other answers: "Whatever thou mayst say; unless thou now warn thy lion, and make him stand quietly to one side, there is no use of thy longer staying here, but begone at once, and so shalt thou be wise; for throughout this country every one is aware how this girl betrayed her lady, and it is right that she receive her due reward in fire and flame." "May the Holy Spirit forbid!" says he who knows the truth; "may God not let me stir from here until I have delivered her!" Then he tells the lion to withdraw and to lie down quietly, and he does so obediently.

The lion now withdrew, and the parley and quarrel being ended between them two, they all took their distance for the charge. The three together spurred toward him, and he went to meet them at a walk. He did not wish to be overturned or hurt at this first encounter. So he let them split their lances, while keeping his entire, making for them a target of his shield, whereon each one broke his lance. Then he galloped off until he was separated from them by the space of an acre; but he soon returned to the business in hand, having no desire to delay. On his coming up the second time, he reached the seneschal before his two brothers, and breaking his lance upon his body, he carried him to earth in spite of himself, and he gave him such a powerful blow that for a long while he lay stunned, incapable of doing him any harm. And then the other two came at him with their swords bared, and both deal him great blows, but they receive still heavier blows from him. For a single one of the blows he deals is more than a match for two of theirs; thus he defends himself so well that they have no advantage over him, until the seneschal gets up and does his best to injure him, in which attempt the others join, until they begin to press him and get the upper hand. Then the lion, who is looking on, delays no longer to lend him aid; for it seems to him that he needs it now. And all the ladies, who are devoted to the damsel, beseech God repeatedly and pray to Him earnestly not to allow the death or the defeat of him who has entered the fray on her account. The ladies, having no other weapons, thus assist him with their prayers. And the lion brings him such effective aid, that at his first attack, he strikes so fiercely the seneschal, who was now on his feet, that he makes the meshes fly from the hauberk like straw, and he drags him down with such violence that he tears the soft flesh from his shoulder and all down his side. He strips whatever he touches, so that the entrails lie exposed. The other two avenge this blow.

Now they are all even on the field. The seneschal is marked for death, as he turns and welters in the red stream of warm blood pouring from his body. The lion attacks the others; for my lord Yvain is quite unable, though he did his best by beating or by threatening him, to drive him back; but the lion doubtless feels confident that his master does not dislike his aid, but rather loves him the more for it: so he fiercely attacks them, until they have reason to complain of his blows, and they wound him in turn and use him badly. When my lord Yvain sees his lion wounded, his heart is wroth within his breast, and rightly so; but he makes such efforts to avenge him, and presses them so hard, that he completely reduces them; they no longer resist him, but surrender to him at discretion, because of the lion's help, who is now in great distress; for he was wounded everywhere, and had good cause to be in pain. For his part, my lord Yvain was by no means in a healthy state, for his body bore many a wound. But he is not so anxious about himself as about his lion, which is in distress. Now he has delivered the damsel exactly in accordance with his wish, and the lady has very willingly dismissed the grudge that she bore her. And those men were burned upon the pyre which had been kindled for the damsel's death; for it is right and just that he who has misjudged another, should suffer the same manner of death as that to which he had condemned the other. Now Lunete is joyous and glad at being reconciled with her mistress, and together they were more happy than any one ever was before. Without recognising him, all present offered to him, who was their lord, their service so long as life should last; even the lady, who possessed unknowingly his heart, begged him insistently to tarry there until his lion and he had quite recovered. And he replied: "Lady, I shall not now tarry here until my lady removes from me her displeasure and anger: then the end of all my labours will come." "Indeed," she said, "that grieves me. I think the lady cannot be very courteous who cherishes ill-will against you. She ought not to close her door against so valorous a knight as you, unless he had done her some great wrong." "Lady," he replies, "however great the hardship be, I am pleased by what ever may be her will. But speak to me no more of that; for I shall say nothing of the cause or crime, except to those who are informed of it." "Does any one know it, then, beside you two?" "Yes, truly, lady." "Well, tell us at least your name, fair sir; then you will be free to go." "Quite free, my lady? No, I shall not be free. I owe more than I can pay. Yet, I ought not to conceal from you my name. You will never hear of 'The Knight with the Lion' without hearing of me; for I wish to be known by that name." "For God's sake, sir, what does that name mean? For we never saw you before, nor have we ever heard mentioned this name of yours." "My lady, you may from that infer that my fame is not widespread." Then the lady says: "Once more, if it did not oppose your will, I would pray you to tarry here." "Really, my lady, I should not dare, until I knew certainly that I had regained my lady's good-will." "Well, then, go in God's name, fair sir; and, if it be His will, may He convert your grief and sorrow into joy." "Lady," says he, "may God hear your prayer." Then he added softly under his breath: "Lady, it is you who hold the key, and, though you know it not, you hold the casket in which my happiness is kept under lock."

Then he goes away in great distress, and there is no one who recognises him save Lunete, who accompanied him a long distance. Lunete alone keeps him company, and he begs her insistently never to reveal the name of her champion. "Sire," says she, "I will never do so." Then he further requested her that she should not forget him, and that she should keep a place for him in his mistress' heart, whenever the chance arose. She tells him to be at ease on that score; for she will never be forgetful, nor unfaithful, nor idle. Then he thanks her a thousand times, and he departs pensive and oppressed, because of his lion that he must needs carry, being unable to follow him on foot. He makes for him a litter of moss and ferns in his shield. When he has made a bed for him there, he lays him in it as gently as he can, and carries him thus stretched out full length on the inner side of his shield. Thus, in his shield he bears him off, until he arrives before the gate of a mansion, strong and fair. Finding it closed, he called, and the porter opened it so promptly that he had no need to call but once. He reaches out to take his rein, and greets him thus: "Come in, fair sire. I offer you the dwelling of my lord, if it please you to dismount." "I accept the offer gladly," he replies, "for I stand in great need of it, and it is time to find a lodging."

Thereupon, he passed through the gate, and saw the retainers in a mass coming to meet him. They greeted him and helped him from his horse, and laid down upon the pavement his shield with the lion on it. And some, taking his horse, put it in a stable: while others very properly relieved him of his arms and took them. Then the lord of the castle heard the news, and at once came down into the courtyard, and greeted him. And his lady came down, too, with all her sons and daughters and a great crowd of other people, who all rejoiced to offer him a lodging. They gave him a quiet room, because they deemed that he was sick; but their good nature was put to a test when they allowed the lion to go with him. His cure was undertaken by two maidens skilled in surgery, who were daughters of the lord. I do not know how many days he stayed there, until he and his lion, being cured, were compelled to proceed upon their way.

But within this time it came about that my lord of Noire Espine had a struggle with Death, and so fierce was Death's attack that he was forced to die. After his death it happened that the elder of two daughters whom he had, announced that she would possess uncontested all the estates for herself during her entire lifetime, and that she would give no share to her sister. And the other one said that she would go to King Arthur's court to seek help for the defence of her claim to the land. When the former saw that her sister would by no means concede all the estates to her without contest, she was greatly concerned, and thought that, if possible, she would get to court before her. At once she prepared and equipped herself, and without any tarrying or delay, she proceeded to the court. The other followed her, and made all the haste she could; but her journey was all in vain, for her elder sister had already presented her case to my lord Gawain, and he had promised to execute her will. But there was an agreement between them that if any one should learn of the facts from her, he would never again take arms for her, and to this arrangement she gave consent.

Just then the other sister arrived at court, clad in a short mantle of scarlet cloth and fresh ermine. It happened to be the third day after the Queen had returned from the captivity in which Maleagant had detained her with all the other prisoners; but Lancelot had remained behind, treacherously confined within a tower. And on that very day, when the damsel came to court, news was received of the cruel and wicked giant whom the knight with the lion had killed in battle. In his name, my lord Gawain was greeted by his nephews and niece, who told him in detail of all the great service and great deeds of prowess he had done for them for his sake, and how that he was well acquainted with him, though not aware of his identity.

All this was heard by her, who was plunged thereby into great despair and sorrow and dejection; for, since the best of the knights was absent, she thought she would find no aid or counsel at the court. She had already made several loving and insistent appeals to my lord Gawain; but he had said to her: "My dear, it is useless to appeal to me; I cannot do it; I have another affair on hand, which I shall in no wise give up." Then the damsel at once left him, and presented herself before the King. "O King," said she, "I have come to thee and to thy court for aid. But I find none, and I am very much mazed that I can get no counsel here. Yet it would not be right for me to go away without taking leave. My sister may know, however, that she might obtain by kindness whatever she desired of my property; but I will never surrender my heritage to her by force, if I can help it, and if I can find any aid or counsel." "You have spoken wisely," said the King; "since she is present here, I advise, recommend, and urge her to surrender to you what is your right." Then the other, who was confident of the best knight in the world, replied: "Sire, may God confound me, if ever I bestow on her from my estates any castle, town, clearing, forest, land, or anything else. But if any knight dares to take arms on her behalf and desires to defend her cause, let him step forth at once." "Your offer to her is not fair; she needs more time," the King replied; "if she desires, she may have forty days to secure a champion, according to the practice of all courts." To which the elder sister replied: "Fair King, my lord, you may establish your laws as it pleases you, and as seems good, nor is it my place to gainsay you, so I must consent to the postponement, if she desires it." Whereupon, the other says that she does desire it, and she makes formal request for it. Then she commended the King to God, and left the court resolving to devote her life to the search through all the land for the Knight with the Lion, who devotes himself to succouring women in need of aid.

Thus she entered upon her quest, and traversed many a country without hearing any news of him, which caused her such grief that she fell sick. But it was well for her that it happened so; for she came to the dwelling of a friend of hers, by whom she was dearly loved. By this time her face showed clearly that she was not in good health. They insisted upon detaining her until she told them of her plight; whereupon, another damsel took up the quest wherein she had been engaged, and continued the search on her behalf. So while the one remained in this retreat, the other rode rapidly all day long, until the darkness of night came on, and caused her great anxiety. And her trouble was doubled when the rain came on with terrible violence, as if God Himself were doing His worst, while she was in the depths of the forest. The night and the woods cause her great distress, but she is more tormented by the rain than by either the woods or the night. And the road was so bad that her horse was often up to the girth in mud; any damsel might well be terrified to be in the woods, without escort, in such bad weather and in such darkness that she could not see the horse she was riding. So she called on God first, and His mother next, and then on all the saints in turn, and offered up many a prayer that God would lead her out from this forest and conduct her to some lodging-place. She continued in prayer until she heard a horn, at which she greatly rejoiced; for she thought now she would find shelter, if she could only reach the place. So she turned in the direction of the sound, and came upon a paved road which led straight toward the horn whose sound she heard; for the horn had given three long, loud blasts. And she made her way straight toward the sound, until she came to a cross which stood on the right side of the road, and there she thought that she might find the horn and the person who had sounded it. So she spurred her horse in that direction, until she drew near a bridge, and descried the white walls and the barbican of a circular castle. Thus, by chance she came upon the castle, setting her course by the sound which had led her thither. She had been attracted by the sound of the horn blown by a watchman upon the walls. As soon as the watchman caught sight of her, he called to her, then came down, and taking the key of the gate, opened it for her and said: "Welcome, damsel, whoe'er you be. You shall be well lodged this night." "I have no other desire than that," the damsel replied, as he let her in. After the toil and anxiety she had endured that day, she was fortunate to find such a lodging-place; for she was very comfortable there. After the meal the host addressed her, and inquired where she was going and what was her quest. Whereupon, she thus replied: "I am seeking one whom I never saw, so far as I am aware, and never knew; but he has a lion with him, and I am told that, if I find him, I can place great confidence in him." "I can testify to that," the other said: "for the day before yesterday God sent him here to me in my dire need. Blessed be the paths which led him to my dwelling. For he made me glad by avenging me of a mortal enemy and killing him before my eyes. Outside yonder gate you may see to-morrow the body of a mighty giant, whom he slew with such ease that he hardly had to sweat." "For God's sake, sire," the damsel said, "tell me now the truth, if you know whither he went, and where he is." "I don't know," he said, "as God sees me here; but to-morrow I will start you on the road by which he went away from here." "And may God," said she, "lead me where I may hear true news of him. For if I find him, I shall be very glad."

Thus they continued in long converse until at last they went to bed. When the day dawned, the maid arose, being in great concern to find the object of her quest. And the master of the house arose with all his companions, and set her upon the road which led straight to the spring beneath the pine. And she, hastening on her way toward the town, came and asked the first men whom she met, if they could tell her where she would find the lion and the knight who travelled in company. And they told her that they had seen him defeat three knights in that very place. Whereupon, she said at once: "For God's sake, since you have said so much, do not keep back from me anything that you can add." "No," they replied; "we know nothing more than we have said, nor do we know what became of him. If she for whose sake he came here, cannot give you further news, there will be no one here to enlighten you. You will not have far to go, if you wish to speak with her; for she has gone to make prayer to God and to hear Mass in yonder church, and judging by the time she has been inside, her orisons have been prolonged."

While they were talking thus, Lunete came out from the church, and they said: "There she is." Then she went to meet her, and they greeted each other. She asked Lunete at once for the information she desired; and Lunete said that she would have a palfrey saddled; for she wished to accompany her, and would take her to an enclosure where she had left him. The other maiden thanked her heartily. Lunete mounts the palfrey which is brought without delay, and, as they ride, she tells her how she had been accused and charged with treason, and how the pyre was already kindled upon which she was to be laid, and how he had come to help her in just the moment of her need. While speaking thus, she escorted her to the road which led directly to the spot where my lord Yvain had parted from her. When she had accompanied her thus far, she said: "Follow this road until you come to a place where, if it please God and the Holy Spirit, you will hear more reliable news of him than I can tell. I very well remember that I left him either near here, or exactly here, where we are now; we have not seen each other since then, and I do not know what he has done. When he left me, he was in sore need of a plaster for his wounds. So I will send you along after him, and if it be God's will, may He grant that you find him to-night or to-morrow in good health. Now go: I commend you to God. I must not follow you any farther, lest my mistress be displeased with me." Then Lunete leaves her and turns back; while the other pushed on until she found a house, where my lord Yvain had tarried until he was restored to health. She saw people gathered before the gate, knights, ladies and men-at-arms, and the master of the house; she saluted them, and asked them to tell her, if possible, news of a knight for whom she sought. "Who is he?" they ask. "I have heard it said that he is never without a lion." "Upon my word, damsel," the master says, "he has just now left us. You can come up with him to-night, if you are able to keep his tracks in sight, and are careful not to lose any time." "Sire," she answers, "God forbid. But tell me now in what direction I must follow him." And they tell her: "This way, straight ahead," and they beg her to greet him on their behalf. But their courtesy was not of much avail; for, without giving any heed, she galloped off at once. The pace seemed much too slow to her, though her palfrey made good time. So she galloped through the mud just the same as where the road was good and smooth, until she caught sight of him with the lion as his companion. Then in her gladness she exclaims: "God, help me now. At last I see him whom I have so long pursued, and whose trace I have long followed. But if I pursue and nothing gain, what will it profit me to come up with him? Little or nothing, upon my word. If he does not join in my enterprise, I have wasted all my pains." Thus saying, she pressed on so fast that her palfrey was all in a sweat; but she caught up with him and saluted him. He thus at once replied to her: "God save you, fair one, and deliver you from grief and woe." "The same to you, sire, who, I hope, will soon be able to deliver me." Then she draws nearer to him, and says: "Sire, I have long searched for you. The great fame of your merit has made me traverse many a county in my weary search for you. But I continued my quest so long, thank God, that at last I have found you here. And if I brought any anxiety with me, I am no longer concerned about it, nor do I complain or remember it now. I am entirely relieved; my worry has taken flight the moment I met with you. Moreover, the affair is none of mine: I come to you from one that is better than I, a woman who is more noble and excellent. But if she be disappointed in her hopes of you, then she has been betrayed by your fair renown, for she has no expectation of other aid. My damsel, who is deprived of her inheritance by a sister, expects with your help to win her suit; she will have none but you defend her cause. No one can make her believe that any one else could bear her aid. By securing her share of the heritage, you will have won and acquired the love of her who is now disinherited, and you will also increase your own renown. She herself was going in search for you to secure the boon for which she hoped; no one else would have taken her place, had she not been detained by an illness which compels her to keep her bed. Now tell me, please, whether you will dare to come, or whether you will decline." "No," he says; "no man can win praise in a life of ease; and I will not hold back, but will follow you gladly, my sweet friend, whithersoever it may please you. And if she for whose sake you have sought me out stands in some great need of me, have no fear that I shall not do all I can for her. Now may God grant me the happiness and grace to settle in her favour her rightful claim."

Thus conversing, they two rode away until they approached the town of Pesme Avanture. They had no desire to pass it by, for the day was already drawing to a close. They came riding to the castle, when all the people, seeing them approach, called out to the knight: "Ill come, sire, ill come. This lodging-place was pointed out to you in order that you might suffer harm and shame. An abbot might take his oath to that." "Ah," he replied, "foolish and vulgar folk, full of all mischief, and devoid of honour, why have you thus assailed me?" "Why? you will find out soon enough, if you will go a little farther. But you shall learn nothing more until you have ascended to the fortress." At once my lord Yvain turns toward the tower, and the crowd cries out, all shouting aloud at him: "Eh, eh, wretch, whither goest thou? If ever in thy life thou hast encountered one who worked thee shame and woe, such will be done thee there, whither thou art going, as will never be told again by thee." My lord Yvain, who is listening, says: "Base and pitiless people, miserable and impudent, why do you assail me thus, why do you attack me so? What do you wish of me, what do you want, that you growl this way after me?" A lady, who was somewhat advanced in years, who was courteous and sensible, said: "Thou hast no cause to be enraged: they mean no harm in what they say; but, if thou understoodest them aright, they are warning thee not to spend the night up there; they dare not tell thee the reason for this, but they are warning and blaming thee because they wish to arouse thy fears. This they are accustomed to do in the case of all who come, so that they may not go inside. And the custom is such that we dare not receive in our own houses, for any reason whatsoever, any gentleman who comes here from a distance. The responsibility now is thine alone; no one will stand in thy way. If thou wishest, thou mayst go up now; but my advice is to turn back again." "Lady," he says, "doubtless it would be to my honour and advantage to follow your advice; but I do not know where I should find a lodging-place to-night." "Upon my word," says she, "I'll say no more, for the concern is none of mine. Go wherever you please. Nevertheless, I should be very glad to see you return from inside without too great shame; but that could hardly be." "Lady," he says, "may God reward you for the wish. However, my wayward heart leads me on inside, and I shall do what my heart desires." Thereupon, he approaches the gate, accompanied by his lion and his damsel. Then the porter calls to him, and says: "Come quickly, come. You are on your way to a place where you will be securely detained, and may your visit be accursed."

The porter, after addressing him with this very ungracious welcome, hurried upstairs. But my lord Yvain, without making reply, passed straight on, and found a new and lofty hall; in front of it there was a yard enclosed with large, round, pointed stakes, and seated inside the stakes he saw as many as three hundred maidens, working at different kinds of embroidery. Each one was sewing with golden thread and silk, as best she could. But such was their poverty, that many of them wore no girdle, and looked slovenly, because so poor; and their garments were torn about their breasts and at the elbows, and their shifts were soiled about their necks. Their necks were thin, and their faces pale with hunger and privation. They see him, as he looks at them, and they weep, and are unable for some time to do anything or to raise their eyes from the ground, so bowed down they are with woe. When he had contemplated them for a while, my lord Yvain turned about and moved toward the door; but the porter barred the way, and cried: "It is no use, fair master; you shall not get out now. You would like to be outside: but, by my head, it is of no use. Before you escape you will have suffered such great shame that you could not easily suffer more; so you were not wise to enter here, for there is no question of escaping now." "Nor do I wish to do so, fair brother," said he; "but tell me, by thy father's soul, whence came the damsels whom I saw in the yard, weaving cloths of silk and gold. I enjoy seeing the work they do, but I am much distressed to see their bodies so thin, and their faces so pale and sad. I imagine they would be fair and charming, if they had what they desire." "I will tell you nothing," was the reply; "seek some one else to tell you." "That will I do, since there is no better way." Then he searches until he finds the entrance of the yard where the damsels were at work: and coming before them, he greets them all, and sees tears flowing from their eyes, as they weep. Then he says to them: "May it please God to remove from your hearts, and turn to joy, this grief, the cause of which I do not know." One of them answers: "May you be heard by God, to whom you have addressed your prayer. It shall not be concealed from you who we are, and from what land: I suppose that is what you wish to know." "For no other purpose came I here," says he. "Sire, it happened a long while ago that the king of the Isle of Damsels went seeking news through divers courts and countries, and he kept on his travels like a dunce until he encountered this perilous place. It was an unlucky hour when he first came here, for we wretched captives who are here receive all the shame and misery which we have in no wise deserved. And rest assured that you yourself may expect great shame, unless a ransom for you be accepted. But, at any rate, so it came about that my lord came to this town, where there are two sons of the devil (do not take it as a jest) who were born of a woman and an imp. These two were about to fight with the king, whose terror was great, for he was not yet eighteen years old, and they would have been able to cleave him through like a tender lamb. So the king, in his terror, escaped his fate as best he could, by swearing that he would send hither each year, as required, thirty of his damsels, and with this rent he freed himself. And when he swore, it was agreed that this arrangement should remain in force as long as the two devils lived. But upon the day when they should be conquered and defeated in battle, he would be relieved from this tribute, and we should be delivered who are now shamefully given over to distress and misery. Never again shall we know what pleasure is. But I spoke folly just now in referring to our deliverance, for we shall never more leave this place. We shall spend our days weaving cloths of silk, without ever being better clad. We shall always be poor and naked, and shall always suffer from hunger and thirst, for we shall never be able to earn enough to procure for ourselves any better food. Our bread supply is very scarce--a little in the morning and less at night, for none of us can gain by her handiwork more than fourpence a day for her daily bread. And with this we cannot provide ourselves with sufficient food and clothes. For though there is not one of us who does not earn as much as twenty sous a week, yet we cannot live without hardship. Now you must know that there is not a single one of us who does not do twenty sous worth of work or more, and with such a sum even a duke would be considered rich. So while we are reduced to such poverty, he, for whom we work, is rich with the product of our toil. We sit up many nights, as well as every day, to earn the more, for they threaten to do us injury, when we seek some rest, so we do not dare to rest ourselves. But why should I tell you more? We are so shamefully treated and insulted that I cannot tell you the fifth part of it all. But what makes us almost wild with rage is that we very often see rich and excellent knights, who fight with the two devils, lose their lives on our account. They pay dearly for the lodging they receive, as you will do to-morrow. For, whether you wish to do so or not, you will have to fight singlehanded and lose your fair renown with these two devils." "May God, the true and spiritual, protect me," said my lord Yvain, "and give you back your honour and happiness, if it be His will. I must go now and see the people inside there, and find out what sort of entertainment they will offer me." "Go now, sire, and may He protect you who gives and distributes all good things."

Then he went until he came to the hall where he found no one, good or bad, to address him. Then he and his companion passed through the house until they came to a garden. They never spoke of, or mentioned, stabling their horses. But what matters it? For those who considered them already as their own had stabled them carefully. I do not know whether their expectation was wise, for the horses' owners are still perfectly hale. The horses, however, have oats and hay, and stand in litter up to their belly. My lord Yvain and his company enter the garden. There he sees, reclining upon his elbow upon a silken rug, a gentleman, to whom a maiden was reading from a romance about I know not whom. There had come to recline there with them and listen to the romance a lady, who was the mother of the damsel, as the gentleman was her father; they had good reason to enjoy seeing and hearing her, for they had no other children. She was not yet sixteen years old, and was so fair and full of grace that the god of Love would have devoted himself entirely to her service, if he had seen her, and would never have made her fall in love with anybody except himself. For her sake he would have become a man, and would lay aside his deity, and would smite his own body with that dart whose wound never heals unless some base physician attends to it. It is not fitting that any one should recover until he meets with faithlessness. Any one who is cured by other means is not honestly in love. I could tell you so much about this wound, if you were pleased to listen to it, that I would not get through my tale to-day. But there would be some one who would promptly say that I was telling you but an idle tale; for people don't fall in love nowadays, nor do they love as they used to do, so they do not care to hear of it. But hear now in what fashion and with what manner of hospitality my lord Yvain was received. All those who were in the garden leaped to their feet when they saw him come, and cried out: "This way, fair sire. May you and all you love be blessed with all that God can do or say." I know not if they were deceiving him, but they receive him joyfully and act as if they are pleased that he should be comfortably lodged. Even the lord's daughter serves him very honourably, as one should treat a worthy guest. She relieves him of all his arms, nor was it the least attention she bestowed on him when she herself washed his neck and face. The lord wishes that all honour should be shown him, as indeed they do. She gets out from her wardrobe a folded shirt, white drawers, needle and thread for his sleeves, which she sews on, thus clothing him. May God want now that this attention and service may not prove too costly to him! She gave him a handsome jacket to put on over his shirt, and about his neck she placed a brand new spotted mantle of scarlet stuff. She takes such pains to serve him well that he feels ashamed and embarrassed. But the damsel is so courteous and open-hearted and polite that she feels she is doing very little. And she knows well that it is her mother's will that she shall leave nothing undone for him which she thinks may win his gratitude. That night at table he was so well served with so many dishes that there were too many. The servants who brought in the dishes might well have been wearied by serving them. That night they did him all manner of honour, putting him comfortably to bed, and not once going near him again after he had retired. His lion lay at his feet, as his custom was. In the morning, when God lighted His great light for the world, as early as was consistent in one who was always considerate, my lord Yvain quickly arose, as did his damsel too. They heard Mass in a chapel, where it was promptly said for them in honour of the Holy Spirit.

After the Mass my lord Yvain heard bad news, when he thought the time had come for him to leave and that nothing would stand in his way; but it could not be in accordance with his wish. When he said: "Sire, if it be your will, and with your permission, I am going now," the master of the house replied: "Friend, I will not grant you permission yet. There is a reason why I cannot do so, for there is established in this castle a very terrible practice which I am bound to observe. I shall now cause to approach two great, strong fellows of mine, against whom, whether right or wrong, you must take arms. If you can defend yourself against them, and conquer and slay them both, my daughter desires you as her lord, and the suzerainty of this town and all its dependencies awaits you." "Sire," said he, "for all this I have no desire. So may God never bestow your daughter upon me, but may she remain with you; for she is so fair and so elegant that the Emperor of Germany would be fortunate to win her as his wife." "No more, fair guest," the lord replied: "there is no need of my listening to your refusal, for you cannot escape. He who can defeat the two, who are about to attack you, must by right receive my castle, and all my land, and my daughter as his wife. There is no way of avoiding or renouncing the battle. But I feel sure that your refusal of my daughter is due to cowardice, for you think that in this manner you can completely avoid the battle. Know, however, without fail that you must surely fight. No knight who lodges here can possibly escape. This is a settled custom and statute, which will endure yet for many a year, for my daughter will never be married until I see them dead or defeated." "Then I must fight them in spite of myself. But I assure you that I should very gladly give it up. In spite of my reluctance, however, I shall accept the battle, since it is inevitable." Thereupon, the two hideous, black sons of the devil come in, both armed with a crooked club of a cornelian cherry-tree, which they had covered with copper and wound with brass. They were armed from the shoulders to the knees, but their head and face were bare, as well as their brawny legs. Thus armed, they advanced, bearing in their hands round shields, stout and light for fighting. The lion begins to quiver as soon as he sees them, for he sees the arms they have, and perceives that they come to fight his master. He is aroused, and bristles up at once, and, trembling with rage and bold impulse, he thrashes the earth with his tail, desiring to rescue his master before they kill him. And when they see him they say: "Vassal, remove the lion from here that he may not do us harm. Either surrender to us at once, or else, we adjure you, that lion must be put where he can take no part in aiding you or in harming us. You must come alone to enjoy our sport, for the lion would gladly help you, if he could." My lord Yvain then replies to them: "Take him away yourselves if you are afraid of him. For I shall be well pleased and satisfied if he can contrive to injure you, and I shall be grateful for his aid." They answer: "Upon my word that will not do; you shall never receive any help from him. Do the best you can alone, without the help of any one. You must fight single-handed against us two. If you were not alone, it would be two against two; so you must follow our orders, and remove your lion from here at once, however much you may dislike to do so." "Where do you wish him to be?" he asks, "or where do you wish me to put him?" Then they show him a small room, and say: "Shut him up in there." "It shall be done, since it is your will." Then he takes him and shuts him up. And now they bring him arms for his body, and lead out his horse, which they give to him, and he mounts. The two champions, being now assured about the lion, which is shut up in the room, come at him to injure him and do him harm. They give him such blows with the maces that his shield and helmet are of little use, for when they hit him on the helmet they batter it in and break it; and the shield is broken and dissolved like ice, for they make such holes in it that one could thrust his fists through it: their onslaught is truly terrible. And he--what does he do against these two devils? Urged on by shame and fear, he defends himself with all his strength. He strains every nerve, and exerts himself to deal heavy, and telling blows; they lost nothing by his gifts, for he returned their attentions with double measure. In his room, the lion's heart is heavy and sad, for he remembers the kind deed done for him by this noble man, who now must stand in great need of his service and aid. If now he could escape from there, he would return him the kindness with full measure and full bushel, without any discount whatsoever. He looks about in all directions, but sees no way of escape. He hears the blows of the dangerous and desperate fight, and in his grief he rages and is beside himself. He investigates, until he comes to the threshold, which was beginning to grow rotten; and he scratches at it until he can squeeze himself in as far as his haunches, when he sticks fast. Meanwhile, my lord Yvain was hard pressed and sweating freely, for he found that the two fellows were very strong, fierce, and persistent. He had received many a blow, and repaid it as best he could, but without doing them any harm, for they were well skilled in fencing, and their shields were not of a kind to be hacked by any sword, however sharp and well tempered it might be. So my lord Yvain had good reason to fear his death, yet he managed to hold his own until the lion extricated himself by continued scratching beneath the thresh-old. If the rascals are not killed now, surely they will never be. For so long as the lion knows them to be alive, they can never obtain truce or peace with him. He seizes one of them, and pulls him down to earth like a tree-trunk. The wretches are terrified, and there is not a man present who does not rejoice. For he whom the lion has dragged down will never be able to rise again, unless the other succours him. He runs up to bring him aid, and at the same time to protect himself, lest the lion should attack him as soon as he had despatched the one whom he had thrown down; he was more afraid of the lion than of his master. But my lord Yvain will be foolish now if he allows him longer life, when he sees him turn his back, and sees his neck bare and exposed; this chance turned out well for him. When the rascal exposed to him his bare head and neck, he dealt him such a blow that he smote his head from his shoulders so quietly that the fellow never knew a word about it. Then he dismounts, wishing to help and save the other one from the lion, who holds him fast. But it is of no use, for already he is in such straits that a physician can never arrive in time; for the lion, coming at him furiously, so wounded him at the first attack, that he was in a dreadful state. Nevertheless, he drags the lion back, and sees that he had torn his shoulder from its place. He is in no fear of the fellow now, for his club has fallen from his hand, and he lies like a dead man without action or movement; still he has enough strength to speak, and he said as clearly as he could: "Please take your lion away, fair sire, that he may not do me further harm. Henceforth you may do with me whatever may be your desire. Whoever begs and prays for mercy, ought not to have his prayer refused, unless he addresses a heartless man. I will no longer defend myself, nor will I ever get up from here with my own strength; so I put myself in your hands." "Speak out then," he says, "if thou dost admit that thou art conquered and defeated." "Sire," he says, "it is evident. I am defeated in spite of myself, and I surrender, I promise you." "Then thou needest have no further fear of me, and my lion will leave thee alone." Then he is surrounded by all the crowd, who arrive on the scene in haste. And both the lord and his lady rejoice over him, and embrace him, and speak to him of their daughter, saying: "Now you will be the lord and master of us all, and our daughter will be your wife, for we bestow her upon you as your spouse." "And for my part," he says. "I restore her to you. Let him who has her keep her. I have no concern with her, though I say it not in disparagement. Take it not amiss if I do not accept her, for I cannot and must not do so. But deliver to me now, if you will, the wretched maidens in your possession. The agreement, as you well know, is that they shall all go free." "What you say is true," he says: "and I resign and deliver them freely to you: there will be no dispute on that score. But you will be wise to take my daughter with all my wealth, for she is fair, and charming, and sensible. You will never find again such a rich marriage as this." "Sire," he replies, "you do not know of my engagements and my affairs, and I do not dare to explain them to you. But, you may be sure, when I refuse what would never be refused by any one who was free to devote his heart and intentions to such a fair and charming girl, that I too would willingly accept her hand if I could, or if I were free to accept her or any other maid. But I assure you that I cannot do it: so let me depart in peace. For the damsel, who escorted me hither, is awaiting me. She has kept me company, and I would not willingly desert her whatever the future may have in store." "You wish to go, fair sire? But how? My gate will never be opened for you unless my judgment bids me give the command; rather shall you remain here as my prisoner. You are acting haughtily and making a mistake when you disdain to take my daughter at my request." "Disdain, my lord? Upon my soul, I do not disdain her. Whatever the penalty may be, I cannot marry a wife or tarry here. I shall follow the damsel who is my guide: for otherwise it cannot be. But, with your consent, I will pledge you my right hand, and you may take my word, that, just as you see me now, I will return if possible, and then will accept your daughter's hand, whenever it may seem good ro you." "Confound any one," he says, "who asks you for your word or promise or pledge. If my daughter pleases you, you will return quickly enough. You will not return any sooner. I think, for having given your word or sworn an oath. Begone now. I release you from all oaths and promises. If you are detained by rain or wind, or by nothing at all, it is of no consequence to me. I do not hold my daughter so cheap as to bestow her upon you forcibly. Now go about your business. For it is quite the same to me whether you go or whether you stay."

Thereupon my lord Yvain turns away and delays no longer in the castle. He escorted the poor and ill-clad wretches, who were now released from captivity, and whom the lord committed to his care. These maidens feel that now they are rich, as they file out in pairs before him from the castle. I do not believe that they would rejoice so much as they do now were He who created the whole world to descend to earth from Heaven. Now all those people who had insulted him in every possible way come to beseech him for mercy and peace, and escort him on his way. He replies that he knows nothing of what they mean. "I do not understand what you mean," he says; "but I have nothing against you. I do not remember that you ever said anything that harmed me." They are very glad for what they hear, and loudly praise his courtesy, and after escorting him a long distance, they all commend him to God. Then the damsels, after asking his permission, separated from him. When they left him, they all bowed to him, and prayed and expressed the wish that God might grant him joy and health, and the accomplishment of his desire, wherever in the future he should go. Then he, who is anxious to be gone, says that he hopes God will save them all. "Go," he says, "and may God conduct you into your countries safe and happy." Then they continue their way joyfully; and my lord Yvain departs in the other direction. All the days of that week he never ceases to hurry on under the escort of the maid, who was well acquainted with the road, and with the retired place where she had left the unhappy and disconsolate damsel who had been deprived of her inheritance. But when she heard news of the arrival of the maiden and of the Knight with the Lion. There never was such joy as she felt within her heart. For now she thinks that, if she insists, her sister will cede her a part of her inheritance. The damsel had long lain sick, and had just recovered from her malady. It had seriously affected her, as was apparent from her face. Straightway she went forth to meet them, greeting them and honouring them in every way she could. There is no need to speak of the happiness that prevailed that night in the house. No mention will be made of it, for the story would be too long to tell. I pass over all that, until they mounted next morning and went away. They rode until they saw the town where King Arthur had been staying for a fortnight or more. And there, too, was the damsel who had deprived her sister of her heritage, for she had kept close to the court, waiting for the arrival of her sister, who now draws near. But she does not worry much, for she does not think that her sister can find any knight who can withstand my lord Gawain's attack, and only one day of the forty yet remains. If this single day had passed, she would have had the reasonable and legal right to claim the heritage for herself alone. But more stands in the way than she thinks or believes. That night they spent outside the town in a small and humble house, where, in accordance with their desire, they were not recognised. At the first sign of dawn the next morning they necessarily issue forth, but ensconce themselves in hiding until broad daylight.

I know not how many days had passed since my lord Gawain had so completely disappeared that no one at court knew anything about him, except only the damsel in whose cause he was to fight. He had concealed himself three or four leagues from the court, and when he returned he was so equipped that even those who knew him perfectly could not recognise him by the arms he bore. The damsel, whose injustice toward her sister was evident, presented him at court in the sight of all, for she intended with his help to triumph in the dispute where she had no rights. So she said to the King: "My lord, time passes. The noon hour will soon be gone, and this is the last day. As you see, I am prepared to defend my claim. If my sister were going to return, there would be nothing to do but await her arrival. But I may praise God that she is not coming back again. It is evident that she cannot better her affairs, and that her trouble has been for naught. For my part, I have been ready all the time up to this last day, to prove my claim to what is mine. I have proved my point entirely without a fight, and now I may rightfully go to accept my heritage in peace; for I shall render no accounting for it to my sister as long as I live, and she will lead a wretched and miserable existence." Then the King, who well knew that the damsel was disloyally unjust toward her sister, said to her: "My dear, upon my word, in a royal court one must wait as long as the king's justice sits and deliberates upon the verdict. It is not yet time to pack up, for it is my belief that your sister will yet arrive in time." Before the King had finished, he saw the Knight with the Lion and the damsel with him. They two were advancing alone, having slipped away from the lion, who had stayed where they spent the night.

The King saw the damsel whom he did not fail to recognise, and he was greatly pleased and delighted to see her, for he was on her side of the quarrel, because he had regard for what was right. Joyfully he cried out to her as soon as he could: "Come forward, fair one: may God save you!" When the other sister hears these words, she turns trembling, and sees her with the knight whom she had brought to defend in her claim: then she turned blacker than the earth. The damsel, after being kindly welcomed by all, went to where the King was sitting. When she had come before him, she spoke to him thus: "God save the King and his household. If my rights in this dispute can be settled by a champion, then it will be done by this knight who has followed me hither. This frank and courteous knight had many other things to do elsewhere; but he felt such pity for me that he cast aside all his other affairs for the sake of mine. Now, madame, my very dear sister, whom I love as much as my own heart, would do the right and courteous thing if she would let me have so much of what is mine by right that there might be peace between me and her; for I ask for nothing that is hers." "Nor do I ask for anything that is thine," the other replied; "for thou hast nothing, and nothing shalt thou have. Thou canst never talk so much as to gain anything by thy words. Thou mayest dry up with grief." Then the other, who was very polite and sensible and courteous, replied with the words: "Certainly I am sorry that two such gentlemen as these should fight on our behalf over so small a disagreement. But I cannot disregard my claim, for I am in too great need of it. So I should be much obliged to you if you would give me what is rightly mine." "Surely," the other said, "any one would be a fool to consider thy demands. May I burn in evil fire and flame if I give thee anything to ease thy life! The banks of the Seine will meet, and the hour of prime will be called noon, before I refuse to carry out the fight." "May God and the right, which I have in this cause, and in which I trust and have trusted till the present time, aid him, who in charity and courtesy has offered himself in my service, though he knows not who I am, and though we are ignorant of each other's identity."

So they talked until their conversation ceased, and then produced the knights in the middle of the court. Then all the people crowd about, as people are wont to do when they wish to witness blows in battle or in joust. But those who were about to fight did not recognise each other, though their relations were wont to be very affectionate. Then do they not love each other now? I would answer you both "yes" and "no." And I shall prove that each answer is correct. In truth, my lord Gawain loves Yvain and regards him as his companion, and so does Yvain regard him, wherever he may be. Even here, if he knew who he was, he would make much of him, and either one of them would lay down his head for the other before he would allow any harm to come to him. Is not that a perfect and lofty love? Yes, surely. But, on the other hand, is not their hate equally manifest? Yes; for it is a certain thing that doubtless each would be glad to have broken the other's head, and so to have injured him as to cause his humiliation. Upon my word, it is a wondrous thing, that Love and mortal Hate should dwell together. God! How can two things so opposed find lodging in the same dwelling-place? It seems to me they cannot live together; for one could not dwell with the other, without giving rise to noise and contention, as soon as each knew of the other's presence. But upon the ground-floor there may be several apartments: for there are halls and sleeping-rooms. It may be the same in this case: I think Love had ensconced himself in some hidden room, while Hate had betaken herself to the balconies looking on the high-road, because she wishes to be seen. Just now Hate is in the saddle, and spurs and pricks forward as she can, to get ahead of Love who is indisposed to move. Ah! Love, what has become of thee? Come out now, and thou shalt see what a host has been brought up and opposed to thee by the enemies of thy friends. The enemies are these very men who love each other with such a holy love for love, which is neither false nor feigned, is a precious and a holy thing. In this case Love is completely blind, and Hate, too, is deprived of sight. For if Love had recognised these two men, he must have forbidden each to attack the other, or to do any thing to cause him harm. In this respect, then, Love is blind and discomfited and beguiled; for, though he sees them, he fails to recognise those who rightly belong to him. And though Hate is unable to tell why one of them should hate the other, yet she tries to engage them wrongfully, so that each hates the other mortally. You know, of course, that he cannot be said to love a man who would wish to harm him and see him dead. How then? Does Yvain wish to kill his friend, my lord Gawain? Yes, and the desire is mutual. Would, then, my lord Gawain desire to kill Yvain with his own hands, or do even worse than I have said? Nay, not really, I swear and protest. One would not wish to injure or harm the other, in return for all that God has done for man, or for all the empire of Rome. But this, in turn, is a lie of mine, for it is plainly to be seen that, with lance raised high in rest, each is ready to attack the other, and there will be no restraint of the desire of each to wound the other with intent to injure him and work him woe. Now tell me! When one will have defeated the other, of whom can he complain who has the worst of it? For if they go so far as to come to blows, I am very much afraid that they will continue the battle and the strife until victory be definitely decided. If he is defeated, will Yvain be justified in saying that he has been harmed and wronged by a man who counts him among his friends, and who has never mentioned him but by the name of friend or companion? Or, if it comes about perchance that Yvain should hurt him in turn, or defeat him in any way, will Gawain have the right to complain? Nay, for he will not know whose fault it is. In ignorance of each other's identity, they both drew off and took their distance. At this first shock, their lances break, though they were stout, and made of ash. Not a word do they exchange, for if they had stopped to converse their meeting would have been different. In that case, no blow would have been dealt with lance or sword; they would have kissed and embraced each other rather than sought each other's harm. For now they attack each other with injurious intent. The condition of the swords is not improved, nor that of the helmets and shields, which are dented and split; and the edges of the swords are nicked and dulled. For they strike each other violently, not with the fiat of the swords, but with the edge, and they deal such blows with the pommels upon the nose-guards and upon the neck, forehead and cheeks, that they are all marked black and blue where the blood collects beneath the skin. And their hauberks are so torn, and their shields so broken in pieces, that neither one escaped without wounds. Their breath is almost exhausted with the labour of the strife; they hammer away at each other so lustily that every hyacinth and emerald set in their helmets is crushed and smashed. For they give each other such a battering with their pommels upon the helmets that they are quite stunned, as they almost beat out each other's brains. The eyes in their heads gleam like sparks, as, with stout square fists, and strong nerves, and hard bones, they strike each other upon the mouth as long as they can grip their swords, which are of great service to them in dealing their heavy blows.

When they had for a long time strained themselves, until the helmets were crushed, and the hauberks' meshes were torn apart with the hammering of the swords, and the shields were split and cracked, they drew apart a little to give their pulse a rest and to catch their breath again. However, they do not long delay, but run at each other again more fiercely than before. And all declare that they never saw two more courageous knights. "This fight between them is no jest, but they are in grim earnest. They will never be repaid for their merits and deserts." The two friends, in their bitter struggle, heard these words, and heard how the people were talking of reconciling the two sisters; but they had no success in placating the elder one. And the younger one said she would leave it to the King, and would not gainsay him in anything. But the elder one was so obstinate that even the Queen Guinevere and the knights and the King and the ladies and the townspeople side with the younger sister, and all join in beseeching the King to give her a third or a fourth part of the land in spite of the elder sister, and to separate the two knights who had displayed such bravery, for it would be too bad if one should injure the other or deprive him of any honour. And the King replied that he would take no hand in making peace, for the elder sister is so cruel that she has no desire for it. All these words were heard by the two, who were attacking each other so bitterly that all were astonished thereat; for the battle is waged so evenly that it is impossible to judge which has the better and which the worse. Even the two men themselves, who fight, and who are purchasing honour with agony, are filled with amazement and stand aghast, for they are so well matched in their attack, that each wonders who it can be that withstands him with such bravery. They fight so long that the day draws on to night, while their arms grow weary and their bodies sore, and the hot, boiling blood flows from many a spot and trickles down beneath their hauberks: they are in such distress that it is no wonder if they wish to rest. Then both withdraw to rest themselves, each thinking within himself that, however long he has had to wait, he now at last has met his match. For some time they thus seek repose, without daring to resume the fight. They feel no further desire to fight, because of the night which is growing dark, and because of the respect they feel for each other's might. These two considerations keep them apart, and urge them to keep the peace. But before they leave the field they will discover each other's identity, and joy and mercy will be established between them.

My brave and courteous lord Yvain was the first to speak. But his good friend was unable to recognise him by his utterance; for he was prevented by his low tone and by his voice which was hoarse, weak, and broken; for his blood was all stirred up by the blows he had received. "My lord," he says, "the night comes on! I think no blame or reproach will attach to us if the night comes between us. But I am willing to admit, for my own part, that I feel great respect and admiration for you, and never in my life have I engaged in a battle which has made me smart so much, nor did I ever expect to see a knight whose acquaintance I should so yearn to make. You know well how to land your blows and how to make good use of them: I have never known a knight who was so skilled in dealing blows. It was against my will that I received all the blows you have bestowed on me to-day; I am stunned by the blows you have I struck upon my head." "Upon my word," my lord Gawain replies, "you are not so stunned and faint but that I am as much so, or more. And if I should tell you the simple truth, I think you would not be loath to hear it, for if I have lent you anything of mine, you have fully paid me back, principal and interest; for you were more ready to pay back than I was to accept the payment. But however that may be, since you wish me to inform you of my name, it shall not be kept from you: my name is Gawain the son of King Lot." As soon as my lord Yvain heard that, he was amazed and sorely troubled; angry and grief-stricken, he cast upon the ground his bloody sword and broken shield, then dismounted from his horse, and cried: "Alas, what mischance is this! Through what unhappy ignorance in not recognising each other have we waged this battle! For if I had known who you were,

I should never have fought with you; but, upon my word, I should have surrendered without a blow." "How is that?" my lord Gawain inquires, "who are you, then?" "I am Yvain, who love you more than any man in the whole wide world, for you have always been fond of me and shown me honour in every court. But I wish to make you such amends and do you such honour in this affair that I will confess myself to have been defeated." "Will you do so much for my sake?" my gentle lord Gawain asks him; "surely I should be presumptuous to accept any such amends from you. This honour shall never be claimed as mine, but it shall be yours, to whom I resign it." "Ah, fair sire, do not speak so. For that could never be. I am so wounded and exhausted that I cannot endure more." "Surely, you have no cause to be concerned." his friend and companion replies; "but for my part, I am defeated and over-come; I say it not as a compliment; for there is no stranger in the world, to whom I would not say as much, rather than receive any more blows." Thus saying, he got down from his horse, and they threw their arms about each other's neck, kissing each other, and each con-tinuing to assert that it is he who has met defeat. The argument is still in progress when the King and the knights come running up from every side, at the sight of their reconciliation; and great is their desire to hear how this can be, and who these men are who manifest such happiness. The King says: "Gentlemen, tell us now who it is that has so suddenly brought about this friendship and harmony between you two, after the hatred and strife there has been this day?" Then his nephew, my lord Gawain, thus answers him: "My lord, you shall be informed of the misfortune and mischance which have been the cause of our strife. Since you have tarried in order to hear and learn the cause of it, it is right to let you know the truth. I, Gawain, who am your nephew, did not recognise this companion of mine, my lord Yvain, until he fortunately, by the will of God, asked me my name. After each had informed the other of his name, we recognised each other, but not until we had fought it out. Our struggle already has been long; and if we had fought yet a little longer, it would have fared ill with me, for, by my head, he would have killed me, what with his prowess and the evil cause of her who chose me as her champion. But I would rather be defeated than killed by a friend in battle." Then my lord Yvain's blood was stirred, as he said to him in reply: "Fair dear sire, so help me God, you have no right to say so much. Let my lord, The King, well know in this battle I am surely the one who has been defeated and overcome!" "I am the one" "No, I am." Thus each cries out, and both are so honest and courteous that each allows the victory and crown to be the other's prize, while neither one of them will accept it. Thus each strives to convince the King and all the people that he has been defeated and overthrown. But when he had listened to them for a while, the King terminated the dispute. He was well pleased with what he heard and with the sight of them in each other's arms, though they had wounded and injured each other in several places. "My lords," he says, "there is deep affection between you two. You give clear evidence of that, when each insists that it is he who has been defeated. Now leave it all to me! For I think I can arrange it in such a way that it will redound to your honour, and every one will give consent." Then they both prom-ised him that they would do his will in every particular. And the King says that he will decide the quarrel fairly and faithfully. "Where is the damsel," he inquires, "who has ejected her sister from her land, and has forcibly and cruelly disinherited her?" "My lord," she answers, "here I am." "Are you there? Then draw near to me! I saw plainly some time ago that you were disinheriting her. But her right shall no longer be denied; for you yourself have avowed the truth to me. You must now resign her share to her." "Sire," she says, "if I uttered a fool-ish and thoughtless word, you ought not to take me up in it. For God's sake, sire, do not be hard on me! You are a king, and you ought to guard against wrong and error." The King replies: "That is precisely why I wish to give your sister her rights; for I have never defended what is wrong. And you have surely heard how your knight and hers have left the matter in my hands. I shall not say what is altogether pleasing to you; for your injustice is well known. In his desire to honour the other, each one says that he has been defeated. But there is no need to delay further: since the matter has been left to me, either you will do in all respects what I say, without resistance, or I shall announce that my nephew has been defeated in the fight. That would be the worst thing that could happen to your cause, and I shall be sorry to make such a declaration." In reality, he would not have said it for anything; but he spoke thus in order to see if he could frighten her into restoring the heritage to her sister; for he clearly saw that she never would surrender anything to her for any words of his unless she was influenced by force or fear. In fear and apprehension, she replied to him: "Fair lord, I must now respect your desire, though my heart is very loath to yield. Yet, however hard it may go with me, I shall do it, and my sister shall have what belongs to her. I give her your own person as a pledge of her share in my inheritance, in order that she may be more assured of it." "Endow her with it, then, at once," the King replies; "let her receive it from your hands, and let her vow fidelity to you! Do you love her as your vassal, and let her love you as her sovereign lady and as her sister." Thus the King conducts the affair until the damsel takes possession of her land, and offers her thanks to him for it. Then the King asked the valiant and brave knight who was his nephew to allow himself to be disarmed; and he requested my lord Yvain to lay aside his arms also; for now they may well dispense with them. Then the two vassals lay aside their arms and separate on equal terms. And while they are taking off their armour, they see the lion running up in search of his master. As soon as he catches sight of him, he begins to show his joy. Then you would have seen people draw aside, and the boldest among them takes to flight. My lord Yvain cries out: "Stand still, all! Why do you flee? No one is chasing you. Have no fear that yonder lion will do you harm. Believe me, please, when I say that he is mine, and I am his, and we are both companions." Then it was known of a truth by all those who had heard tell of the adventures of the lion and of his companion that this must be the very man who had killed the wicked giant. And my lord Gawain said to him: "Sir companion, so help me God, you have overwhelmed me with shame this day. I did not deserve the service that you did me in killing the giant to save my nephews and my niece. I have been thinking about you for some time, and I was troubled because it was said that we were acquainted as loving friends. I have surely thought much upon the subject: but I could not hit upon the truth, and had never heard of any knight that I had known in any land where I had been, who was called 'The Knight with the Lion.'" While they chatted thus they took their armour off, and the lion came with no slow step to the place where his master sat, and showed such joy as a dumb beast could. Then the two knights had to be removed to a sick-room and infirmary, for they needed a doctor and piaster to cure their wounds. King Arthur, who loved them well, had them both brought before him, and summoned a surgeon whose knowledge of surgery was supreme. He exercised his art in curing them, until he had healed their wounds as well and as quickly as possible. When he had cured them both, my lord Yvain, who had his heart set fast on love, saw clearly that he could not live, but that he finally would die unless his lady took pity upon him; for he was dying for love of her; so he thought he would go away from the court alone, and would go to fight at the spring that belonged to her, where he would cause such a storm of wind and rain that she would be compelled perforce to make peace with him; otherwise, there would be no end to the disturbance of the spring, and to the rain and wind.

As soon as my lord Yvain felt that he was cured and sound again, he departed without the knowledge of any one. But he had with him his lion, who never in his life wished to desert him. They travelled until they saw the spring and made the rain descend. Think not that this is a lie of mine, when I tell you that the disturbance was so violent that no one could tell the tenth part of it: for it seemed as if the whole forest must surely be engulfed. The lady fears for her town, lest it, too, will crumble away; the walls totter, and the tower rocks so that it is on the verge of falling down. The bravest Turk would rather be a captive in Persia than be shut up within those walls. The people are so stricken with terror that they curse all their ancestors, saying: "Confounded be the man who first constructed a house in this neighbourhood, and all those who built this town! For in the wide world they could not have found so detestable a spot, for a single man is able here to invade and worry and harry us." "You must take counsel in this matter, my lady," says Lunete; "you will find no one who will undertake to aid you in this time of need unless you seek for him afar. In the future we shall never be secure in this town, nor dare to pass beyond the walls and gate. You know full well that, were some one to summon together all your knights for this cause, the best of them would not dare to step forward. If it is true that you have no one to defend your spring, you will appear ridiculous and humiliated. It will redound greatly to your honour, forsooth, if he who has attacked you shall retire without a fight! Surely you are in a bad predicament if you do not devise some other plan to benefit yourself." The lady replies: "Do thou, who art so wise, tell me what plan I can devise, and I will follow thy advice." "Indeed, lady, if I had any plan, I should gladly propose it to you. But you have great need of a wiser counsellor. So I shall certainly not dare to intrude, and in common with the others I shall endure the rain and wind until, if it please God, I shall see some worthy man appear here in your court who will assume the responsibility and burden of the battle; but I do not believe that that will happen to-day, and we have not yet seen the worst of your urgent need." Then the lady replies at once: "Damsel, speak now of something else! Say no more of the people of my household; for I cherish no further expectation that the spring and its marble brim will ever be defended by any of them. But, if it please God, let us hear now what is your opinion and plan; for people always say that in time of need one can test his friend." "My lady, if there is any one who thinks he could find him who slew the giant and defeated the three knights, he would do well to go to search for him. But so long as he shall incur the enmity, wrath, and displeasure of his lady, I fancy there is not under heaven any man or woman whom he would follow, until he had been assured upon oath that everything possible would be done to appease the hostility which his lady feels for him, and which is so bitter that he is dying of the grief and anxiety it causes him." And the lady said: "Before you enter upon the quest, I am prepared to promise you upon my word and to swear that, if he will return to me, I will openly and frankly do all I can to bring about his peace of mind." Then Lunete replies to her: "Lady, have no fear that you cannot easily effect his reconciliation, when once it is your desire to do so; but, if you do not object, I will take your oath before I start." "I have no objection," the lady says. With delicate courtesy, Lunete procured at once for her a very precious relic, and the lady fell upon her knees. Thus Lunete very courteously accepted her upon her oath. In administering the oath, she forgot nothing which it might be an advantage to insert. "Lady," she says, "now raise your hand! I do not wish that the day after to-morrow you should lay any charge upon me; for you are not doing anything for me, but you are acting for your own good. If you please now, you shall swear that you will exert yourself in the interests of the Knight with the Lion until he recover his lady's love as completely as he ever possessed it." The lady then raised her right hand and said: "I swear to all that thou hast said, so help me God and His holy saint, that my heart may never fail to do all within my power. If I have the strength and ability, I will restore to him the love and favour which with his lady he once enjoyed."

Lunete has now done well her work; there was nothing which she had desired so much as the object which she had now attained. They had already got out for her a palfrey with an easy pace. Gladly and in a happy frame of mind Lunete mounts and rides away, until she finds beneath the pine-tree him whom she did not expect to find so near at hand. Indeed, she had thought that she would have to seek afar before discovering him. As soon as she saw him, she recognised him by the lion, and coming toward him rapidly, she dismounted upon the solid earth. And my lord Yvain recognised her as soon as he saw her, and greeted her, as she saluted him with the words: "Sire, I am very happy to have found you so near at hand." And my lord Yvain said in reply: "How is that? Were you looking for me, then?" "Yes, sire, and in all my life I have never felt so glad, for I have made my mistress promise, if she does not go back upon her word, that she will be again your lady as was once the case, and that you shall be her lord; this truth I make bold to tell." My lord Yvain was greatly elated at the news he hears, and which he had never expected to hear again. He could not sufficiently show his gratitude to her who had accomplished this for him. He kisses her eyes, and then her face, saying: "Surely, my sweet friend, I can never repay you for this service. I fear that ability and time will fail me to do you the honour and service which is your due." "Sire," she replies, "have no concern, and let not that thought worry you! For you will have an abundance of strength and time to show me and others your good will. If I have paid this debt I owed, I am entitled to only so much gratitude as the man who borrows another's goods and then discharges the obligation. Even now I do not consider that I have paid you the debt I owed." "Indeed you have, as God sees me, more than five hundred thousand times. Now, when you are ready, let us go. But have you told her who I am?" "No, I have not, upon my word. She knows you only by the name of 'The Knight with the Lion.'"

Thus conversing they went along, with the lion following after them, until they all three came to the town. They said not a word to any man or woman there, until they arrived where the lady was. And the lady was greatly pleased as soon as she heard that the damsel was approaching, and that she was bringing with her the lion and the knight, whom she was very anxious to meet and know and see. All clad in his arms, my lord Yvain fell at her feet upon his knees, while Lunete, who was standing by, said to her: "Raise him up, lady, and apply all your efforts and strength and skill in procuring that peace and pardon which no one in the world, except you, can secure for him." Then the lady bade him rise, and said: "He may dispose of all my power! I shall be very happy, if possible, to accomplish his wish and his desire." "Surely, my lady," Lunete replied, "I would not say it if it were not true. But all this is even more possible for you than I have said: but now I will tell you the whole truth, and you shall see: you never had and you never will have such a good friend as this gentleman. God, whose will it is that there should be unending peace and love between you and him, has caused me to find him this day so near at hand. In order to test the truth of this, I have only one thing to say: lady, dismiss the grudge you bear him! For he has no other mistress than you. This is your husband, my lord Yvain."

The lady, trembling at these words, replied: "God save me! You have caught me neatly in a trap! You will make me love, in spite of myself, a man who neither loves nor esteems me. This is a fine piece of work, and a charming way of serving me! I would rather endure the winds and the tempests all my life: And if it were not a mean and ugly thing to break one's word, he would never make his peace or be reconciled with me. This purpose would have always lurked within me, as a fire smoulders in the ashes; but I do not wish to renew it now, nor do I care to refer to it, since I must be reconciled with him."

My lord Yvain hears and understands that his cause is going well, and that he will be peacefully reconciled with her. So he says: "Lady, one ought to have mercy on a sinner. I have had to pay, and dearly to pay, for my mad act. It was madness that made me stay away, and I now admit my guilt and sin. I have been bold, indeed, in daring to present myself to you; but if you will deign to keep me now, I never again shall do you any wrong." She replied: "I will surely consent to that; for if I did not do all I could to establish peace between you and me, I should be guilty of perjury. So, if you please, I grant your request." "Lady," says he, "so truly as God in this mortal life could not otherwise restore me to happiness, so may the Holy Spirit bless me five hundred times!"

Now my lord Yvain is reconciled, and you may believe that, in spite of the trouble he has endured, he was never so happy for anything. All has turned out well at last; for he is beloved and treasured by his lady, and she by him. His troubles no longer are in his mind; for he forgets them all in the joy he feels with his precious wife. And Lunete, for her part, is happy too: all her desires are satisfied when once she had made an enduring peace between my polite lord Yvain and his sweetheart so dear and so elegant.

Thus Chretien concludes his romance of the Knight with the Lion; for I never heard any more told of it, nor will you ever hear any further particulars, unless some one wishes to add some lies.

# Lancelot: The Knight of the Cart

Since my lady of Champagne wishes me to undertake to write a romance, I shall very gladly do so, being so devoted to her service as to do anything in the world for her, without any intention of flattery. But if one were to introduce any flattery upon such an occasion, he might say, and I would subscribe to it, that this lady surpasses all others who are alive, just as the south wind which blows in May or April is more lovely than any other wind. But upon my word, I am not one to wish to flatter my lady. I will simply say: "The Countess is worth as many queens as a gem is worth of pearls and sards." Nay I shall make no comparison, and yet it is true in spite of me; I will say, however, that her command has more to do with this work than any thought or pains that I may expend upon it. Here Chretien begins his book about the Knight of the Cart. The material and the treatment of it are given and furnished to him by the Countess, and he is simply trying to carry out her concern and intention. Here he begins the story.

Upon a certain Ascension Day King Arthur had come from Caerleon, and had held a very magnificent court at Camelot as was fitting on such a day. After the feast the King did not quit his noble companions, of whom there were many in the hall. The Queen was present, too, and with her many a courteous lady able to converse in French. And Kay, who had furnished the meal, was eating with the others who had served the food. While Kay was sitting there at meat, behold there came to court a knight, well equipped and fully armed, and thus the knight appeared before the King as he sat among his lords. He gave him no greeting, but spoke out thus: "King Arthur, I hold in captivity knights, ladies, and damsels who belong to thy dominion and household; but it is not because of any intention to restore them to thee that I make reference to them here; rather do I wish to proclaim and serve thee notice that thou hast not the strength or the resources to enable thee to secure them again. And be assured that thou shalt die before thou canst ever succour them." The King replies that he must needs endure what he has not the power to change; nevertheless, he is filled with grief. Then the knight makes as if to go away, and turns about, without tarrying longer before the King; but after reaching the door of the hall, he does not go down the stairs, but stops and speaks from there these words: "King, if in thy court there is a single knight in whom thou hast such confidence that thou wouldst dare to entrust to him the Queen that he might escort her after me out into the woods whither I am going, I will promise to await him there, and will surrender to thee all the prisoners whom I hold in exile in my country if he is able to defend the Queen and if he succeeds in bringing her back again." Many who were in the palace heard this challenge, and the whole court was in an uproar. Kay, too, heard the news as he sat at meat with those who served. Leaving the table, he came straight to the King, and as if greatly enraged, he began to say: "O King, I have served thee long, faithfully, and loyally; now I take my leave, and shall go away, having no desire to serve thee more." The King was grieved at what he heard, and as soon as he could, he thus replied to him: "Is this serious, or a joke?" And Kay replied: "O King, fair sire, I have no desire to jest, and I take my leave quite seriously. No other reward or wages do I wish in return for the service I have given you. My mind is quite made up to go away immediately." "Is it in anger or in spite that you wish to go?" the King inquired; "seneschal, remain at court, as you have done hitherto, and be assured that I have nothing in the world which I would not give

161

you at once in return for your consent to stay." "Sire," says Kay, "no need of that. I would not accept for each day's pay a measure of fine pure gold." Thereupon, the King in great dismay went off to seek the Queen. "My lady," he says, "you do not know the demand that the seneschal makes of me. He asks me for leave to go away, and says he will no longer stay at court; the reason of this I do not know. But he will do at your request what he will not do for me. Go to him now, my lady dear. Since he will not consent to stay for my sake, pray him to remain on your account, and if need be, fall at his feet, for I should never again be happy if I should lose his company." The King sends the Queen to the seneschal, and she goes to him. Finding him with the rest, she went up to him, and said: "Kay, you may be very sure that I am greatly troubled by the news I have heard of you. I am grieved to say that I have been told it is your intention to leave the King. How does this come about? What motive have you in your mind? I cannot think that you are so sensible or courteous as usual. I want to ask you to remain: stay with us here, and grant my prayer." "Lady," he says, "I give you thanks; nevertheless, I shall not remain." The Queen again makes her request, and is joined by all the other knights. And Kay informs her that he is growing tired of a service which is unprofitable. Then the Queen prostrates herself at full length before his feet. Kay beseeches her to rise, but she says that she will never do so until he grants her request. Then Kay promises her to remain, provided the King and she will grant in advance a favour he is about to ask. "Kay," she says, "he will grant it, whatever it may be. Come now, and we shall tell him that upon this condition you will remain." So Kay goes away with the Queen to the King's presence. The Queen says: "I have had hard work to detain Kay; but I have brought him here to you with the understanding that you will do what he is going to ask." The King sighed with satisfaction, and said that he would perform whatever request he might make.

"Sire," says Kay, "hear now what I desire, and what is the gift you have promised me. I esteem myself very fortunate to gain such a boon with your consent. Sire, you have pledged your word that you would entrust to me my lady here, and that we should go after the knight who awaits us in the forest." Though the King is grieved, he trusts him with the charge, for he never went back upon his word. But it made him so ill-humoured and displeased that it plainly showed in his countenance. The Queen, for her part, was sorry too, and all those of the household say that Kay had made a proud, outrageous, and mad request. Then the King took the Queen by the hand, and said: "My lady, you must accompany Kay without making objection." And Kay said: "Hand her over to me now, and have no fear, for I shall bring her back perfectly happy and safe." The King gives her into his charge, and he takes her off. After them all the rest go out, and there is not one who is not sad. You must know that the seneschal was fully armed, and his horse was led into the middle of the courtyard, together with a palfrey, as is fitting, for the Queen. The Queen walked up to the palfrey, which was neither restive nor hard-mouthed. Grieving and sad, with a sigh the Queen mounts, saying to herself in a low voice, so that no one could hear: "Alas, alas, if you only knew it, I am sure you would never allow me without interference to be led away a step." She thought she had spoken in a very low tone; but Count Guinable heard her, who was standing by when she mounted. When they started away, as great a lament was made by all the men and women present as if she already lay dead upon a bier. They do not believe that she will ever in her life come back. The seneschal in his impudence takes her where that other knight is awaiting her. But no one was so much concerned as to undertake to follow him; until at last my lord Gawain thus addressed the King his uncle: "Sire," he says, "you have done a very foolish thing, which causes me great surprise; but if you will take my advice, while they are still near by, I and you will ride after them, and all those who wish to accompany us. For my part, I cannot restrain myself from going in pursuit of them at once. It would not be proper for us not to go after them, at least far enough to learn what is to become of the Queen, and how Kay is going to comport himself." "Ah, fair nephew," the King replied, "you have spoken courteously. And since you have undertaken the affair, order our horses to be led out bridled and saddled that there may be no delay in setting out."

The horses are at once brought out, all ready and with the saddles on. First the King mounts, then my lord Gawain, and all the others rapidly. Each one, wishing to be of the party, follows his own will and starts away. Some were armed, but there were not a few without their arms. My lord Gawain was armed, and he bade two squires lead by the bridle two extra steeds. And as they thus approached the forest, they saw Kay's horse running out; and they recognised him, and saw that both reins of the bridle were broken. The horse was running wild, the stirrup-straps all stained with blood, and the saddle-bow was broken and damaged. Every one was chagrined at this, and they nudged each other and shook their heads. My lord Gawain was riding far in advance of the rest of the party, and it was not long before he saw coming slowly a knight on a horse that was sore, painfully tired, and covered with sweat. The knight first saluted my lord Gawain, and his greeting my lord Gawain returned. Then the knight, recognising my lord Gawain, stopped and thus spoke to him: "You see, sir, my horse is in a sweat and in such case as to be no longer serviceable. I suppose that those two horses belong to you now, with the understanding that I shall return the service and the favour, I beg you to let me have one or the other of them, either as a loan or outright as a gift." And he answers him: "Choose whichever you prefer." Then he who was in dire distress did not try to select the better or the fairer or the larger of the horses, but leaped quickly upon the one which was nearer to him, and rode him off. Then the one he had just left fell dead, for he had ridden him hard that day, so that he was used up and overworked. The knight without delay goes pricking through the forest, and my lord Gawain follows in pursuit of him with all speed, until he reaches the bottom of a hill. And when he had gone some distance, he found the horse dead which he had given to the knight, and noticed that the ground had been trampled by horses, and that broken shields and lances lay strewn about, so that it seemed that there had been a great combat between several knights, and he was very sorry and grieved not to have been there. However, he did not stay there long, but rapidly passed on until he saw again by chance the knight all alone on foot, completely armed, with helmet laced, shield hanging from his neck, and with his sword girt on. He had overtaken a cart. In those days such a cart served the same purpose as does a pillory now; and in each good town where there are more than three thousand such carts nowadays, in those times there was only one, and this, like our pillories, had to do service for all those who commit murder or treason, and those who are guilty of any delinquency, and for thieves who have stolen others' property or have forcibly seized it on the roads. Whoever was convicted of any crime was placed upon a cart and dragged through all the streets, and he lost henceforth all his legal rights, and was never afterward heard, honoured, or welcomed in any court. The carts were so dreadful in those days that the saying was then first used: "When thou dost see and meet a cart, cross thyself and call upon God, that no evil may befall thee." The knight on foot, and without a lance, walked behind the cart, and saw a dwarf sitting on the shafts, who held, as a driver does, a long goad in his hand. Then he cries out: "Dwarf, for God's sake, tell me now if thou hast seen my lady, the Queen, pass by here." The miserable, low-born dwarf would not give him any news of her, but replied: "If thou wilt get up into the cart I am driving thou shalt hear to-morrow what has happened to the Queen." Then he kept on his way without giving further heed. The knight hesitated only for a couple of steps before getting in. Yet, it was unlucky for him that he shrank from the disgrace, and did not jump in at once; for he will later rue his delay. But common sense, which is inconsistent with love's dictates, bids him refrain from getting in, warning him and counselling him to do and undertake nothing for which he may reap shame and disgrace. Reason, which dares thus speak to him, reaches only his lips, but not his heart; but love is enclosed within his heart, bidding him and urging him to mount at once upon the cart. So he jumps in, since love will have it so, feeling no concern about the shame, since he is prompted by love's commands. And my lord Gawain presses on in haste after the cart, and when he finds the knight sitting in it, his surprise is great. "Tell me," he shouted to the dwarf, "if thou knowest anything of the Queen." And he replied: "If thou art so much thy own enemy as is this knight who is sitting here, get in with him, if it be thy pleasure, and I will drive thee along with him." When my lord Gawain heard that, he considered it great foolishness, and said that he would not get in, for it would be dishonourable to exchange a horse for a cart: "Go on, and wherever thy journey lies, I will follow after thee."

Thereupon they start ahead, one mounted on his horse, the other two riding in the cart, and thus they proceed in company. Late in the afternoon they arrive at a town, which, you must know, was very rich and beautiful. All three entered through the gate; the people are greatly amazed to see the knight borne upon the cart, and they take no pains to conceal their feelings, but small and great and old and young shout taunts at him in the streets, so that the knight hears many vile and scornful words at his expense. They all inquire: "To what punishment is this knight to be consigned? Is he to be rayed, or hanged, or drowned, or burned upon a fire of thorns? Tell us, thou dwarf, who art driving him, in what crime was he caught? Is he convicted of robbery? Is he a murderer, or a criminal?" And to all this the dwarf made no response, vouchsafing to them no reply. He conducts the knight to a lodging-place; and Gawain follows the dwarf closely to a tower, which stood on the same level over against the town. Beyond there stretched a meadow, and the tower was built close by, up on a lofty eminence of rock, whose face formed a sharp precipice. Following the horse and cart, Gawain entered the tower. In the hall they met a damsel elegantly attired, than whom there was none fairer in the land, and with her they saw coming two fair and charming maidens. As soon as they saw my lord Gawain, they received him joyously and saluted him, and then asked news about the other knight: "Dwarf, of what crime is this knight guilty, whom thou dost drive like a lame man?" He would not answer her question, but he made the knight get out of the cart, and then he withdrew, without their knowing whither he went. Then my lord Gawain dismounts, and valets come forward to relieve the two knights of their armour. The damsel ordered two green mantles to be brought, which they put on. When the hour for supper came, a sumptuous repast was set. The damsel sat at table beside my lord Gawain. They would not have changed their lodging-place to seek any other, for all that evening the damsel showed them gear honour, and provided them with fair and pleasant company.

When they had sat up long enough, two long, high beds were prepared in the middle of the hall; and there was another bed alongside, fairer and more splendid than the rest; for, as the story testifies, it possessed all the excellence that one could think of in a bed. When the time came to retire, the damsel took both the guests to whom she had offered her hospitality; she shows them the two fine, long, wide beds, and says: "These two beds are set up here for the accommodation of your bodies; but in that one yonder no one ever lay who did not merit it: it was not set up to be used by you." The knight who came riding on the cart replies at once: "Tell me," he says, "for what cause this bed is inaccessible." Being thoroughly informed of this, she answers unhesitatingly: "It is not your place to ask or make such an inquiry. Any knight is disgraced in the land after being in a cart, and it is not fitting that he should concern himself with the matter upon which you have questioned me; and most of all it is not right that he should lie upon the bed, for he would soon pay dearly for his act. So rich a couch has not been prepared for you, and you would pay dearly for ever harbouring such a thought." He replies: "You will see about that presently.".... "Am I to see it?".... "Yes.".... "It will soon appear.".... "By my head," the knight replies, "I know not who is to pay the penalty. But whoever may object or disapprove, I intend to lie upon this bed and repose there at my ease." Then he at once disrobed in the bed, which was long and raised half an ell above the other two, and was covered with a yellow cloth of silk and a coverlet with gilded stars. The furs were not of skinned vair but of sable; the covering he had on him would have been fitting for a king. The mattress was not made of straw or rushes or of old mats. At midnight there descended from the rafters suddenly a lance, as with the intention of pinning the knight through the flanks to the coverlet and the white sheets where he lay. To the lance there was attached a pennon all ablaze. The coverlet, the bedclothes, and the bed itself all caught fire at once. And the tip of the lance passed so close to the knight's side that it cut the skin a little, without seriously wounding him. Then the knight got up, put out the fire and, taking the lance, swung it in the middle of the hall, all this without leaving his bed; rather did he lie down again and slept as securely as at first.

In the morning, at daybreak, the damsel of the tower had Mass celebrated on their account, and had them rise and dress. When Mass had been celebrated for them, the knight who had ridden in the cart sat down pensively at a window, which looked out upon the meadow, and he gazed upon the fields below. The damsel came to another window close by, and there my lord Gawain conversed with her privately for a while about something, I know not what. I do not know what words were uttered, but while they were leaning on the window-sill they saw carried along the river through the fields a bier, upon which there lay a knight, and alongside three damsels walked, mourning bitterly. Behind the bier they saw a crowd approaching, with a tall knight in front, leading a fair lady by the horse's rein. The knight at the window knew that it was the Queen. He continued to gaze at her attentively and with delight as long as she was visible. And when he could no longer see her, he was minded to throw himself out and break his body down below. And he would have let himself fall out had not my lord Gawain seen him, and drawn him back, saying: "I beg you, sire, be quiet now. For God's sake, never think again of committing such a mad deed. It is wrong for you to despise your life." "He is perfectly right," the damsel says; "for will not the news of his disgrace be known everywhere? Since he has been upon the cart, he has good reason to wish to die, for he would be better dead than alive. His life henceforth is sure to be one of shame, vexation, and unhappiness." Then the knights asked for their armour, and armed themselves, the damsel treating them courteously, with distinction and generosity; for when she had joked with the knight and ridiculed him enough, she presented him with a horse and lance as a token of her goodwill. The knights then courteously and politely took leave of the damsel, first saluting her, and then going off in the direction taken by the crowd they had seen. Thus they rode out from the town without addressing them. They proceeded quickly in the direction they had seen taken by the Queen, but they did not overtake the procession, which had advanced rapidly. After leaving the fields, the knights enter an enclosed place, and find a beaten road. They advanced through the woods until it might be six o'clock, and then at a crossroads they met a damsel, whom they both saluted, each asking and requesting her to tell them, if she knows, whither the Queen has been taken. Replying intelligently, she said to them: "If you would pledge me your word, I could set you on the right road and path, and I would tell you the name of the country and of the knight who is conducting her; but whoever would essay to enter that country must endure sore trials, for before he could reach there he must suffer much." Then my lord Gawain replies: "Damsel, so help me God, I promise to place all my strength at your disposal and service, whenever you please, if you will tell me now the truth." And he who had been on the cart did not say that he would pledge her all his strength; but he proclaims, like one whom love makes rich, powerful and bold for any enterprise, that at once and without hesitation he will promise her anything she desires, and he puts himself altogether at her disposal. "Then I will tell you the truth," says she. Then the damsel relates to them the following story: "In truth, my lords, Meleagant, a tall and powerful knight, son of the King of Gorre, has taken her off into the kingdom whence no foreigner returns, but where he must perforce remain in servitude and banishment." Then they ask her: "Damsel, where is this country? Where can we find the way thither?" She replies: "That you shall quickly learn; but you may be sure that you will meet with many obstacles and difficult passages, for it is not easy to enter there except with the permission of the king, whose name is Bademagu; however, it is possible to enter by two very perilous paths and by two very difficult passage-ways. One is called the water-bridge, because the bridge is under water, and there is the same amount of water beneath it as above it, so that the bridge is exactly in the middle; and it is only a foot and a half in width and in thickness. This choice is certainly to be avoided, and yet it is the less dangerous of the two. In addition there are a number of other obstacles of which I will say nothing. The other bridge is still more impracticable and much more perilous, never having been crossed by man. It is just like a sharp sword, and therefore all the people call it 'the sword-bridge'. Now I have told you all the truth I know." But they ask of her once again: "Damsel, deign to show us these two passages." To which the damsel makes reply: "This road here is the most direct to the water-bridge, and that one yonder leads straight to the sword-bridge." Then the knight, who had been on the cart, says: "Sire, I am ready to share with you without prejudice: take one of these two routes, and leave the other one to me; take whichever you prefer." "In truth," my lord Gawain replies, "both of them are hard and dangerous: I am not skilled in making such a choice, and hardly know which of them to take; but it is not right for me to hesitate when you have left the choice to me: I will choose the water-bridge." The other answers: "Then I must go uncomplainingly to the sword-bridge, which I agree to do." Thereupon, they all three part, each one commending the others very courteously to God. And when she sees them departing, she says: "Each one of you owes me a favour of my choosing, whenever I may choose to ask it. Take care not to forget that." "We shall surely not forget it, sweet friend," both the knights call out. Then each one goes his own way, and he of the cart is occupied with deep reflections, like one who has no strength or defence against love which holds him in its sway. His thoughts are such that he totally forgets himself, and he knows not whether he is alive or dead, forgetting even his own name, not knowing whether he is armed or not, or whither he is going or whence he came. Only one creature he has in mind, and for her his thought is so occupied that he neither sees nor hears aught else. And his horse bears him along rapidly, following no crooked road, but the best and the most direct; and thus proceeding unguided, he brings him into an open plain. In this plain there was a ford, on the other side of which a knight stood armed, who guarded it, and in his company there was a damsel who had come on a palfrey. By this time the afternoon was well advanced, and yet the knight, unchanged and unwearied, pursued his thoughts. The horse, being very thirsty, sees clearly the ford, and as soon as he sees it, hastens toward it. Then he on the other side cries out: "Knight, I am guarding the ford, and forbid you to cross." He neither gives him heed, nor hears his words, being still deep in thought. In the meantime, his horse advanced rapidly toward the water. The knight calls out to him that he will do wisely to keep at a distance from the ford, for there is no passage that way; and he swears by the heart within his breast that he will smite him if he enters the water. But his threats are not heard, and he calls out to him a third time: "Knight, do not enter the ford against my will and prohibition; for, by my head, I shall strike you as soon as I see you in the ford." But he is so deep in thought that he does not hear him. And the horse, quickly leaving the bank, leaps into the ford and greedily begins to drink. And the knight says he shall pay for this, that his shield and the hauberk he wears upon his back shall afford him no protection. First, he puts his horse at a gallop, and from a gallop he urges him to a run, and he strikes the knight so hard that he knocks him down flat in the ford which he had forbidden him to cross. His lance flew from his hand and the shield from his neck. When he feels the water, he shivers, and though stunned, he jumps to his feet, like one aroused from sleep, listening and looking about him with astonishment, to see who it can be who has struck him. Then face to face with the other knight, he said: "Vassal, tell me why you have struck me, when I was not aware of your presence, and when I had done you no harm." "Upon my word, you had wronged me," the other says: "did you not treat me disdainfully when I forbade you three times to cross the ford, shouting at you as loudly as I could? You surely heard me challenge you at least two or three times, and you entered in spite of me, though I told you I should strike you as soon as I saw you in the ford." Then the knight replies to him: "Whoever heard you or saw you, let him be damned, so far as I am concerned. I was probably deep in thought when you forbade me to cross the ford. But be assured that I would make you reset it, if I could just lay one of my hands on your bridle." And the other replies: "Why, what of that? If you dare, you may seize my bridle here and now. I do not esteem your proud threats so much as a handful of ashes." And he replies: "That suits me perfectly. However the affair may turn out, I should like to lay my hands on you." Then the other knight advances to the middle of the ford, where the other lays his left hand upon his bridle, and his right hand upon his leg, pulling, dragging, and pressing him so roughly that he remonstrates, thinking that he would pull his leg out of his body. Then he begs him to let go, saying: "Knight, if it please thee to fight me on even terms, take thy shield and horse and lance, and joust with me." He answers: "That will I not do, upon my word; for I suppose thou wouldst run away as soon as thou hadst escaped my grip." Hearing this, he was much ashamed, and said: "Knight, mount thy horse, in confidence for I will pledge thee loyally my word that I shall not flinch or run away." Then once again he answers him: "First, thou wilt have to swear to that, and I insist upon receiving thy oath that thou wilt neither run away nor flinch, nor touch me, nor come near me until thou shalt see me on my horse; I shall be treating thee very generously, if, when thou art in my hands, I let thee go." He can do nothing but give his oath; and when the other hears him swear, he gathers up his shield and lance which were floating in the ford and by this time had drifted well down-stream; then he returns and takes his horse. After catching and mounting him, he seizes the shield by the shoulder-straps and lays his lance in rest. Then each spurs toward the other as fast as their horses can carry them. And he who had to defend the ford first attacks the other, striking him so hard that his lance is completely splintered. The other strikes him in return so that he throws him prostrate into the ford, and the water closes over him. Having accomplished that, he draws back and dismounts, thinking he could drive and chase away a hundred such. While he draws from the scabbard his sword of steel, the other jumps up and draws his excellent flashing blade. Then they clash again, advancing and covering themselves with the shields which gleam with gold. Ceaselessly and without repose they wield their swords; they have the courage to deal so many blows that the battle finally is so protracted that the Knight of the Cart is greatly ashamed in his heart, thinking that he is making a sorry start in the way he has undertaken, when he has spent so much time in defeating a single knight. If he had met yesterday a hundred such, he does not think or believe that they could have withstood him; so now he is much grieved and wroth to be in such an exhausted state that he is missing his strokes and losing time. Then he runs at him and presses him so hard that the other knight gives way and flees. However reluctant he may be, he leaves the ford and crossing free. But the other follows him in pursuit until he falls forward upon his hands; then he of the cart runs up to him, swearing by all he sees that he shall rue the day when he upset him in the ford and disturbed his revery. The damsel, whom the knight had with him, upon hearing the threats, is in great fear, and begs him for her sake to forbear from killing him; but he tells her that he must do so, and can show him no mercy for her sake, in view of the shameful wrong that he has done him. Then, with sword drawn, he approaches the knight who cries in sore dismay: "For God's sake and for my own, show me the mercy I ask of you." And he replies: "As God may save me, no one ever sinned so against me that I would not show him mercy once, for God's sake as is right, if he asked it of me in God's name. And so on thee I will have mercy; for I ought not to refuse thee when thou hast besought me. But first, thou shalt give me thy word to constitute thyself my prisoner whenever I may wish to summon thee." Though it was hard to do so, he promised him. At once the damsel said: "O knight, since thou hast granted the mercy he asked of thee, if ever thou hast broken any bonds, for my sake now be merciful and release this prisoner from his parole. Set him free at my request, upon condition that when the time comes, I shall do my utmost to repay thee in any way that thou shalt choose." Then he declares himself satisfied with the promise she has made, and sets the knight at liberty. Then she is ashamed and anxious, thinking that he will recognise her, which she did not wish. But he goes away at once, the knight and the damsel commending him to God, and taking leave of him. He grants them leave to go, while he himself pursues his way, until late in the afternoon he met a damsel coming, who was very fair and charming, well attired and richly dressed. The damsel greets him prudently and courteously, and he replies: "Damsel, God grant you health and happiness." Then the damsel said to him: "Sire, my house is prepared for you, if you will accept my hospitality, but you shall find shelter there only on condition that you will lie with me; upon these terms I propose and make the offer." Not a few there are who would have thanked her five hundred times for such a gift; but he is much displeased, and made a very different answer: "Damsel, I thank you for the offer of your house, and esteem it highly, but, if you please, I should be very sorry to lie with you." "By my eyes," the damsel says, "then I retract my offer." And he, since it is unavoidable, lets her have her way, though his heart grieves to give consent. He feels only reluctance now; but greater distress will be his when it is time to go to bed. The damsel, too, who leads him away, will pass through sorrow and heaviness. For it is possible that she will love him so that she will not wish to part with him. As soon as he had granted her wish and desire, she escorts him to a fortified place, than which there was none fairer in Thessaly; for it was entirely enclosed by a high wall and a deep moat, and there was no man within except him whom she brought with her.

Here she had constructed for her residence a quantity of handsome rooms, and a large and roomy hall. Riding along a river bank, they approached their lodging-place, and a drawbridge was lowered to allow them to pass. Crossing the bridge, they entered in, and found the hall open with its roof of tiles. Through the open door they pass, and see a table laid with a broad white cloth, upon which the dishes were set, and the candles burning in their stands, and the gilded silver drinking-cups, and two pots of wine, one red and one white. Standing beside the table, at the end of a bench, they found two basins of warm water in which to wash their hands, with a richly embroidered towel, all white and clean, with which to dry their hands. No valets, servants, or squires were to be found or seen. The knight, removing his shield from about his neck, hangs it upon a hook, and, taking his lance, lays it above upon a rack. Then he dismounts from his horse, as does the damsel from hers. The knight, for his part, was pleased that she did not care to wait for him to help her to dismount. Having dismounted, she runs directly to a room and brings him a short mantle of scarlet cloth which she puts on him. The hall was by no means dark; for beside the light from the stars, there were many large twisted candles lighted there, so that the illumination was very bright. When she had thrown the mantle about his shoulders, she said to him: "Friend, here is the water and the towel; there is no one to present or offer it to you except me whom you see. Wash your hands, and then sit down, when you feel like doing so. The hour and the meal, as you can see, demand that you should do so." He washes, and then gladly and readily takes his seat, and she sits down beside him, and they eat and drink together, until the time comes to leave the table.

When they had risen from the table, the damsel said to the knight: "Sire, if you do not object, go outside and amuse yourself; but, if you please, do not stay after you think I must be in bed. Feel no concern or embarrassment; for then you may come to me at once, if you will keep the promise you have made." And he replies: "I will keep my word, and will return when I think the time has come." Then he went out, and stayed in the courtyard until he thought it was time to return and keep the promise he had made. Going back into the hall, he sees nothing of her who would be his mistress; for she was not there. Not finding or seeing her, he said: "Wherever she may be, I shall look for her until I find her." He makes no delay in his search, being bound by the promise he had made her. Entering one of the rooms, he hears a damsel cry aloud, and it was the very one with whom he was about to lie. At the same time, he sees the door of another room standing open, and stepping toward it, he sees right before his eyes a knight who had thrown her down, and was holding her naked and prostrate upon the bed. She, thinking that he had come of course to help her, cried aloud: "Help, help, thou knight, who art my guest. If thou dost not take this man away from me, I shall find no one to do so; if thou dost not succour me speedily, he will wrong me before thy eyes. Thou art the one to lie with me, in accordance with thy promise; and shall this man by force accomplish his wish before thy eyes? Gentle knight, exert thyself, and make haste to bear me aid." He sees that the other man held the damsel brutally uncovered to the waist, and he is ashamed and angered to see him assault her so; yet it is not jealousy he feels, nor will he be made a cuckold by him. At the door there stood as guards two knights completely armed and with swords drawn. Behind them there stood four men-at-arms, each armed with an axe the sort with which you could split a cow down the back as easily as a root of juniper or broom. The knight hesitated at the door, and thought: "God, what can I do? I am engaged in no less an affair than the quest of Queen Guinevere. I ought not to have the heart of a hare, when for her sake I have engaged in such a quest. If cowardice puts its heart in me, and if I follow its dictates, I shall never attain what I seek. I am disgraced, if I stand here; indeed, I am ashamed even to have thought of holding back. My heart is very sad and oppressed: now I am so ashamed and distressed that I would gladly die for having hesitated here so long. I say it not in pride: but may God have mercy on me if I do not prefer to die honourably rather than live a life of shame! If my path were unobstructed, and if these men gave me leave to pass through without restraint, what honour would I gain? Truly, in that case the greatest coward alive would pass through; and all the while I hear this poor creature calling for help constantly, and reminding me of my promise, and reproaching me with bitter taunts." Then he steps to the door, thrusting in his head and shoulders; glancing up, he sees two swords descending. He draws back, and the knights could not check their strokes: they had wielded them with such force that the swords struck the floor, and both were broken in pieces. When he sees that the swords are broken, he pays less attention to the axes, fearing and dreading them much less. Rushing in among them, he strikes first one guard in the side and then another. The two who are nearest him he jostles and thrusts aside, throwing them both down flat; the third missed his stroke at him, but the fourth, who attacked him, strikes him so that he cuts his mantle and shirt, and slices the white flesh on his shoulder so that the blood trickles down from the wound. But he, without delay, and without complaining of his wound, presses on more rapidly, until he strikes between the temples him who was assaulting his hostess. Before he departs, he will try to keep his pledge to her. He makes him stand up reluctantly. Meanwhile, he who had missed striking him comes at him as fast as he can and, raising his arm again, expects to split his head to the teeth with the axe. But the other, alert to defend himself, thrusts the knight toward him in such a way that he receives the axe just where the shoulder joins the neck, so that they are cleaved apart. Then the knight seizes the axe, wresting it quickly from him who holds it; then he lets go the knight whom he still held, and looks to his own defence; for the knights from the door, and the three men with axes are all attacking him fiercely. So he leaped quickly between the bed and the wall, and called to them: "Come on now, all of you. If there were thirty-seven of you, you would have all the fight you wish, with me so favourably placed; I shall never be overcome by you." And the damsel watching him, exclaimed: "By my eyes, you need have no thought of that henceforth where I am." Then at once she dismisses the knights and the men-at-arms, who retire from there at once, without delay or objection. And the damsel continues: "Sire you have well defended me against the men of my household. Come now, and I'll lead you on." Hand in hand they enter the hall, but he was not at all pleased, and would have willingly dispensed with her.

In the midst of the hall a bed had been set up, the sheets of which were by no means soiled, but were white and wide and well spread out. The bed was not of shredded straw or of coarse spreads. But a covering of two silk cloths had been laid upon the couch. The damsel lay down first, but without removing her chemise. He had great trouble in removing his hose and in untying the knots. He sweated with the trouble of it all; yet, in the midst of all the trouble, his promise impels and drives him on. Is this then an actual force? Yes, virtually so; for he feels that he is in duty bound to take his place by the damsel's side. It is his promise that urges him and dictates his act. So he lies down at once, but like her, he does not remove his shirt. He takes good care not to touch her; and when he is in bed, he turns away from her as far as possible, and speaks not a word to her, like a monk to whom speech is forbidden. Not once does he look at her, nor show her any courtesy. Why not? Because his heart does not go out to her. She was certainly very fair and winsome, but not every one is pleased and touched by what is fair and winsome. The knight has only one heart, and this one is really no longer his, but has been entrusted to some one else, so that he cannot bestow it elsewhere. Love, which holds all hearts beneath its sway, requires it to be lodged in a single place. All hearts? No, only those which it esteems. And he whom love deigns to control ought to prize himself the more. Love prized his heart so highly that it constrained it in a special manner, and made him so proud of this distinction that I am not inclined to find fault with him, if he lets alone what love forbids, and remains fixed where it desires. The maiden clearly sees and knows that he dislikes her company and would gladly dispense with it, and that, having no desire to win her love, he would not attempt to woo her. So she said: "My lord, if you will not feel hurt, I will leave and return to bed in my own room, and you will be more comfortable. I do not believe that you are pleased with my company and society. Do not esteem me less if I tell you what I think. Now take your rest all night, for you have so well kept your promise that I have no right to make further request of you. So I commend you to God; and shall go away." Thereupon she arises: the knight does not object, but rather gladly lets her go, like one who is the devoted lover of some one else; the damsel clearly perceived this, and went to her room, where she undressed completely and retired, saying to herself: "Of all the knights I have ever known, I never knew a single knight whom I would value the third part of an angevin in comparison with this one. As I understand the case, he has on hand a more perilous and grave affair than any ever undertaken by a knight; and may God grant that he succeed in it." Then she fell asleep, and remained in bed until the next day's dawn appeared.

At daybreak she awakes and gets up. The knight awakes too, dressing, and putting on his arms, without waiting for any help. Then the damsel comes and sees that he is already dressed. Upon seeing him, she says: "May this day be a happy one for you." "And may it be the same to you, damsel," the knight replies, adding that he is waiting anxiously for some one to bring out his horse. The maiden has some one fetch the horse, and says: "Sire, I should like to accompany you for some distance along the road, if you would agree to escort and conduct me according to the customs and practices which were observed before we were made captive in the kingdom of Logres." In those days the customs and privileges were such that, if a knight found a damsel or lorn maid alone, and if he cared for his fair name, he would no more treat her with dishonour than he would cut his own throat. And if he assaulted her, he would be disgraced for ever in every court. But if, while she was under his escort, she should be won at arms by another who engaged him in battle, then this other knight might do with her what he pleased without receiving shame or blame. This is why the damsel said she would go with him, if he had the courage and willingness to safe guard her in his company, so that no one should do her any harm. And he says to her: "No one shall harm you, I promise you, unless he harm me first." "Then," she says, "I will go with you." She orders her palfrey to be saddled, and her command is obeyed at once. Her palfrey was brought together with the knight's horse. Without the aid of any squire, they both mount, and rapidly ride away. She talks to him, but not caring for her words, he pays no attention to what she says. He likes to think, but dislikes to talk. Love very often inflicts afresh the wound it has given him. Yet, he applied no poultice to the wound to cure it and make it comfortable, having no intention or desire to secure a poultice or to seek a physician, unless the wound becomes more painful. Yet, there is one whose remedy he would gladly seek .... They follow the roads and paths in the right direction until they come to a spring, situated in the middle of a field, and bordered by a stone basin. Some one had forgotten upon the stone a comb of gilded ivory. Never since ancient times has wise man or fool seen such a comb. In its teeth there was almost a handful of hair belonging to her who had used the comb.

When the damsel notices the spring, and sees the stone, she does not wish her companion to see it; so she turns off in another direction. And he, agreeably occupied with his own thoughts, does not at once remark that she is leading him aside; but when at last he notices it, he is afraid of being beguiled, thinking that she is yielding and is going out of the way in order to avoid some danger. "See here, damsel," he cries, "you are not going right; come this way! No one, I think, ever went straight who left this road." "Sire, this is a better way for us," the damsel says, "I am sure of it." Then he replies to her: "I don't know, damsel, what you think; but you can plainly see that the beaten path lies this way; and since I have started to follow it, I shall not turn aside. So come now, if you will, for I shall continue along this way." Then they go forward until they come near the stone basin and see the comb. The knight says: "I surely never remember to have seen so beautiful a comb as this." "Let me have it," the damsel says. "Willingly, damsel," he replies. Then he stoops over and picks it up. While holding it, he looks at it steadfastly, gazing at the hair until the damsel begins to laugh. When he sees her doing so, he begs her to tell him why she laughs. And she says: "Never mind, for I will never tell you." "Why not?" he asks. "Because I don't wish to do so." And when he hears that, he implores her like one who holds that lovers ought to keep faith mutually: "Damsel, if you love anything passionately, by that I implore and conjure and beg you not to conceal from me the reason why you laugh." "Your appeal is so strong," she says, "that I will tell you and keep nothing back. I am sure, as I am of anything, that this comb belonged to the Queen. And you may take my word that those are strands of the Queen's hair which you see to be so fair and light and radiant, and which are clinging in the teeth of the comb; they surely never grew anywhere else." Then the knight replied: "Upon my word, there are plenty of queens and kings; what queen do you mean?" And she answered: "In truth, fair sire, it is of King Arthur's wife I speak." When he hears that, he has not strength to keep from bowing his head over his saddle-bow. And when the damsel sees him thus, she is amazed and terrified, thinking he is about to fall. Do not blame her for her fear, for she thought him in a faint. He might as well have swooned, so near was he to doing so; for in his heart he felt such grief that for a long time he lost his colour and power of speech. And the damsel dismounts, and runs as quickly as possible to support and succour him; for she would not have wished for anything to see him fall. When he saw her, he felt ashamed, and said: "Why do you need to bear me aid?" You must not suppose that the damsel told him why; for he would have been ashamed and distressed, and it would have annoyed and troubled him, if she had confessed to him the truth. So she took good care not to tell the truth, but tactfully answered him: "Sire, I dismounted to get the comb; for I was so anxious to hold it in my hand that I could not longer wait." Willing that she should have the comb, he gives it to her, first pulling out the hair so carefully that he tears none of it. Never will the eye of man see anything receive such honour as when he begins to adore these tresses. A hundred thousand times he raises them to his eyes and mouth, to his forehead and face: he manifests his joy in every way, considering himself rich and happy now. He lays them in his bosom near his heart, between the shirt and the flesh. He would not exchange them for a cartload of emeralds and carbuncles, nor does he think that any sore or illness can afflict him now; he holds in contempt essence of pearl, treacle, and the cure for pleurisy; even for St. Martin and St. James he has no need; for he has such confidence in this hair that he requires no other aid. But what was this hair like? If I tell the truth about it, you will think I am a mad teller of lies. When the mart is full at the yearly fair of St. Denis, and when the goods are most abundantly displayed, even then the knight would not take all this wealth, unless he had found these tresses too. And if you wish to know the truth, gold a hundred thousand times refined, and melted down as many times, would be darker than is night compared with the brightest summer day we have had this year, if one were to see the gold and set it beside this hair. But why should I make a long story of it? The damsel mounts again with the comb in her possession; while he revels and delights in the tresses in his bosom. Leaving the plain, they come to a forest and take a short cut through it until they come to a narrow place, where they have to go in single file; for it would have been impossible to ride two horses abreast. Just where the way was narrowest, they see a knight approach. As soon as she saw him, the damsel recognised him, and said: "Sir knight, do you see him who yonder comes against us all armed and ready for a battle? I know what his intention is: he thinks now that he cannot fail to take me off defenceless with him. He loves me, but he is very foolish to do so. In person, and by messenger, he has been long wooing me. But my love is not within his reach, for I would not love him under any consideration, so help me God! I would kill myself rather than bestow my love on him. I do not doubt that he is delighted now, and is as satisfied as if he had me already in his power. But now I shall see what you can do, and I shall see how brave you are, and it will become apparent whether your escort can protect me. If you can protect me now, I shall not fail to proclaim that you are brave and very worthy." And he answered her: "Go on, go on!" which was as much as to say: "I am not concerned; there is no need of your being worried about what you have said."

While they were proceeding, talking thus, the knight, who was alone, rode rapidly toward them on the run. He was the more eager to make haste, because he felt more sure of success; he felt that he was lucky now to see her whom he most dearly loves. As soon as he approaches her, he greets her with words that come from his heart: "Welcome to her, whence-soever she comes, whom I most desire, but who has hitherto caused me least joy and most distress!" It is not fitting that she should be so stingy of her speech as not to return his greeting, at least by word of mouth. The knight is greatly elated when the damsel greets him; though she does not take the words seriously, and the effort costs her nothing. Yet, if he had at this moment been victor in a tournament, he would not have so highly esteemed himself, nor thought he had won such honour and renown. Being now more confident of his worth, he grasped the bridle rein, and said: "Now I shall lead you away: I have to-day sailed well on my course to have arrived at last at so good a port. Now my troubles are at an end: after dangers, I have reached a haven; after sorrow, I have attained happiness; after pain, I have perfect health; now I have accomplished my desire, when I find you in such case that I can without resistance lead you away with me at once." Then she says: "You have no advantage; for I am under this knight's escort." "Surely, the escort is not worth much," he says, "and I am going to lead you off at once. This knight would have time to eat a bushel of salt before he could defend you from me; I think I could never meet a knight from whom I should not win you. And since I find you here so opportunely, though he too may do his best to prevent it, yet I will take you before his very eyes, however disgruntled he may be." The other is not angered by all the pride he hears expressed, but without any impudence or boasting, he begins thus to challenge him for her: "Sire, don't be in a hurry, and don't waste your words, but speak a little reasonably. You shall not be deprived of as much of her as rightly belongs to you. You must know, however, that the damsel has come hither under my protection. Let her alone now, for you have detained her long enough!" The other gives them leave to burn him, if he does not take her away in spite of him. Then the other says: "It would not be right for me to let you take her away; I would sooner fight with you. But if we should wish to fight, we could not possibly do it in this narrow road. Let us go to some level place--a meadow or an open field." And he replies that that will suit him perfectly: "Certainly, I agree to that: you are quite right, this road is too narrow. My horse is so much hampered here that I am afraid he will crush his flank before I can turn him around." Then with great difficulty he turns, and his horse escapes without any wound or harm. Then he says: "To be sure, I am much chagrined that we have not met in a favourable spot and in the presence of other men, for I should have been glad to have them see which is the better of us two. Come on now, let us begin our search: we shall find in the vicinity some large, broad, and open space." Then they proceed to a meadow, where there were maids, knights, and damsels playing at divers games in this pleasant place. They were not all engaged in idle sport, but were playing backgammon and chess or dice, and were evidently agreeably employed. Most were engaged in such games as these; but the others there were engaged in sports, dancing, singing, tumbling, leaping, and wrestling with each other.

A knight somewhat advanced in years was on the other side of the meadow, seared upon a sorrel Spanish steed. His bridle and saddle were of gold, and his hair was turning grey. One hand hung at his side with easy grace. The weather being fine, he was in his shirt sleeves, with a short mantle of scarlet cloth and fur slung over his shoulders, and thus he watched the games and dances. On the other side of the field, close by a path, there were twenty-three knights mounted on good Irish steeds. As soon as the three new arrivals come into view, they all cease their play and shout across the fields: "See, yonder comes the knight who was driven in the cart! Let no one continue his sport while he is in our midst. A curse upon him who cares or deigns to play so long as he is here!" Meanwhile he who loved the damsel and claimed her as his own, approached the old knight, and said: "Sire, I have attained great happiness; let all who will now hear me say that God has granted me the thing that I have always most desired; His gift would not have been so great had He crowned me as king, nor would I have been so indebted to Him, nor would I have so profited; for what I have gained is fair and good." "I know not yet if it be thine," the knight replies to his son. But the latter answers him: "Don't you know? Can't you see it, then? For God's sake, sire, have no further doubt, when you see that I have her in my possession. In this forest, whence I come, I met her as she was on her way. I think God had fetched her there for me, and I have taken her for my own." "I do not know whether this will be allowed by him whom I see coming after thee; he looks as if he is coming to demand her of thee." During this conversation the dancing had ceased because of the knight whom they saw, nor were they gaily playing any more because of the disgust and scorn they felt for him. But the knight without delay came up quickly after the damsel, and said: "Let the damsel alone, knight, for you have no right to her! If you dare, I am willing at once to fight with you in her defence." Then the old knight remarked: "Did I not know it? Fair son, detain the damsel no longer, but let her go." He does not relish this advice, and swears that he will not give her up: "May God never grant me joy if I give her up to him! I have her, and I shall hold on to her as something that is mine own. The shoulder-strap and all the armlets of my shield shall first be broken, and I shall have lost all confidence in my strength and arms, my sword and lance, before I will surrender my mistress to him." And his father says: "I shall not let thee fight for any reason thou mayest urge. Thou art too confident of thy bravery. So obey my command." But he in his pride replies: "What? Am I a child to be terrified? Rather will I make my boast that there is not within the sea-girt land any knight, wheresoever he may dwell, so excellent that I would let him have her, and whom I should not expect speedily to defeat." The father answers: "Fair son, I do not doubt that thou dost really think so, for thou art so confident of thy strength. But I do not wish to see thee enter a contest with this knight." Then he replies: "I shall be disgraced if I follow your advice. Curse me if I heed your counsel and turn recreant because of you, and do not do my utmost in the fight. It is true that a man fares ill among his relatives: I could drive a better bargain somewhere else, for you are trying to take me in. I am sure that where I am not known, I could act with better grace. No one, who did not know me, would try to thwart my will; whereas you are annoying and tormenting me. I am vexed by your finding fault with me. You know well enough that when any one is blamed, he breaks out still more passionately. But may God never give me joy if I renounce my purpose because of you; rather will I fight in spite of you!" "By the faith I bear the Apostle St. Peter," his father says, "now I see that my request is of no avail. I waste my time in rebuking thee; but I shall soon devise such means as shall compel thee against thy will to obey my commands and submit to them." Straightway summoning all the knights to approach, he bids them lay hands upon his son whom he cannot correct, saying: "I will have him bound rather than let him fight. You here are all my men, and you owe me your devotion and service: by all the fiefs you hold from me, I hold you responsible, and I add my prayer. It seems to me that he must be mad, and that he shows excessive pride, when he refuses to respect my will." Then they promise to take care of him, and say that never, while he is in their charge, shall he wish to fight, but that he must renounce the damsel in spite of himself. Then they all join and seize him by the arms and neck. "Dost thou not think thyself foolish now?" his father asks; "confess the truth: thou hast not the strength or power to fight or joust, however distasteful and hard it may be for thee to admit it. Thou wilt be wise to consent to my will and pleasure. Dost thou know what my intention is? In order somewhat to mitigate thy disappointment, I am willing to join thee, if thou wilt, in following the knight to-day and to-morrow, through wood and plain, each one mounted on his horse. Perhaps we shall soon find him to be of such a character and bearing that I might let thee have thy way and fight with him." To this proposal the other must perforce consent. Like the man who has no alternative, he says that he will give in, provided they both shall follow him. And when the people in the field see how this adventure has turned out, they all exclaim: "Did you see? He who was mounted on the cart has gained such honour here that he is leading away the mistress of the son of my lord, and he himself is allowing it. We may well suppose that he finds in him some merit, when he lets him take her off. Now cursed a hundred times be he who ceases longer his sport on his account! Come, let us go back to our games again." Then they resume their games and dances.

Thereupon the knight turns away, without longer remaining in the field, and the damsel accompanies him. They leave in haste, while the father and his son ride after them through the mown fields until toward three o'clock, when in a very pleasant spot they come upon a church; beside the chancel there was a cemetery enclosed by a wall. The knight was both courteous and wise to enter the church on foot and make his prayer to God, while the damsel held his horse for him until he returned. When he had made his prayer, and while he was coming back, a very old monk suddenly presented himself; whereupon the knight politely requests him to tell him what this place is; for he does not know. And he tells him it is a cemetery. And the other says: "Take me in, so help you God!" "Gladly, sire," and he takes him in. Following the monk's lead, the knight beholds the most beautiful tombs that one could find as far as Dombes or Pampelune; and on each tomb there were letters cut, telling the names of those who were destined to be buried there. And he began in order to read the names, and came upon some which said: "Here Gawain is to lie, here Louis, and here Yvain." After these three, he read the names of many others among the most famed and cherished knights of this or any other land. Among the others, he finds one of marble, which appears to be new, and is more rich and handsome than all the rest. Calling the monk, the knight inquired: "Of what use are these tombs here?" And the monk replied: "You have already read the inscriptions; if you have understood, you must know what they say, and what is the meaning of the tombs." "Now tell me, what is this large one for?" And the hermit answered: "I will tell you. That is a very large sarcophagus, larger than any that ever was made; one so rich and well-carved was never seen. It is magnificent without, and still more so within. But you need not be concerned with that, for it can never do you any good; you will never see inside of it; for it would require seven strong men to raise the lid of stone, if any one wished to open it. And you may be sure that to raise it would require seven men stronger than you and I. There is an inscription on it which says that any one who can lift this stone of his own unaided strength will set free all the men and women who are captives in the land, whence no slave or noble can issue forth, unless he is a native of that land. No one has ever come back from there, but they are detained in foreign prisons; whereas they of the country go and come in and out as they please." At once the knight goes to grasp the stone, and raises it without the slightest trouble, more easily than ten men would do who exerted all their strength. And the monk was amazed, and nearly fell down at the sight of this marvellous thing; for he thought he would never see the like again, and said: "Sire, I am very anxious to know your name. Will you tell me what it is?" "Not I," says the knight, "upon my word." "I am certainly sorry, for that," he says; "but if you would tell me, you would do me a great favour, and might benefit yourself. Who are you, and where do you come from?" "I am a knight, as you may see, and I was born in the kingdom of Logre. After so much information, I should prefer to be excused. Now please tell me, for your part, who is to lie within this tomb." "Sire, he who shall deliver all those who are held captive in the kingdom whence none escapes." And when he had told him all this, the knight commended him to God and all His saints. And then, for the first time, he felt free to return to the damsel. The old white-haired monk escorts him out of the church, and they resume their way. While the damsel is mounting, however, the hermit relates to her all that the knight had done inside, and then he begged her to tell him, if she knew, what his name was; but she assured him that she did not know, but that there was one sure thing she could say, namely, that there was not such a knight alive where the four winds of heaven blow.

Then the damsel takes leave of him, and rides swiftly after the knight. Then those who were following them come up and see the hermit standing alone before the church. The old knight in his shirt sleeves said: "Sire, tell us, have you seen a knight with a damsel in his company?" And he replies: "I shall not be loath to tell you all I know, for they have just passed on from here. The knight was inside yonder, and did a very marvellous thing in raising the stone from the huge marble tomb, quite unaided and without the least effort. He is bent upon the rescue of the Queen, and doubtless he will rescue her, as well as all the other people. You know well that this must be so, for you have often read the inscription upon the stone. No knight was ever born of man and woman, and no knight ever sat in a saddle, who was the equal of this man." Then the father turns to his son, and says: "Son, what dost thou think about him now? Is he not a man to be respected who has performed such a feat? Now thou knowest who was wrong, and whether it was thou or I. I would not have thee fight with him for all the town of Amiens; and yet thou didst struggle hard, before any one could dissuade thee from thy purpose. Now we may as well go back, for we should be very foolish to follow him any farther." And he replies: "I agree to that. It would be useless to follow him. Since it is your pleasure, let us return." They were very wise to retrace their steps. And all the time the damsel rides close beside the knight, wishing to compel him to give heed to her. She is anxious to learn his name, and she begs and beseeches him again and again to tell her, until in his annoyance he answers her: "Have I not already told you that I belong in King Arthur's realm? I swear by God and His goodness that you shall not learn my name." Then she bids him give her leave to go, and she will turn back, which request he gladly grants.

Thereupon the damsel departs, and he rides on alone until it grew very late. After vespers, about compline, as he pursued his way, he saw a knight returning from the wood where he had been hunting. With helmet unlaced, he rode along upon his big grey hunter, to which he had tied the game which God had permitted him to take. This gentleman came quickly to meet the knight, offering him hospitality. "Sire," he says, "night will soon be here. It is time for you to be reasonable and seek a place to spend the night. I have a house of mine near at hand, whither I shall take you. No one ever lodged you better than I shall do, to the extent of my resources: I shall be very glad, if you consent." "For my part, I gladly accept," he says. The gentleman at once sends his son ahead, to prepare the house and start the preparations for supper. The lad willingly executes his command forthwith, and goes off at a rapid pace, while the others, who are in no haste, follow the road leisurely until they arrive at the house. The gentleman's wife was a very accomplished lady; and he had five sons, whom he dearly loved, three of them mere lads, and two already knights; and he had two fair and charming daughters, who were still unmarried. They were not natives of the land, but were there in durance, having been long kept there as prisoners away from their native land of Logres. When the gentleman led the knight into his yard, the lady with her sons and daughters jumped up and ran to meet them, vying in their efforts to do him honour, as they greeted him and helped him to dismount. Neither the sisters nor the five brothers paid much attention to their father, for they knew well enough that he would have it so. They honoured the knight and welcomed him; and when they had relieved him of his armour, one of his host's two daughters threw her own mantle about him, taking it from her own shoulders and throwing it about his neck. I do not need to tell how well he was served at supper; but when the meal was finished, they felt no further hesitation in speaking of various matters. First, the host began to ask him who he was, and from what land, but he did not inquire about his name.

The knight promptly answered him: "I am from the kingdom of Logres, and have never been in this land before." And when the gentleman heard that, he was greatly amazed, as were his wife and children too, and each one of them was sore distressed. Then they began to say to him: "Woe that you have come here, fair sire, for only trouble will come of it! For, like us, you will be reduced to servitude and exile." "Where do you come from, then?" he asked. "Sire, we belong in your country. Many men from your country are held in servitude in this land. Cursed be the custom, together with those who keep it up! No stranger comes here who is not compelled to stay here in the land where he is detained. For whoever wishes may come in, but once in, he has to stay. About your own fate, you may be at rest, you will doubtless never escape from here." He replies: "Indeed, I shall do so, if possible." To this the gentleman replies: "How? Do you think you can escape?" "Yes, indeed, if it be God's will; and I shall do all within my power." "In that case, doubtless all the rest would be set free; for, as soon as one succeeds in fairly escaping from this durance, then all the rest may go forth unchallenged." Then the gentleman recalled that he had been told and informed that a knight of great excellence was making his way into the country to seek for the Queen, who was held by the king's son, Meleagant; and he said to himself: "Upon my word, I believe it is he, and I'll tell him so." So he said to him: "Sire, do not conceal from me your business, if I promise to give you the best advice I know. I too shall profit by any success you may attain. Reveal to me the truth about your errand, that it may be to your advantage as well as mine. I am persuaded that you have come in search of the Queen into this land and among these heathen people, who are worse than the Saracens." And the knight replies: "For no other purpose have I come. I know not where my lady is confined, but I am striving hard to rescue her, and am in dire need of advice. Give me any counsel you can." And he says: "Sire, you have undertaken a very grievous task. The road you are travelling will lead you straight to the sword-bridge. You surely need advice. If you would heed my counsel, you would proceed to the sword-bridge by a surer way, and I would have you escorted thither." Then he, whose mind is fixed upon the most direct way, asks him: "Is the road of which you speak as direct as the other way?" "No, it is not," he says; "it is longer, but more sure." Then he says: "I have no use for it; tell me about this road I am following!" "I am ready to do so," he replies; "but I am sure you will not fare well if you take any other than the road I recommend. To-morrow you will reach a place where you will have trouble: it is called 'the stony passage'. Shall I tell you how bad a place it is to pass? Only one horse can go through at a time; even two men could not pass abreast, and the passage is well guarded and defended. You will meet with resistance as soon as you arrive. You will sustain many a blow of sword and lance, and will have to return full measure before you succeed in passing through." And when he had completed the account, one of the gentleman's sons, who was a knight, stepped forward, saying: "Sire, if you do not object, I will go with this gentleman." Then one of the lads jumps up, and says: "I too will go." And the father gladly gives them both consent. Now the knight will not have to go alone, and he expresses his gratitude, being much pleased with the company.

Then the conversation ceases, and they take the knight to bed, where he was glad to fall asleep. As soon as daylight was visible he got up, and those who were to accompany him got up too. The two knights donned their armour and took their leave, while the young fellow started on ahead. Together they pursued their way until they came at the hour of prime to "the stony passage." In the middle of it they found a wooden tower, where there was always a man on guard. Before they drew near, he who was on the tower saw them and cried twice aloud: "Woe to this man who comes!" And then behold! A knight issued from the tower, mounted and armed with fresh armour, and escorted on either side by servants carrying sharp axes. Then, when the other draws near the passage, he who defends it begins to heap him with abuse about the cart, saying: "Vassal, thou art bold and foolish, indeed, to have entered this country. No man ought ever to come here who had ridden upon a cart, and may God withhold from him His blessing!" Then they spur toward each other at the top of their horses' speed. And he who was to guard the passage-way at once breaks his lance and lets the two pieces fall; the other strikes him in the neck, reaching him beneath the shield, and throws him over prostrate upon the stones. Then the servants come forward with the axes, but they intentionally fail to strike him, having no desire to harm or damage him; so he does not deign to draw his sword, and quickly passes on with his companions. One of them remarks to the other: "No one has ever seen so good a knight, nor has he any equal. Is not this a marvellous thing, that he has forced a passage here?" And the knight says to his brother: "Fair brother, for God's sake, make haste to go and tell our father of this adventure." But the lad asserts and swears that he will not go with the message, and will never leave the knight until he has dubbed and knighted him; let his brother go with the message, if he is so much concerned.

Then they go on together until about three o'clock, when they come upon a man, who asks them who they are. And they answer: "We are knights, busy about our own affairs." Then the man says to the knight: "Sire, I should be glad to offer hospitality to you and your companions here." This invitation he delivers to him whom he takes to be the lord and master of the others. And this one replies to him: "I could not seek shelter for the night at such an hour as this; for it is not well to tarry and seek one's ease when one has undertaken some great task. And I have such business on hand that I shall not stop for the night for some time yet." Then the man continues: "My house is not near here, but is some distance ahead. It will be late when you reach there, so you may proceed, assured that you will find a place to lodge just when it suits you." "In that case," he says, "I will go thither." Thereupon the man starts ahead as guide, and the knight follows along the path. And when they had proceeded some distance, they met a squire who was coming along at a gallop, mounted upon a nag that was as fat and round as an apple. And the squire calls out to the man: "Sire, sire, make haste! For the people of Logres have attacked in force the inhabitants of this land, and war and strife have already broken out; and they say that this country has been invaded by a knight who has been in many battles, and that wherever he wishes to go, no one, however reluctantly, is able to deny him passage. And they further say that he will deliver those who are in this country, and will subdue our people. Now take my advice and make haste!" Then the man starts at a gallop, and the others are greatly delighted at the words they have heard, for they are eager to help their side. And the vavasor's son says: "Hear what this squire says! Come and let us aid our people who are fighting their enemies!" Meanwhile the man rides off, without waiting for them, and makes his way rapidly toward a fortress which stood upon a fortified hill; thither he hastens, till he comes to the gate, while the others spur after him. The castle was surrounded by a high wall and moat. As soon as they had got inside, a gate was lowered upon their heels, so that they could not get out again. Then they say: "Come on, come on! Let us not stop here!" and they rapidly pursue the man until they reach another gate which was not closed against them. But as soon as the man had passed through, a portcullis dropped behind him. Then the others were much dismayed to see themselves shut in, and they think they must be bewitched. But he, of whom I have more to tell, wore upon his finger a ring, whose stone was of such virtue that any one who gazed at it was freed from the power of enchantment. Holding the ring before his eyes, he gazed at it, and said: "Lady, lady, so help me God, now I have great need of your succour!" This lady was a fairy, who had given it to him, and who had cared for him in his infancy. And he had great confidence that, wherever he might be, she would aid and succour him. But after appealing to her and gazing upon the ring, he realises that there is no enchantment here, but that they are actually shut in and confined. Then they come to the barred door of a low and narrow postern gate. Drawing their swords, they all strike it with such violence that they cut the bar. As soon as they were outside the tower, they see that a fierce strife was already begun down in the meadows, and that there are at least a thousand knights engaged, beside the low-bred infantry. While they were descending to the plain, the wise and moderate son of the vavasor remarked: "Sire, before we arrive upon the field, it would be wise for us, it seems to me, to find out and learn on which side our people are. I do not know where they are placed, but I will go and find out, if you wish it so." "I wish you would do so," he replies, "go quickly, and do not fail to come back again at once." He goes and returns at once, saying: "It has turned out well for us, for I have plainly seen that these are our troops on this side of the field." Then the knight at once rode into the fight and jousted with a knight who was approaching him, striking him in the eye with such violence that he knocked him lifeless to the ground. Then the lad dismounts, and taking the dead knight's horse and arms, he arms himself with skill and cleverness. When he was armed, he straightway mounts, taking the shield and the lance, which was heavy, stiff, and decorated, and about his waist he girt a sharp, bright, and flashing sword. Then he followed his brother and lord into the fight. The latter demeaned himself bravely in the melee for some time, breaking, splitting, and crushing shields, helmets and hauberks. No wood or steel protected the man whom he struck; he either wounded him or knocked him lifeless from the horse. Unassisted, he did so well that he discomfited all whom he met, while his companions did their part as well. The people of Logres, not knowing him, are amazed at what they see, and ask the vavasor's sons about the stranger knight. This reply is made to them: "Gentlemen, this is he who is to deliver us all from durance and misery, in which we have so long been confined, and we ought to do him great honour when, to set us free, he has passed through so many perils and is ready to face many more. He has done much, and will do yet more." Every one is overjoyed at hearing this welcome news. The news travelled fast, and was noised about, until it was known by all. Their strength and courage rise, so that they slay many of those still alive, and apparently because of the example of a single knight they work greater havoc than because of all the rest combined. And if it had not been so near evening, all would have gone away defeated; but night came on so dark that they had to separate.

When the battle was over, all the captives pressed about the knight, grasping his rein on either side, and thus addressing him: "Welcome, fair sire," and each one adds: "Sire, for the name of God, do not fail to lodge with me!" What one says they all repeat, for young and old alike insist that he must lodge with them, saying: "You will be more comfortably lodged with me than with any one else." Thus each one addresses him to his face, and in the desire to capture him, each one drags him from the rest, until they almost come to blows. Then he tells them that they are very foolish and silly to struggle so. "Cease this wrangling among yourselves, for it does no good to me or you. Instead of quarrelling among ourselves, we ought rather to lend one another aid. You must not dispute about the privilege of lodging me, but rather consider how to lodge me in such a place that it may be to your general advantage, and that I may be advanced upon my way." Then each one exclaims at once: "That is my house, or, No, it is mine," until the knight replies: "Follow my advice and say nothing more; the wisest of you is foolish to contend this way. You ought to be concerned to further my affairs, and instead you are seeking to turn me aside. If you had each individually done me all the honour and service it is possible to do, and I had accepted your kindness, by all the saints of Rome I swear that I could not be more obliged to you than I am now for your good-will. So may God give me joy and health, your good intentions please me as much as if each one of you had already shown me great honour and kindness: so let the will stand for the deed!" Thus he persuades and appeases them all. Then they take him quickly along the road to a knight's residence, where they seek to serve him: all rejoice to honour and serve him throughout the evening until bedtime, for they hold him very dear. Next morning, when the time came to separate, each one offers and presents himself, with the desire to accompany him; but it is not his will or pleasure that any one shall go with him except the two whom he had brought with him. Accompanied by them alone, he resumed his journey. That day they rode from morn till evening without encountering any adventure. When it was now very late, and while they were riding rapidly out of a forest, they saw a house belonging to a knight, and seated at the door they saw his wife, who had the bearing of a gentle lady. As soon as she espied them coming, she rose to her feet to meet them, and greeted them joyfully with a smile: "Welcome! I wish you to accept my house; this is your lodging; pray dismount" "Lady, since it is your will, we thank you, and will dismount; we accept your hospitality for the night." When they had dismounted, the lady had the horses taken by members of her well-ordered household. She calls her sons and daughters who come at once: the youths were courteous, handsome, and well-behaved, and the daughters were fair. She bids the lads remove the saddles and curry the horses well; no one refused to do this, but each carried out her instructions willingly. When she ordered the knights to be disarmed, her daughters step forward to perform this service. They remove their armour, and hand them three short mantles to put on. Then at once they take them into the house which was very handsome. The master was not at home, being out in the woods with two of his sons. But he presently returned, and his household, which was well-ordered, ran to meet him outside the door. Quickly they untie and unpack the game he brings, and tell him the news: "Sire, sire, you do not know that you have three knights for guests." "God be praised for that," he says. Then the knight and his two sons extend a glad welcome to their guests. The rest of the household were not backward, for even the least among them prepared to perform his special task. While some run to prepare the meal, others light the candles in profusion; still others get a towel and basins, and offer water for the hands: they are not niggardly in all this. When all had washed, they take their seats. Nothing that was done there seemed to be any trouble or burdensome. But at the first course there came a surprise in the form of a knight outside the door. As he sat on his charger, all armed from head to feet, he looked prouder than a bull, and a bull is a yew proud beast. One leg was fixed in the stirrup, but the other he had thrown over the mane of his horse's neck, to give himself a careless and jaunty air. Behold him advancing thus, though no one noticed him until he came forward with the words: "I wish to know which is the man who is so foolish and proud a numskull that he has come to this country and intends to cross the sword-bridge. All his pains will come to naught, and his expedition is in vain." Then he, who felt no fear at all, thus replies with confidence: "I am he who intends to cross the bridge." "Thou? Thou? How didst thou dare to think of such a thing? Before undertaking such a course, thou oughtest to have thought of the end that is in store for thee, and thou oughtest to have in mind the memory of the cart on which thou didst ride. I know not whether thou feelest shame for the ride thou hadst on it, but no sensible man would have embarked on such an enterprise as this if he had felt the reproach of his action."

Not a word does he deign to reply to what he hears the other say; but the master of the house and all the others express their surprise openly: "Ah, God, what a misfortune this is," each one of them says to himself; "cursed be the hour when first a cart was conceived or made! For it is a very vile and hateful thing. Ah, God, of what was he accused? Why was he carried in a cart? For what sin, or for what crime? He will always suffer the reproach. If he were only clear of this disgrace, no knight could be found in all the world, however his valour might be proved, who would equal the merit of this knight. If all good knights could be compared, and if the truth were to be known, you could find none so handsome or so expert." Thus they expressed their sentiments. Then he began his speech of impudence: "Listen, thou knight, who art bound for the sword-bridge! If thou wishest, thou shalt cross the water very easily and comfortably. I will quickly have thee ferried over in a skiff. But once on the other side, I will make thee pay me toll, and I will take thy head, if I please to do so, or if not, thou shalt be held at my discretion." And he replies that he is not seeking trouble, and that he will never risk his head in such an adventure for any consideration. To which the other answers at once: "Since thou wilt not do this, whosesoever the shame and loss may be, thou must come outside with me and there engage me hand to hand." Then, to beguile him. the other says: "If I could refuse, I would very gladly excuse myself; but in truth I would rather fight than be compelled to do what is wrong." Before he arose from the table where they were sitting, he told the youths who were serving him, to saddle his horse at once, and fetch his arms and give them to him. This order they promptly execute: some devote themselves to arming him, while others go to fetch his horse. As he slowly rode along completely armed, holding his shield tight by the straps, you must know that he was evidently to be included in the list of the brave and fair. His horse became him so well that it is evident he must be his own, and as for the shield he held by the straps and the helmet laced upon his head, which fitted him so well, you would never for a moment have thought that he had borrowed it or received it as a loan; rather, you would be so pleased with him that you would maintain that he had been thus born and raised: for all this I should like you to take my word.

Outside the gate, where the battle was to be fought, there was a stretch of level ground well adapted for the encounter. When they catch sight of each other, they spur hotly to the attack and come together with such a shock, dealing such blows with their lances, that they first bend, then buckle up, and finally fly into splinters. With their swords they then hew away at their shields, helmets, and hauberks. The wood is cut and the steel gives way, so that they wound each other in several places. They pay each other such angry blows that it seems as if they had made a bargain. The swords often descend upon the horses' croups, where they drink and feast upon their blood; their riders strike them upon the flanks until at last they kill them both. And when both have fallen to earth, they attack each other afoot; and if they had cherished a mortal hatred, they could not have assailed each other more fiercely with their swords. They deal their blows with greater frequency than the man who stakes his money at dice and never fails to double the stakes every time he loses; yet, this game of theirs was very different; for there were no losses here, but only fierce blows and cruel strife. All the people came out from the house: the master, his lady, his sons and daughters; no man or woman, friend or stranger, stayed behind, but all stood in line to see the fight in progress in the broad, level field. The Knight of the Cart blames and reproaches himself for faintheartedness when he sees his host watching him and notices all the others looking on. His heart is stirred with anger, for it seems to him that he ought long since to have beaten his adversary. Then he strikes him, rushing in like a storm and bringing his sword down close by his head; he pushes and presses him so hard that he drives him from his ground and reduces him to such a state of exhaustion that he has little strength to defend himself. Then the knight recalls how the other had basely reproached him about the cart; so he assails him and drubs him so soundly that not a string or strap remains unbroken about the neck-band of his hauberk, and he knocks the helmet and ventail from his head. His wounds and distress are so great that he has to cry for mercy. Just as the lark cannot withstand or protect itself against the hawk which outflies it and attacks it from above, so he in his helplessness and shame, must invoke him and sue for mercy. And when he hears him beg for mercy, he ceases his attack and says: "Dost thou wish for mercy?" He replies: "You have asked a very clever question; any fool could ask that. I never wished for anything so much as I now wish for mercy." Then he says to him: "Thou must mount, then, upon a cart. Nothing thou couldst say would have any influence with me, unless thou mountest the cart, to atone for the vile reproaches thou didst address to me with thy silly mouth." And the knight thus answers him: "May it never please God that I mount a cart!" "No?" he asks; "then you shall die." "Sire, you can easily put me to death; but I beg and beseech you for God's sake to show me mercy and not compel me to mount a cart. I will agree to anything, however grievous, excepting that. I would rather die a hundred times than undergo such a disgrace. In your goodness and mercy you can tell me nothing so distasteful that I will not do it."

While he is thus beseeching him, behold across the field a maiden riding on a tawny mule, her head uncovered and her dress disarranged. In her hand she held a whip with which she belaboured the mule; and in truth no horse could have galloped so fast as was the pace of the mule. The damsel called out to the Knight of the Cart: "May God bless thy heart, Sir Knight, with whatever delights thee most!" And he, who heard her gladly, says: "May God bless you, damsel, and give you joy and health!" Then she tells him of her desire. "Knight," she says, "in urgent need I have come from afar to thee to ask a favour, for which thou wilt deserve the best guerdon I can make to thee; and I believe that thou wilt yet have need of my assistance." And he replies: "Tell me what it is you wish; and if I have it, you shall have it at once, provided it be not something extravagant." Then she says: "It is the head of the knight whom thou hast just defeated; in truth, thou hast never dealt with such a wicked and faithless man. Thou wilt be committing no sin or wrong, but rather doing a deed of charity, for he is the basest creature that ever was or ever shall be." And when he who had been vanquished hears that she wishes him to be killed, he says to him: "Don't believe her, for she hates me; but by that God who was at once Father and Son, and who chose for His mother her who was His daughter and handmaiden, I beg you to have mercy upon me!" "Ah, knight!" the maid exclaims, "pay no attention to what this traitor says! May God give thee all the joy and honour to which thou dost aspire, and may He give thee good success in thy undertaking." Then the knight is in a predicament, as he thinks and ponders over the question: whether to present to her the head she asks him to cut off, or whether he shall allow himself to be touched by pity for him. He wishes to respect the wishes of both her and him. Generosity and pity each command him to do their will; for he was both generous and tender-hearted. But if she carries off the head, then will pity be defeated and put to death; whereas, if she does not carry off the head, generosity will be discomfited. Thus, pity and generosity hold him so confined and so distressed that he is tormented and spurred on by each of them in turn. The damsel asks him to give her the head, and on the other hand the knight makes his request, appealing to his pity and kindness. And, since he has implored him, shall he not receive mercy? Yes, for it never happened that, when he had put down an enemy and compelled him to sue for mercy, he would refuse such an one his mercy or longer bear him any grudge. Since this is his custom, he will not refuse his mercy to him who now begs and sues for it. And shall she have the head she covets? Yes, if it be possible. "Knight," he says, "it is necessary for thee to fight me again, and if thou dost care to defend thy head again, I will show thee such mercy as to allow thee to resume the helmet; and I will give thee time to arm thy body and thy head as well as possible. But, if I conquer thee again, know that thou shalt surely die." And he replies: "I desire nothing better than that, and ask for no further favour." "And I will give thee this advantage," he adds: "I will fight thee as I stand, without changing my present position." Then the other knight makes ready, and they begin the fight again eagerly. But this time the knight triumphed more quickly than he had done at first. And the damsel at once cries out: "Do not spare him, knight, for anything he may say to thee. Surely he would not have spared thee, had he once defeated thee. If thou heedest what he says, be sure that he will again beguile thee. Fair knight, cut off the head of the most faithless man in the empire and kingdom, and give it to me! Thou shouldst present it to me, in view of the guerdon I intend for thee. For another day may well come when, if he can, he will beguile thee again with his words." He, thinking his end is near, cries aloud to him for mercy; but his cry is of no avail, nor anything that he can say. The other drags him by the helmet, tearing all the fastening, and he strikes from his head the ventail and the gleaming coif. Then he cries out more loudly still: "Mercy, for God's sake! Mercy, sir!" But the other answers: "So help me, I shall never again show thee pity, after having once let thee off." "Ah," he says, "thou wouldst do wrong to heed my enemy and kill me thus." While she, intent upon his death, admonishes him to cut off his head, and not to believe a word he says. He strikes: the head flies across the sward and the body fails. Then the damsel is pleased and satisfied. Grasping the head by the hair, the knight presents it to the damsel, who takes it joyfully with the words: "May thy heart receive such delight from whatever it most desires as my heart now receives from what I most coveted. I had only one grief in life, and that was that this man was still alive. I have a reward laid up for thee which thou shalt receive at the proper time. I promise thee that thou shalt have a worthy reward for the service thou hast rendered me. Now I will go away, with the prayer that God may guard thee from harm." Then the damsel leaves him, as each commends the other to God. But all those who had seen the battle in the plain are overjoyed, and in their joy they at once relieve the knight of his armour, and honour him in every way they can. Then they wash their hands again and take their places at the meal, which they eat with better cheer than is their wont. When they had been eating for some time, the gentleman turned to his guest at his side, and said: "Sire, a long while ago we came hither from the kingdom of Logres. We were born your countrymen, and we should like to see you win honour and fortune and joy in this country; for we should profit by it as well as you, and it would be to the advantage of many others, if you should gain honour and fortune in the enterprise you have undertaken in this land." And he makes answer: "May God hear your desire."

When the host had dropped his voice and ceased speaking, one of his sons followed him and said: "Sire, we ought to place all our resources at your service, and give them outright rather than promise them; if you have any need of our assistance, we ought not to wait until you ask for it. Sire, be not concerned over your horse which is dead. We have good strong horses here. I want you to take anything of ours which you need, and you shall choose the best of our horses in place of yours." And he replies: "I willingly accept." Thereupon, they have the beds prepared and retire for the night. The next morning they rise early, and dress, after which they prepare to start. Upon leaving, they fail in no act of courtesy, but take leave of the lady, her lord, and all the rest. But in order to omit nothing, I must remark that the knight was unwilling to mount the borrowed steed which was standing ready at the door; rather, he caused him to be ridden by one of the two knights who had come with him, while he took the latter's horse instead, for thus it pleased him best to do. When each was seated on his horse, they all asked for leave to depart from their host who had served them so honourably. Then they ride along the road until the day draws to a close, and late in the afternoon they reach the sword-bridge.

At the end of this very difficult bridge they dismount from their steeds and gaze at the wicked-looking stream, which is as swift and raging, as black and turgid, as fierce and terrible as if it were the devil's stream; and it is so dangerous and bottomless that anything failing into it would be as completely lost as if it fell into the salt sea. And the bridge, which spans it, is different from any other bridge; for there never was such a one as this. If any one asks of me the truth, there never was such a bad bridge, nor one whose flooring was so bad. The bridge across the cold stream consisted of a polished, gleaming sword; but the sword was stout and stiff, and was as long as two lances. At each end there was a tree-trunk in which the sword was firmly fixed. No one need fear to fall because of its breaking or bending, for its excellence was such that it could support a great weight. But the two knights who were with the third were much discouraged; for they surmised that two lions or two leopards would be found tied to a great rock at the other end of the bridge. The water and the bridge and the lions combine so to terrify them that they both tremble with fear, and say: "Fair sire, consider well what confronts you; for it is necessary and needful to do so. This bridge is badly made and built, and the construction of it is bad. If you do not change your mind in time, it will be too late to repent. You must consider which of several alternatives you will choose. Suppose that you once get across (but that cannot possibly come to pass, any more than one could hold in the winds and forbid them to blow, or keep the birds from singing, or re-enter one's mother's womb and be born again--all of which is as impossible as to empty the sea of its water); but even supposing that you got across, can you think and suppose that those two fierce lions that are chained on the other side will not kill you, and suck the blood from your veins, and eat your flesh and then gnaw your bones? For my part, I am bold enough, when I even dare to look and gaze at them. If you do not take care, they will certainly devour you. Your body will soon be torn and rent apart, for they will show you no mercy. So take pity on us now, and stay here in our company! It would be wrong for you to expose yourself intentionally to such mortal peril." And he, laughing, replies to them: "Gentlemen, receive my thanks and gratitude for the concern you feel for me: it comes from your love and kind hearts. I know full well that you would not like to see any mishap come to me; but I have faith and confidence in God, that He will protect me to the end. I fear the bridge and stream no more than I fear this dry land; so I intend to prepare and make the dangerous attempt to cross. I would rather die than turn back now." The others have nothing more to say; but each weeps with pity and heaves a sigh. Meanwhile he prepares, as best he may, to cross the stream, and he does a very marvellous thing in removing the armour from his feet and hands. He will be in a sorry state when he reaches the other side. He is going to support himself with his bare hands and feet upon the sword, which was sharper than a scythe, for he had not kept on his feet either sole or upper or hose. But he felt no fear of wounds upon his hands or feet; he preferred to maim himself rather than to fall from the bridge and be plunged in the water from which he could never escape. In accordance with this determination, he passes over with great pain and agony, being wounded in the hands, knees, and feet. But even this suffering is sweet to him: for Love, who conducts and leads him on, assuages and relieves the pain. Creeping on his hands, feet, and knees, he proceeds until he reaches the other side. Then he recalls and recollects the two lions which he thought he had seen from the other side; but, on looking about, he does not see so much as a lizard or anything else to do him harm. He raises his hand before his face and looks at his ring, and by this test he proves that neither of the lions is there which he thought he had seen, and that he had been enchanted and deceived; for there was not a living creature there. When those who had remained behind upon the bank saw that he had safely crossed, their joy was natural; but they do not know of his injuries. He, however, considers himself fortunate not to have suffered anything worse. The blood from his wounds drips on his shirt on all sides. Then he sees before him a tower, which was so strong that never had he seen such a strong one before: indeed, it could not have been a better tower. At the window there sat King Bademagu, who was very scrupulous and precise about matters of honour and what was right, and who was careful to observe and practise loyalty above all else; and beside him stood his son, who always did precisely the opposite so far as possible, for he found his pleasure in disloyalty, and never wearied of villainy, treason, and felony. From their point of vantage they had seen the knight cross the bridge with trouble and pain. Meleagant's colour changed with the rage and displeasure he felt; for he knows now that he will be challenged for the Queen; but his character was such that he feared no man, however strong or formidable. If he were not base and disloyal, there could no better knight be found; but he had a heart of wood, without gentleness and pity. What enraged his son and roused his ire, made the king happy and glad. The king knew of a truth that he who had crossed the bridge was much better than any one else. For no one would dare to pass over it in whom there dwelt any of that evil nature which brings more shame upon those who possess it than prowess brings of honour to the virtuous. For prowess cannot accomplish so much as wickedness and sloth can do: it is true beyond a doubt that it is possible to do more evil than good.

I could say more on these two heads, if it did not cause me to delay. But I must turn to something else and resume my subject, and you shall hear how the king speaks profitably to his son: "Son," he says, "it was fortunate that thou and I came to look out this window; our reward has been to witness the boldest deed that ever entered the mind of man. Tell me now if thou art not well disposed toward him who has performed such a marvellous feat. Make peace and be reconciled with him, and deliver the Queen into his hands. Thou shalt gain no glory in battle with him, but rather mayst thou incur great loss. Show thyself to be courteous and sensible, and send the Queen to meet him before he sees thee. Show him honour in this land of thine, and before he asks it, present to him what he has come to seek. Thou knowest well enough that he has come for the Queen Guinevere. Do not act so that people will take thee to be obstinate, foolish, or proud. If this man has entered thy land alone, thou shouldst bear him company, for one gentleman ought not to avoid another, but rather attract him and honour him with courtesy. One receives honour by himself showing it; be sure that the honour will be thine, if thou doest honour and service to him who is plainly the best knight in the world." And he replies: "May God confound me, if there is not as good a knight, or even a better one than he!" It was too bad that he did not mention himself, of whom he entertains no mean opinion. And he adds: "I suppose you wish me to clasp my hands and kneel before him as his liegeman, and to hold my lands from him? So help me God, I would rather become his man than surrender to him the Queen! God forbid that in such a fashion I should deliver her to him! She shall never be given up by me, but rather contested and defended against all who are so foolish as to dare to come in quest of her." Then again the king says to him: "Son, thou wouldst act very courteously to renounce this pretension. I advise thee and beg thee to keep the peace. Thou knowest well that the honour will belong to the knight, if he wins the Queen from thee in battle. He would doubtless rather win her in battle than as a gift, for it will thus enhance his fame. It is my opinion that he is seeking her, not to receive her peaceably, but because he wishes to win her by force of arms. So it would be wise on thy part to deprive him of the satisfaction of fighting thee. I am sorry to see thee so foolish; but if thou dost not heed my advice, evil will come of it, and the ensuing misfortune will be worse for thee. For the knight need fear no hostility from any one here save thee. On behalf of myself and all my men, I will grant him a truce and security. I have never yet done a disloyal deed or practised treason and felony, and I shall not begin to do so now on thy account any more than I would for any stranger. I do not wish to flatter thee, for I promise that the knight shall not lack any arms, or horse or anything else he needs, in view of the boldness he has displayed in coming thus far. He shall be securely guarded and well defended against all men here excepting thee. I wish him clearly to understand that, if he can maintain himself against thee, he need have no fear of any one else." "I have listened to you in silence long enough," says Meleagant, "and you may say what you please. But little do I care for all you say. I am not a hermit, nor so compassionate and charitable, and I have no desire to be so honourable as to give him what I most love. His task will not be performed so quickly or so lightly; rather will it turn out otherwise than as you and he expect. You and I need not quarrel because you aid him against me. Even if he enjoys peace and a truce with you and all your men, what matters that to me? My heart does not quail on that account; rather, so help me God, I am glad that he need not feel concern for any one here but me; I do not wish you to do on my account anything which might be construed as disloyalty or treachery. Be as compassionate as you please, but let me be cruel." "What? Wilt thou not change thy mind?" "No," he says. "Then I will say nothing more. I will leave thee alone to do thy best and will go now to speak with the knight. I wish to offer and present to him my aid and counsel in all respects; for I am altogether on his side."

Then the king goes down and orders them to bring his horse. A large steed is brought to him, upon which he springs by the stirrup, and he rides off with some of his men: three knights and two squires he bade to go with him. They did not stop their ride downhill until they came to the bridge, where they see him stanching his wounds and wiping the blood from them. The king expects to keep him as his guest for a long time while his wounds are healing; but he might as well expect to drain the sea. The king hastens to dismount, and he who was grievously wounded, stood up at once to meet him, though he did not know him, and he gave no more evidence of the pain he felt in his feet and hands than if he had been actually sound. The king sees that he is exerting himself, and quickly runs to greet him with the words: "Sire, I am greatly amazed that you have fallen upon us in this land. But be welcome, for no one will ever repeat the attempt: it never happened in the past, and it will never happen in the future that any one should perform such a hardy feat or expose himself to such peril. And know that I admire you greatly for having executed what no one before ever dared to conceive. You will find me very kindly disposed, and loyal and courteous toward you. I am the king of this land, and offer you freely all my counsel and service; and I think I know pretty well what you have come here to seek. You come, I am sure, to seek the Queen." "Sire," he replies, "your surmise is correct; no other cause brings me here." "Friend, you must suffer hardship to obtain her," he replies; "and you are sorely wounded, as I see by the wounds and the flowing blood. You will not find him who brought her hither so generous as to give her up without a struggle; but you must tarry, and have your wounds cared for until they are completely healed. I will give you some of 'the three Marys' ointment, and something still better, if it can be found, for I am very solicitous about your comfort and your recovery. And the Queen is so confined that no mortal man has access to her--not even my son, who brought her here with him and who resents such treatment, for never was a man so beside himself and so desperate as he. But I am well disposed toward you, and will gladly give you, so help me God, all of which you stand in need. My son himself will not have such good arms but that I will give you some that are just as good, and a horse, too, such as you will need, though my son will be angry with me. Despite the feelings of any one, I will protect you against all men. You will have no cause to fear any one excepting him who brought the Queen here. No man ever menaced another as I have menaced him, and I came near driving him from my land, in my displeasure because he will not surrender her to you. To be sure, he is my son; but feel no concern, for unless he defeats you in battle, he can never do you the slightest harm against my will." "Sire," he says, "I thank you. But I am losing time here which I do not wish to waste. I have no cause to complain, and have no wound which is paining me. Take me where I can find him; for with such arms as I have, I am ready to divert myself by giving and receiving blows." "Friend, you had better wait two or three weeks until your wounds are healed, for it would be well for you to tarry here at least two weeks, and not on any account could I allow it, or look on, while you fought in my presence with such arms and with such an outfit." And he replies: "With your permission, no other arms would be used than these, for I should prefer to fight with them, and I should not ask for the slightest postponement, adjournment or delay. However, in deference to you, I will consent to wait until to-morrow; but despite what any one may say, longer I will not wait." Then the king assured him that all would be done as he wished; then he has the lodging-place prepared, and insistently requests his men, who are in the company, to serve him, which they do devotedly. And the king, who would gladly have made peace, had it been possible, went at once to his son and spoke to him like one who desires peace and harmony, saying: "Fair son, be reconciled now with this knight without a fight! He has not come here to disport himself or to hunt or chase, but he comes in search of honour and to increase his fame and renown, and I have seen that he stands in great need of rest. If he had taken my advice, he would not have rashly undertaken, either this month or the next, the battle which he so greatly desires. If thou makest over the Queen to him, dost thou fear any dishonour in the deed? Have no fear of that, for no blame can attach to thee; rather is it wrong to keep that to which one has no rightful claim. He would gladly have entered the battle at once, though his hands and feet are not sound, but cut and wounded." Meleagant answers his father thus: "You are foolish to be concerned. By the faith I owe St. Peter, I will not take your advice in this matter. I should deserve to be drawn apart with horses, if I heeded your advice. If he is seeking his honour, so do I seek mine; if he is in search of glory, so am I; if he is anxious for the battle, so am I a hundred times more so than he." "I see plainly," says the king, "that thou art intent upon thy mad enterprise, and thou shalt have thy fill of it. Since such is thy pleasure, to-morrow thou shalt try thy strength with the knight." "May no greater hardship ever visit me than that!" Meleagant replies; "I would much rather it were to-day than to-morrow. Just see how much more downcast I am than is usual! My eyes are wild, and my face is pale! I shall have no joy or satisfaction or any cause for happiness until I am actually engaged with him."

The king understands that further advice and prayers are of no avail, so reluctantly he leaves his son and, taking a good, strong horse and handsome arms, he sends them to him who well deserves them, together with a surgeon who was a loyal and Christian man. There was in the world no more trusty man, and he was more skilled in the cure of wounds than all the doctors of Montpeilier. That night he treated the knight as best he could, in accordance with the king's command. Already the news was known by the knights and damsels, the ladies and barons of all the country-side, and all through the night until daybreak strangers and friends were making long journeys from all the country round. When morning came, there was such a press before the castle that there was not room to move one's foot. And the king, rising early in his distress about the battle, goes directly to his son, who had already laced upon his head the helmet which was of Poitiers make. No delay or peace is possible, for though the king did his best, his efforts are of no effect. In the middle of the castle-square, where all the people are assembled, the battle will be fought in compliance with the king's wish and command. The king sends at once for the stranger knight, and he is conducted to the grounds which were filled with people from the kingdom of Logres. For just as people are accustomed to go to church to hear the organ on the annual feast-days of Pentecost or Christmas, so they had all assembled now. All the foreign maidens from King Arthur's realm had fasted three days and gone barefoot in their shifts, in order that God might endow with strength and courage the knight who was to fight his adversary on behalf of the captives. Very early, before prime had yet been sounded, both of the knights fully armed were led to the place, mounted upon two horses equally protected. Meleagant was very graceful, alert, and shapely; the hauberk with its fine meshes, the helmet, and the shield hanging from his neck--all these became him well. All the spectators, however, favoured the other knight, even those who wished him ill, and they say that Meleagant is worth nothing compared with him. As soon as they were both on the ground, the king comes and detains them as long as possible in an effort to make peace between them, but he is unable to persuade his son. Then he says to them: "Hold in your horses until I reach the top of the tower. It will be only a slight favour, if you will wait so long for me." Then in sorrowful mood he leaves them and goes directly to the place where he knew he would find the Queen. She had begged him the evening before to place her where she might have an unobstructed view of the battle; he had granted her the boon, and went now to seek and fetch her, for he was very anxious to show her honour and courtesy. He placed her at one window, and took his place at another window on her right. Beside them, there were gathered there many knights and prudent dames and damsels, who were natives of that land; and there were many others, who were captives, and who were intent upon their orisons and prayers. Those who were prisoners were praying for their lord, for to God and to him they entrusted their succour and deliverance. Then the combatants without delay make all the people stand aside; then they clash the shields with their elbows, and thrust their arms into the straps, and spur at each other so violently that each sends his lance two arms' length through his opponent's shield, causing the lance to split and splinter like a flying spark. And the horses meet head on, clashing breast to breast, and the shields and helmets crash with such a noise that it seems like a mighty thunder-clap; not a breast-strap, girth, rein or surcingle remains unbroken, and the saddle-bows, though strong, are broken to pieces. The combatants felt no shame in falling to earth, in view of their mishaps, but they quickly spring to their feet, and without waste of threatening words rush at each other more fiercely than two wild boars, and deal great blows with their swords of steel like men whose hate is violent. Repeatedly they trim the helmets and shining hauberks so fiercely that after the sword the blood spurts out. They furnished an excellent battle, indeed, as they stunned and wounded each other with their heavy, wicked blows. Many fierce, hard, long bouts they sustained with equal honour, so that the onlookers could discern no advantage on either side. But it was inevitable that he who had crossed the bridge should be much weakened by his wounded hands. The people who sided with him were much dismayed, for they notice that his strokes are growing weaker, and they fear he will get the worst of it; it seemed to them that he was weakening, while Meleagant was triumphing, and they began to murmur all around. But up at the window of the tower there was a wise maiden who thought within herself that the knight had not undertaken the battle either on her account or for the sake of the common herd who had gathered about the list, but that his only incentive had been the Queen; and she thought that, if he knew that she was at the window seeing and watching him, his strength and courage would increase. And if she had known his name, she would gladly have called to him to look about him. Then she came to the Queen and said: "Lady, for God's sake and your own as well as ours, I beseech you to tell me, if you know, the name of yonder knight, to the end that it may be of some help to him." "Damsel," the Queen replies, "you have asked me a question in which I see no hate or evil, but rather good intent; the name of the knight, I know, is Lancelot of the Lake." "God, how happy and glad at heart I am!" the damsel says. Then she leans forward and calls to him by name so loudly that all the people hear: "Lancelot, turn about and see who is here taking note of thee!"

When Lancelot heard his name, he was not slow to turn around: he turns and sees seated up there at the window of the tower her whom he desired most in the world to see. From the moment he caught sight of her, he did not turn or take his eyes and face from her, defending himself with backhand blows. And Meleagant meanwhile attacked him as fiercely as he could, delighted to think that the other cannot withstand him now; and they of the country are well pleased too, while the foreigners are so distressed that they can no longer support themselves, and many of them fall to earth either upon their knees or stretched out prone; thus some are glad, and some distressed. Then the damsel cried again from the window: "Ah, Lancelot, how is it that thou dost now conduct thyself so foolishly? Once thou wert the embodiment of prowess and of all that is good, and I do not think God ever made a knight who could equal thee in valour and in worth. But now we see thee so distressed that thou dealest back-hand blows and fightest thy adversary, behind thy back. Turn, so as to be on the other side, and so that thou canst face toward this tower, for it will help thee to keep it in view." Then Lancelot is so ashamed and mortified that he hates himself, for he knows full well that all have seen how, for some time past, he has had the worst of the fight. Thereupon he leaps backward and so manoeuvres as to force Meleagant into a position between him and the tower. Meleagant makes every effort to regain his former position. But Lancelot rushes upon him, and strikes him so violently upon his body and shield whenever he tries to get around him, that he compels him to whirl about two or three times in spite of himself. Lancelot's strength and courage grow, partly because he has love's aid, and partly because he never hated any one so much as him with whom he is engaged. Love and mortal hate, so fierce that never before was such hate seen, make him so fiery and bold that Meleagant ceases to treat it as a jest and begins to stand in awe of him, for he had never met or known so doughty a knight, nor had any knight ever wounded or injured him as this one does. He is glad to get away from him, and he winces and sidesteps, fearing his blows and avoiding them. And Lancelot does not idly threaten him, but drives him rapidly toward the tower where the Queen was stationed on the watch. There upon the tower he did her the homage of his blows until he came so close that, if he advanced another step, he would lose sight of her. Thus Lancelot drove him back and forth repeatedly in whatever direction he pleased, always stopping before the Queen, his lady, who had kindled the flame which compels him to fix his gaze upon her. And this same flame so stirred him against Meleagant that he was enabled to lead and drive him wherever he pleased. In spite of himself he drives him on like a blind man or a man with a wooden leg. The king sees his son so hard pressed that he is sorry for him and he pities him, and he will not deny him aid and assistance if possible; but if he wishes to proceed courteously, he must first beg the Queen's permission. So he began to say to her: "Lady, since I have had you in my power, I have loved you and faithfully served and honoured you. I never consciously left anything undone in which I saw your honour involved; now repay me for what I have done. For I am about to ask you a favour which you should not grant unless you do so willingly. I plainly see that my son is getting the worst of this battle; I do not speak so because of the chagrin I feel, but in order that Lancelot, who has him in his power, may not kill him. Nor ought you to wish to see him killed; not because he has not wronged both you and him, but because I make the request of you: so tell him, please, to stop beating him. If you will, you can thus repay me for what I have done for you." "Fair sire, I am willing to do so at your request," the Queen replies; "had I mortal hatred for your son, whom it is true I do not love, yet you have served me so well that, to please you, I am quite willing that he should desist." These words were not spoken privately, but Lancelot and Meleagrant heard what was said. The man who is a perfect lover is always obedient and quickly and gladly does his mistress' pleasure. So Lancelot was constrained to do his Lady's will, for he loved more than Pyramus, if that were possible for any man to do. Lancelot heard what was said, and as soon as the last word had issued from her mouth, "since you wish him to desist, I am willing that he should do so," Lancelot would not have touched him or made a movement for anything, even if the other had killed him. He does not touch him or raise his hand. But Meleagant, beside himself with rage and shame when he hears that it has been necessary to intercede in his behalf, strikes him with all the strength he can muster. And the king went down from the tower to upbraid his son, and entering the list he addressed him thus: "How now? Is this becoming, to strike him when he is not touching thee? Thou art too cruel and savage, and thy prowess is now out of place! For we all know beyond a doubt that he is thy superior." Then Meleagant, choking with shame, says to the king: "I think you must be blind! I do not believe you see a thing. Any one must indeed be blind to think I am not better than he." "Seek some one to believe thy words!" the king replies, "for all the people know whether thou speakest the truth or a lie. All of us know full well the truth." Then the king bids his barons lead his son away, which they do at once in execution of his command: they led away Meleagant. But it was not necessary to use force to induce Lancelot to withdraw, for Meleagant might have harmed him grievously, before he would have sought to defend himself. Then the king says to his son: "So help me God, now thou must make peace and surrender the Queen. Thou must cease this quarrel once for all and withdraw thy claim." "That is great nonsense you have uttered! I hear you speak foolishly. Stand aside! Let us fight, and do not mix in our affairs!" But the king says he will take a hand, for he knows well that, were the fight to continue, Lancelot would kill his son. "He kill me! Rather would I soon defeat and kill him, if you would leave us alone and let us fight." Then the king says: "So help me God, all that thou sayest is of no avail." "Why is that?" he asks. "Because I will not consent. I will not so trust in thy folly and pride as to allow thee to be killed. A man is a fool to court death, as thou dost in thy ignorance. I know well that thou hatest me because I wish to save thy life. God will not let me see and witness thy death, if I can help it, for it would cause me too much grief." He talks to him and reproves him until finally peace and good-will are restored. The terms of the peace are these: he will surrender the Queen to Lancelot, provided that the latter without reluctance will fight them again within a year of such time as he shall choose to summon him: this is no trial to Lancelot. When peace is made, all the people press about, and it is decided that the battle shall be fought at the court of King Arthur, who holds Britain and Cornwall in his sway: there they decide that it shall be. And the Queen has to consent, and Lancelot has to promise, that if Meleagant can prove him recreant, she shall come back with him again without the interference of any one. When the Queen and Lancelot had both agreed to this, the arrangement was concluded, and they both retired and removed their arms. Now the custom in the country was that when one issued forth, all the others might do so too. All called down blessings upon Lancelot: and you may know that he must have felt great joy, as in truth he did. All the strangers assemble and rejoice over Lancelot, speaking so as to be heard by him: "Sire, in truth we were joyful as soon as we heard your name, for we felt sure at once that we should all be set free." There was a great crowd present at this glad scene, as each one strives and presses forward to touch him if possible. Any one who succeeded in touching him was more delighted than he could tell. There was plenty of joy, and of sorrow too; those who were now set free rejoiced unrestrainedly; but Meleagant and his followers have not anything they want, but are pensive, gloomy, and downcast. The king turns away from the list, taking with him Lancelot, who begs him to take him to the Queen. "I shall not fail to do so," the king replies; "for it seems to me the proper thing to do. And if you like, I will show you Kay the seneschal." At this Lancelot is so glad that he almost falls at his feet. Then the king took him at once into the hall, where the Queen had come to wait for him.

When the Queen saw the king holding Lancelot by the hand, she rose before the king, but she looked displeased with clouded brow, and she spoke not a word. "Lady, here is Lancelot come to see you," says the king; "you ought to be pleased and satisfied." "I, sire? He cannot please me. I care nothing about seeing him." "Come now, lady," says the king who was very frank and courteous, "what induces you to act like this? You are too scornful toward a man who has served you so faithfully that he has repeatedly exposed his life to mortal danger on this journey for your sake, and who has defended and rescued you from my son Meleagant who had deeply wronged you." "Sire, truly he has made poor use of his time. I shall never deny that I feel no gratitude toward him." Now Lancelot is dumbfounded; but he replies very humbly like a polished lover: "Lady, certainly I am grieved at this, but I dare not ask your reason." The Queen listened as Lancelot voiced his disappointment, but in order to grieve and confound him, she would not answer a single word, but returned to her room. And Lancelot followed her with his eyes and heart until she reached the door; but she was not long in sight, for the room was close by. His eyes would gladly have followed her, had that been possible; but the heart, which is more lordly and masterful in its strength, went through the door after her, while the eyes remained behind weeping with the body. And the king said privily to him: "Lancelot, I am amazed at what this means: and how it comes about that the Queen cannot endure the sight of you, and that she is so unwilling to speak with you. If she is ever accustomed to speak with you, she ought not to be niggardly now or avoid conversation with you, after what you have done for her. Now tell me, if you know, why and for what misdeed she has shown you such a countenance." "Sire, I did not notice that just now; but she will not look at me or hear my words, and that distresses and grieves me much." "Surely," says the king, "she is in the wrong, for you have risked your life for her. Come away now, fair sweet friend, and we shall go to speak with the seneschal." "I shall be glad to do so," he replies. Then they both go to the seneschal. As soon as Lancelot came where he was, the seneschal's first exclamation was: "How thou hast shamed me!" "I? How so?" Lancelot inquires; "tell me what disgrace have I brought upon you?" "A very great disgrace, for thou hast carried out what I could not accomplish, and thou hast done what I could not do."

Then the king left them together in the room, and went out alone. And Lancelot inquires of the seneschal if he has been badly off. "Yes," he answers, "and I still am so. I was never more wretched than I am now. And I should have died a long time ago, had it not been for the king, who in his compassion has shown me so much gentleness and kindness that he willingly let me lack nothing of which I stood in need; but I was furnished at once with everything that I desired. But opposed to the kindness which he showed me, was Meleagant his son, who is full of wickedness, and who summoned the physicians to him and bade them apply such ointments as would kill me. Such a father and stepfather have I had! For when the king had a good plaster applied to my wounds in his desire that I should soon be cured, his treacherous son, wishing to put me to death, had it promptly taken off and some harmful salve applied. But I am very sure that the king was ignorant of this; he would not tolerate such base and murderous tricks. But you do not know how courteous he has been to my lady: no frontier tower since the time that Noah built the ark was ever so carefully guarded, for he has guarded her so vigilantly that, though his son chafed under the restraint, he would nor let him see her except in the presence of the king himself. Up to the present time the king in his mercy has shown her all the marks of consideration which she herself proposed. She alone had the disposition of her affairs. And the king esteemed her all the more for the loyalty she showed. But is it true, as I am told, that she is so angry with you that she has publicly refused to speak with you?" "You have been told the exact truth," Lancelot replies, "but for God's sake, can you tell me why she is so displeased with me?" He replies that he does not know, and that he is greatly surprised at it. "Well, let it be as she pleases," says Lancelot, feeling his helplessness; "I must now take my leave, and I shall go to seek my lord Gawain who has entered this land, and who arranged with me that he would proceed directly to the waterbridge." Then, leaving the room, he appeared before the king and asked for leave to proceed in that direction. And the king willingly grants him leave to go. Then those whom Lancelot had set free and delivered from prison ask him what they are to do. And he replies: "All those who desire may come with me, and those who wish to stay with the Queen may do so: there is no reason why they should accompany me." Then all those, who so desire, accompany him, more glad and joyous than is their wont. With the Queen remain her damsels who are light of heart, and many knights and ladies too. But there is not one of those who stay behind, who would not have preferred to return to his own country to staying there. But on my lord Gawain's account, whose arrival is expected, the Queen keeps them, saying that she will never stir until she has news of him.

The news spreads everywhere that the Queen is free to go, and that all the other prisoners have been set at liberty and are free to go whenever it suits and pleases them. Wherever the people of the land gather together, they ask each other about the truth of this report, and never talk of anything else. They are very much enraged that all the dangerous passes have been overcome, and that any one may come and go as he pleases. But when the natives of the country, who had not been present at the battle, learned how Lancelot had been the victor, they all betook themselves to the place where they knew he must pass by, thinking that the king would be well pleased if they should seize Lancelot and hale him back to him. All of his own men were without their arms, and therefore they were at a disadvantage when they saw the natives of the country coming under arms. It was not strange that they seized Lancelot, who was without his arms. They lead him back prisoner, his feet lashed together beneath his horse. Then his own men say: "Gentlemen, this is an evil deed; for the king has given us his safe-conduct, and we are under his protection." But the others reply: "We do not know how that may be; but as we have taken you, you must return with us to court." The rumour, which swiftly flies and runs, reaches the king, that his men have seized Lancelot and put him to death. When the king hears it, he is sorely grieved and swears angrily by his head that they who have killed him shall surely die for the deed; and that, if he can seize or catch them, it shall be their fate to be hanged, burned, or drowned. And if they attempt to deny their deed, he will not believe what they say, for they have brought him such grief and shame that he would be disgraced were vengeance not to be exacted from them; but he will be avenged without a doubt. The news of this spread until it reached the Queen, who was sitting at meat. She almost killed herself on hearing the false report about Lancelot, but she supposes it to be true, and therefore she is in such dismay that she almost loses the power to speak; but, because of those present, she forces herself to say: "In truth, I am sorry for his death, and it is no wonder that I grieve, for he came into this country for my sake, and therefore I should mourn for him." Then she says to herself, so that the others should not hear, that no one need ask her to drink or eat, if it is true that he is dead, in whose life she found her own. Then grieving she rises from the table, and makes her lament, but so that no one hears or notices her. She is so beside herself that she repeatedly grasps her throat with the desire to kill herself; but first she confesses to herself, and repents with self-reproach, blaming and censuring herself for the wrong she had done him, who, as she knew, had always been hers, and would still be hers, if he were alive. She is so distressed at the thought of her cruelty, that her beauty is seriously impaired. Her cruelty and meanness affected her and marred her beauty more than all the vigils and fastings with which she afflicted herself. When all her sins rise up before her, she gathers them together, and as she reviews them, she repeatedly exclaims: "Alas! of what was I thinking when my lover stood before me and I should have welcomed him, that I would not listen to his words? Was I not a fool, when I refused to look at or speak to him? Foolish indeed? Rather was I base and cruel, so help me God. I intended it as a jest, but he did not take it so, and has not pardoned me. I am sure it was no one but me who gave him his death-blow. When he came before me smiling and expecting that I would be glad to see him and would welcome him, and when I would not look at him, was not that a mortal blow? When I refused to speak with him, then doubtless at one blow I deprived him of his heart and life. These two strokes have killed him, I am sure; no other bandits have caused his death. God! can I ever make amends for this murder and this crime? No, indeed; sooner will the rivers and the sea dry up. Alas! how much better I should feel, and how much comfort I should take, if only once before he died I had held him in my arms! What? Yes, certainly, quite unclad, in order the better to enjoy him. If he is dead, I am very wicked not to destroy myself. Why? Can it harm my lover for me to live on after he is dead, if I take no pleasure in anything but in the woe I bear for him? In giving myself up to grief after his death, the very woes I court would be sweet to me, if he were only still alive. It is wrong for a woman to wish to die rather than to suffer for her lover's sake. It is certainly sweet for me to mourn him long. I would rather be beaten alive than die and be at rest."

For two days the Queen thus mourned for him without eating or drinking, until they thought she too would die. There are plenty of people ready to carry bad news rather than good. The news reaches Lancelot that his lady and sweetheart is dead. You need have no doubt of the grief he felt; every one may feel sure that he was afflicted and overcome with grief. Indeed, if you would know the truth, he was so downcast that he held his life in slight esteem. He wished to kill himself at once, but first he uttered a brief lament. He makes a running noose at one end of the belt he wore, and then tearfully communes thus with himself: "Ah, death, how hast thou spied me out and undone me, when in the bloom of health! I am undone, and yet I feel no pain except the grief within my heart. This is a terrible mortal grief. I am willing that it should be so, and if God will, I shall die of it. Then can I not die some other way, without God's consent? Yes, if he will let me tie this noose around my neck. I think I can compel death, even against her will, to take my life. Death, who covets only those who fear her, will not come to me; but my belt will bring her within my power, and as soon as she is mine, she will execute my desire. But, in truth, she will come too tardily for me, for I yearn to have her now!" Then he delays and hesitates no longer, but adjusts his head within the noose until it rests about his neck; and in order that he may not fail to harm himself, he fastens the end of the belt tightly about the saddle-bow, without attracting the attention of any one. Then he let himself slide to earth, intending his horse to drag him until he was lifeless, for he disdains to live another hour. When those who ride with him see him fallen to earth, they suppose him to be in a faint, for no one sees the noose which he had attached about his neck. At once they caught him in their arms and, on raising him, they found the noose which he had put around his neck and with which he sought to kill himself. They quickly cut the noose; but the noose had so hurt his throat that for some time he could not speak; the veins of his neck and throat are almost broken. Now he could not harm himself, even had he wished to do so; however, he is grieved that they have laid hands on him, and he almost burns up with rage, for willingly would he have killed himself had no one chanced to notice him. And now when he cannot harm himself, he cries: "Ah, vile and shameless death! For God's sake, why hadst thou not the power and might to kill me before my lady died? I suppose it was because thou wouldst not deign to do what might be a kindly deed. If thou didst spare me, it must be attributed to thy wickedness. Ah, what kind of service and kindness is that! How well hast thou employed them here! A curse upon him who thanks thee or feels gratitude for such a service! I know not which is more my enemy: life, which detains me, or death, which will not slay me. Each one torments me mortally; and it serves me right, so help me God, that in spite of myself I should still live on. For I ought to have killed myself as soon as my lady the Queen showed her hate for me; she did not do it without cause, but she had some good reason, though I know not what it is. And if I had known what it was before her soul went to God, I should have made her such rich amends as would have pleased her and gained her mercy. God! what could my crime have been? I think she must have known that I mounted upon the cart. I do not know what other cause she can have to blame me. This has been my undoing. If this is the reason of her hate, God! what harm could this crime do? Any one who would reproach me for such an act never knew what love is, for no one could mention anything which, if prompted by love, ought to be turned into a reproach. Rather, everything that one can do for his lady-love is to be regarded as a token of his love and courtesy. Yet, I did not do it for my 'lady-love'. I know not by what name to call her, whether 'lady-love', or not. I do not dare to call her by this name. But I think I know this much of love: that if she loved me, she ought not to esteem me less for this crime, but rather call me her true lover, inasmuch as I regarded it as an honour to do all love bade me do, even to mount upon a cart. She ought to ascribe this to love; and this is a certain proof that love thus tries his devotees and thus learns who is really his. But this service did not please my lady, as I discovered by her countenance. And yet her lover did for her that for which many have shamefully reproached and blamed him, though she was the cause of it; and many blame me for the part I have played, and have turned my sweetness into bitterness. In truth, such is the custom of those who know so little of love, that even honour they wash in shame. But whoever dips honour into shame, does not wash it, but rather sullies it. But they, who maltreat him so, are quite ignorant of love; and he, who fears not his commands, boasts himself very superior to him. For unquestionably he fares well who obeys the commands of love, and whatever he does is pardonable, but he is the coward who does not dare."

Thus Lancelot makes his lament, and his men stand grieving by his side, keeping hold of him and guarding him. Then the news comes that the Queen is not dead. Thereupon Lancelot at once takes comfort, and if his grief for her death had before been intense and deep, now his joy for her life was a hundred thousand times as great. And when they arrived within six or seven leagues of the castle where King Bademagu was, grateful news of Lancelot was told him, how he was alive and was coming hale and hearty, and this news the king was glad to hear. He did a very courteous thing in going at once to appraise the Queen. And she replies: "Fair sire, since you say so, I believe it is true, but I assure you that, if he were dead, I should never be happy again. All my joy would be cut off, if a knight had been killed in my service."

Then the king leaves her, and the Queen yearns ardently for the arrival of her lover and her joy. She has no desire this time to bear him any grudge. But rumour, which never rests but runs always unceasingly, again reaches the Queen to the effect that Lancelot would have killed himself for her sake, if he had had the chance. She is happy at the thought that this is true, but she would not have had it happen so for anything, for her sorrow would have been too great. Thereupon Lancelot arrived in haste. As soon as the king sees him, he runs to kiss and embrace him. He feels as if he ought to fly, borne along by the buoyancy of his joy. But his satisfaction is cut short by those who had taken and bound his guest, and the king tells them they have come in an evil hour, for they shall all be killed and confounded. Then they made answer that they thought he would have it so. "It is I whom you have insulted in doing your pleasure. He has no reason to complain," the king replies; "you have not shamed him at all, but only me who was protecting him. However you look at it, the shame is mine. But if you escape me now, you will see no joke in this." When Lancelot hears his wrath, he puts forth every effort to make peace and adjust matters; when his efforts have met with success, the king takes him away to see the Queen. This time the Queen did not lower her eyes to the ground, but she went to meet him cheerfully, honouring him all she could, and making him sit down by her side. Then they talked together at length of all that was upon their hearts, and love furnished them with so much to say that topics did not lack. And when Lancelot sees how well he stands, and that all he says finds favour with the Queen, he says to her in confidence: "Lady, I marvel greatly why you received me with such a countenance when you saw me the day before yesterday, and why you would not speak a word to me: I almost died of the blow you gave me, and I had not the courage to dare to question you about it, as I now venture to do. I am ready now, lady, to make amends, when you have told me what has been the crime which has caused me such distress." Then the Queen replies: "What? Did you not hesitate for shame to mount the cart? You showed you were loath to get in, when you hesitated for two whole steps. That is the reason why I would neither address nor look at you." "May God save me from such a crime again," Lancelot replies, "and may God show me no mercy, if you were not quite right! For God's sake, lady, receive my amends at once, and tell me, for God's sake, if you can ever pardon me." "Friend, you are quite forgiven," the Queen replies; "I pardon you willingly." "Thank you for that, lady," he then says; "but I cannot tell you here all that I should like to say; I should like to talk with you more at leisure, if possible." Then the Queen indicates a window by her glance rather than with her finger, and says: "Come through the garden to-night and speak with me at yonder window, when every one inside has gone to sleep. You will not be able to get in: I shall be inside and you outside: to gain entrance will be impossible. I shall be able to touch you only with my lips or hand, but, if you please, I will stay there until morning for love of you. Our bodies cannot be joined, for close beside me in my room lies Kay the seneschal, who is still suffering from his wounds. And the door is not open, but is tightly closed and guarded well. When you come, take care to let no spy catch sight of you." "Lady," says he, "if I can help it, no spy shall see me who might think or speak evil of us." Then, having agreed upon this plan, they separate very joyfully.

Lancelot leaves the room in such a happy frame that all his past troubles are forgotten. But he was so impatient for the night to come that his restlessness made the day seem longer than a hundred ordinary days or than an entire year. If night had only come, he would gladly have gone to the trysting place. Dark and sombre night at last won its struggle with the day, and wrapped it up in its covering, and laid it away beneath its cloak. When he saw the light of day obscured, he pretended to be tired and worn, and said that, in view of his protracted vigils, he needed rest. You, who have ever done the same, may well understand and guess that he pretends to be tired and goes to bed in order to deceive the people of the house; but he cared nothing about his bed, nor would he have sought rest there for anything, for he could not have done so and would not have dared, and furthermore he would not have cared to possess the courage or the power to do so. Soon he softly rose, and was pleased to find that no moon or star was shining, and that in the house there was no candle, lamp, or lantern burning. Thus he went out and looked about, but there was no one on the watch for him, for all thought that he would sleep in his bed all night. Without escort or company he quickly went out into the garden, meeting no one on the way, and he was so fortunate as to find that a part of the garden-wall had recently fallen down. Through this break he passes quickly and proceeds to the window, where he stands, taking good care not to cough or sneeze, until the Queen arrives clad in a very white chemise. She wore no cloak or coat, but had thrown over her a short cape of scarlet cloth and shrew-mouse fur. As soon as Lancelot saw the Queen leaning on the window-sill behind the great iron bars, he honoured her with a gentle salute. She promptly returned his greeting, for he was desirous of her, and she of him. Their talk and conversation are not of vulgar, tiresome affairs. They draw close to one another, until each holds the other's hand. But they are so distressed at not being able to come together more completely, that they curse the iron bars. Then Lancelot asserts that, with the Queen's consent, he will come inside to be with her, and that the bars cannot keep him out. And the Queen replies: "Do you not see how the bars are stiff to bend and hard to break? You could never so twist, pull or drag at them as to dislodge one of them." "Lady," says he, "have no fear of that. It would take more than these bars to keep me out. Nothing but your command could thwart my power to come to you. If you will but grant me your permission, the way will open before me. But if it is not your pleasure, then the way is so obstructed that I could not possibly pass through." "Certainly," she says, "I consent. My will need not stand in your way; but you must wait until I retire to my bed again, so that no harm may come to you, for it would be no joke or jest if the seneschal, who is sleeping here, should wake up on hearing you. So it is best for me to withdraw, for no good could come of it, if he should see me standing here." "Go then, lady," he replies; "but have no fear that I shall make any noise. I think I can draw out the bars so softly and with so little effort that no one shall be aroused."

Then the Queen retires, and he prepares to loosen the window. Seizing the bars, he pulls and wrenches them until he makes them bend and drags them from their places. But the iron was so sharp that the end of his little finger was cut to the nerve, and the first joint of the next finger was torn; but he who is intent upon something else paid no heed to any of his wounds or to the blood which trickled down. Though the window is not low, Lancelot gets through it quickly and easily. First he finds Kay asleep in his bed, then he comes to the bed of the Queen, whom he adores and before whom he kneels, holding her more dear than the relic of any saint. And the Queen extends her arms to him and, embracing him, presses him tightly against her bosom, drawing him into the bed beside her and showing him every possible satisfaction; her love and her heart go out to him. It is love that prompts her to treat him so; and if she feels great love for him, he feels a hundred thousand times as much for her. For there is no love at all in other hearts compared with what there is in his; in his heart love was so completely embodied that it was niggardly toward all other hearts. Now Lancelot possesses all he wants, when the Queen voluntarily seeks his company and love, and when he holds her in his arms, and she holds him in hers. Their sport is so agreeable and sweet, as they kiss and fondle each other, that in truth such a marvellous joy comes over them as was never heard or known. But their joy will not be revealed by me, for in a story, it has no place. Yet, the most choice and delightful satisfaction was precisely that of which our story must not speak. That night Lancelot's joy and pleasure were very great. But, to his sorrow, day comes when he must leave his mistress' side. It cost him such pain to leave her that he suffered a real martyr's agony. His heart now stays where the Queen remains; he has not the power to lead it away, for it finds such pleasure in the Queen that it has no desire to leave her: so his body goes, and his heart remains. But enough of his body stays behind to spot and stain the sheets with the blood which has fallen from his fingers. Full of sighs and tears, Lancelot leaves in great distress. He grieves that no time is fixed for another meeting, but it cannot be. Regretfully he leaves by the window through which he had entered so happily. He was so badly wounded in the fingers that they were in sorry, state; yet he straightened the bars and set them in their place again, so that from neither side, either before or behind, was it evident that any one had drawn out or bent any of the bars. When he leaves the room, he bows and acts precisely as if he were before a shrine; then he goes with a heavy heart, and reaches his lodgings without being recognised by any one. He throws himself naked upon his bed without awaking any one, and then for the first time he is surprised to notice the cuts in his fingers; but he is not at all concerned, for he is very sure that the wound was caused by dragging the window bars from the wall. Therefore he was not at all worried, for he would rather have had both arms dragged from his body than not enter through the window. But he would have been very angry and distressed, if he had thus injured and wounded himself under any other circumstances.

In the morning, within her curtained room, the Queen had fallen into a gentle sleep; she had not noticed that her sheets were spotted with blood, but she supposed them to be perfectly white and clean and presentable. Now Meleagant, as soon as he was dressed and ready, went to the room where the Queen lay. He finds her awake, and he sees the sheets spotted with fresh drops of blood, whereupon he nudges his companions and, suspicious of some mischief, looks at the bed of Kay the seneschal, and sees that his sheets are blood-stained too, for you must know that in the night his wounds had begun to bleed afresh. Then he said: "Lady, now I have found the evidence that I desired. It is very true that any man is a fool to try to confine a woman: he wastes his efforts and his pains. He who tries to keep her under guard loses her sooner than the man who takes no thought of her. A fine watch, indeed, has been kept by my father, who is guarding you on my behalf! He has succeeded in keeping you from me, but, in spite of him, Kay the seneschal has looked upon you last night, and has done what he pleased with you, as can readily be proved." "What is that?"

she asks. "Since I must speak, I find blood on your sheets, which proves the fact. I know it and can prove it, because I find on both your sheets and his the blood which issued from his wounds: the evidence is very strong." Then the Queen saw on both beds the bloody sheets, and marvelling, she blushed with shame and said: "So help me God, this blood which I see upon my sheets was never brought here by Kay, but my nose bled during the night, and I suppose it must be from my nose." In saying so, she thinks she tells the truth. "By my head," says Meleagant, "there is nothing in what you say. Swearing is of no avail, for you are taken in your guilt, and the truth will soon be proved." Then he said to the guards who were present: "Gentlemen, do not move, and see to it that the sheets are not taken from the bed until I return. I wish the king to do me justice, as soon as he has seen the truth." Then he searched until he found him, and failing at his feet, he said: "Sire, come to see what you have failed to guard. Come to see the Queen, and you shall see the certain marvels which I have already seen and tested. But, before you go, I beg you not to fail to be just and upright toward me. You know well to what danger I have exposed myself for the Queen; yet, you are no friend of mine and keep her from me under guard. This morning I went to see her in her bed, and I remarked that Kay lies with her every night. Sire, for God's sake, be not angry, if I am disgruntled and if I complain. For it is very humiliating for me to be hated and despised by one with whom Kay is allowed to lie." "Silence!" says the king; "I don't believe it." "Then come, my lord, and see the sheets and the state in which Kay has left them. Since you will not believe my words, and since you think I am lying, I will show you the sheets and the quilt covered with blood from Kay's wounds." "Come now," says the king, "I wish to see for myself, and my eyes will judge of the truth." Then the king goes directly to the room, where the Queen got up at his approach. He sees that the sheets are blood-stained on her bed and on Kay's alike and he says: "Lady, it is going badly now, if what my son has said is true." Then she replies: "So help me God, never even in a dream was uttered such a monstrous lie. I think Kay the seneschal is courteous and loyal enough not to commit such a deed, and besides, I do not expose my body in the market-place, nor offer it of my own free will. Surely, Kay is not the man to make an insulting proposal to me, and I have never desired and shall never desire to do such a thing myself." "Sire, I shall be much obliged to you," says Meleagant to his father, "if Kay shall be made to atone for this outrage, and the Queen's shame thus be exposed. It devolves upon you to see that justice is done, and this justice I now request and claim. Kay has betrayed King Arthur, his lord, who had such confidence in him that he entrusted to him what he loved most in the world." "Let me answer, sire," says Kay, "and I shall exonerate myself. May God have no mercy upon my soul when I leave this world, if I ever lay with my lady! Indeed, I should rather be dead than ever do my lord such an ugly wrong, and may God never grant me better health than I have now but rather kill me on the spot, if such a thought ever entered my mind! But I know that my wounds bled profusely last night, and that is the reason why my sheets are stained with blood. That is why your son suspects me, but surely he has no right to do so." And Meleagant answers him: "So help me God, the devils and demons have betrayed you. You grew too heated last night and, as a result of your exertions, your wounds have doubtless bled afresh. There is no use in your denying it; we can see it, and it is perfectly evident. It is right that he should atone for his crime, who is so plainly taken in his guilt. Never did a knight with so fair a name commit such iniquities as this, and yours is the shame for it." "Sire, sire," says Kay to the king, "I will defend the Queen and myself against the accusation of your son. He harasses and distresses me, though he has no ground to treat me so." "You cannot fight," the king replies, "you are too ill." "Sire, if you will allow it, I will fight with him, ill as I am, and will show him that I am not guilty of the crime which he imputes to me." But the Queen, having secretly sent word to Lancelot, tells the king that she will present a knight who will defend the seneschal, if Meleagant dares to urge this charge. Then Meleagant said at once: "There is no knight without exception, even were he a giant, whom I will not fight until one of us is defeated." Then Lancelot came in, and with him such a rout of knights that the whole hall was filled with them. As soon as he had entered, in the hearing of all, both young and old, the Queen told what had happened, and said: "Lancelot, this insult has been done me by Meleagant. In the presence of all who hear his words he says I have lied, if you do not make him take it back. Last night, he asserted, Kay lay with me, because he found my sheets, like his, all stained with blood; and he says that he stands convicted, unless he will undertake his own defence, or unless some one else will fight the battle on his behalf." Lancelot says: "You need never use arguments with me. May it not please God that either you or he should be thus discredited! I am ready to fight and to prove to the extent of my power that he never was guilty of such a thought. I am ready to employ my strength in his behalf, and to defend him against this charge." Then Meleagant jumped up and said: "So help me God, I am pleased and well satisfied with that: no one need think that I object." And Lancelot said: "My lord king, I am well acquainted with suits and laws, with trials and verdicts: in a question of veracity an oath should be taken before the fight." Meleagant at once replies: "I agree to take an oath; so let the relics be brought at once, for I know well that I am right." And Lancelot answers him: "So help me God, no one who ever knew Kay the seneschal would doubt his word on such a point." Then they call for their horses, and ask that their arms be brought. This is promptly done, and when the valets had armed them, they were ready for the fight. Then the holy relics are brought forth: Meleagant steps forward, with Lancelot by his side, and both fall on their knees. Then Meleagant, laying his hands upon the relics, swears unreservedly: "So help me God and this holy relic, Kay the seneschal lay with the Queen in her bed last night and, had his pleasure with her." "And I swear that thou liest," says Lancelot, "and furthermore I swear that he neither lay with her nor touched her. And may it please God to take vengeance upon him who has lied, and may He bring the truth to light! Moreover, I will take another oath and swear, whoever may dislike it or be displeased, that if I am permitted to vanquish Meleagant to-day, I will show him no mercy, so help me God and these relics here!" The king felt no joy when he heard this oath.

When the oaths had been taken, their horses were brought forward, which were fair and good in every way. Each man mounts his own home, and they ride at once at each other as fast as the steeds can carry them; and when the horses are in mid-career, the knights strike each other so fiercely that there is nothing left of the lances in their hands. Each brings the other to earth; however, they are not dismayed, but they rise at once and attack each other with their sharp drawn swords. The burning sparks fly in the air from their helmets. They assail each other so bitterly with the drawn swords in their hands that, as they thrust and draw, they encounter each other with their blows and will not pause even to catch their breath. The king in his grief and anxiety called the Queen, who had gone up in the tower to look out from the balcony: he begged her for God's sake, the Creator, to let them be separated. "Whatever is your pleasure is agreeable to me," the Queen says honestly: "I shall not object to anything you do." Lancelot plainly heard what reply the Queen made to the king's request, and from that time he ceased to fight and renounced the struggle at once. But Meleagant does not wish to stop, and continues to strike and hew at him. But the king rushes between them and stops his son, who declares with an oath that he has no desire for peace. He wants to fight, and cares not for peace. Then the king says to him: "Be quiet, and take my advice, and be sensible. No shame or harm shall come to thee, if thou wilt do what is right and heed my words. Dost thou not remember that thou hast agreed to fight him at King Arthur's court? And dost thou not suppose that it would be a much greater honour for thee to defeat him there than anywhere else?" The king says this to see if he can so influence him as to appease him and separate them. And Lancelot, who was impatient to go in search of my lord Gawain, requests leave of the king and Queen to depart. With their permission he goes away toward the water-bridge, and after him there followed a great company of knights. But it would have suited him very well, if many of those who went had stayed behind. They make long days' journeys until they approach the water-bridge, but are still about a league from it. Before they came in sight of the bridge, a dwarf came to meet them on a mighty hunter, holding a scourge with which to urge on and incite his steed. In accordance with his instructions, he at once inquired: "Which of you is Lancelot? Don't conceal him from me; I am of your party; tell me confidently, for I ask the question for your good." Lancelot replies in his own behalf, and says: "I am he whom thou seekest and askest for." "Ah," says the dwarf, "frank knight, leave these people, and trust in me. Come along with me alone, for I will take thee to a goodly place. Let no one follow thee for anything, but let them wait here; for we shall return presently." He, suspecting no harm in this, bids all his men stay there, and follows the dwarf who has betrayed him. Meanwhile his men who wait for him may continue to expect him long in vain, for they, who have taken and seized him, have no desire to give him up. And his men are in such a state of grief at his failure to return that they do not know what steps to take. They all say sorrowfully that the dwarf has betrayed them. It would be useless to inquire for him: with heavy hearts they begin to search, but they know not where to look for him with any hope of finding him. So they all take counsel, and the most reasonable and sensible agree on this, it seems: to go to the passage of the water-bridge, which is close by, to see if they can find my lord Gawain in wood or plain, and then with his advice search for Lancelot. Upon this plan they all agree without dissension. Toward the water-bridge they go, and as soon as they reach the bridge, they see my lord Gawain overturned and fallen from the bridge into the stream which is very deep. One moment he rises, and the next he sinks; one moment they see him, and the next they lose him from sight. They make such efforts that they succeed in raising him with branches, poles and hooks. He had nothing but his hauberk on his back, and on his head was fixed his helmet, which was worth ten of the common sort, and he wore his iron greaves, which were all rusty with his sweat, for he had endured great trials, and had passed victoriously through many perils and assaults. His lance, his shield, and horse were all behind on the other bank. Those who have rescued him do not believe he is alive. For his body was full of water, and until he got rid of it, they did not hear him speak a word. But when his speech and voice and the passageway to his heart are free, and as soon, as what he said could be heard and understood, he tried to speak he inquired at once for the Queen, whether those present had any news of her. And they replied that she is still with King Bademagu, who serves her well and honourably. "Has no one come to seek her in this land?" my lord Gawain then inquires of them. And they answer him: "Yes, indeed." "Who?" "Lancelot of the Lake," they say, "who crossed the sword-bridge, and rescued and delivered her as well as all the rest of us. But we have been betrayed by a pot-bellied, humpbacked, and crabbed dwarf. He has deceived us shamefully in seducing Lancelot from us, and we do not know what he has done with him." "When was that?" my lord Gawain inquires. "Sire, near here this very day this trick was played on us, while he was coming with us to meet you." "And how has Lancelot been occupied since he entered this land?" Then they begin to tell him all about him in detail, and then they tell him about the Queen, how she is waiting for him and asserting that nothing could induce her to leave the country, until she sees him or hears some credible news of him. To them my lord Gawain replies: "When we leave this bridge, we shall go to search for Lancelot." There is not one who does not advise rather that they go to the Queen at once, and have the king seek Lancelot, for it is their opinion that his son Meleagant has shown his enmity by having him cast into prison. But if the king can learn where he is, he will certainly make him surrender him: they can rely upon this with confidence.

They all agreed upon this plan, and started at once upon their way until they drew near the court where the Queen and king were. There, too, was Kay the seneschal, and that disloyal man, full to overflowing of treachery, who has aroused the greatest anxiety for Lancelot on the part of the party which now arrives. They feel they have been discomfited and betrayed, and they make great lament in their misery. It is not a gracious message which reports this mourning to the Queen. Nevertheless, she deports herself with as good a grace as possible. She resolves to endure it, as she must, for the sake of my lord Gawain. However, she does not so conceal her grief that it does not somewhat appear. She has to show both joy and grief at once: her heart is empty for Lancelot, and to my lord Gawain she shows excessive joy. Every one who hears of the loss of Lancelot is grief-stricken and distracted. The king would have rejoiced at the coming of my lord Gawain and would have been delighted with his acquaintance; but he is so sorrowful and distressed over the betrayal of Lancelot that he is prostrated and full of grief. And the Queen beseeches him insistently to have him searched for, up and down throughout the land, without postponement or delay. My lord Gawain and Kay and all the others join in this prayer and request. "Leave this care to me, and speak no more of it," the king replies, "for I have been ready to do so for some time. Without need of request or prayer this search shall be made with thoroughness." Everyone bows in sign of gratitude, and the king at once sends messengers through his realm, sagacious and prudent men-at-arms, who inquired for him throughout the land. They made inquiry for him everywhere, but gained no certain news of him. Not finding any, they come back to the place where the knights remain; then Gawain and Kay and all the others say that they will go in search of him, fully armed and lance in rest; they will not trust to sending some one else.

One day after dinner they were all in the hall putting on their arms, and the point had been reached where there was nothing to do but start, when a valet entered and passed by them all until he came before the Queen, whose cheeks were by no means rosy! For she was in such mourning for Lancelot, of whom she had no news, that she had lost all her colour. The valet greeted her as well as the king, who was by her side, and then all the others and Kay and my lord Gawain. He held a letter in his hand which he gave to the king, who took it. The king had it read in the hearing of all by one who made no mistake in reading it. The reader knew full well how to communicate to them what was written in the parchment: he says that Lancelot sends greetings to the king as his kind lord, and thanks him for the honour and kindness he has shown him, and that he now places himself at the king's orders. And know that he is now hale and hearty at King Arthur's court, and he bids him tell the Queen to come thither, if she will consent, in company with my lord Gawain and Kay. In proof of which, he affixed his signature which they should recognise, as indeed they did. At this they were very happy and glad; the whole court resounds with their jubilation, and they say they will start next day as soon as it is light. So, when the day broke, they make ready and prepare: they rise and mount and start. With great joy and jubilee the king escorts them for a long distance on their way. When he has conducted them to the frontier and has seen them safely across the border, he takes leave of the Queen, and likewise of all the rest. And when he comes to take his leave, the Queen is careful to express her gratitude for all the kindness he has shown to her, and throwing her arms about his neck, she offers and promises him her own service and that of her lord: no greater promise can she make. And my lord Gawain promises his service to him, as to his lord and friend, and then Kay does likewise, and all the rest. Then the king commends them to God as they start upon their way. After these three, he bids the rest farewell, and then turns his face toward home. The Queen and her company do not tarry a single day until news of them reaches the court. King Arthur was delighted at the news of the Queen's approach, and he is happy and pleased at the thought that his nephew had brought about the Queen's return, as well as that of Kay and of the lesser folk. But the truth is quite different from what he thinks. All the town is cleared as they go to meet them, and knights and vassals join in shouting as they approach: "Welcome to my lord Gawain, who has brought back the Queen and many another captive lady, and has freed for us many prisoners!" Then Gawain answered them: "Gentlemen, I do not deserve your praise. Do not trouble ever to say this again, for the compliment does not apply to me. This honour causes me only shame, for I did not reach the Queen in time; my detention made me late. But Lancelot reached there in time, and won such honour as was never won by any other knight." "Where is he, then, fair dear sire, for we do not see him here?" "Where?" echoes my lord Gawain; "at the court of my lord the King, to be sure. Is he not?" "No, he is not here, or anywhere else in this country. Since my lady was taken away, we have had no news of him." Then for the first time my lord Gawain realised that the letter had been forged, and that they had been betrayed and deceived: by the letter they had been misled. Then they all begin to lament, and they come thus weeping to the court, where the King at once asks for information about the affair. There were plenty who could tell him how much Lancelot had done, how the Queen and all the captives were delivered from durance by him, and by what treachery the dwarf had stolen him and drawn him away from them. This news is not pleasing to the King, and he is very sorry and full of grief; but his heart is so lightened by the pleasure he takes in the Queen's return, that his grief concludes in joy. When he has what he most desires, he cares little for the rest.

While the Queen was out of the country, I believe, the ladies and the damsels who were disconsolate, decided among themselves that they would marry, soon, and they organised a contest and a tournament. The lady of Noauz was patroness of it, with the lady of Pomeglegloi. They will have nothing to do with those who fare ill, but they assert that they will accept those who comport themselves well in the tournament. And they had the date of the contest proclaimed s long while in advance in all the countries near and far, in order that there might be more participants. Now the Queen arrived before the date they had set, and as soon as the ladies heard of the Queen's return, most of them came at once to the King and besought him to grant them a favour and boon, which he did. He promised to do whatever they wished, before he knew what their desire might be. Then they told him that they wished him to let the Queen come to be present at their contest. And he who was not accustomed to forbid, said he was willing, if she wished ir so. In happy mood they go to the Queen and say to her: "Lady, do not deprive us of the boon which the King has granted us." Then she asks them: "What is that? Don't fail to tell!" Then they say to her: "If you will come to our tournament, he will not gainsay you nor stand in the way." Then she said that she would come, since he was willing that she should. Promptly the dames send word throughout the realm that they are going to bring the Queen on the day set for the tournament. The news spread far and near, here and there, until it reached the kingdom whence no one used to return--but now whoever wished might enter or pass out unopposed. The news travelled in this kingdom until it came to a seneschal of the faithless Meleagant may an evil fire burn him! This seneschal had Lancelot in his keeping, for to him he had been entrusted by his enemy Meleagant, who hated him with deadly hate. Lancelot learned the hour and date of the tournament, and as soon as he heard of it, his eyes were not tearless nor was his heart glad. The lady of the house, seeing Lancelot sad and pensive, thus spoke to him: "Sire, for God's sake and for your own soul's good, tell me truly," the lady said, "why you are so changed. You won't eat or drink anything, and I see that you do not make merry or laugh. You can tell me with confidence why you are so sad and troubled." "Ah, lady, for God's sake, do not be surprised that I am sad! Truly, I am very much downcast, since I cannot be present where all that is good in the world will be assembled: that is, at the tournament where there will be a gathering of the people who make the earth tremble. Nevertheless, if it pleased you, and if God should incline your heart to let me go thither, you might rest assured that I should be careful to return to my captivity here." "I would gladly do it," she replied, "if I did not see that my death and destruction would result. But I am in such terror of my lord, the despicable Meleagant, that I would not dare to do it, for he would kill my husband at once. It is not strange that I am afraid of him, for, as you know, he is very bad." "Lady, if you are afraid that I may not return to you at once after the tournament, I will take an oath which I will never break, that nothing will detain me from returning at once to my prison here immediately after the tournament." "Upon my word," said she, "I will allow it upon one condition." "Lady, what condition is that?" Then she replies: "Sire, upon condition that you wilt swear to return to me, and promise that I shall have your love." "Lady, I give you all the love I have, and swear to come back." Then the lady laughs and says: "I have no cause to boast of such a gift, for I know you have bestowed upon some one else the love for which I have just made request. However, I do not disdain to take so much of it as I can get. I shall be satisfied with what I can have, and will accept your oath that you will be so considerate of me as to return hither a prisoner."

In accordance with her wish, Lancelot swears by Holy Church that he will return without fail. And the lady at once gives him the vermilion arms of her lord, and his horse which was marvellously good and strong and brave. He mounts and leaves, armed with handsome, new arms, and proceeds until he comes to Noauz. He espoused this side in the tournament, and took his lodging outside the town. Never did such a noble man choose such a small and lowly lodging-place; but he did not wish to lodge where he might be recognised. There were many good and excellent knights gathered within the town. But there were many more outside, for so many had come on account of the presence of the Queen that the fifth part could not be accommodated inside. For every one who would have been there under ordinary circumstances, there were seven who would not have come excepting on the Queen's account. The barons were quartered in tents, lodges, and pavilions for five leagues around. Moreover, it was wonderful how many gentle ladies and damsels were there. Lancelot placed his shield outside the door of his lodging-place, and then, to make himself more comfortable, he took off his arms and lay down upon a bed which he held in slight esteem; for it was narrow and had a thin mattress, and was covered with a coarse hempen cloth. Lancelot had thrown himself upon the bed all disarmed, and as he lay there in such poor estate, behold! a fellow came in in his shirt-sleeves; he was a herald-at-arms, and had left his coat and shoes in the tavern as a pledge; so he came running barefoot and exposed to the wind. He saw the shield hanging outside the door, and looked at it: but naturally he did not recognise it or know to whom it belonged, or who was the bearer of it. He sees the door of the house standing open, and upon entering, he sees Lancelot upon the bed, and as soon as he saw him, he recognised him and crossed himself. And Lancelot made a sign to him, and ordered him not to speak of him wherever he might go, for if he should tell that he knew him, it would be better for him to have his eyes put out or his neck broken. "Sire," the herald says, "I have always held you in high esteem, and so long as I live, I shall never do anything to cause you displeasure." Then he runs from the house and cries aloud: "Now there has come one who will take the measure! Now there has come one who will take the measure!" The fellow shouts this everywhere, and the people come from every side and ask him what is the meaning of his cry. He is not so rash as to answer them, but goes on shouting the same words: "Now there has come one who will take the measure!" This herald was the master of us all, when he taught us to use the phrase, for he was the first to make use of it.

Now the crowd was assembled, including the Queen and all the ladies, the knights and the other people, and there were many men-at-arms everywhere, to the right and left. At the place where the tournament was to be, there were some large wooden stands for the use of the Queen with her ladies and damsels. Such fine stands were never seen before they were so long and well constructed. Thither the ladies betook themselves with the Queen, wishing to see who would fare better or worse in the combat. Knights arrive by tens, twenties, and thirties, here eighty and there ninety, here a hundred, there still more, and yonder twice as many yet; so that the press is so great in front of the stands and all around that they decide to begin the joust. As they assemble, armed and unarmed, their lances suggest the appearance of a wood, for those who have come to the sport brought so many lances that there is nothing in sight but lances, banners, and standards. Those who are going to take part begin to joust, and they find plenty of their companions who had come with similar intent. Still others prepare to perform other feats of chivalry. The fields, meadows, and fallow lands are so full of knights that it is impossible to estimate how many of them are there. But there was no sign of Lancelot at this first gathering of the knights; but later, when he entered the middle of the field, the herald saw him and could not refrain from crying out: "Behold him who will take the measure! Behold him who will take the measure!" And the people ask him who he is, but he will not tell them anything.

When Lancelot entered the tournament, he was as good as twenty of the best, and he began to fight so doughtily that no one could take his eyes from him, wherever he was. On the Pomelegloi side there was a brave and valorous knight, and his horse was spirited and swifter than a wild stag. He was the son of the Irish king, and fought well and handsomely. But the unknown knight pleased them all more a hundred times. In wonder they all make haste to ask: "Who is this knight who fights so well?" And the Queen privily called a clever and wise damsel to her and said: "Damsel, you must carry a message, and do it quickly and with few words. Go down from the stand, and approach yonder knight with the vermilion shield, and tell him privately that I bid him do his 'worst'." She goes quickly, and with intelligence executes the Queen's command. She sought the knight until she came up close to him; then she said to him prudently and in a voice so low that no one standing by might hear: "Sire, my lady the Queen sends you word by me that you shall do your 'worst'." When he heard this, he replied: "Very willingly," like one who is altogether hers. Then he rides at another knight as hard as his horse can carry him, and misses his thrust which should have struck him. From that time till evening fell he continued to do as badly as possible in accordance with the Queen's desire. But the other, who fought with him, did not miss his thrust, but struck him with such violence that he was roughly handled. Thereupon he took to flight, and after that he never turned his horse's head toward any knight, and were he to die for it, he would never do anything unless he saw in it his shame, disgrace, and dishonour; he even pretends to be afraid of all the knights who pass to and fro. And the very knights who formerly esteemed him now hurled jests and jibes at him. And the herald who had been saying: "He will beat them all in turn!" is greatly dejected and discomfited when he hears the scornful jokes of those who shout: "Friend, say no more! This fellow will not take any one's measure again. He has measured so much that his yardstick is broken, of which thou hast boasted to us so much." Many say: "What is he going to do? He was so brave just now; but now he is so cowardly that there is not a knight whom he dares to face. The cause of his first success must have been that he never engaged at arms before, and he was so brave at his first attack that the most skilled knight dared not withstand him, for he fought like a wild man. But now he has learned so much of arms that he will never wish to bear them again his whole life long. His heart cannot longer endure the thought, for there is nothing more cowardly than his heart." And the Queen, as she watches him, is happy and well-pleased, for she knows full well, though she does not say it, that this is surely Lancelot. Thus all day long till evening he played his coward's part, and late in the afternoon they separated. At parting there was a great discussion as to who had done the best. The son of the Irish king thinks that without doubt or contradiction he has all the glory and renown. But he is grievously mistaken, for there were plenty of others as good as he. Even the vermilion knight so pleased the fairest and gentlest of the ladies and damsels that they had gazed at him more than at any other knight, for they had remarked how well he fought at first, and how excellent and brave he was; then he had become so cowardly that he dared not face a single knight, and even the worst of them could defeat and capture him at will. But knights and ladies all agreed that on the morrow they should return to the list, and the damsels should choose as their lords those who should win honour in that day's fight: on this arrangement they all agree. Then they turn toward their lodgings, and when they had returned, here and there men began to say: "What has become of the worst, the most craven and despised of knights? Whither did he go? Where is he concealed? Where is he to be found? Where shall we search for him? We shall probably never see him again. For he has been driven off by cowardice, with which he is so filled that there is no greater craven in the world than he. And he is not wrong, for a coward is a hundred times more at ease than a valorous fighting man. Cowardice is easy of entreaty, and that is the reason he has given her the kiss of peace and has taken from her all she has to give. Courage never so debased herself as to lodge in his breast or take quarters near him. But cowardice is altogether lodged with him, and she has found a host who will honour her and serve her so faithfully that he is willing to resign his own fair name for hers." Thus they wrangle all night, vying with each other in slander. But often one man maligns another, and yet is much worse himself than the object of his blame and scorn. Thus, every one said what he pleased about him. And when the next day dawned, all the people prepared and came again to the jousting place. The Queen was in the stand again, accompanied by her ladies and damsels and many knights without their arms, who had been captured or defeated, and these explained to them the armorial bearings of the knights whom they most esteem. Thus they talk among themselves: "Do you see that knight yonder with a golden band across the middle of his red shield? That is Governauz of Roberdic. And do you see that other one, who has an eagle and a dragon painted side by side upon his shield? That is the son of the King of Aragon, who has come to this land in search of glory and renown. And do you see that one beside him, who thrusts and jousts so well, bearing a shield with a leopard painted on a green ground on one part, and the other half is azure blue? That is Ignaures the well-beloved, a lover himself and jovial. And he who bears the shield with the pheasants portrayed beak to beak is Coguillanz of Mautirec. Do you see those two side by side, with their dappled steeds, and golden shields showing black lions? One is named Semiramis, and the other is his companion; their shields are painted alike. And do you see the one who has a shield with a gate painted on it, through which a stag appears to be passing out? That is King Ider, in truth." Thus they talk up in the stand. "That shield was made at Limoges, whence it was brought by Pilades, who is very ardent and keen to be always in the fight. That shield, bridle, and breast-strap were made at Toulouse, and were brought here by Kay of Estraus. The other came from Lyons on the Rhone, and there is no better under heaven; for his great merit it was presented to Taulas of the Desert, who bears it well and protects himself with it skilfully. Yonder shield is of English workmanship and was made at London; you see on it two swallows which appear as if about to fly; yet they do not move, but receive many blows from the Poitevin lances of steel; he who has it is poor Thoas." Thus they point out and describe the arms of those they know; but they see nothing of him whom they had held in such contempt, and, not remarking him in the fray, they suppose that he has slipped away. When the Queen sees that he is not there, she feels inclined to send some one to search for him in the crowd until he be found. She knows of no one better to send in search of him than she who yesterday performed her errand. So, straightway calling her, she said to her: "Damsel, go and mount your palfrey! I send you to the same knight as I sent you yesterday, and do you seek him until you find him. Do not delay for any cause, and tell him again to do his 'worst'. And when you have given him this message, mark well what reply he makes." The damsel makes no delay, for she had carefully noticed the direction he took the night before, knowing well that she would be sent to him again. She made her way through the ranks until she saw the knight, whom she instructs at once to do his "worst" again, if he desires the love and favour of the Queen which she sends him. And he makes answer: "My thanks to her, since such is her will." Then the damsel went away, and the valets, sergeants, and squires begin to shout: "See this marvellous thing! He of yesterday with the vermilion arms is back again. What can he want? Never in the world was there such a vile, despicable, and craven wretch! He is so in the power of cowardice that resistance is useless on his part." And the damsel returns to the Queen, who detained her and would not let her go until she heard what his response had been; then she heartily rejoiced, feeling no longer any doubt that this is he to whom she altogether belongs, and he is hers in like manner. Then she bids the damsel quickly return and tell him that it is her command and prayer that he shall do his "best "; and she says she will go at once without delay. She came down from the stand to where her valet with the palfrey was awaiting her. She mounted and rode until she found the knight, to whom she said at once: "Sire, my lady now sends word that you shall do the 'best' you can!" And he replies: "Tell her now that it is never a hardship to do her will, for whatever pleases her is my delight." The maiden was not slow in bearing back this message, for she thinks it will greatly please and delight the Queen. She made her way as directly as possible to the stand, where the Queen rose and started to meet her, however, she did not go down, but waited for her at the top of the steps. And the damsel came happy in the message she had to bear. When she had climbed the steps and reached her side, she said: "Lady, I never saw so courteous g knight, for he is more than ready to obey every command you send to him, for, if the truth be known, he accepts good and evil with the same countenance." "Indeed," says the Queen, "that may well be so." Then she returns to the balcony to watch the knights. And Lancelot without delay seizes his shield by the leather straps, for he is kindled and consumed by the desire to show his prowess. Guiding his horse's head, he lets him run between two lines. All those mistaken and deluded men, who have spent a large part of the day and night in heaping him with ridicule, will soon be disconcerted. For a long time they have had their sport and joke and fun. The son of the King of Ireland held his shield closely gripped by the leather straps, as he spurs fiercely to meet him from the opposite direction. They come together with such violence that the son of the Irish king having broken and splintered his lance, wishes no more of the tournament; for it was not moss he struck, but hard, dry boards. In this encounter Lancelot taught him one of his thrusts, when he pinned his shield to his arm, and his arm to his side, and brought him down from his horse to earth. Like arrows the knights at once fly out, spurring and pricking from either side, some to relieve this knight, others to add to his distress. While some thus try to aid their lords, many a saddle is left empty in the strife and fray. But all that day Gawain took no hand at arms, though he was with the others there, for he took such pleasure in watching the deeds of him with the red painted arms that what the others did seemed to him pale in comparison. And the herald cheered up again, as he shouted aloud so that all could hear: "Here there has one come who will take the measure! To-day you shall see what he can do. To-day his prowess shall appear." Then the knight directs his steed and makes a very skilful thrust against a certain knight, whom he strikes so hard that he carries him a hundred feet or more from his horse. His feats with sword and lance are so well performed that there is none of the onlookers who does not find pleasure in watching him. Many even of those who bear arms find pleasure and satisfaction in what he does, for it is great sport to see how he makes horses and knights tumble and fall. He encounters hardly a single knight who is able to keep his seat, and he gives the horses he wins to those who want them. Then those who had been making game of him said: "Now we are disgraced and mortified. It was a great mistake for us to deride and vilify this man, for he is surely worth a thousand such as we are on this field; for he has defeated and outdone all the knights in the world, so that there is no one now that opposes him." And the damsels, who amazed were watching him, all said that he might take them to wife; but they did not dare to trust in their beauty or wealth, or power or highness, for not for her beauty or wealth would this peerless knight deign to choose any one of them. Yet, most of them are so enamoured of him that they say that, unless they marry him, they will not be bestowed upon any man this year. And the Queen, who hears them boast, laughs to herself and enjoy the fun, for well she knows that if all the gold of Arabia should be set before him, yet he who is beloved by them all would not select the best, the fairest, or the most charming of the group. One wish is common to them all--each wishes to have him as her spouse. One is jealous of another, as if she were already his wife; and all this is because they see him so adroit that in their opinion no mortal man could perform such deeds as he had done. He did so well that when the time came to leave the list, they admitted freely on both sides that no one had equalled the knight with the vermilion shield. All said this, and it was true. But when he left, he allowed his shield and lance and trappings to fall where he saw the thickest press, then he rode off hastily with such secrecy that no one of all the host noticed that he had disappeared. But he went straight back to the place whence he had come, to keep his oath. When the tournament broke up, they all searched and asked for him, but without success, for he fled away, having no desire to be recognised. The knights are disappointed and distressed, for they would have rejoiced to have him there. But if the knights were grieved to have been deserted thus, still greater was the damsels' grief when they learned the truth, and they asserted by St. John that they would not marry at all that year. If they can't have him whom they truly love, then all the others may be dismissed. Thus the tourney was adjourned without any of them choosing a husband. Meanwhile Lancelot without delay repairs to his prison. But the seneschal arrived two or three days before Lancelot, and inquired where he was. And his wife, who had given to Lancelot his fair and well-equipped vermilion arms, as well as his harness and his horse, told the truth to the seneschal--how she had sent him where there had been jousting at the tourney of Noauz. "Lady," the seneschal replies, "you could truly have done nothing worse than that. Doubtless, I shall smart for this, for my lord Meleagant will treat me worse than the beach-combers' law would treat me were I a mariner in distress. I shall be killed or banished the moment he hears the news, and he will have no pity for me." "Fair sire, be not now dismayed," the lady said; "there is no occasion for the fear you feel. There is no possibility of his detention, for he swore to me by the saints that he would return as soon as possible."

Then the seneschal mounts, and coming to his lord, tells him the whole story of the episode; but at the same time, he emphatically reassures him, telling how his wife had received his oath that he would return to his prison. "He will not break his word, I know," says Meleagant: "and yet I am very much displeased at what your wife has done. Not for any consideration would I have had him present at that tournament. But return now, and see to it that, when he comes back, he be so strictly guarded that he shall not escape from his prison or have any freedom of body: and send me word at once." "Your orders shall be obeyed," says the seneschal. Then he goes away and finds Lancelot returned as prisoner in his yard. A messenger, sent by the seneschal, runs back at once to Meleagant, appraising him of Lancelot's return. When he heard this news, he took masons and carpenters who unwillingly or of their own free-will executed his commands. He summoned the best artisans in the land, and commanded them to build a tower, and exert themselves to build it well. The stone was quarried by the seaside; for near Gorre on this side there runs a big broad arm of the sea, in the midst of which an island stood, as Meleagant well knew. He ordered the stone to be carried thither and the material for the construction of the tower. In less than fifty-seven days the tower was completely built, high and thick and well-founded. When it was completed, he had Lancelot brought thither by night, and after putting him in the tower, he ordered the doors to be walled up, and made all the masons swear that they would never utter a word about this tower. It was his will that it should be thus sealed up, and that no door or opening should remain, except one small window. Here Lancelot was compelled to stay, and they gave him poor and meagre fare through this little window at certain hours, as the disloyal wretch had ordered and commanded them.

Now Meleagant has carried out all his purpose, and he betakes himself to King Arthur's court: behold him now arrived! And when he was before the King, he thus spoke with pride and arrogance: "King, I have scheduled a battle to take place in thy presence and in thy court. But I see nothing of Lancelot who agreed to be my antagonist. Nevertheless, as my duty is, in the hearing of all who are present here, I offer myself to fight this battle. And if he is here, let him now step forth and agree to meet me in your court a year from now. I know not if any one has told you how this battle was agreed upon. But I see knights here who were present at our conference, and who, if they would, could tell you the truth. If he should try to deny the truth, I should employ no hireling to take my place, but would prove it to him hand to hand." The Queen, who was seated beside the King, draws him to her as she says: "Sire, do you know who that knight is? It is Meleagant who carried me away while escorted by Kay the seneschal; he caused him plenty of shame and mischief too." And the King answered her: "Lady, I understand; I know full well that it is he who held my people in distress." The Queen says no more, but the King addresses Meleagant: "Friend," he says, "so help me God, we are very sad because we know nothing of Lancelot." "My lord King," says Meleagant, "Lancelot told me that I should surely find him here. Nowhere but in your court must I issue the call to this battle, and I desire all your knights here to bear me witness that I summon him to fight a year from to-day, as stipulated when we agreed to fight."

At this my lord Gawain gets up, much distressed at what he hears: "Sire, there is nothing known of Lancelot in all this land," he says; "but we shall send in search of him and, if God will, we shall find him yet, before the end of the year is reached, unless he be dead or in prison. And if he does not appear, then grant me the battle, and I will fight for him: I will arm myself in place of Lancelot, if he does not return before that day." "Ah," says Meleagant, "for God's sake, my fair lord King, grant him the boon. I join my request to his desire, for I know no knight in all the world with whom I would more gladly try my strength, excepting only Lancelot. But bear in mind that, if I do not fight with one of them, I will accept no exchange or substitution for either one." And the King says that this is understood, if Lancelot does not return within the time. Then Meleagant left the royal court and journeyed until he found his father, King Bademagu. In order to appear brave and of consideration in his presence, he began by making a great pretence and by assuming an expression of marvellous cheer. That day the king was holding a joyous court at his city of Bade; it was his birthday, which he celebrated with splendour and generosity, and there were many people of divers sorts gathered with him. All the palace was filled with knights and damsels, and among them was the sister of Meleagant, of whom I shall tell you, farther on, what is my thought and reason for mentioning her here. But it is not fitting that I should explain it here, for I do not wish to confuse or entangle my material, but rather to treat it straight forwardly. Now I must tell you that Meleagant in the hearing of all, both great and small, spoke thus to his father boastingly: "Father," he says, "so help me God, please tell me truly now whether he ought not to be well-content, and whether he is not truly brave, who can cause his arms to be feared at King Arthur's court?" To this question his father replies at once: "Son," he says, "all good men ought to honour and serve and seek the company of one whose deserts are such." Then he flattered him with the request that he should not conceal why he has alluded to this, what he wishes, and whence he comes. "Sire, I know not whether you remember," Meleagant begins, "the agreements and stipulations which were recorded when Lancelot and I made peace. It was then agreed, I believe, and in the presence of many we were told, that we should present ourselves at the end of a year at Arthur's court. I went thither at the appointed time, ready equipped for my business there. I did everything that had been prescribed: I called and searched for Lancelot, with whom I was to fight, but I could not gain a sight of him: he had fled and run away. When I came away, Gawain pledged his word that, if Lancelot is not alive and does not return within the time agreed upon, no further postponement will be asked, but that he himself will fight the battle against me in place of Lancelot. Arthur has no knight, as is well known, whose fame equals his, but before the flowers bloom again, I shall see, when we come to blows, whether his fame and his deeds are in accord: I only wish it could be settled now!" "Son," says his father, "thou art acting exactly like a fool. Any one, who knew it not before, may learn of thy madness from thy own lips. A good heart truly humbles itself, but the fool and the boastful never lose their folly. Son, to thee I direct my words, for the traits of thy character are so hard and dry, that there is no place for sweetness or friendship. Thy heart is altogether pitiless: thou art altogether in folly's grasp. This accounts for my slight respect for thee, and this is what will cast thee down. If thou art brave, there will be plenty of men to say so in time of need. A virtuous man need not praise his heart in order to enhance his deed; the deed itself will speak in its own praise. Thy self-praise does not aid thee a whit to increase in any one's esteem; indeed, I hold thee in less esteem. Son, I chasten thee; but to what end? It is of little use to advise a fool. He only wastes his strength in vain who tries to cure the madness of a fool, and the wisdom that one teaches and expounds is worthless, wasted and unemployed, unless it is expressed in works." Then Meleagant was sorely enraged and furious. I may truly say that never could you see a mortal man so full of anger as he was; the last bond between them was broken then, as he spoke to his father these ungracious words: "Are you in a dream or trance, when you say that I am mad to tell you how my matters stand? I thought I had come to you as to my lord and my father; but that does not seem to be the case, for you insult me more outrageously than I think you have any right to do; moreover, you can give no reason for having addressed me thus." "Indeed, I can." "What is it, then?" "Because I see nothing in thee but folly and wrath. I know very well what thy courage is like, and that it will cause thee great trouble yet. A curse upon him who supposes that the elegant Lancelot, who is esteemed by all but thee, has ever fled from thee through fear. I am sure that he is buried or confined in some prison whose door is barred so tight that he cannot escape without leave. I should surely be sorely grieved if he were dead or in distress. It would surely be too bad, were a creature so splendidly equipped, so fair, so bold, yet so serene, to perish thus before his time. But, may it please God, this is not true." Then Bademagu said no more; but a daughter of his had listened attentively to all his words, and you must know that it was she whom I mentioned earlier in my tale, and who is not happy now to hear such news of Lancelot. It is quite clear to her that he is shut up, since no one knows any news of him or his wanderings. "May God never look upon me, if I rest until I have some sure and certain news of him!" Straightway, without making any noise or disturbance, she runs and mounts a fair and easy-stepping mule. But I must say that when she leaves the court, she knows not which way to turn. However, she asks no advice in her predicament, but takes the first road she finds, and rides along at random rapidly, unaccompanied by knight or squire. In her eagerness she makes haste to attain the object of her search. Keenly she presses forward in her quest, but it will not soon terminate. She may not rest or delay long in any single place, if she wishes to carry out her plan, to release Lancelot from his prison, if she can find him and if it is possible. But in my opinion, before she finds him she will have searched in many a land, after many a journey and many a quest, before she has any news of him. But what would be the use of my telling you of her lodgings and her journeyings? Finally, she travelled so far through hill and dale, up and down, that more than a month had passed, and as yet she had learned only so much as she knew before--that is, absolutely nothing. One day she was crossing a field in a sad and pensive mood, when she saw a tower in the distance standing by the shore of an arm of the sea. Not within a league around about was there any house, cottage, or dwelling-place. Meleagant had had it built, and had confined Lancelot within. But of all this she still was unaware. As soon as she espied the tower, she fixed her attention upon it to the exclusion of all else. And her heart gives her assurance that here is the object of her quest; now at last she has reached her goal, to which Fortune through many trials has at last directed her.

The damsel draws so near to the tower that she can touch it with her hands. She walks about, listening attentively, I suppose, if perchance she may hear some welcome sound. She looks down and she gazes up, and she sees that the tower is strong and high and thick. She is amazed to see no door or window, except one little narrow opening. Moreover, there was no ladder or steps about this high, sheer tower. For this reason she surmises that it was made so intentionally, and that Lancelot is confined inside. But she resolves that before she tastes of food, she will learn whether this is so or not. She thinks she will call Lancelot by name, and is about to do so when she is deterred by hearing from the tower a voice which was making a marvellously sad moan as it called on death. It implores death to come, and complains of misery unbearable. In contempt of the body and life, it weakly piped in a low, hoarse tone: "Ah, fortune, how disastrously thy wheel has turned for me! Thou hast mocked me shamefully: a while ago I was up, but now I am down; I was well off of late, but now I am in a sorry state; not long since thou didst smile on me, but now thy eyes are filled with tears. Alas, poor wretch, why didst thou trust in her, when so soon she has deserted thee! Behold, in a very little while she has cast thee down from thy high estate! Fortune, it was wrong of thee to mock me thus; but what carest thou! Thou carest not how it may turn out. Ah, sacred Cross! All, Holy Ghost! How am I wretched and undone! How completely has my career been closed! Ah, Gawain, you who possess such worth, and whose goodness is unparalleled, surely I may well be amazed that you do not come to succour me. Surely you delay too long and are not showing courtesy. He ought indeed to receive your aid whom you used to love so devotedly! For my part I may truly say that there is no lodging place or retreat on either side of the sea, where I would not have searched for you at least seven or ten years before finding you, if I knew you to be in prison. But why do I thus torment myself? You do not care for me even enough to take this trouble. The rustic is right when he says that it is hard nowadays to find a friend! It is easy to rest the true friend in time of need. Alas! more than a year has passed since first I was put inside this tower. I feel hurt, Gawain, that you have so long deserted me! But doubtless you know nothing of all this, and I have no ground for blaming you. Yes, when I think of it, this must be the case, and I was very wrong to imagine such a thing; for I am confident that not for all the world contains would you and your men have failed to come to release me from this trouble and distress, if you were aware of it. If for no other reason, you would be bound to do this out of love for me, your companion. But it is idle to talk about it--it cannot be. Ah, may the curse and the damnation of God and St. Sylvester rest upon him who has shut me up so shamefully! He is the vilest man alive, this envious Meleagant, to treat me as evilly as possible!" Then he, who is wearing out his life in grief, ceases speaking and holds his peace. But when she, who was lingering at the base of the tower, heard what he said, she did not delay, but acted wisely and called him thus: "Lancelot," as loudly as she could; "friend, up there, speak to one who is your friend!" But inside he did not hear her words. Then she called out louder yet, until he in his weakness faintly heard her, and wondered who could be calling him. He heard the voice and heard his name pronounced, but he did not know who was calling him: he thinks it must be a spirit. He looks all about him to see, I suppose, if he could espy any one; but there is nothing to be seen but the tower and himself. "God," says he, "what is that I heard? I heard some one speak, but see nothing! Indeed, this is passing marvellous, for I am not asleep, but wide awake. Of course, if this happened in a dream, I should consider it an illusion; but I am awake, and therefore I am distressed." Then with some trouble he gets up, and with slow and feeble steps he moves toward the little opening. Once there, he peers through it, up and down and to either side. When he had looked out as best he might, he caught sight of her who had hailed him. He did not recognise her by sight. But she knew him at once and said: "Lancelot, I have come from afar in search of you. Now, thank God, at last I have found you. I am she who asked of you a boon as you were on your way to the sword-bridge, and you very gladly granted it at my request; it was the head I bade you cut from the conquered knight whom I hated so. Because of this boon and this service you did me, I have gone to this trouble. As a guerdon I shall deliver you from here." "Damsel, many thanks to you," the prisoner then replied; "the service I did you will be well repaid if I am set at liberty. If you can get me out of here, I promise and engage to be henceforth always yours, so help me the holy Apostle Paul! And as I may see God face to face, I shall never fail to obey your commands in accordance with your will. You may ask for anything I have, and receive it without delay." "Friend, have no fear that you will not be released from here. You shall be loosed and set free this very day. Not for a thousand pounds would I renounce the expectation of seeing you free before the datum of another day. Then I shall take you to a pleasant place, where you may rest and take your ease. There you shall have everything you desire, whatever it be. So have no fear. But first I must see if I can find some tool any- where hereabouts with which you might enlarge this hole, at least enough to let you pass." "God grant that you find something," he said, agreeing to this plan; "I have plenty of rope in here, which the rascals gave me to pull up my food--hard barley bread and dirty water, which sicken my stomach and heart." Then the daughter of Bademagu sought and found a strong, stout, sharp pick, which she handed to him. He pounded, and hammered and struck and dug, notwithstanding the pain it caused him, until he could get out comfortably. Now he is greatly relieved and glad, you may be sure, to be out Of prison and to get away from the place where he has been so long confined. Now he is at large in the open air. You may be sure that he would not go back again, were some one to gather in a pile and give to him all the gold there is scattered in the world.

Behold Lancelot now released, but so feeble that he staggered from his weakness and disability. Gently, without hurting him, she sets him before her on her mule, and then they ride off rapidly. But the damsel purposely avoids the beaten track, that they may not be seen, and proceeds by a hidden path; for if she had travelled openly, doubtless some one would have recognised them and done them harm, and she would not have wished that to happen. So she avoided the dangerous places and came to a mansion where she often makes her sojourn because of its beauty and charm. The entire estate and the people on it belonged to her, and the place was well furnished, safe, and private. There Lancelot arrived. And as soon as he had come, and had laid aside his clothes, the damsel gently laid him on a lofty, handsome couch, then bathed and rubbed him so carefully that I could not describe half the care she took. She handled and treated him as gently as if he had been her father. Her treatment makes a new man of him, as she revives him with her cares. Now he is no less fair than an angel and is more nimble and more spry than anything you ever saw. When he arose, he was no longer mangy and haggard, but strong and handsome. And the damsel sought out for him the finest robe she could find, with which she clothed him when he arose. And he was glad to put it on, quicker than a bird in flight. He kissed and embraced the maid, and then said to her graciously: "My dear, I have only God and you to thank for being restored to health again. Since I owe my liberty to you, you may take and command at will my heart and body, my service and estate. I belong to you in return for what you have done for me; but it is long since I have been at the court of my lord Arthur, who has shown me great honour; and there is plenty there for me to do. Now, my sweet gentle friend, I beg you affectionately for leave to go; then, with your consent, I should feel free to go." "Lancelot, fair, sweet dear friend, I am quite willing," the damsel says; "I desire your honour and welfare above everything everywhere." Then she gives him a wonderful horse she has, the best horse that ever was seen, and he leaps up without so much as saying to the stirrups "by your leave": he was up without considering them. Then to God, who never lies, they commend each other with good intent.

Lancelot was so glad to be on the road that, if I should take an oath, I could not possibly describe the joy he felt at having escaped from his trap. But he said to himself repeatedly that woe was the traitor, the reprobate, whom now he has tricked and ridiculed, "for in spite of him I have escaped." Then he swears by the heart and body of Him who made the world that not for all the riches and wealth from Babylon to Ghent would he let Meleagant escape, if he once got him in his power: for he has him to thank for too much harm and shame! But events will soon turn out so as to make this possible; for this very Meleagant, whom he threatens and presses hard, had already come to court that day without being summoned by any one; and the first thing he did was to search until he found my lord Gawain. Then the rascally proven traitor asks him about Lancelot, whether he had been seen or found, as if he himself did not know the truth. As a matter of fact, he did not know the truth, although he thought he knew it well enough. And Gawain told him, as was true, that he had not been seen, and that he had not come. "Well, since I don't find him," says Meleagant, "do you come and keep the promise you made me: I shall not longer wait for you." Then Gawain makes answer: "I will keep presently my word with you, if it please God in whom I place my trust. I expect to discharge my debt to you. But if it comes to throwing dice for points, and I should throw a higher number than you, so help me God and the holy faith, I'll not withdraw, but will keep on until I pocket all the stakes." Then without delay Gawain orders a rug to be thrown down and spread before him. There was no snivelling or attempt to run away when the squires heard this command, but without grumbling or complaint they execute what he commands. They bring the rug and spread it out in the place indicated; then he who had sent for it takes his seat upon it and gives orders to be armed by the young men who were standing unarmed before him. There were two of them, his cousins or nephews, I know not which, but they were accomplished and knew what to do. They arm him so skilfully and well that no one could find any fault in the world with them for any mistake in what they did. When they finished arming him, one of them went to fetch a Spanish steed able to cross the fields, woods, hills, and valleys more swiftly than the good Bucephalus. Upon a horse such as you have heard Gawain took his seat--the admired and most accomplished knight upon whom the sign of the Cross was ever made. Already he was about to seize his shield, when he saw Lancelot dismount before him, whom he was not expecting to see. He looked at him in amazement, because he had come so unexpectedly; and, if I am not wrong, he was as much surprised as if he had fallen from the clouds. However, no business of his own can detain him, as soon as he sees Lancelot, from dismounting and extending his arms to him, as he embraces, salutes and kisses him. Now he is happy and at ease, when he has found his companion. Now I will tell you the truth, and you must not think I lie, that Gawain would not wish to be chosen king, unless he had Lancelot with him. The King and all the rest now learn that, in spite of all, Lancelot, for whom they so long have watched, has come back quite safe and sound. Therefore they all rejoice, and the court, which so long has looked for him, comes together to honour him. Their happiness dispels and drives away the sorrow which formerly was theirs. Grief takes flight and is replaced by an awakening joy. And how about the Queen? Does she not share in the general jubilee? Yes, verily, she first of all. How so? For God's sake, where, then, could she be keeping herself? She was never so glad in her life as she was for his return. And did she not even go to him? Certainly she did; she is so close to him that her body came near following her heart. Where is her heart, then? It was kissing and welcoming Lancelot. And why did the body conceal itself? Why is not her joy complete? Is it mingled with anger or hate? No, certainly, not at all; but it may be that the King or some of the others who are there, and who are watching what takes place, would have taken the whole situation in, if, while all were looking on, she had followed the dictates of her heart. If common-sense had not banished this mad impulse and rash desire, her heart would have been revealed and her folly would have been complete. Therefore reason closes up and binds her fond heart and her rash intent, and made it more reasonable, postponing the greeting until it shall see and espy a suitable and more private place where they would fare better than here and now. The King highly honoured Lancelot, and after welcoming him, thus spoke: "I have not heard for a long time news of any man which were so welcome as news of you; yet I am much concerned to learn in what region and in what land you have tarried so long a time. I have had search made for you up and down, all the winter and summer through, but no one could find a trace of you." "Indeed, fair sire," says Lancelot, "I can inform you in a few words exactly how it has fared with me. The miserable traitor Meleagant has kept me in prison ever since the hour of the deliverance of the prisoners in his land, and has condemned me to a life of shame in a tower of his beside the sea. There he put me and shut me in, and there I should still be dragging out my weary life, if it were not for a friend of mine, a damsel for whom I once performed a slight service. In return for the little favour I did her, she has repaid me liberally: she has bestowed upon me great honour and blessing. But I wish to repay without delay him for whom I have no love, who has sought out and devised for me this shame and injury. He need not wait, for the sum is all ready, principal and interest; but God forbid that he find in it cause to rejoice!" Then Gawain said to Lancelot: "Friend, it will be only a slight favour for me, who am in your debt, to make this payment for you. Moreover, I am all ready and mounted, as you see. Fair, sweet friend, do not deny me the boon I desire and request." But Lancelot replies that he would rather have his eye plucked out, or even both of them, than be persuaded to do this: he swears it shall never be so. He owes the debt and he will pay it himself: for with his own hand he promised it. Gawain plainly sees that nothing he can say is of any avail, so he loosens and takes off his hauberk from his back, and completely disarms himself. Lancelot at once arms himself without delay; for he is impatient to settle and discharge his debt. Meleagant, who is amazed beyond measure at what he sees, has reached the end of his good fortunes, and is about to receive what is owing him. He is almost beside himself and comes near fainting. "Surely I was a fool," he says, "not to go, before coming here, to see if I still held imprisoned in my tower him who now has played this trick on me. But, God, why should I have gone? What cause had I to think that he could possibly escape? Is not the wall built strong enough, and is not the tower sufficiently strong and high? There was no hole or crevice in it, through which he could pass, unless he was aided from outside. I am sure his hiding-place was revealed. If the wall were worn away and had fallen into decay, would he not have been caught and injured or killed at the same time? Yes, so help me God, if it had fallen down, he would certainly have been killed. But I guess, before that wall gives away without being torn down, that all the water in the sea will dry up without leaving a drop and the world will come to an end. No, that is not it: it happened otherwise: he was helped to escape, and could not have got out otherwise: I have been outwitted through some trickery. At any rate, he has escaped; but if I had been on my guard, all this would never have happened, and he would never have come to court. But it's too late now to repent. The rustic, who seldom errs, pertinently remarks that it is too late to close the stable when the horse is out. I know I shall now be exposed to great shame and humiliation, if indeed I do not suffer and endure something worse. What shall I suffer and endure? Rather, so long as I live, I will give him full measure, if it please God, in whom I trust." Thus he consoles himself, and has no other desire than to meet his antagonist on the field. And he will not have long to wait, I think, for Lancelot goes in search of him, expecting soon to conquer him. But before the assault begins, the King bids them go down into the plain where the tower stands, the prettiest place this side of Ireland for a fight. So they did, and soon found themselves on the plain below. The King goes down too, and all the rest, men and women in crowds. No one stays behind; but many go up to the windows of the tower, among them the Queen, her ladies and damsels, of whom she had many with her who were fair.

In the field there stood a sycamore as fair as any tree could be; it was wide-spread and covered a large area, and around it grew a fine border of thick fresh grass which was green at all seasons of the year. Under this fair and stately sycamore, which was planted back in Abel's time, there rises a clear spring of water which flows away hurriedly. The bed of the spring is beautiful and as bright as silver, and the channel through which the water flows is formed, I think, of refined and tested gold, and it stretches away across the field down into a valley between the woods. There it pleases the King to take his seat where nothing unpleasant is in sight. After the crowd has drawn back at the King's command, Lancelot rushes furiously at Meleagant as at one whom he hates cordially, but before striking him, he shouted with a loud and commanding voice: "Take your stand, I defy you! And take my word, this time you shall not be spared." Then he spurs his steed and draws back the distance of a bow-shot. Then they drive their horses toward each other at top speed, and strike each other so fiercely upon their resisting shields that they pierced and punctured them. But neither one is wounded, nor is the flesh touched in this first assault. They pass each other without delay, and come back at the top of their horses: speed to renew their blows on the strong, stout shields. Both of the knights are strong and brave, and both of the horses are stout and fast. So mighty are the blows they deal on the shields about their necks that the lances passed clean through, without breaking or splintering, until the cold steel reached their flesh. Each strikes the other with such force that both are borne to earth, and no breast-strap, girth, or stirrup could save them from falling backward over their saddle-bow, leaving the saddle without an occupant. The horses run riderless over hill and dale, but they kick and bite each other, thus showing their mortal hatred. As for the knights who fell to earth, they leaped up as quickly as possible and drew their swords, which were engraved with chiselled lettering. Holding their shields before the face, they strive to wound each other with their swords of steel. Lancelot stands in no fear of him, for he knew half as much again about fencing as did his antagonist, having learned it in his youth. Both dealt such blows on the shield slung from their necks, and upon their helmets barred with gold, that they crushed and damaged them. But Lancelot presses him hard and gives him a mighty blow upon his right arm which, though encased in mail, was unprotected by the shield, severing it with one clean stroke. And when he felt the loss of his right arm, he said that it should be dearly sold. If it is at all possible, he will not fail to exact the price; he is in such pain and wrath and rage that he is well-nigh beside himself, and he has a poor opinion of himself, if he cannot score on his rival now. He rushes at him with the intent to seize him, but Lancelot forestalls his plan, for with his trenchant sword he deals his body such a cut as he will not recover from until April and May be passed. He smashes his nose-guard against his teeth, breaking three of them in his mouth. And Meleagant's rage is such that he cannot speak or say a word; nor does he deign to cry for mercy, for his foolish heart holds tight in such constraint that even now it deludes him still. Lancelot approaches and, unlacing his helmet, cuts off his head. Never more will this man trouble him; it is all over with him as he falls dead. Not a soul who was present there felt any pity at the sight. The King and all the others there are jubilant and express their joy. Happier than they ever were before, they relieve Lancelot of his arms, and lead him away exultingly.

My lords, if I should prolong my tale, it would be beside the purpose, and so I will conclude. Godefroi de Leigni, the clerk, has written the conclusion of "the Cart"; but let no one find fault with him for having embroidered on Chretien's theme, for it was done with the consent of Chretien who started it. Godefroi has finished it from the point where Lancelot was imprisoned in the tower. So much he wrote; but he would fain add nothing more, for fear of disfiguring the tale.

Made in the USA
Lexington, KY
18 January 2018